STUDIES IN CHRISTIAN HISTORY AND THOUGHT

Puritan Evangelism

Preaching for Conversion in Late Seventeenth-Century English
Puritanism as seen in the Works of John Flavel

STUDIES IN CHRISTIAN HISTORY AND THOUGHT

Series Editors

Alan P.F. Sell	Visiting Professor at Acadia University Divinity College, Nova Scotia
D.W. Bebbington	University of Stirling, Stirling, Scotland
Clyde Binfield	Professor Associate in History, University of Sheffield, UK
Gerald Bray	Anglican Professor of Divinity, Beeson Divinity School, Samford University, Birmingham, Alabama, USA
Grayson Carter	Associate Professor of Church History, Fuller Theological Seminary SW, Phoenix, Arizona, USA
Dennis Ngien	Professor of Theology, Tyndale University College and Seminary, Founder of the Centre for Mentorship and Theological Reflection, Toronto, Canada

STUDIES IN CHRISTIAN HISTORY AND THOUGHT

Puritan Evangelism

Preaching for Conversion in Late Seventeenth-Century English
Puritanism as seen in the Works of John Flavel

Clifford B. Boone

Copyright © Clifford B. Boone 2013

First published 2013 by Paternoster

Paternoster is an imprint of Authentic Media
52 Presley Way
Crownhill
Milton Keynes MK8 0ES

09 08 07 06 05 04 03   8 7 6 5 4 3 2 1

The right of Clifford B. Boone to be identified as the Author of this Work
has been asserted by him in accordance with the Copyright, Designs
and Patents Act 1988.

*All rights reserved. No part of this publication may be reproduced, stored in a retrieval
system, or transmitted, in any form or by any means, electronic, mechanical, photocopying,
recording or otherwise, without the prior permission of the publisher or a license permitting
restricted copying. In the UK such licenses are issued by the Copyright Licensing Agency,
90 Tottenham Court Road, London W1P 9HE.*

British Library Cataloguing in Publication Data
A catalogue record for this book is available from the British Library

ISBN 9781842277843

Typeset by Tim Grass
Printed and bound in Great Britain
for Paternoster
by Lightning Source, Milton Keynes

Series Preface

This series complements the specialist series of Studies in Evangelical History and Thought and Studies in Baptist History and Thought for which Paternoster is becoming increasingly well known by offering works that cover the wider field of Christian history and thought. It encompasses accounts of Christian witness at various periods, studies of individual Christians and movements, and works which concern the relations of church and society through history, and the history of Christian thought.

The series includes monographs, revised dissertations and theses, and collections of papers by individuals and groups. As well as 'free standing' volumes, works on particular running themes are being commissioned; authors will be engaged for these from around the world and from a variety of Christian traditions.

A high academic standard combined with lively writing will commend the volumes in this series both to scholars and to a wider readership.

To my wife, Becky
Now I know why so many men
dedicate their first book to their wife.
I couldn't have done it without you!
Thank you!

Contents

List of Tables	xv
Acknowledgements	xvii
Abbreviations	xviii

PART ONE Introduction   1

Chapter 1 Studies of Puritan Preaching   3
  Preliminary Issues: Focus and Definition   3
  Descriptions of Puritan Preaching   5
  Non-Theological Explanations of Puritan Preaching   9
  Theological Explanations of Puritan Preaching which do not include the Effectual Call   11
    TWO EXCEPTIONS   11
    STUDIES OF PURITAN PREACHING WHICH OMIT ITS RELATIONSHIP TO THE EFFECTUAL CALL   17
    STUDIES OF THE PURITAN VIEW OF THE EFFECTUAL CALL WHICH OMIT ITS RELATIONSHIP TO PREACHING   27
  Summary   31

Chapter 2 John Flavel and the Rationale for using him in this Study   32
  Biographical Sketch   32
  Flavel's Significance in Seventeenth-Century Puritanism   36
    THE TESTIMONY OF FOE AND FRIEND   36
    FLAVEL'S INVOLVEMENT IN EVANGELISM   39
    THE POPULARITY AND USE OF FLAVEL'S WRITTEN WORKS   41
    WILLS AND NAMES IN THE NEW WORLD   46
    THE OBSERVATIONS OF SCHOLARLY INVESTIGATION   47
  Introductory Issues concerning Flavel's Works   51
  Evangelistic Intent in Flavel's Publications   53
  Summary   58

PART TWO The Theology of John Flavel   61

Chapter 3 The Human Constitution   63
   The 'Image of God'   63
   The Faculties of the Soul   67
      PURITAN 'FACULTY PSYCHOLOGY'   67
      THE NUMBER OF FACULTIES IN THE SOUL   72
      THE INTELLECT (INCLUDING THE CONSCIENCE)   73
         Discernment: A Function of the Intellect   74
         Direction of the Will: Another Function of the Intellect   75
         Thoughts: Another Function of the Intellect   75
         Conscience: Another Function of the Intellect   76
      THE WILL   81
      THE AFFECTIONS   85
      THE RELATIONSHIP BETWEEN THE INTELLECT, THE WILL, AND THE AFFECTIONS   88
         The Will's Place as 'Queen of the Soul'   88
         The Influence of Will and Intellect upon the Affections   89
         The Affections' Influence upon the Will   89
         The Relationship between the Will and the Mind   91
      SUMMARY   96

Chapter 4 The Doctrine of Sin   97
   Introductory Issues   97
      THE ORIGIN OF THE SOUL'S SINFULNESS   97
      THE THREE ASPECTS OF SIN   100
      SIN'S EFFECT ON THE SOUL'S FACULTIES   101
   Sin's Effect on the Intellect   102
      JUDICIAL BLINDING   103
      SPIRITUAL IGNORANCE   104
      ILLUMINATION   104
      NATURAL VS SPIRITUAL KNOWLEDGE   105
      THE RELATIONSHIP BETWEEN FAITH AND REASON   107
   Sin's Effect on the Will   108
   Sin's Effect on the Affections   110
   Summary   112

Chapter 5 Effectual Call: Overview and First Step   115
  Flavel's Terminology which relates to the Effectual Call   115
  The Steps of the Effectual Call   117
  The Order of the Steps of the Effectual Call   118
  Illumination   123
      FLAVEL'S TERMINOLOGY WHICH RELATES TO ILLUMINATION   124
      THE DATA REGARDING WHICH ILLUMINATION TAKES PLACE   126
      THE MEANS OF ILLUMINATION   128
      ILLUMINATION AS EFFECTUAL   129
      'PARTIAL CONVICTIONS'   130
      SUMMARY CONCERNING ILLUMINATION   132

Chapter 6 Effectual Call: Last Steps and Summary   134
  Conviction   134
      DEFINITION   134
      COMPUNCTION: THE INTENSE EFFECT OF CONVICTION UPON THE AFFECTIONS   135
      THE AIM OF CONVICTION   137
      THE NECESSITY OF CONVICTION   137
      THE MEANS OF CONVICTION   138
      THE EFFICACY OF CONVICTION   139
      'PARTIAL CONVICTION' VS PREPARATORY WORK OF THE SPIRIT   140
      OPPOSITION TO CONVICTION   145
      SUMMARY CONCERNING CONVICTION   146
  Renewing of the Will   146
      RENEWING OF THE WILL: CLEARLY THE THIRD AND FINAL STEP IN VOCATION   147
      RENEWING OF THE WILL AS EFFICACIOUS   147
      RENEWING OF THE WILL AS CONGRUENT WITH THE NATURE OF THE HUMAN SOUL   148
      PROVIDENCE AS AN INSTRUMENT IN THE EFFECTUAL CALL   148
      THE RESULT OF THE RENEWING OF THE WILL: FAITH   149
  Faith   150
      WHICH FACULTY OF THE SOUL IS THE SEAT OF FAITH?   151
      FAITH AND THE AFFECTIONS   154
      THE OBJECT OF FAITH   156

FAITH AS AN INSTRUMENTAL CONDITION OF SALVATION	157
THE NECESSITY OF FAITH FOR SALVATION	159
FAITH AS SPIRIT-GIVEN YET TRULY A HUMAN ACT	160
SUMMARY CONCERNING THE RENEWING OF THE WILL AND FAITH	
	161
Summary of Flavel's View of the Effectual Call	162

PART THREE The Preaching of John Flavel: The Application of his Theology to the Work of Preaching for Conversion 165

Chapter 7 Factors other than the Effectual Call which influenced Puritan Sermon Construction 167
Ramism	167
The Puritan 'plain style'	172
Flavel's View of the Role of the Minister	177

Chapter 8 Flavel's Alignment of the Matter and Manner of his Sermons with his View of the Effectual Call 182
The Importance of the Steps of the Effectual Call and their Order	182
Shaping the Sermon in the Light of Illumination	182
Shaping the Sermon in the Light of Conviction	190
Shaping the Sermon in the Light of the Renewing of the Will and Faith	197
PREACHING TO THE AFFECTIONS TO EVOKE A DESIRE FOR CHRIST	
	198
THE PREACHER'S EMOTIONS	200
PREACHING IN THE LIGHT OF THE ISSUE OF ASSENT VS CONSENT	
	201
HOW DID FLAVEL PREACH IN THE LIGHT OF THE PASSIVE ASPECT OF THE THIRD STEP?	202
HOW DID FLAVEL PREACH IN THE LIGHT OF THE ACTIVE ASPECT OF THE THIRD STEP?	203
Summary	212

PART FOUR Conclusion

Chapter 9 Summary and Conclusion of this Study 217

Appendixes
Appendix 1: The Compass of *Navigation Spiritualized* 225
Appendix 2: Outline of *Fountain of Life* 229
Appendix 3: Outline of *Method of Grace* 230
Appendix 4: Outline of *Soul of Man* 231
Appendix 5: Annotated Chronological List of Flavel's Works 233

Bibliography 261

Index 275

List of Tables

Table 1: Flavel's View of the Effectual Call   163
Table 2: Flavel's View of the Responsibility of the Preacher in the
    First Step of the Effectual Call   187
Table 3: Flavel's View of the Responsibility of the Preacher in the
    Second Step of the Effectual Call   195
Table 4: Flavel's View of the Responsibility of the Preacher in the
    Third Step of the Effectual Call   209
Table 5: Flavel's View of the Responsibilities of the Preacher throughout
    the Effectual Call   213

Acknowledgements

The bibliography is an appropriate expression of my indebtedness for the intellectual property of others with which I have interacted. There is, however, additional indebtedness which is due a more personal expression of gratitude. I wish to thank the librarians and staff of the Montgomery Library of Westminster Theological Seminary, Reeves Library of Moravian College and Theological Seminary, The Library of Congress, Highland Theological College, Dr. Williams's Library, and the Bodleian Library, for their patience, carefulness and invaluable assistance. I wish to thank Andrew McGowan for his initial counsel which steered me in the direction of researching John Flavel. I thank also Francis Knight, Susan Hardman Moore, and John Morgan-Guy for their valuable advice which shaped my study. And I wish to express my profound gratitude to Nick Needham: his piercing eye and perceptive questions honed me while his belief in me and in my work continually fortified me in what became a very long process.

I thank Ellen Pearce for her painstakingly accurate proof-reading, Tim Grass for his editorial work, and Mike Parsons and Paternoster for their confidence in the value of this particular academic inquiry.

I thank the elders, fellow pastors, and people of Cedar Crest Bible Fellowship Church who allowed me the time I needed to work on this project, Carl Cassel for his unwavering encouragement, Nicholas Beadles for just the right word at just the right time, Rob Black for his continual prayers, my parents for their cheers, and my sister for her understanding (she has walked the same road) and timely encouragement.

Lastly, I thank my children for the sacrifice they did not choose yet underwent – your understanding and enthusiasm is precious. And my wife … words cannot express what I owe you.

Clifford B. Boone
Cedar Crest Bible Fellowship Church, Allentown, Pennsylvania
October 2012

Abbreviations

BT *Banner of Truth*
ChH *Church History*
EQ *Evangelical Quarterly*
JEH *Journal of Ecclesiastical History*
ODNB *Oxford Dictionary of National Biography*
WTJ *Westminster Theological Journal*

PART ONE

Introduction

Chapter 1

Studies of Puritan Preaching

Preliminary Issues: Focus and Definition

This study explores the influence that the theology believed by the Puritan preacher had on the manner and matter of his preaching. The particular kind of preaching we are concerned with is Puritan evangelistic preaching – sermons presented to those whom the preacher considered unconverted with the aim of seeing their conversions take place. The aspect of the Puritan preacher's theology on which we will focus is his understanding of how the unconverted become converted – specifically, the effectual call. Our contention is that within the generally accepted homiletic framework of this tradition the Puritan preacher's understanding of the effectual call was the main factor that influenced the content, arrangement and presentation of his sermons to the unconverted. The works of one particular late seventeenth-century English Puritan, John Flavel (1628–91), will serve as the object of our investigation.

It is necessary to explain what definition of Puritanism we are using. The author of the biblical book of Ecclesiastes wrote: 'But beyond this, my son, be warned: the writing of books is endless.' Those scholars intent on arriving at a conclusive definition of Puritanism seem destined to prove this ancient Scripture true. The written discussion concerning the essence of Puritanism continues unabated. It is not within the scope of this work to enter into that debate, but we will explain the choice of the definition we are using.[1]

---

[1] The following sources provide a sample of the issues and intricacies involved in the discussion on the definition of Puritanism. They are listed in chronological order. J. Gregory, *Puritanism in the Old World and in the New* (New York: Fleming H. Revell, 1869); Jerald Brauer, 'Reflections on the Nature of English Puritanism,' *ChH* 23 (1954), pp. 99–108; Christopher Hill, *Society and Puritanism in Pre-Revolutionary England* (London: Secker & Warburg, 1964); Geoffrey F. Nuttall, *The Puritan Spirit: Essays and Addresses* (London: Epworth Press, 1967); John Coolidge, *The Pauline Renaissance in England* (Oxford: Clarendon Press, 1970); Peter Toon, *Puritans and Calvinism* (Swengel: Reiner Publications, 1973); Nicholas Tyacke, 'Puritanism, Arminianism and Counter-Revolution,' in Conrad Russel, ed., *The Origins of the English Civil War* (London: Macmillan, 1973), pp. 119–44; E. Brooks Holifield, *The Covenant Sealed: The Development of Puritan Sacramental Theology in Old and New England, 1570–1720* (New Haven: Yale University Press, 1974); Peter Lewis, *The Genius of Puritanism* (Morgan: Soli Deo Gloria, 1996); Paul Christianson, 'Reformers and the Church of England under Elizabeth and the early Stuarts', and Patrick Collinson, 'A Comment: Concerning the Name Puritan', *JEH* 31

Patrick Collinson explains the elusiveness of a precise definition in terms of the 'unstable and dynamic situation'[2] in which Puritanism took place. After acknowledging and discussing the changing situation in which Puritanism existed and the difficulties of using the term 'Puritan' or other terms which have been suggested in its place, Collinson closes his careful article without proposing a definition of his own.

Peter Lake, in his 'Defining Puritanism – again?,' puts previous attempts at defining Puritanism in three categories and then makes his own suggestion of a way to approach the problem.[3] His first category includes definitions which focus on the Puritans' commitment to further reform the government and liturgy of the church. The second category is made up of definitions which focus on the 'style of piety' which the Puritans possessed. This piety, Lake asserts, must be acknowledged to contain emotional as well as ideological components. The third category is made up of those who observe that many attempts to define Puritanism inevitably describe non-Puritans of the same period, and who therefore conclude that 'notions of Puritanism as a free-standing view of the world are best jettisoned.' Lake's own suggestion is that Puritanism be understood as a style of piety and divinity which is best understood as a synthesis of various strands of both tenets and practices. It is not the tenets and practices themselves which are distinctive, Lake suggests, but the particular synthesis that the Puritans embodied.

(1980), pp. 483–88; Barrington R. White, ed., *The English Puritan Tradition* (Nashville: Broadman Press, 1980); Charles E. Hambrick-Stowe, *The Practice of Piety: Puritan Devotional Disciplines in Seventeenth-Century New England* (Chapel Hill: University of North Carolina Press, 1982); Harry L. Poe, 'Evangelistic Fervency among the Puritans in Stuart England, 1603–1688' (Ph.D. diss., Southern Baptist Theological Seminary, 1982); Alan Heimert and Andrew Delbanco, eds, *The Puritans in America: A Narrative Anthology* (Cambridge, MA: Harvard University Press, 1985); Baird Tipson, 'The Elusiveness of "Puritanism"', *Religious Studies Review* 11 (1985), pp. 245–56; Gavin J. McGrath, 'Puritans and the Human Will: Voluntarism within Mid-Seventeenth Century English Puritanism as seen in the Works of Richard Baxter and John Owen' (Ph.D. diss., University of Durham, 1989); I.M. Green, 'Bunyan in Context: The Changing Face of Protestantism in Seventeenth-Century England', in *Bunyan in England and Abroad: Papers delivered at the John Bunyan Tercentenary Symposium, Vrije Universiteit Amsterdam, 1988*, ed. M. van Os and G.J. Schutte (Amsterdam: VU Press, 1990); Francis J. Bremer, ed., *Puritanism: Transatlantic Perspectives on a Seventeenth-Century Anglo-American Faith* (Boston: Massachusetts Historical Society, 1993). For additional works concerning the definition issue, see Patrick Collinson's bibliography in his *English Puritanism* (London: Historical Association, 1983), p. 43, and Joel Beeke's annotated bibliographic footnote in his *The Quest for Full Assurance: The Legacy of Calvin and his Successors* (Edinburgh: Banner of Truth, 1999), pp. 82–83.

[2] Collinson, 'Comment', p. 488.
[3] Peter Lake, 'Defining Puritanism – again?', in Bremer, ed., *Puritanism: Transatlantic Perspectives*, pp. 3–29.

Studies of Puritan Preaching 5

In the face of the uncertainty concerning the definition of Puritanism, Christopher Hill suggests that: 'The word "Puritan" too is an admirable refuge from clarity of thought.'[4] In an effort to avoid a retreat into Hill's 'refuge' we accept for our discussion the four distinguishing marks of Puritanism suggested by Jerald Brauer:

> There appear to be at least four characteristics which taken together mark the Puritan movement as a distinct entity in English life from 1570–1680. They are: (1) a deep dissatisfaction with the Anglican conception of the Reformation and with the Roman Catholic interpretation of the faith. (2) The root of this dissatisfaction is founded primarily and initially on a deep religious experience which is of dramatic intensity for every individual in the movement. (3) Out of this personal experience arises a zeal for reform which spreads from vestments and worship to include every facet of contemporary life. (4) The use of covenant theology as the primary vehicle for structuring their experience of and understanding of the Christian faith.[5]

Although proposed in the mid-twentieth century, this definition fits within Peter Lake's suggested framework for defining Puritanism. We accept it for this reason, and also because it acknowledges the strong element of a Puritan desire to reform the established church which was evident in the late sixteenth and early seventeenth centuries, but also gives room for the 'spirit' of Puritanism which can be seen in late seventeenth-century England as well as in the New World.[6]

Descriptions of Puritan Preaching

There have been numerous studies of Puritan preaching but none have drawn the correlation between the particular view the Puritans held of the effectual call and the manner and matter of their preaching. Some studies describe the phenomena of Puritan preaching but make no attempt to explain why such preaching came to hold certain distinctive characteristics. Other studies suggest

---

[4] Hill, *Society and Puritanism*, p. 13.
[5] Brauer, 'Reflections on the Nature of English Puritanism,' p. 100.
[6] Peter Toon, although arguing for a definition that is tied to the hope of a reformed national church in a reformed nation and thus questioning the validity of the use of the term 'Puritan' for those living after 1662, nevertheless identified what he called the 'Puritan spirit' and mentioned the particular Puritan upon whom we focus in our study as being illustrative of that spirit. He wrote: 'If a much more restricted definition is used which covers only the emphasis (the 'Puritan spirit'?) which William Perkins, John Dod, John Preston and Richard Sibbes and many others urged in the years 1590–1630 (that is, Bible-reading, practical divinity, household religion, sabbatarianism, anti-Arminianism, etc.), then perhaps it may be used to describe men like John Flavell and John Bunyan in the period after 1662.' Toon, *Puritans and Calvinism*, p. 50.

reasons for the distinctive organization and delivery of Puritan preaching but not in terms of the theological framework within which the Puritan preacher carried out his work. Finally, some scholars do indeed suggest theological reasons for the manner and matter of Puritan sermons yet, with two important exceptions, none include the effectual call in their theories.

Neil Keeble, in an examination of the sermons of Richard Baxter (1615–91),[7] sets out to describe 'his homiletic concerns and manner.'[8] He sees a difference in emphasis between the sermons Baxter preached before and after 1662. In his discussion of the pre-1662 sermons, Keeble writes: 'Whatever their occasion, and whether delivered in Kidderminster or London, the sermons Baxter preached up to 1662 are directed primarily to those who are "strangers to the New birth."'[9] Keeble examines the preparation that Baxter put into the sermons, Baxter's belief that many church attendees were unregenerate even though they thought of themselves as Christians, and the effort he took to convince the listeners of their needy spiritual state. Keeble's examination continues by discussing Baxter's very personal and pointed analysis of the state of his hearer's hearts during the sermon, his emphasis on the love of God over the terrors of hell, and the movement of his sermon to a moment of decision. After briefly showing Baxter's general adherence to the sermon format advocated by William Perkins (1558–1602),[10] Keeble demonstrates that Baxter spent more preaching time on the 'Uses' section of the sermon than on the 'Doctrine' section. An emphasis on application was undoubtedly Baxter's intent. Finally, Keeble explores Baxter's use of emotive language within the framework of holding rational argument in high regard.

Yet, during this entire discussion Keeble does not attempt to explain these observations by linking them to any aspect of Baxter's theology. The one

---

[7] Richard Baxter, minister at Kidderminster, was ejected in 1662. He was continually involved in theological controversy, but spent considerable energy working for unity among the Protestant factions. He was a prolific writer, publishing approximately 130 different titles. His influence through his preaching, his involvement as a chaplain during the Civil War years, his participation in conferences dealing with theological and ecclesiological issues, and the widespread reception of his writings render him one of the most influential figures in seventeenth-century nonconformity. N.H. Keeble, 'Baxter, Richard (1615–1691),' *ODNB*, http://www.oxforddnb.com/view/article/1734, accessed 21 November 2009.

[8] N.H. Keeble, 'Richard Baxter's Preaching Ministry: Its History and Texts,' *JEH* 35 (1984), pp. 539–59, at 542.

[9] Keeble, 'Baxter's Preaching Ministry,' p. 549.

[10] William Perkins, theologian and Church of England clergyman, taught for ten years (1584–94) at Christ's College, Cambridge, and is known for his influence upon his students, many of whom became influential clergymen themselves, and his theological books which popularized a variety of theological and moral issues. Michael Jinkins, 'Perkins, William (1558–1602),' *ODNB*, http://www.oxforddnb.com/view/article/21973, accessed 21 November 2009.

notable exception was his tying of Baxter's belief in the possibility of churched people being unregenerate with Baxter's emphasis upon explaining the lost condition of men to his audiences. However, Keeble does not investigate how Baxter's beliefs concerning conversion impinged upon his sermon construction. Were Baxter's pointed probes into the listeners' hearts, his emphasis on the love of God, his movement towards a point of decision, his weighting of the sermon on the side of application, and his use of emotion tied in any way to his theology of how a person moves from an unregenerate to a regenerate state? Keeble does not ask, nor does he answer, this question.

Horton Davies, in his extensive *Worship and Theology in England: From Cranmer to Baxter and Fox, 1534–1690*, spends at least fifty-seven pages discussing Puritan preaching.[11] He begins his discussion by identifying the primacy in worship that the Puritans gave to preaching. This primacy, according to Davies, was 'due to their conviction that this was God's primary way of winning men to His allegiance.'[12] After an exploration of the dearth of preaching at the beginning of the English Reformation, the limitations of the practice of reading prepared homilies, and the evident effectiveness of a personal presentation over against a written sermon, Davies concludes:

> the Puritans believed that preaching was the means chosen by God for illuminating the minds, mollifying the hearts, sensitizing the consciences, strengthening the faith, quelling the doubts, and saving the souls of mankind. To that end the Puritan brethren dedicated their chief energies to preaching clearly, faithfully, sincerely, and movingly, trusting that the Holy Spirit would take their human words and make them the 'lively oracles of God' to their congregation.[13]

Thus Davies ties the emphasis that the Puritans placed on preaching to their conviction concerning a theological position – namely, that God had ordained the preaching of the word as an instrument to bring about salvation in humankind. But what of the manner and matter of the Puritan sermon? Was it, as well as the priority given to preaching, tied to a particular theological understanding in the Puritan preacher's mind? To use Davies's own terminology to press our question further: what theological understanding of the Puritan preacher made the mind's illumination, the heart's mollification, the conscience's sensitizing, and so on, important? And, given that theological understanding, what was the preacher's role in those activities? And, did that understanding impact how the preacher organized and delivered the sermon? It is our intent to address these questions.

In sections entitled 'The Structure of the Sermon' and 'Sermon Style'

---

[11] H. Davies, *Worship and Theology in England: From Cranmer to Baxter and Fox, 1534–1690* (2 vols in 1, Grand Rapids: William B. Eerdmans, 1996), Vol. 1, pp. 294–324; Vol. 2, pp. 133–42, 161–77.
[12] Davies, *Worship and Theology in England*, Vol. 1. p. 295.
[13] Davies, *Worship and Theology in England*, Vol. 1. p. 301.

Davies explicates several identifying marks of the Puritan sermon.[14] He does not, however, answer our questions. He comes close to the issue that we are raising when he momentarily mentions the various faculties of the soul in the context of discussing the aim of the Puritan preacher. 'As such, it [the Puritan sermon] aimed to produce light and heat, illumination of the mind and warming of the affections.'[15] Davies suggests that the hearer's mind and affections are intentional targets of the Puritan preacher. He later adds one additional faculty of the soul when stating that Puritan preaching was 'being directed to the conversion of the will and the betterment of behaviour.'[16] And so, Davies asserts that the hearer's mind, affections and will are being deliberately aimed at by the Puritan preacher.

No discussion follows, no doubt because it is not within the scope of his work, that shows the correlation between the preacher's concern with those three faculties of the hearer's soul and a theological understanding of how the hearer is moved from an unregenerate to a regenerate state. Does the Puritan preacher actually have such a theology in mind as he prepares and presents his sermons? Davies does not ask or answer that question. These questions are precisely the ones we will attempt to answer.

Similarly, Bruce Shelley, in his discussion of early New England preaching, directs his readers' attention to various facets of Puritan preaching without addressing the types of questions we are asking. After a brief overview of the distinctive elements of Puritanism salient to his discussion, he explores the standards of preaching excellence, the doctrine in Puritan pulpits, the 'plain style' of Puritan preaching, and the aim of Puritan preaching.[17] In the entire discussion there is no attempt to correlate his observations with the theological framework within which the Puritan preacher approached his work.

The works of Keeble, Davies, and Shelley cited above are examples of scholarly attention given to Puritan preaching without any extended consideration of the possibility that it was aspects of the Puritan preacher's theology that had the most significant influence on the organization and delivery of his sermon.

Non-Theological Explanations of Puritan Preaching

We now turn our attention to some studies which do explore underlying reasons for the particular manner and matter of Puritan preaching, but formulate explanations based upon non-theological factors.

---

[14] Davies, *Worship and Theology in England*, Vol. 1, pp. 305–16.
[15] Davies, *Worship and Theology in England*, Vol. 1, p. 304.
[16] Davies, *Worship and Theology in England*, Vol. 1, p. 308.
[17] Bruce L. Shelley, 'Preaching in early New England', in *Evangelical Roots: A Tribute to Wilbur Smith*, ed. Kenneth S. Kantzer (New York: Thomas Nelson, 1978), pp. 17–33.

Patricia Ruth Meyers, in her 'Rhetoric of Seventeenth-Century New England Puritan Occasional Sermons,' analyzes Puritan occasional sermons and concludes that changes in sermon content and style can be attributed to the audience and to the specific occasion in which the sermon was delivered. Meyers explains that her focus excludes the type of sermons in which we are interested: 'This study does not examine Sunday sermons, which were more likely to deal with issues of personal salvation, but it focuses instead on the political use of preaching.'[18] Thus we are not surprised to find her discussion devoid of any recognition of the importance of the preacher's view of the effectual call.

Nevertheless, she does investigate the causes underlying the development of Puritan sermons aimed at persuasion. She attributes the elements of sermon arrangement meant to increase persuasive appeal to the Puritan preacher's awareness of the principles of rhetoric. According to Myers, 'For persuasive purposes, the preachers did use the inartistic proofs of Aristotle: *ethos*, *logos*, and *pathos*. In employing all these appeals, the preachers were demonstrating their understanding of what is involved in simple persuasion.'[19] In the course of her discussion she mentions the importance of Puritan fidelity to *sola scriptura*, as well as their dedication to 'the major tenets of covenant theology,'[20] but does not explicitly analyze those theological understandings or tie them specifically to certain homiletic practices. Her emphasis is on an analysis of rhetorical practices. She does not raise nor answer the specific questions with which we are concerned.

Anders Lunt, in his 'The Reinvention of Preaching: A Study of Sixteenth and Seventeenth Century English Preaching Theories,' asserts that a discernible distinct preaching theory arose from within the Puritan movement and later spread to almost all English preaching.[21] He bases this conclusion on his careful examination of over one hundred English preaching treatises from the sixteenth and seventeenth centuries. In this examination he articulates the most important contributions to rhetorical theory made by Puritan preaching, and suggests that there was a strong 'faculty psychology' present within that Puritan preaching theory.[22]

For our purposes it is important to draw attention to the fact that Lunt purposefully avoids explanations of the Puritan preaching model that proposed theological underpinnings for that model:

---

[18] Patricia R. Meyers, 'Rhetoric of Seventeenth-Century New England Puritan Occasional Sermons' (Ph.D. diss., Arizona State University, 1992), p. iii.
[19] Myers, 'Rhetoric,' p. 165.
[20] Myers, 'Rhetoric,' p. 199.
[21] Anders Robert Lunt, 'The Reinvention of Preaching: A Study of Sixteenth and Seventeenth Century English Preaching Theories' (Ph.D. diss., University of Maryland, 1998).
[22] Lunt, 'Reinvention of Preaching,' p. 13.

> While articulating these arguments, I shall maintain a distinctly rhetorical perspective. From among the more than one-hundred treatises which have been discovered, I will choose for close study those which best exemplify the development of a unique rhetorical theory within English preaching. Then, I will approach the selected treatises as rhetorical theories, though they are grounded in theological ideas and manifested in the practice of preaching.[23]

Lunt acknowledges that the preaching treatises were grounded in theological ideas but does not identify those ideas nor pursue his examination of the treatises in light of those ideas. His choice to approach the Puritan preaching from purely a rhetorical framework is valid. His study, however, leaves our questions unasked and unanswered. What were those theological ideas, and how did they manifest themselves in the sermons of the Puritans? It is our intent to address those questions.

In reference to his mention of a 'faculty psychology' we once again see a discussion of an important aspect of Puritan preaching without the corresponding theological connection being investigated. In the summary of his examination of critical preaching treatises, Lunt includes his impression of the Puritans' awareness of the various faculties of the soul. 'Simplicity and plainness, though, affected only the mind and beliefs. Changing behavior required a new sermon part, application, in which the preacher sought to take the truths drawn from Scripture and "drive them home" to the emotions and will.'[24] The mind, the emotions, and the will are all mentioned as being a part of the Puritan preacher's awareness as he preached.

Lunt furthers this observation by explaining: 'The scope of this contribution is broadened, however, by the tendency of many among the seventeenth century preaching theorists to link the explication of scripture, or doctrine, to the understanding and to aim the application, or uses, to the emotions and will of their listeners.'[25] This discussion of the faculties of the soul and their place in Puritan preaching is more developed than that of Davies, yet leaves the theological foundation of this issue unexplored. Is there a theological grid by which the various faculties of the soul are understood? Is there a theological understanding of how the faculties of the soul are involved in the process by which an unbelieving person becomes a believer? Did the Puritan preacher have this theological understanding in mind as he formulated and presented his sermons to an unbelieving audience? Lunt does not ask nor does he answer these questions. We intend to do so.

John Rechtien looks at Puritan sermon construction from the perspective of the influence of Ramist logic upon the Puritan 'plain style.' His discussion is extensive and detailed. For our purposes we note that any exploration of the influence of the preacher's theological persuasions upon his sermon style,

---

[23] Lunt, 'Reinvention of Preaching,' p. 13.
[24] Lunt, 'Reinvention of Preaching,' p. 118.
[25] Lunt, 'Reinvention of Preaching,' p. 119.

organization or delivery lies outside Rechtien's chosen framework for examining Puritan sermons. When commenting on authors who would change styles from oratorical to analytical, Rechtien states: 'Neither style is intrinsically determined by a theological position.'[26] Although we understand that this statement is intended to apply to those two examples of style, it does nevertheless represent his approach to the examination of Puritan sermons. Possible theological underpinnings of Puritan preaching are not part of Rechtien's consideration.

The works of Meyers, Lunt and Rechtien are examples of scholarly attention given to Puritan preaching in which factors other than the preacher's theology were propounded as being influential in the formation and delivery of the sermons. In none of the above cases were theological factors disputed. Theological factors were merely not a decisive part of their discussion.

Theological Explanations of Puritan Preaching which do not include the Effectual Call

We now turn our attention to studies that explore underlying reasons for the particular manner and matter of Puritan preaching and do indeed formulate explanations based upon theological factors. Significant for our study is the observation that, although various aspects of theology are linked to Puritan preaching, with two important exceptions, none of the studies address the influence of the Puritan view of the effectual call on sermon development and delivery.

Two Exceptions

Perry Miller's extensive and seminal work concerning Puritanism, *The New England Mind: The Seventeenth Century*, is one of the exceptions.[27] Since its first publication in 1939 his work has been the subject of continual interaction by scholars of Puritanism and still commands respect today. The editor who eventually facilitated the publication of Miller's footnotes,[28] James Hoopes, comments: 'His [i.e. Miller's] two-volume *New England Mind* (1939, 1953) is honored by challenge or correction every publishing season, which proves the book is still very much alive.'[29] It is not surprising, therefore, that we would

---

[26] J.G. Rechtien, 'Logic in Puritan Sermons in the Late Sixteenth Century and Plain Style', *Style* 13 (1979), pp. 237–58, at 237.
[27] Perry Miller, *The New England Mind: The Seventeenth Century* (Cambridge, MA: Belknap Press, 1982).
[28] Miller's annotations and footnotes were originally bound in a separate volume and placed in the Harvard College library.
[29] J. Hoopes, ed., *Sources for* The New England Mind: The Seventeenth Century (Williamsburg: Institute of Early American History and Culture, 1981), p. vii.

find Perry Miller's discussion intersecting closely with ours.

We have found that on certain points our conclusion concerning Puritan theology differs from Miller's presentation of Puritanism. Those differences will be explored at the proper place in this study. For the moment it is important to point out that Miller does indeed draw a connection between the theology of conversion held by the Puritan preacher and the way he preached.

Miller does not use the term effectual call. In a chapter entitled, 'The Means of Conversion,' Miller points to what he calls 'the doctrine of means,' and emphasizes that this doctrine informed the Puritan preacher in his task. 'Though the grace of God is free and unpredictable, capricious and terrible, yet it does not work upon physical bodies without physical agents. It comes to men through what Puritans called the "means."'[30] After discussing the church and the sacraments as means, he highlights the priority that the minister's sermon held in Puritan thinking. 'Therefore sermons are the chief means for salvation because they are best accommodated to God's treating with men as with rational creatures.'[31]

Miller asserts that the 'doctrine of means' was combined with an understanding of the human being's faculties – what he calls 'the traditional and inherited psychological theory.'[32] Miller attempts to show how this theory had its roots in Aristotle, even at times calling it 'Peripatetic psychology.'[33] Our concern is not with his assertion that the Puritan understanding of the human faculties had an Aristotelian heritage, but with his claim that this understanding affected their preaching. In a chapter entitled 'The Nature of Man,' he discusses the Puritan understanding of the human faculties and observes a link between that understanding and the task of preaching. 'The faculties could not be quickened until ministers knew what they were, and the manner of teaching depended entirely upon what concept of the faculties the ministers were taught.'[34] Our examination of Puritan theology discovers a different view of what place each faculty played in conversion than what Miller suggests is the normative Puritan position. This difference will be discussed later. Nevertheless, Miller's explicit assertion that the Puritan preacher's view of the human faculties was a factor in shaping his preaching is echoed in our book.

Later in our study we will point out the differences between Miller's description of the place of the various faculties in the conversion process, the details of the process itself, and one influential Puritan's understanding of the same. The differences, we contend, become evident when the precise order of the effectual call is carefully delineated within the context of understanding what changes take place in each faculty of the soul during the process of

---

[30] Miller, *New England Mind*, p. 288.
[31] Miller, *New England Mind*, p. 292.
[32] Miller, *New England Mind*, p. 255.
[33] Miller, *New England Mind*, p. 305.
[34] Miller, *New England Mind*, p. 244.

conversion. Given Miller's different focus – his examination of Puritan sermons as data through which to discover their intellectual heritage and to further define the corporate mind of seventeenth-century New England – such details of the effectual call are not the subject of his investigation.

As was already stated, Miller never refers to the effectual call per se. He uses terms such as 'doctrine of means,'[35] 'means of conversion,'[36] or 'the process and phases of regeneration.'[37] These terms are useful, but we note that they were not used as synonyms for the effectual call. His discussion of the Puritan view of conversion is done without a detailed, systematic delineation of all the facets of the Puritan view of the effectual call. Although one would hesitate to use the adjective 'superficial' when referring to Professor Miller's work, in this particular case it is perhaps appropriate. In his discussion of the psychology of the human being – what we will refer to within the theological category of human constitution – he mentions the three faculties that become the focus of the particular Puritan whom we have chosen to study. Our subject, however, goes into elaborate detail. In Miller's discussion of the 'means of conversion' there is not a meticulous delineation of what phase of the sinner's transition from an unconverted state to a converted state takes place in what faculty. Indeed, this level of detail on one particular aspect of theology should not be expected from a work with the scope of *The New England Mind*. It is, however, within our scope and was, as we shall endeavour to show, clearly understood and explained by at least one influential English Puritan preacher of the late seventeenth century.

Given this absence of detail concerning the Puritan view of the nature of the effectual call, and the different aim of Miller's work, it is not surprising that his discussion of the interrelatedness of the preacher's theology with his sermon construction leaves much room for further investigation. Miller devotes an entire chapter to the place that the Puritans gave to rhetoric in their thinking and preaching,[38] and devotes another chapter to the Puritan 'plain style,'[39] which focuses upon the influence of Ramist logic on William Perkins and, via his preaching manual, on the Puritan movement. Both chapters touch upon the relationship between what the preacher understood and how he preached. However, consistent with the aim of his book, he explores more thoroughly the intellectual heritage of the Puritans than he does the exact nature of the effect that their theology of the effectual call had on their sermon development.

In our examination of one particular Puritan's precisely defined theology concerning the human constitution, the effects of sin on that constitution, the steps and order of the effectual call, and then the preacher's role in the effectual

---

[35] Miller, *New England Mind*, p. 288.
[36] Miller, *New England Mind*, p. 280.
[37] Miller, *New England Mind*, p. 280.
[38] Miller, *New England Mind*, pp. 300–30.
[39] Miller, *New England Mind*, pp. 331–62.

call as it relates to those steps and that process, significant differences from Miller's analysis are revealed, significant additional details of the Puritan understanding of the effectual call are delineated, and the application of that understanding by Puritan preachers to their task of preaching to the unconverted is explored.

In our estimation, it is noteworthy that very little of the scholarship subsequent to Perry Miller has directly addressed the relationship between the Puritan view of the effectual call and the formation of the Puritan sermon.

The one person in addition to Miller who did investigate this relationship in more than a cursory manner is John Fulcher. In his 'Puritan Piety in early New England,'[40] Fulcher examines the dynamics of Puritan piety in early New England and concludes that it was of such import that it must be understood, along with issues such as the Puritan view of covenant theology and Congregational polity, in order to assess accurately the early New England Puritan movement. In his evaluation of Puritan piety he has a chapter entitled, 'The Anatomy of Regeneration.' It is in this chapter that his discussion involves the effectual call. This chapter is followed by one entitled 'The Means of Grace,' and it is here that the correlation between the Puritan view of the effectual call and the work of preaching is probed.

In 'The Anatomy of Regeneration,' Fulcher asserts that the early New England Puritans accepted the 'theological formula by the divines of the Westminster Assembly' to explain the doctrine of conversion. It is important for our purposes to note that he does not offer a more detailed delineation of the steps of salvation than that of the Westminster Confession of Faith. He states that formula as describing 'conversion as a process of effectual calling, justification, adoption, and sanctification.'[41] He then uses the writings of Thomas Hooker (1586–1647)[42] and Thomas Shepard (1605–49)[43] in

---

[40] John Rodney Fulcher, 'Puritan Piety in early New England: A Study in Spiritual Regeneration from the Antinomian Controversy to the Cambridge Synod of 1648 in the Massachusetts Bay Colony' (Ph.D. diss., Princeton University, 1963).

[41] Fulcher, 'Puritan Piety,' p. 183.

[42] Thomas Hooker, educated at Cambridge, served in Esher, Surrey, and then Chelmsford, Essex, until increasing pressure from Bishop Laud forced him into exile in the Netherlands. After two years he returned to England, and soon emigrated to New England, where he ministered first in the Massachusetts Bay colony and then in Connecticut. His influence as a preacher, counsellor to colonial magistrates, and writer was significant. Sargent Bush Jr, 'Hooker, Thomas (1586?–1647),' *ODNB*, http://www.oxforddnb. com/ view/article/13697, accessed 21 November 2009.

[43] Thomas Shepard was born in England, educated at Cambridge, and involved in a parochial apprenticeship in Terling, Essex, where he came under the influence of Thomas Hooker. He became minister at Earls Colne, Essex, but soon came under pressure from Bishop Laud. Eventually Shepard emigrated to New England. There he became minister at Newton (later renamed Cambridge), participated in the antinomian controversy of 1636–38, helped establish Harvard College, and published

comparison to the writings of John Cotton (1584–1652)[44] to illustrate how this formula was expressed and applied by the Puritans of that day.

Fulcher begins his examination of Shepard and Hooker by focusing upon those stages which follow the effectual call, namely justification and sanctification. His special concern is the nature of faith and the view of it as continuing throughout the believer's life, not merely exercised momentarily at conversion.[45] Within this discussion he briefly relates this view of faith to the effectual call and comments upon how preaching fits into this scheme.[46]

Fulcher then delves into a discussion of the issue of 'preparation' for conversion, leaning on Miller's ideas as his starting point. He points out the controversy of this subject: 'How can the unconverted be prepared for the work of saving grace when the natural man is indisposed to accept the grace offered in Christ?'[47] During his summary of Hooker's views he intersects with our study when he touches upon the various faculties of the soul in which this work of preparation takes place. We will show at the appropriate point in our argument that at least one seventeenth-century Puritan avoided that controversy by understanding 'preparation' as actually within the boundaries of the effectual call. Fulcher, seeing certain early stages through which an unregenerate person passes on his or her way to being regenerate as a separate issue from the effectual call, does not arrive at the same conclusions as ours.

It should be noted that in his discussion Fulcher has only briefly examined the details of the Puritan view of the effectual call. He comments that it consists of 'both an inward word of the Spirit and an outward word of the minister.'[48] He does not go further to investigate what steps or stages may be included in

---

    sermon series as books. Jinkins writes: 'His influence on religious thought in the New World was considerable.' Michael Jinkins, 'Shepard, Thomas (1605–1649),' *ODNB*, http://www.oxforddnb.com/ view/article/25325, accessed 21 November 2009.

[44] John Cotton was educated at Cambridge and became vicar at St Botolph's, Boston, Lincolnshire, in 1612. For the next twenty-one years he ministered there, wrote treatises, and sheltered and trained aspiring clergy with nonconformist sympathies. Eventually pressure from Bishop Laud forced him to emigrate to New England. He began to minister in the prominent First Church, Boston, Massachusetts, where he quickly rose to the 'front ranks of colonial clergy.' His involvement in the Anne Hutchinson trials, his counselling of magistrates, his preaching, and his books, kept him as, 'along with Hooker and Davenport, the most widely known and respected of the first generation of colonial clergy.' Francis J. Bremer, 'Cotton, John (1585–1652),' *ODNB*, http://www.oxforddnb.com/view/article/6416, accessed 21 November 2009.

[45] Fulcher, 'Puritan Piety,' pp. 185–98.
[46] Fulcher, 'Puritan Piety,' p. 196. This treatment of the relationship between the effectual call and preaching is only one paragraph long.
[47] Fulcher, 'Puritan Piety,' pp. 209–14.
[48] Fulcher, 'Puritan Piety,' p. 197.

that inward calling. This is somewhat surprising since the Westminster Confession of Faith, which he carefully points out to be the accepted doctrine of those whose works he examined, does indeed delineate subcategories within the doctrine of the effectual call. These subcategories are not acknowledged by Fulcher.

His failure to explain the effectual call as containing steps or stages is no doubt partly due to the fact that he has separated preparation from the effectual call. Nevertheless, we do find him explaining stages within the category of preparation when he examines Shepard's writings. He states: 'Shepard distinguishes between conviction of sin and compunction for sin, the second phase of preparation.'[49] He does not give us, however, a summary statement on the various phases of preparation. It seems not to be his aim. Even in his discussion of preparation he is primarily concerned with the question of whether or not the human will's response of faith contradicts the Puritan theology of grace. This concern is tied to his purpose of examining the piety of the early New England Puritans.

Our study goes further than Fulcher's in defining the Puritan view of the effectual call. That more detailed definition will be expounded in Part 2 of this study. It is sufficient here to say that we agree with his observation that the Puritan view of how God moved a person from an unregenerate state to a regenerate state was an extremely important aspect of the Puritan mindset.

In Fulcher's chapter entitled 'The Means of Grace,' he has a subsection devoted to the Puritan practice of preaching.[50] As with Miller, Puritan preaching is not the focus of his entire work, but he does see it as connected to his thesis and therefore devotes considerable attention to it. It is here that he builds on Miller's observation that there was a correlation between the Puritan's faculty psychology and his preaching. Fulcher takes particular interest in the preacher's deliberate aim at the listeners' emotions. He suggests reasons for this which were grounded in the views of preparation and conversion that the preacher held.

We make two observations here about Fulcher's discussion. First, he approaches this subject with the overriding intent of investigating the Puritan understanding of preaching's efficacy. Was the sermon's usefulness in bringing conversion to people due to an inherent efficacy or was it due to the sovereign work of the Spirit of God? And if it was merely a means used by God, why then was an appeal to the emotions important? Fulcher was not making a direct correlation between the effectual call and preaching, nor did he discover the place of the emotions in the effectual call. Secondly, he noted primarily the place of the listener's emotions, without offering an equal treatment of the Puritan view of the intellect and will. The resulting conclusions differ significantly from ours on certain points. We will delineate those differences at

---

[49] Fulcher, 'Puritan Piety,' p. 233.
[50] Fulcher, 'Puritan Piety,' pp. 248–60.

the appropriate point in our study.

Although we have found that our conclusions differ from Fulcher's on some important points, nevertheless we echo his observation that the Puritan's theology of conversion affected the way he preached. His discussion of the interrelatedness of the preacher's theology with his sermon construction, like Miller's, leaves much room for further investigation. Our study is designed to explore this interrelatedness, especially in light of the definition of the effectual call which our research reveals.

It is noteworthy that very little scholarship subsequent to Miller and Fulcher has directly addressed the relationship between the Puritan view of the effectual call and the formation of the Puritan sermon. No one that we are aware of has come as close to this issue as Perry Miller and John Fulcher did in the mid-twentieth century. Our study is intended to address this neglected area of academic inquiry.

Studies of Puritan Preaching which omit its Relationship to the Effectual Call

Scholarship since Miller and Fulcher that has investigated Puritan preaching and has suggested a link between that preaching and the Puritans' theology has exhibited an overwhelming silence concerning the effectual call.

A cursory look at the table of contents of William Haller's *The Rise of Puritanism* suggests that perhaps he addresses our topic of study. Two successive chapters are titled 'The Calling of the Saints' and 'The Rhetoric of the Spirit.' Would Haller tie together the implications of the Puritans' view of the effectual call to their 'rhetoric' or preaching? After a perusal of those chapters it is clear that the answer is no.

Haller acknowledges that vocation, or the effectual call, was an important part of the theological framework within which the Puritan preacher worked:

> Election, vocation, justification, sanctification, glorification, here was the perfect formula explaining what happened to every human soul born to be saved ... . In sermons and popular treatises almost beyond number, the Puritan preachers described the psychological pattern which exemplified the working of the formula, which all the saints were supposed to have exemplified and which every man who desired to be saved must hope would be exemplified again in his own case.[51]

Haller's acknowledgement of the 'formula,' however, leads him to examine the experiences of Puritan preachers as recorded in their diaries rather than the theology with which they explained their experiences.

Haller justifies this approach by taking what he sees as the same tack as the Puritan preachers.

---

[51] W. Haller, *The Rise of Puritanism* (New York: Harper & Row, 1957), p. 90.

The preachers themselves asserted again and again that only so much doctrine was important to be understood as could be understood by men of least knowledge and capacity when set forth in plain English. What, therefore, is important for us to understand is less how learned doctors argued among themselves than what they succeeded in conveying to the people, not what their doctrine was but what it meant and did.[52]

Haller does not delve into any detailed explanation of the theology of the 'formula' (i.e. election, vocation, justification, sanctification, and glorification), much less explore in detail the theology of one part of the formula – vocation.

Due to this approach, we are not surprised to find his discussion of Puritan preaching disconnected from any extensive understanding of the effectual call. Haller does indeed acknowledge that the Puritan's theology affected his preaching, but he collects all the facets of that theology under the title 'doctrine of predestination,' developing his discussion along very broad theological lines. 'What all this meant in practical effect was that the spiritual preacher lavished his strength on turning the currents of emotion in his audience into the molds defined by the doctrine of predestination.'[53] The 'molds' he discusses had to do with the clarity of speech and use of expression to move the emotions of the hearers, but this clarity and use of emotion are never linked to the Puritan view of the effectual call and the place of the preacher in that call.

Bruce Bickel, in his examination of Puritan preaching, *Light and Heat: The Puritan View of the Pulpit*,[54] presents his ideas in two parts. In the first part he points to the Puritans' understanding of God as a major factor in their view of their ministry of preaching. 'The scope of their ministry in and from the pulpit was dictated and defined by their vision of the holy character of God.'[55] Bickel titles the second part of his book 'The Focus of the Gospel in Puritan Preaching,' and it is here that we would expect him to interact with an awareness of the Puritan view of the effectual call. Instead, he only gives the effectual call a cursory mention.

Bickel's concern is with comparing modern evangelism with Puritan evangelism. His thesis is that much modern evangelism has as its foundation the theology and associated methodology of Charles Finney (1792–1875).[56]

---

[52] Haller, *Rise of Puritanism*, p. 86.
[53] Haller, *Rise of Puritanism*, p. 135.
[54] R.B. Bickel, *Light and Heat: The Puritan View of the Pulpit* (Morgan: Soli Deo Gloria, 1999).
[55] Bickel, *Light and Heat*, p. 71.
[56] Charles Finney, an American, began a career in law but became a central figure in the religious revival movement of the early nineteenth century after his personal conversion. He eventually pastored the Broadway Temple in New York City, and was professor of theology and president of Oberlin College. 'Finney, Charles Grandison,' *Encyclopædia Britannica Online*, 2009 edn, http://search.eb.com/eb/article-9034304, accessed 27 November 2009.

Throughout his discussion he is concerned with contrasting the beliefs and methodology of what he calls 'Finneyism' with those of the Puritan movement. He illustrates from Puritan writings their views of God, man, the person and work of Christ, repentance and faith, and assurance. He compares these views with present-day evangelistic views and preaching, tracing what he considers present-day shortcomings to Finneyism.

During his discussion he touches upon aspects of our study. We will comment upon those intersections later. Here it is sufficient to point out that although Bickel's discussion includes topics such as Puritan preaching, evangelism, the nature of man, the affect of sin on human ability, faith and repentance, all topics that are vitally related to the effectual call, he does not include a detailed understanding of the Puritan view of the effectual call.

David Jussely, in his extensive cataloguing of seventeenth-century Puritan sermons, focuses his attention on the strategy used by the Puritan preachers in choosing the texts of Scripture for their sermons. His attention rests on the use of *lectio continua* sermons. *Lectio continua* is 'a rhetorical strategy of homiletic invention ... by which preachers develop consecutive, continuous expository sermons through various books, chapters, or sections of the Bible.'[57] It is Jussely's contention that 'there were two distinct, yet intimately related phenomena in Puritan pulpit rhetoric: the use of the new Reformed method or "plain style" ... and the use of the *lectio continua*.'[58] The presentation of his research supports his thesis that 'Puritans of this era used the *lectio continua* as a predominant strategy of invention for locating sermon texts in preaching.'[59]

Noteworthy for our purposes is the fact that the overwhelming weight of his research was spent in showing the reality of the predominance of the Puritan use of *lectio continua* in sermon text selection. Very little attention was given to the possibility of there being theological reasons in the mind of the Puritan preacher for such a method. Jussely makes a brief exception to this in his conclusion when he states that 'Puritan preaching was governed by their presuppositions concerning the nature of scripture.'[60] This acknowledgment of the presence of a theological foundation for a certain aspect of Puritan preaching is not supported by any preceding examination or proof of the contention. The connection between the use of *lectio continua* in Puritan preaching and the theological convictions of the preachers is not the subject of Jussely's dissertation. Although we are examining a different aspect of Puritan preaching, namely, the arrangement and presentation of sermons to the unconverted, our focus will be on the connection between this aspect of Puritan preaching and the theological convictions of the preachers.

---

[57] D.H. Jussely, 'The Puritan Use of the Lectio Continua in Sermon Invention (1640–1700)' (Ph.D. diss., University of Southern Mississippi, 1997), p. 1.
[58] Jussely, '*Lectio Continua*,' p. 3.
[59] Jussely, '*Lectio Continua*,' p. 123.
[60] Jussely, '*Lectio Continua*,' p. 129.

Peter Toon, in his examination of hyper-Calvinism in England, briefly acknowledges the influence of the preacher's theological understanding concerning salvation on his sermon construction. In a short section entitled 'The Preaching of the Gospel,' he points out that the hyper-Calvinist, of whom Tobias Crisp (1600–43)[61] was an example, would not labour in his sermons to convince the listeners of their spiritual need so as to see signs of conviction in them, but rather would offer grace immediately.[62] He draws attention to the fact that this contrasted with 'Middle-Way' Calvinists, implying that the difference in the two parties' theology could be seen in the manner of their preaching.

Toon's comment upon the effect the various forms of Calvinism had upon the preaching of the day is brief – consisting of just four paragraphs. The thrust of the book lies elsewhere. An exploration of the connection between nonconformist theology and the preaching of those who believed that theology would have to wait for another day. It is precisely this investigation that we have undertaken.

Harry L. Poe, in his 'Evangelistic Fervency Among the Puritans in Stuart England, 1603–1688,' proposes reasons for the eventual loss of evangelistic fervency among later Puritans. His discussion includes an acknowledgement of an interconnection between the theology held by the preacher and the preacher's evangelistic sermonizing. 'The Puritans knew the importance of theology for evangelism. Evangelism must have a theological framework.'[63]

This interest in the theological framework for evangelism takes Poe in a different direction from our study. Instead of looking at the effectual call he directs some attention to the theological issues relating to the relationship between justification and sanctification. He points out the different views among the Puritans concerning what place Christian practice held for an individual's assurance of salvation. 'While the most traditional Calvinists stressed faith as the basis for assurance, a belief developed among the Puritans that practice formed the basis for assurance.'[64] This issue had implications concerning the content and arrangement of evangelistic sermons. Poe does not delineate those implications, nor does he examine the writings or sermons of individual Puritans to show that those implications were consciously dealt with

---

[61] Tobias Crisp was educated at both Cambridge (BA) and Oxford (MA) and became rector of Newington, Surrey, in 1627. During the Civil War he moved to London and took up a heavy preaching schedule. He died soon afterwards of smallpox. He became controversial after his death with the publication of his writings. His emphasis on the righteousness of Christ over against any contribution of man brought him under the accusation of Antinomianism. Roger Pooley, 'Crisp, Tobias (1600–1643),' *ODNB*, http://www.oxforddnb.com/ view/article/6708, accessed 21 November 2009.

[62] Peter Toon, *The Emergence of Hyper-Calvinism in English Nonconformity 1689–1765* (London: Olive Tree, 1967), p. 63.

[63] Poe, 'Evangelistic Fervency,' p. 261.

[64] Poe, 'Evangelistic Fervency,' p. 261.

in their preaching.

The other doctrinal issue Poe mentions is the impact that Arminianism had on the later Puritan movement. Consistent with the direction of his thesis, Poe does not investigate seventeenth-century writings to show relationships between either Arminianism or Calvinism and their proponents' preaching. Rather, he contends that the Arminianism–Calvinism debate was a distraction to Puritan evangelism. 'When pressed by the rival theological claims of the Arminians, this practical thrust [i.e. evangelism] of Puritan Calvinism took on a scholastically doctrinal emphasis ... . The ensuing theological debate diverted the Puritans from the practice of evangelism as they devoted themselves increasingly to the defense of the doctrines of Dort.'[65]

Thus Poe leaves uninvestigated the questions that we are discussing in our study. Was the Puritan understanding of the effectual call clear in the minds of Puritan preachers? Was it taken into consideration as they shaped and delivered their evangelistic sermons?

W. Fraser Mitchell, in his *English Pulpit Oratory from Andrewes to Tillotson: A Study of its Literary Aspects*, focuses on the literary contributions of the sermons of that era. His discussion is concerned mainly with non-Puritan sermons. Due to the 'plain style' of the Puritan preachers Mitchell finds little in their sermons relating to his topic. 'Voluminous as the output of these divines was, and prominent as were the parts played by many of them in the national affairs of their own day, amid the hundreds of printed sermons which they have left us comparatively few are of any literary importance.'[66] Briefly Mitchell acknowledges that the Puritans' theology had an effect on the types of sermons they delivered. 'The change from rhetoric to sacred rhetoric was coloured by theological prepossessions, and that being so, a difference in theological outlook naturally led to a difference in style.'[67] Although observing that the Puritan's style was 'coloured' by Puritan theology, he does not investigate this line of thinking further. What was it about the Puritan's 'theological prepossessions' that dictated certain characteristics in his sermons? Mitchell leaves this question uninvestigated. It is precisely this question that underlies our study.

Kim Fedderson, however, professes to investigate this question in the course of his 'The Rhetoric of the Elizabethan Sermon.' Fedderson states his intent to examine 'the principal modifications to the precepts governing the invention, disposition and ornamentation of the Elizabethan sermon as homiletic theory in the latter half of the sixteenth century attempted to respond to the theological

---

[65] Poe, 'Evangelistic Fervency,' p. 262.
[66] W. Fraser Mitchell, *English Pulpit Oratory from Andrewes to Tillotson: A Study of its Literary Aspects* (New York: Russell & Russell, 1962), p. 255.
[67] Mitchell, *English Pulpit Oratory*, p. 347.

and ecclesiastical reforms initiated by Elizabethan Puritanism.'[68] He argues that during the Elizabethan period theological and other reforms originating from the Puritans changed homiletic theory. Those changes in homiletic theory resulted in changes in actual preaching. In short, Fedderson is proposing that Puritan preaching partially reflected theological underpinnings. On the surface, one would expect his thesis to correlate closely with ours.

A self-imposed limitation in his work should be noted. Fedderson intentionally focuses on homiletic theory rather than practice. He writes, 'I should also stress that my concern throughout rests primarily with sermon theory, not practice … . The study of the Elizabethan sermon is in its infancy, and any definitive statements about the varied practices of Elizabethan preachers would be, in my estimation, premature.'[69] Our study does include an examination of practice as well as theory, by investigating the practices of one particular Puritan preacher.

Fedderson proposes that the change in homiletic theory can be documented by examining the preaching manuals of Andreas Hyperius (1511–64),[70] Niels Hemmingsen (1513–1600),[71] and William Perkins. Fedderson explains: 'The works of Hyperius, Hemmingsen and Perkins take us from the beginning to the end of Elizabeth's reign and reflect its theological mutations. All three writers belong to a common homiletic tradition … . However, they represented this homiletic tradition at different stages of its evolution.'[72]

Fedderson promises to investigate the relationship between the preacher's theology and his shaping of sermons. After commenting on James O'Malley's 'agenda for future scholarship'[73] related to this matter, he says: 'I will touch on a number of the topics O'Malley identifies – two in particular, the evolution of reformation homiletic theory and the relation of theological doctrine to the art of sacred oratory.'[74] Here again our expectations are raised that he will speak to the issues we investigate in our study.

---

[68] Kim Fedderson, 'The Rhetoric of the Elizabethan Sermon' (Ph.D. diss., York University, Ontario, 1985), p. iv.

[69] Fedderson, 'Elizabethan Sermon,' p. 5.

[70] Andreas Hyperius was a Flemish Protestant theologian, otherwise known as Andreas Gheeraerdts. His influence on English preaching followed the translation of his homiletic manual from Latin into English by John Ludham, vicar of Wethersfield. Fedderson, 'Elizabethan Sermon,' p.5.

[71] Niels Hemmingsen was a Danish Lutheran theologian who studied at the University of Wittenberg under Melanchthon. Upon his return to Denmark he wrote numerous works in Latin. His books on homiletics were translated into English by John Horsfall. Fedderson, 'Elizabethan Sermon,' p. 6.

[72] Fedderson, 'Elizabethan Sermon,' p. 7.

[73] See James W. O'Malley, 'Content and Rhetorical Forms in Sixteenth-Century Treatises on Preaching', in James Murphy, ed., *Renaissance Rhetoric* (Berkeley: University of California Press, 1983), p. 252.

[74] Fedderson, 'Elizabethan Sermon,' p. 8.

Studies of Puritan Preaching 23

However, Fedderson also refers to factors other than theology which, in his opinion, affected Puritan homiletics. These factors include the 'Puritan insistence that the church must be stripped of all human innovations and restored to its original apostolic simplicity.'[75] This insistence had consequences on Puritan homiletics. 'Puritan homiletic theory attempted to strip the sermon of its oratorical vestments and turn it into a purely functional instrument of the exposition of God's word.'[76]

Fedderson then borrows a phrase from Edward Dowden[77] and contrasts the Catholic and Puritan 'family of mind.' He affirms, while quoting Dowden, that the Puritan family of mind is such that 'the natural and supernatural exist in an unmediated dualism, and it is a difficulty with him to clothe the naked idea – religious or ethical – in any sensuous medium or body. Hence, Puritanism in itself is ill fitted to produce great art.' He quickly asserts: 'It is this Puritan family of mind or sensibility that triggers the transformation in the theory of Protestant pulpit oratory during the reign of Elizabeth.'[78] This assertion belies Fedderson's approach. He attributes the change in preaching to a non-theological factor. He follows this assertion with a discussion of the importance of a 'distinctly Puritan theory of language,' and tells us his 'aim is to trace some of the sixteenth-century sources that contributed to its development.'[79] He thus points to a Puritan 'sensibility' and 'theory of language' as that which influenced Puritan preaching. Where is his promised discussion of theological factors? Will he show that it was Puritan theology that contributed to their distinct 'sensibility' and 'theory of language,' or will he propose non-theological reasons for them also?

His introductory comments continue to suggest that he will investigate the relationship between theology and preaching. 'Further, depending on the theology a preacher subscribes to, certain stylistic features, while never presenting themselves as a [*sic*] obligatory choices ... do, nevertheless, become preferred options.'[80] Yet he quickly turns to the theory and vocabulary of rhetoric rather than to theology. He explains that he has arranged his material along the lines of classical rhetoric. 'Each chapter begins with a concise overview of one of the five great rhetorical arts – <u>inventio</u>, <u>dispositio</u>, <u>elocutio</u>, <u>memoria</u>, <u>pronuntatio</u> – and, using the principles of each art as a benchmark, each chapter examines the extent to which the precepts of the various homiletic theories available to Elizabethan preachers either reaffirmed or departed from

---

[75] Fedderson, 'Elizabethan Sermon,' p. 3.
[76] Fedderson, 'Elizabethan Sermon,' p. 4.
[77] Edward Dowden, *Puritan and Anglican* (New York: Books for Libraries Press, 1967), p. 7.
[78] Fedderson, 'Elizabethan Sermon,' p. 9.
[79] Fedderson, 'Elizabethan Sermon,' p. 10.
[80] Fedderson, 'Elizabethan Sermon,' p. 16.

the teachings of traditional rhetoric.'[81] The same focus upon rhetorical theory which informed the arrangement of his entire work can be seen in the discussion within each subsection.

When Fedderson arrives at a discussion of the place of emotions in rhetoric he shows that his pursuit of answers is not primarily in the realm of theology. He writes, 'Recognizing the emotional character of faith, all sermon theorists to a greater or lesser degree recommend that preachers avail themselves of appeals to their audience's emotions. Admitting the need for such appeals, the theorists then search for the precepts necessary to inform homiletic practice, and unsurprisingly it is in the "bookes of the rhetorician."'[82] In this statement it is revealed where he too will search.

The great bulk of his work is in actuality concerned with non-theological factors of sermon construction: matters of rhetoric, of audience type, and the influence of Ramism. His explanations occasionally drift into areas of theology. The most significant example occurs when discussing the preacher's intention to influence the hearer's emotions. He asserts: 'Implicit in Hyperius' insistence that preachers must concern themselves more with moving affections than proving and confirming doctrine is a recognition that the ground upon which faith is based is emotional rather than intellectual. Faith is a feeling towards and not a knowledge of God.'[83] This assertion, which our study suggests is an inaccurate representation of the Puritan view of faith, is made without any examination of theological writings of the early Puritans.

Fedderson examines rhetorical texts and homiletics and logic, not theology. Although he goes to great lengths to substantiate his statements about early Puritan use of rhetoric, he makes assertions about Puritan belief with virtually no substantiation at all. We agree with him that the Puritan preacher's appeal to emotions is significant. However, other than an unsubstantiated claim concerning the Puritans' understanding of the nature of faith, his readers are left to guess at what theological issues underlay the practice of appealing to the audience's emotions. Could there not be a system of theological thought supporting that practice? Fedderson does not answer that question.

It must be noted that during his entire discussion there is no examination of the Puritan view of the effectual call. It is our contention that in understanding this view of the effectual call we realize why the emotions are targeted by the Puritan preacher. There are indeed theological reasons for the way the Puritans preached. Fedderson's focus upon rhetorical theories does not lead him to those reasons. It is precisely those reasons that we intend to investigate.

Of all relatively recent scholars Teresa Toulouse comes closest to our approach when examining Puritan preaching. She is focusing her attention on the New England Puritan, John Cotton (1584–1652). In doing so, she explicitly

---

[81] Fedderson, 'Elizabethan Sermon,' p. 17.
[82] Fedderson, 'Elizabethan Sermon,' p. 64. Fedderson is here quoting Hyperius.
[83] Fedderson, 'Elizabethan Sermon,' p. 62.

states that her approach involves the assumption that the theological convictions of the preacher were one of the main factors that shaped the manner and matter of his sermons. An example of this mentality is seen when she is comparing Cotton's sermon structure with Perkins' sermon model. She asserts: 'There appear to be theological assumptions underlying the Perkins model that Cotton does not share.'[84] She develops her arguments with the conscious premise that Puritan theology informed Puritan preaching.

After stating that a major concern of her study is the exploration of the structure of 'the New England Puritan sermon, and of sermons written in this loosely defined Puritan tradition'[85] Toulouse further defines what she means by sermon structure. 'By structure, I refer most broadly not only to arguments which occur or recur in sermons, but also to methods whereby these arguments are juxtaposed, to the particular language – ornate, plain, mixed – used within these varying juxtapositions, and to the kind of progressive movement or lack of it that occurs within the sermon as a whole.'[86]

Having thus stated her intent to examine Puritan sermon structure, Toulouse then explains her view that the structure itself can tell us about the Puritan preacher's beliefs. 'Such a study rests on the belief that sermon structures do not merely frame the "content" of faith, but can also be used to reconstruct the preacher's sense of his role.'[87] We will include this self-awareness of the preacher's role within our discussion of the preacher's theology. It is a theological understanding of the place of the preacher and his task in God's revealed process for accomplishing his will in the lives of the listeners.

In a review of Toulouse's work, O.C. Edwards Jr says: 'Thus Toulouse demonstrates the interrelatedness of what is believed with the way it is preached.'[88] We agree that such interrelatedness exists and that we can find in it the driving force behind much of the matter and manner of Puritan sermons to the unconverted. In our study, however, we have identified the theological understanding of the effectual call as the primary shaper of the preacher's homiletics. Toulouse goes in another direction.

Toulouse suggests that the aspects of theology that significantly affected the preacher's sermon structure were those which related to the preacher's understanding of saving faith, and his understanding of his audience's spiritual state.

---

[84] Teresa Toulouse, '"The arte of prophesying": John Cotton and the Rhetoric of Election,' *Early American Literature* 19 (1984–85), p. 279.
[85] Teresa Toulouse, *The Art of Prophesying: New England Sermons and the Shaping of Belief* (Athens: University of Georgia Press, 1987), p. 7.
[86] Toulouse, *New England Sermons*, p. 8.
[87] Toulouse, *New England Sermons*, p. 8.
[88] Otis C. Edwards Jr, 'Preaching in New England,' *Anglican Theological Review* 71 (1989), pp. 191–200, at p. 199.

Obviously, the notion of what the form of a sermon should be and the relation that this form might bear to belief and to audience differ for each preacher. What is clear in each case explored here, however, is that ideas about what properly constituted 'faith' led to reactions, sometimes blatant, sometimes very subtle, against one manner of presentation in favor of another and, in the process, came to privilege one conception of audience over another.[89]

It should be stated that Toulouse examines factors other than theology that affected sermon structure – mainly the preacher's role in Puritan New England of maintaining a sense of continuity in a community faced with change. But it is her attempts to show the interrelatedness between the preacher's theology and his homiletics that intersect with our study.

In the above quotation Toulouse asserts that 'ideas about what properly constituted "faith"' affected the preacher's sermon presentation. Her discussion includes preachers outside the Puritan movement as well as an examination of Cotton's sermons. Her examination of Cotton does not detail his view of faith and its relation to the sermon structure. She does, however, focus a good deal of attention on how Cotton viewed his audience theologically and what that view meant for his homiletics.

Toulouse asserts that in Cotton's view there were the elect and the non-elect among the preacher's audience, and each group had differing spiritual capacities for comprehending God's word. Cotton's understanding of these differing capacities, and his understanding of his role as a preacher in speaking God's will to each group, determined how he preached. It is Toulouse's assertion that Cotton diverged from the normal Perkins model of preaching partly because of this theological issue. Cotton understood the elect listener as having a God-given ability to apply the preached word to life, and he therefore de-emphasized the 'Uses' section of the sermon: 'Cotton ... shows very little interest in applying the doctrines he so carefully opens.'[90] His understanding of the spiritual ability of the elect also led Cotton to increasing use of figurative language in order to create an emotional impact, rather than relying on logical argumentation. This departure from the normal Puritan sermon form of the day she calls a 'fragmenting' of the Perkins model.

Her discussion is extensive, but her most salient point for our purposes is that this divergence was due to a theological understanding which Cotton possessed. In a parallel publication she writes: 'Cotton's apparently fragmented structure, then, in which figurative language appears where rational argument might be expected, does not show a simple inability or unwillingness to follow Perkins. It is, I would suggest, the result of certain convictions about listeners who have been granted "eyes to see" and "ears to hear" the "literall" meaning of Scripture.'[91]

---

[89] Toulouse, *New England Sermons*, p. 8.
[90] Toulouse, *New England Sermons*, p. 15.
[91] Toulouse, 'John Cotton,' p. 288.

We agree that the definition of saving faith and the spiritual ability of the audience are areas of the preacher's theology that affect his preaching. Rather than isolate those two aspects of theology for discussion, our study of Puritan theology reveals them as fitting together in the theological scheme of the effectual call. It will be in that broader context that we will examine both these areas of theology and their relation to preaching.

It is important to notice that Toulouse does not discuss the effectual call. In her discussion of Cotton she notes: 'English Puritans like Perkins and Cotton derived a flexible step-by-step movement towards salvation from the writings of St. Paul. While these steps are not necessarily sequential, the regenerate soul must, at some point, experience all of them. These steps have generally been termed election, calling, justification, sanctification, and glorification.'[92] After mentioning these five steps, which include the effectual call, she does not mention it again. She comments briefly on election and glorification. She then spends over four pages on the relationship between justification and sanctification and how the defining of that issue became an important part of the Antinomian controversy of which John Cotton was a part. She omits entirely any pursuit of a fuller understanding of the theological category of 'calling' and its effect on the preacher. It is precisely that issue which our study is designed to explore.

It is noteworthy that these studies of Puritan preaching (Haller, Bickel, Jussely, Toon, Poe, Mitchell, Fedderson and Toulouse) all acknowledge that there is a correlation between the Puritan preacher's theology and his preaching but none of them explore the Puritan view of the effectual call.

Studies of the Puritan View of the Effectual Call which omit its Relationship to Preaching

Two examinations of Puritan theology do discuss the Puritan view of the effectual call and suggest that there is some correlation between that view and Puritan preaching. However, in these two studies Puritan preaching is not the focus of the theses. Cursory acknowledgment is made of the fact that Puritan preaching was impacted by their view of the effectual call, but no comprehensive examination is offered of that impact.

Lynn B. Tipson Jr, in his 'The Development of a Puritan Understanding of Conversion,' examines early Puritanism until the time of William Perkins.[93] After investigating the development of Protestant theological views concerning conversion, Tipson examines what he calls 'a tradition of practical conversion preaching.'[94] He asserts that this tradition is identifiable within a 'virtual

---

[92] Toulouse, *New England Sermons*, p. 24.
[93] Lynn Baird Tipson Jr, 'The Development of a Puritan Understanding of Conversion' (Ph.D. diss., Yale University, 1972).
[94] Tipson, 'Understanding of Conversion,' p. i.

Reformed consensus' concerning the doctrines of conversion. He studies the writings of John Bradford (1510–55),[95] Arthur Dent (1552/3–1603),[96] Thomas Wilcox (1549–1608),[97] Richard Greenham (1531–91),[98] and Richard Rogers (1551–1618)[99] as examples of this kind of Puritan understanding and preaching. The fact that Tipson is acknowledging a link between Puritan understanding of conversion and Puritan preaching brings his study into contact with ours.

What we find especially noteworthy is that Tipson does in fact attempt to describe the Puritan understanding of the effectual call. His description occurs within his larger discussion of Puritan doctrines related to conversion.

---

[95] John Bradford worked as a vice-treasurer of the English army but changed careers after being converted, and entered Cambridge. Although eventually finding a place on the faculty, he was appointed one of the king's chaplains. After Edward VI's death, the government of Queen Mary imprisoned Bradford. During his imprisonment he wrote prolifically, both letters and books. Bradford's prominent leadership role among the Protestants resulted in numerous attempts to secure his recantation. After almost two years of imprisonment and steadfast refusal to recant, he was executed at the stake. D. Andrew Penny, 'Bradford, John (c.1510–1555),' *ODNB*, http://www.oxforddnb.com/view/article/3175, accessed 21 November 2009.

[96] Arthur Dent was educated at Cambridge and was ordained as priest at the age of twenty-four. He ministered in various places within the diocese of London, during which time he received censures of various degrees from Archdeacon John Walker but always avoided imprisonment or worse. His preaching was effective and 'he translated this skill into print, becoming one of the most popular protestant authors of his generation.' Brett Usher, 'Dent, Arthur (1552/3–1603),' *ODNB*, http://www.oxforddnb.com/view/article/7511, accessed 21 November 2009.

[97] Thomas Wilcox was educated at Oxford and 'became part of a militant tendency of younger London preachers' led by John Field. His relationship with Field resulted in shared publications and joint imprisonment. Release from prison gave Wilcox more opportunities to preach, write, and influence the clergy of the day. Collinson describes him as 'one of the most committed, active, and socially and politically well connected of Elizabethan puritan ministers.' Patrick Collinson, 'Wilcox, Thomas (c.1549–1608),' *ODNB*, http://www. oxforddnb.com/view/article/29390, accessed 21 November 2009.

[98] Richard Greenham, after finishing his studies at Cambridge, began his ministry at Dry Drayton in 1567. After defending himself before Bishop Richard Cox, he was allowed to preach as a member of the 'godly' preachers but also worked with Cox in attempting to restore recusants to the church. At Dry Drayton 'he presided over the first known household seminary.' He later moved to London and ministered there until his death. Eric Josef Carlson, 'Greenham, Richard (early 1540s–1594),' *ODNB*, http://www.oxforddnb.com/view/ article/11424, accessed 21 November 2009.

[99] Richard Rogers was educated at Cambridge and ministered at Radwinter and Wethersfield, both in Essex. He was a signer of the Book of Discipline and a member of the Braintree Conference. His *Seven Treatises Containing such Directions as is Gathered out of the Holie Scripture* became widely read and influential. Francis J. Bremer, 'Rogers, Richard (1551–1618),' *ODNB*, http://www.oxforddnb.com/view/article/23995, accessed 21 November 2009.

However, he devotes little more than five pages to this aspect.[100] When exploring the implications of this view of the effectual call, Tipson asserts that it did indeed affect Puritan preaching. This exploration is brief, taking place within the five pages he devotes to the effectual call. His illustration of this effect is seen most clearly in his discussion of the writings of Rogers.[101]

Tipson, although identifying the effectual call as an essential component of the Puritan view of conversion as well as a significant factor in shaping Puritan preaching, does not arrive at a description of the effectual call which involved identifiable steps. He makes a particular point of this fact in his conclusion. 'In addition, and here this dissertation stands counter to a direction frequent in recent studies of Puritanism, the understanding of conversion taught by Perkins and the English practical tradition before him did not reduce conversion to well-defined stages in a morphology.'[102] Tipson consistently resists giving an explanation of conversion that delineates certain steps.

Our research shows a very different picture. As will be detailed later, our findings result in a very precise depiction of well-defined steps in the Puritan view of the effectual call. This becomes extremely significant when the understanding of the effectual call is applied to the task of preaching.

It is also important to note that Tipson does not systematically discuss the Puritan view of the faculties of the soul. He mentions the human intellect, will and affections, but does not explore their functions from a theological perspective, nor does he attempt to explain their interrelatedness precisely. His lack of detailed analysis of this point is illustrated in the fact that he does not identify which faculties are the seats of various aspects of the effectual call. This, of course, is understandable since Tipson does not work with a definition of the effectual call which includes well-defined steps. Our research reveals an important relationship in Puritan thinking between the various faculties of the soul and the steps in the effectual call. This relationship was all-important in the mind of the Puritan preacher as he shaped his sermons for the unconverted. This relationship, however, has not been discovered by Tipson.

Tipson's discussion of Puritan preaching is not direct. He does not address preaching under a separate heading but blends his comments on preaching into his explanation of the effectual call and his descriptions of the views of various Puritans. His main observation is that the Puritan understanding of conversion meant that the Puritan preacher would preach Law as well as Grace. 'It was the preacher's duty to apply both Law and Gospel correctly to his hearers.'[103] The Law was to be preached first. 'After he had prepared his hearers with the Law, the preacher turned to the Gospel.'[104] Tipson does not explain the Puritan's

---

[100] Tipson, 'Understanding of Conversion,' pp. 237–42.
[101] Tipson, 'Understanding of Conversion,' pp. 282–96.
[102] Tipson, 'Understanding of Conversion,' p. 321.
[103] Tipson, 'Understanding of Conversion,' p. 237.
[104] Tipson, 'Understanding of Conversion,' p. 240.

decision to preach the Law first in relation to the Puritan's understanding of the details of the effectual call.

In contrast, our research reveals an important relationship in Puritan thinking between the various faculties of the soul and the steps in the effectual call. We also have discovered that this relationship had significant implications on sermon construction and delivery. Tipson's discussion does not address this relationship, nor does it discover those implications.

Gavin McGrath, in his 'Puritans and the Human Will,' examines certain aspects of the theology of mid-seventeenth-century Puritanism. He studies the works of Richard Baxter and John Owen (1616–83),[105] who were both contemporaries of the particular Puritan whose works are the subject of our study. The central point of McGrath's investigation is not the effectual call, nor its effect on preaching, but voluntarism and its effect on Puritan piety and practice. He states in his conclusion: 'The contribution which this study makes to the knowledge of puritan theology and practice lies principally in the definition of voluntarism offered.'[106] He gives only three pages of attention to discussing the effectual call, approaching the subject within his stated aim of discovering the nuances of Puritan voluntarism. We will interact with his observations concerning the effectual call at the proper place in our discourse. For now we note that although he acknowledges the importance of the effectual call in Puritan thinking, it is not the primary subject of his investigation.

Although McGrath's emphasis does not lead him to a detailed description of the Puritan view of the effectual call, he does at times relate the effectual call to the task of preaching. Like Tipson, he does not devote a particular section of his dissertation to exploring this relationship, nor even to the subject of Puritan preaching, but comments on the relationship between the effectual call and preaching while discussing other issues. For example, within his short section on the effectual call he writes: 'Baxter and Owen were convinced about the importance and priority of preaching: it was for them the chief means of grace and so the primary way in which the effectual call was given.'[107] He does not follow up on this observation with any detailed analysis of the interrelatedness of the effectual call and the practice of preaching.

McGrath's study does intersect with ours at one significant point. Our

---

[105] John Owen studied at Oxford and began active ministry in 1635. His ministry included sermons to Parliament, a close association with Cromwell, and the vice-chancellorship of Oxford University. He came under pressure after 1660 for his nonconformity but continued preaching and writing. He wrote prodigiously on theological subjects, issues of church polity, apologetics for toleration, and issues of practical Christianity. 'He was indisputably the leading proponent of high Calvinism in England in the late seventeenth century.' Richard L. Greaves, 'Owen, John (1616–1683),' *ODNB*, http://www.oxforddnb.com/ view/article/21016, accessed 21 November 2009.

[106] McGrath, 'Puritans and the Human Will,' p. 390.

[107] McGrath, 'Puritans and the Human Will,' p. 266.

investigation involves a detailed description of the Puritan theology of the human constitution. This theology encompasses the faculty psychology which characterized many Puritans of that day. Involved in this psychology is a view of how various faculties of the soul – mind, will, and affections – function and how they relate to each other. It is exactly here that McGrath investigates some of the same questions as we do. We will interact with his ideas in detail at the relevant point in our study.

We also must note that his investigation of the Puritan view of the human will and intellect, valuable and thorough as it is, does not address all our questions. How did these faculties fit into the Puritan view of the effectual call? What implications did that hold for preaching for conversion? In McGrath's comments about preaching, which he makes within a brief consideration of the effectual call, he momentarily touches upon one of the key points of our study. He writes: 'Through the preached word, they [i.e. Baxter and Owen] assumed that God addressed the minds and moved the wills of the congregation.'[108] Was the addressing of the mind and will merely an assumption? Was there an order to the addressing of the mind and will? Was that order tied to the effectual call? Was the Puritan preacher aligning certain aspects of his sermon with an understanding of the effectual call that, in turn, was built upon the belief that certain steps in conversion occurred in certain faculties of the soul? Such detailed questions concerning the relationship between the effectual call and the work of preaching are not the subject of McGrath's discussions. It is precisely such questions that we will investigate.

Summary

In summary, we note that those studies which have focused on Puritan preaching have not drawn a correlation between the particular view the Puritans held of the effectual call and their sermon preparation and presentation. Some studies have described Puritan preaching without attempting to explain the Puritan motivation for sermon organization and delivery. Other studies suggest non-theological reasons for the distinctive Puritan preaching. Some scholars do indeed suggest theological reasons for the manner and matter of Puritan preaching but do not include the effectual call in their theories.

Other than the works of Tipson and McGrath, we are not aware of any relatively recent academic study that has examined the correlation between the Puritan's view of the effectual call and the manner and matter of Puritan preaching for conversion. We assert that this correlation is a vital part of understanding late seventeenth-century Puritan preaching. It is the design of our study to investigate this correlation. We also assert that this correlation and its importance can be clearly seen in the sermons and writings of one particular Puritan preacher. We turn our attention now to that man and his works.

---

[108] McGrath, 'Puritans and the Human Will,' p. 266.

Chapter 2

John Flavel and the Rationale for using him in this Study

Our study of the relationship between the Puritan preacher's understanding of the effectual call and his sermon construction and delivery will proceed by examining the theology and sermons of John Flavel (c.1628–91).

We are not suggesting that the Puritan movement was homogeneous in all points of theology or in its sermon construction and delivery. Recent scholarship has contended that 'it was in the mid-seventeenth century that English Protestantism really began to splinter: not only did the number of groups with differing ideas rise rapidly, as we have seen, but also the number of subjects on which there was serious disagreement increased rapidly too.'[1] McGrath, in his study of voluntarism in Baxter and Owen, observes 'the rather startling absence of studies on puritan theology which pay attention to the theology of particular individuals. It seems that in the attempt to "discover" the pulse of seventeenth century Puritanism many of the finer details (which help constitute the whole) are forfeited for the sake of the "broad picture."'[2] In the conclusion of his dissertation, McGrath mentions the work of Miller as an example of Puritan studies built upon the assumption that Puritan theology was more or less monolithic – an assumption with which McGrath contends.[3]

We agree with McGrath's contention. In an effort to contribute some of those previously forfeited 'finer details' we concentrate our attention on the theology and preaching of John Flavel.

Who was John Flavel? What was his influence through preaching and through his published works? Why is Flavel an ideal subject for the study of the influence of Puritan theology on Puritan preaching for conversion? What sermons and writings of Flavel's do we have available for our examination? We now turn our attention to answering these questions.

Biographical Sketch

John Flavel was born between 1627 and 1630 into the family of Richard Flavel,

---

[1] Green, 'Bunyan in Context,' p. 11.
[2] McGrath, 'Puritans and the Human Will,' p. 66.
[3] McGrath, 'Puritans and the Human Will,' p. 390.

minister at Bromsgrove in Worcestershire. Richard Flavel was at that time associated with the portion of the Church of England which fostered sentiments that in later years would express themselves in nonconformity. By the time of the ejection in 1662 he was located in London. He apparently had no settled congregation at that time but engaged in pastoral ministry whenever and wherever possible. He was known to have been the target of the authorities' attention. Finally, in 1665 his nonconformist practices resulted in his imprisonment. Although eventually released, he and his wife both had contracted the plague in prison and died soon thereafter.

John Flavel spent the years of his childhood at home, being taught the tenets of his faith by his father and apparently absorbing some of his redoubtable spirit. He was sent to Oxford, entering in 1646 when he was around seventeen years old, and was enrolled in University College. Before the age of twenty-three he took the degree of B.A.

In 1650, Mr. Walpate, rector of Diptford in Devon, inquired at Oxford for an assistant. John Flavel was recommended to him and on April 27, 1650, he began his work as assistant minister. In October of the same year Flavel was examined and ordained by a presbytery assembled at Salisbury.

Not long afterwards, Walpate died and Flavel succeeded him in the rectory. He served as minister of the church in Diptford until 1656. During those six years he married twice. His first wife, Jane Randal, and their infant son, died in childbirth. He later married Elizabeth Morrice. During this time he gained a good reputation for his behaviour and his execution of his ministerial duties.

On December 10, 1656, Flavel responded to a call from the church in Dartmouth and began work as minister there along with Allen Geere. Two congregations were served by the men, St. Saviour, where Geere was the vicar, and the church at Townstall, just outside the town, where Flavel was the curate. The two men shared ministerial duties at both places. As in Diptford, Flavel soon gained a reputation as one who was extremely devoted to his studies and to the carrying out of his ministerial duties.

In 1662, following the Act of Uniformity, John Flavel was ejected from his office.[4] Four months later Geere died. Flavel stayed in Dartmouth attempting to

---

[4] The Act of Uniformity was enforced from St Bartholomew's Day, August 24, 1662. Iain Murray, in his introduction to *Sermons of the Great Ejection*, summarized the salient points of the Act of Uniformity: 'The principal terms required by the Act were, a Declaration of "unfeigned assent and consent" to everything contained in the Book of Common Prayer, re-ordination for those not episcopally ordained and a renunciation of the Solemn League and Covenant. Knowing that the Puritans would not submit to such terms, the Authorities framed the Act to secure their expulsion.' (London: Banner of Truth, 1962), p. 7 n. The exact wording of the Act can be found in Henry Gee and William Hardy, ed., *Documents Illustrative of English Church History: Compiled from Original Sources* (London: Macmillan, 1910), pp. 600–19. A succinct discussion of the elements of the act which were offensive to the Puritans is found in John Spurr, 'From Puritanism to Dissent, 1660–1700,' in Christopher

minister to his former congregation in whatever manner possible or through whatever opportunity presented itself.

In 1665 the Oxford Act, or Five-Mile Act, was passed and he was thereby forced to leave Dartmouth.[5] He moved to Slapton, barely beyond the five-mile limit, and continued to maintain communication with the people of his church. There are numerous accounts of the unusual efforts he and the people of his church made to meet together for worship and instruction. These efforts included midnight meetings in a large house near South Molton, meetings in forests and fields, arrests and fines imposed upon the people, and clandestine meetings in Dartmouth after nightfall. Also, worth noting for our purposes, Flavel wrote treatises and began to publish his works during this period.

On March 15, 1672, Charles II issued a Declaration of Indulgence in which he revoked all the laws which punished Roman Catholics and other religious dissenters. The increased freedom resulting from this indulgence allowed Flavel to move back into Dartmouth. He began to hold open meetings again in the town. He continued to write and publish, as well as to preach and perform ministerial duties. Within a year, however, the Parliament forced Charles to withdraw the indulgence and in its place instituted the Test Act.[6] Flavel stayed in Dartmouth and continued preaching but more privately.

His second wife died and he eventually married a widow, Mrs Ann Downe. Two sons were born to Flavel and his third wife.

During the interval between the recalling of the indulgence in 1673 and King James II's Declaration of Liberty of Conscience in 1687,[7] Flavel experienced

---

Durston and Jacqueline Eales, eds, *The Culture of English Puritanism, 1560–1700* (New York: St. Martin's Press, 1996), pp. 234–65.

[5] The Five-Mile Act was enforced beginning on March 24, 1665. This Act prohibited any clergyman who had not submitted to the Act of Uniformity from being within five miles of any city or town, or of any place where he had formerly preached. The text of the act can be found in Gee and Hardy, ed., *Documents*, pp. 620–23.

[6] John Moorman explains that 'in 1673, the *Test Act* was passed, requiring all those holding any civil or military office to receive the Holy Communion according to the rites of the Church of England, to denounce the doctrine of Transubstantiation, and to take the oaths of supremacy and allegiance. This, of course, was aimed at the Roman Catholics who were now becoming a danger to the peace of the realm.' *A History of the Church in England* (New York: Morehouse-Barlow, 1963), p. 253. The text of the Test Act is given in Gee and Hardy, ed., *Documents*, pp. 632–40.

[7] The Declaration of Indulgence can be found in Gee and Hardy, ed., *Documents*, pp. 641–44. The salient sentence expressing the core of the Declaration is as follows (p. 642): 'We do likewise declare, that it is our royal will and pleasure that from henceforth the execution of all and all manner of penal laws in matters ecclesiastical, for not coming to church, or not receiving the Sacrament, or for any other nonconformity to the religion established, or for or by reason of the exercise of religion in any manner whatsoever, be immediately suspended; and the further execution of the said penal laws and every of them is hereby suspended.'

waves of persecution and difficulty. At one point a mob was formed in Dartmouth that burned him in effigy. Richard Greaves, commenting on this period of English history, writes: 'The decade 1678–88, spanning the period from the Popish Plot to the Glorious Revolution, was one of the most turbulent in British history.'[8] Flavel was one of those who rode the waves of that turbulence.

In the early 1680s he decided to leave Dartmouth for London. During the time in London Flavel's third wife died. He was married again, this time to Dorothy Jeffries, 'the widowed daughter of George Jeffries, minister of Kingsbridge.'[9]

While in London he interacted with other nonconformists, often ministering in their congregations, which included a close participation with William Jenkins (1613–85), a well-known leader of Presbyterian nonconformists in London. Flavel narrowly escaped arrest when a secret worship meeting he was attending with Jenkins was interrupted by the authorities. Jenkins was not so fortunate, being caught and imprisoned.

Eventually Flavel moved back to Dartmouth, where he was soon placed under house arrest. Jenkins, like Flavel's parents, contracted a fatal disease while in prison. After Jenkins' death the church over which he had been pastor extended an invitation to Flavel. Flavel refused this call and remained in Dartmouth. The publication dates of Flavel's various books show us that he continued to write during this period.

The liberty of conscience declared by King James II on April 4, 1687, was soon followed by the Glorious Revolution in 1688. Lasting freedom was finally provided to the nonconformists. As a result, Flavel began a more open ministry in Dartmouth. By the testimony of several witnesses, there was a great response to Flavel's preaching during this time of new freedom. He continued in Dartmouth, preaching and carrying on ministerial duties, and putting many of his thoughts into writing for publication.

In 1691 there was an attempt to promote a union between the Presbyterians and the Independents. Flavel was unanimously chosen to be moderator in an assembly of western nonconformist ministers called for this purpose. Flavel prepared an address for this assembly and travelled to Exeter for the meeting. The meetings started with Flavel moderating. However, he died on June 26, 1691, without having delivered the sermon. The sermon text is recorded in his *Works*. He was said to be 64 years old at his death.

Following the Act of Uniformity and his subsequent ejection from the Dartmouth church, Flavel began to put some of his thoughts and teachings into

---

[8] Richard L. Greaves, 'Amid the Holy War: Bunyan and the Ethic of Suffering,' in Anne Laurence, W.R. Owens and Stuart Sim, eds, *John Bunyan and His England, 1628–88* (London and Ronceverte, Hambledon Press, 1990), pp. 63–75, at 63.

[9] J.W. Kelly, 'Flavell, John (*bap.*1630, *d.*1691),' *ODNB*, http://www.oxforddnb.com/view/article/9678, accessed 21 November 2009.

writing for publication. The first treatise, *A Saint Indeed*, was written in 1667 when he was thirty-nine years old. Over the next twenty-five years, he would produce thirty-three more written works. Most of these were published individually as they were completed. He was nearing completion of *An Exposition of the Assembly's Catechism* when he died in 1691. A neighbouring nonconformist minister completed this book, which was published two years later. In 1701, ten years after Flavel's death, his complete works were first collected and published together.[10]

In Appendix 5 of this study we provide an annotated list of all of his works, published and unpublished, that are available to us today.

Flavel's Significance in Seventeenth-Century Puritanism

The Testimony of Foe and Friend

It is our contention that John Flavel was a significant figure in late seventeenth-century Puritanism. We formulate this contention partly as a result of observing the attention paid to him by his critics and those outside the nonconformist movement. These unsympathetic commentators give us a valuable view of Flavel's influence during his day.

One critic was Edmund Elys (1633–1708),[11] a Church of England clergyman living in Exeter, who initiated correspondence with Flavel during 1687.[12] Elys expressed strong and virulent opposition to Flavel's doctrinal views as well as to his nonconformist practices. In 1703 John Walker (1674–1747),[13] Church of England clergyman and historian, was collecting information in an effort to write a book in support of the Church of England clergy who suffered during

---

[10] John Flavel, *The Whole Works of the Reverend Mr. John Flavel, Late Minister at Dartmouth in Devon, in Two Volumes* (London: Parkhurst, Newman, Bell and Cockerill, 1701).

[11] Edmund Elys graduated from Oxford in 1655, was ordained by a deprived bishop in 1659, and began a ministry in which he was pursued by the authorities of the Interregnum for 'being an enemy to the Common Wealth,' and pursued after the Restoration for unmet financial obligations. His writings are known for anti-Socinian polemic and an opposition to strong Calvinistic doctrines. Philip Dixon, 'Elys, Edmund (1633x5–1708),' *ODNB*, http://www.oxforddnb.com/view/article/8783, accessed 21 November 2009.

[12] The correspondence is found in the Bodleian Library (MS J. Walker e.8.39, 40).

[13] John Walker was educated at Oxford, ordained deacon in 1698, and later served as rector of various churches in Devon. He is most known for his effort to record the sufferings and treatment of 'conforming clergy who were deprived and sequestered by the puritans in the period before the Restoration.' This large work earned him the DD of diploma from Oxford and the title 'historian.' Alexander Du Toit, 'Walker, John (*bap.*1674, *d.*1747),' *ODNB*, http://www.oxforddnb.com/view/article/28496, accessed 21 November 2009.

the interregnum.[14] Walker contacted Elys for information concerning the clergymen in Devon. Elys' response to Walker gives us a contemporary's view of the sizeable influence Flavel had in his day:

> Sir, I congratulate to you the virtue of your good design for the service of the church, & I hope I shall be able to give you some assistance in it especially in reference to these three Enemies of the church whose writings have made so much noise in the world, Dr. Owen, R. Baxter, & John Flavel.[15]

We note from the above quotation that this loyal Church of England clergyman put Flavel in the same category as John Owen and Richard Baxter calling them 'these three Enemies of the church.' We also note that Elys recognized the influence that Flavel's writings had exerted, comparing their influence also to that of Owen and Baxter.

The same John Walker also wrote to a Dartmouth resident named Humfries Smith asking for historical information on Flavel. Smith replied: 'He [i.e. Flavel] was mightily admired by the dissenting party in these parts.'[16] Although Smith was not a part of nonconformist circles, Flavel's prominence in those circles was apparently readily observable to him.

Anthony Wood (1632–95),[17] a strong supporter of the Church of England and an unsympathetic commentator on nonconformists, described Flavel as obtaining 'more disciples than ever John Owen the independent, or Rich. Baxter the Presbyterian did.'[18] This is a remarkable evaluation of Flavel's influence. For our purposes it is important to note not only that Wood also compared Flavel to Owens and Baxter, but also that he described Flavel as superseding them in the work of evangelism.

The comments of his fellow nonconformists also suggest that Flavel held a significant influence among late seventeenth-century Puritans. Increase Mather

---

[14] His work was eventually published in 1714 with the title *Attempt Towards Recovering an Account of the Number and Sufferings of the Clergy of the Church of England*.

[15] Bodleian Library, MS J. Walker e.8.32.

[16] H. Smith, 'For the Reverend Mr. John Walker, a minister in Exeter', Bodleian Library, MS J. Walker c.2.422.

[17] Anthony Wood [Anthony à Wood] graduated from Oxford in 1652 and decided to remain in the city for most of his life. Parry writes: 'Wood never had an official base in the university, even though he became over the years the incomparable historian of the place.' He is most well known for his detailed history of the city of Oxford, the university, and his *Athenae Oxonienses*, a compilation of brief biographies of writers and notable graduates of Oxford. Graham Parry, 'Wood, Anthony (1632–1695),' *ODNB*, http://www.oxforddnb.com/view/article/29864, accessed 21 November 2009.

[18] A. Wood, ed., *Athenae Oxoniensis* (4 vols, London: Lackington, Hughes, etc., 1813–20).

(1639–1723),[19] in his preface to Flavel's *England's Duty*, spoke of the widespread influence that Flavel was exerting. 'The worthy author of the discourse emitted herewith, is one whose praise in the gospel is throughout all the churches. His other books have made his name precious and famous in both Englands.'[20] Fellow Puritans considered Flavel's sphere of influence to be widespread and significant.

Richard Baxter also held Flavel in high esteem. Although not personally sharing such esteem, Elys nevertheless expressed Baxter's opinion of Flavel in one of his letters to Walker. He wrote that Flavel 'was no scholar, & yet so impressed upon some that were indeed learned that Mr. Baxter reckons him amongst eminent writers on their side.'[21] It is notable that Baxter considered Flavel as being one of the eminent nonconformist writers.

Flavel's status among nonconformists can also be seen in the fact that he was chosen by them to be the moderator of the Exeter gathering in 1691. Early in that year nearly one hundred London nonconformist ministers had signed a document entitled 'Heads of Agreement' which sought to bring together the Presbyterians and Congregationalists.[22] This document was being presented to nonconformists around the country, and the western nonconformists called a meeting in June to consider it. As already noted, Flavel was chosen to be moderator in this assembly. His esteem was evident not only in his being chosen as moderator, but also in the sway he exerted while holding that position. Brockett explains:

> This desire for Universal Concord was further evident at the second meeting of the Assembly, at Topsham on 23rd–24th June 1691, when those present accepted 'cheerfully and heartily' the Heads of Agreement decided upon that year by the Dissenting Ministers of London, which for the time being brought about a Union between Presbyterians and Independents, the two most numerous of the Nonconformist societies. This Topsham Assembly was held under the moderatorship of John Flavel, the veteran scholar and preacher from Dartmouth,

---

[19] Increase Mather, first child of Cotton Mather, was born in Massachusetts, educated at Harvard, and then moved to England in 1657. He ministered there in several places. Bremer explains that 'his religious views were incompatible with the new regime and he returned to Massachusetts in 1661.' He became teacher at the influential North Church in Boston, eventually became president of Harvard, was involved in the negotiations with the Crown over the charter of Massachusetts, and authored several treatises. Francis J. Bremer, 'Mather, Increase (1639–1723),' *ODNB*, http://www.oxforddnb.com/view/article/18322, accessed 21 November 2009.

[20] Increase Mather in Flavel's *Works*, Vol. 4, p. 16.

[21] E. Elys, letter dated March 6, 1703, Bodleian Library, MS J. Walker e.8.32.

[22] G. Rupp, *Religion in England: 1688–1791* (Oxford: Clarendon Press, 1986), p. 115.

and it was largely due to his eloquent plea for unity that his colleagues followed the example of their London brethren.[23]

Flavel's Involvement in Evangelism

Flavel's importance can be seen, not only in the comments of both sympathetic and adversarial contemporaries but also in his notable involvement in evangelism. John Quick (1636–1706)[24] shared a long friendship with Flavel which began, as he explained, 'when we were neighbour ministers in the south Hames of Devon & continued to the day of his death.'[25] He wrote of the particular success which Flavel had in evangelism – the preaching to unconverted with the aim of seeing them regenerated. 'Few ministers had more spirituall children of their own begetting in the West than Mr. Flavell.'[26]

Frank Lambert, in his *Inventing the 'Great Awakening'*, examines various factors surrounding the conversion of great numbers of people in New England in the eighteenth century. One such factor was the use of printed evangelistic sermons from the previous century. Flavel's sermons were used in this way. Lambert observes that 'Flavel had been one of the leading divines in preaching in a "warm" evangelistic style.'[27]

A description of Flavel's characteristic engagement in evangelistic efforts and his deliberate zeal in that work was published, along with two of his sermons, just three months after his death. In a short biography John Galpine wrote:

> A second thing I observed in this worthy minister was a longing desire after the conversion of souls … . That he might win souls to Christ and build them up in their most holy faith was … the mark that he had in his eye; it was for this that he studied, and labored in the Gospel, and wrestled with God in prayer; and when he perceived that the Spirit of God had been at work upon the souls of any of his people, he did … his utmost both by his counsels and prayers, that the blessed

---

[23] Allan Brockett, *Nonconformity in Exeter, 1650–1875* (Manchester: Manchester University Press, 1962), p. 65.

[24] John Quick graduated from Oxford in 1657 and began preaching in Devon. Following the Restoration he was ejected, but continued preaching whenever he could find opportunity. He was arrested and jailed more than once. His involvement in nonconformity in the West Country continued throughout his life. Alexander Gordon, 'Quick, John (*bap*.1636, *d*.1706),' rev. Stephen Wright, *ODNB*, http://www.oxforddnb.com/view/article/22952, accessed 21 November 2009.

[25] John Quick, *Icones Sacrae Anglicaneae: or The lives & deathss of severall eminent English divines, ministers of the gospell, pastors of churches, & professors of divinity in our own & forreigne universitys*, Vol. 1, Part 2, p. 919. Dr Williams's Library, MS 38.35.

[26] Quick, *Icones Sacrae Anglicaneae*, Vol. 1, Part 2, p. 964.

[27] Frank Lambert, *Inventing the 'Great Awakening'* (Princeton: Princeton University Press, 1999), p. 173.

work might be carried on to perfection. And indeed God was pleased to crown his labors with great success this way. Many souls have been given in as the seal of his ministry, who have owned him to be their spiritual father in Christ, by whom they have been begotten through the Gospel.[28]

Poe suggests that the later Puritans were not known for their evangelistic efforts.

> The old Puritans who survived into the Restoration period would never have said that they were not concerned with salvation. Nonetheless, their concern for salvation had been mitigated by so many other cares that their evangelistic fervency drowned in their concern for competing issues. Their belief in the necessity of conversion persisted, but their practical activity turned from evangelism to theological and ecclesiological debate.[29]

Confuting the assertion that Puritanism as a whole had lost its evangelistic fervency during Flavel's day is not within the scope of our study, but it is our assertion that Flavel himself very clearly does not fit Poe's description. Erroll Hulse, in his 'Adding to the Church: The Puritan Approach to Persuading Souls,' mentions Flavel as an example of one whose life and practice supports the assertion that some Puritans were indeed evangelistic in their outlook.[30] We concur with Hulse's evaluation.

A concern for the conversion of the unregenerate was evident throughout his ministry. Around the year 1668, one of the first works which he published, *Navigation Spiritualized,* had an explicit evangelistic purpose. Twenty-three years later, the treatise published in the year of his death, *Reasonableness and Necessity,* also had an evangelistic purpose. Many of the treatises published during the span of years represented by those two publications included purposeful attempts to influence the conversion of his readers. His sermons, which we will examine later in detail, showed considerable and deliberate attention to the conversion of his hearers.

As late as 1689, just two years prior to his death, we find Flavel using the new-found liberty which followed the coronation of William and Mary to pursue the work of evangelism. It seems that working towards the conversion of the unconverted was the first task to which he directed his attention once real freedom was obtained. The extraordinary results of this effort, and the treatise

---

[28] John Galpine, quoted in John Flavel, *Flavel, the Quaker and the Crown: John Flavel, Clement Lake, and Religious Liberty in 17th Century England* (Cambridge, MA: Rhwymbooks, 2000; first published 1687–92), p. 16, reprinting manuscripts from 1691 and 1692.

[29] Poe, 'Evangelistic Fervency,' p. 260.

[30] Erroll Hulse, 'Adding to the Church: The Puritan Approach to Persuading Souls,' in David Bugden, ed., *Adding to the Church: Being Papers read at the 1973 Westminster Conference* (London: Westminster Conference, 1973), pp. 7–19, at 8.

that resulted from those evangelistic sermons, are commented on in Appendix 5 of this study, in the annotation we provide for his *England's Duty*.

Comment by his contemporaries both inside and outside of the Puritan movement, the opinion of subsequent scholarship, and the examination of his written works and sermons show that John Flavel was deliberately and determinedly involved in evangelism and that he was notably successful in it.

The Popularity and Use of Flavel's Written Works

The significance of John Flavel can be seen not only in the evaluation of him made by his contemporaries and in his particularly fruitful involvement in evangelism but also in the popularity and use of his written works.

The frequent and numerous reprints of his various individual publications and of his collected *Works* speak of a large popularity. As has already been noted, Increase Mather gave testimony to the fact that Flavel's books were being widely received on both sides of the Atlantic. 'His ... books have made his name precious and famous in both Englands.'[31] Flavel's critic, Edmund Elys, lamented the popularity of Flavel's writings, complaining that they, along with the publications of Owen and Baxter, 'have made so much noise in the world.'[32] David Hall, in his study of seventeenth-century popular religion, included Flavel's writings in the category of 'steady-sellers' that thrived in the mid-eighteenth-century marketplace, some of them even into the early 1800s.[33] Ian Green, in his *Print and Protestantism in Early Modern England*, listed Flavel's *A Saint Indeed* as one of the few works of the 'older high Calvinist' genre that sold well in the late seventeenth century.[34]

Theologians and ministers, both of his day and the decades immediately following his death, read his works and referred to his writings.

Cotton Mather (1663–1728)[35] considered Flavel's writings as indispensable for the library of a minister. Hall notes that 'Mather ended his book with a "minimum requirement" reading list for pastors: one much like that in Richard

---

[31] Increase Mather, in Flavel, *Works*, Vol. 4, p. 16.
[32] Bodleian Library, MS J. Walker e.8.32.
[33] David Hall, *Worlds of Wonder, Days of Judgment: Popular Religious Belief in Early New England* (New York: Alfred A. Knopf, 1989), pp. 48–49.
[34] Ian Green, *Print and Protestantism in Early Modern England* (Oxford: Oxford University Press, 2000), pp. 332–33.
[35] Cotton Mather was born in Boston, the son of Increase Mather, entered Harvard at eleven years old, and began distinguishing himself as one with extraordinary mental abilities. He was ordained in his father's Boston North Church in 1685 and ministered there the rest of his life. He and his father were involved in the Salem witch trials and in the politics of Massachusetts. He authored 380 separate titles. Michael Hall writes: 'Cotton Mather was the most influential writer of his generation in America.' 'Mather, Cotton (1663–1728),' *ODNB*, http://www.oxforddnb.com/view/article/18321, accessed 21 November 2009.

Baxter's Christian Directory (1673). It included works by Charnock, Flavel, Pool and Strong (English Puritans).'[36] Thomas Holbrook, in his study of the sources and development of typology in American literature, pointed out the influence Flavel had on Mather. 'In Agricola Mather was emulating the English dissenting clergyman John Flavel (1630?–1691), who had long influenced him.'[37]

Perry Miller, in a discussion of the development in New England of 'a new type of Puritan literature invented after the Restoration,' stated that Flavel's *Husbandry Spiritualized* was its 'chief exemplar.'[38] Miller called this volume 'a best seller among nonconformists for a century after its publication in 1669,' and pointed out its obvious influence on Cotton Mather.[39]

It has already been pointed out that Richard Baxter considered Flavel one of the 'eminent' writers of his day.[40]

Jonathan Edwards (1703–58)[41] also leaned on Flavel's writings. Because of Edwards' prominence in the Puritan theological landscape it is appropriate to note the scholarly discussions surrounding his use of Flavel. Sally Ann Stephenson, in her examination of the relationship between Edwards' thought and his ministry, observed Edwards' respect for and use of Flavel's writings. 'Edwards appears to have read the Puritans – notably Flavel and Charnock – early in his ministerial training.'[42] In her dissertation Stephenson shows a link in thought between Edwards and his theological predecessors, one of whom she shows to be Flavel. This theological relationship to Flavel referred especially to the view of the various faculties of the soul and their involvement in

---

[36] Sally Ann Stephenson, 'The Ministerial and Theological Purposes of Jonathan Edwards' Thought: A Study in Source and Context' (Ph.D. diss., University of Pennsylvania, 1983), p. 49.

[37] Thomas Arthur Holbrook, 'The elaborated Labyrinth: The American Habit of Typology' (Ph.D. diss., University of Maryland, 1984), p. 240.

[38] Miller, *New England Mind*, p. 404.

[39] Jonathan Edwards, *Images or Shadows of Divine Things*, ed. Perry Miller (Westport: Greenwood Press, 1977; first published 1746), p. 13.

[40] E. Elys, letter dated March 6, 1703, Bodleian Library, MS J. Walker e.8.32.

[41] Jonathan Edwards was born in Connecticut and studied at Yale. He held two pastorates prior to being elected to a tutorship at Yale. In 1726 he took a ministerial position at Northampton, Massachusetts, with his grandfather, Solomon Stoddard. His relationship with this church lasted until 1750. During this time he became an instrumental figure in the Great Awakening. He then pastored in Stockbridge until 1757, when he took the position of president of Princeton. During all his adult life he studied and wrote prodigiously. Zakai writes that Edwards 'was the outstanding American theologian and certainly the ablest American philosopher to write before' the mid nineteenth century, and that he 'is recognized as one of the most original thinkers in the American experience.' Avihu Zakai, 'Edwards, Jonathan (1703–1758),' *ODNB*, http://www.oxford dnb.com/view/article/48853, accessed 21 November 2009.

[42] Stephenson, 'Jonathan Edwards' Thought,' p. 76.

conversion. We will take note of this issue later while describing Flavel's theology in detail. Sufficient at this point is the observation that Stephenson maintains that Flavel was studied and quoted by Edwards.

Wallace Anderson, in his introductory comments to the 1993 reprint of Edwards' *Images of Divine Things*, mentioned Flavel, 'whose writings Edwards respected and used but did not accept unquestioningly.'[43] Edwards did not accept anyone's writings unquestioningly, but that he respected and used Flavel's is significant.

John E. Smith edited the 1959 reprint of Edwards' *Religious Affections*. In his comments Smith examines the authors whom Edwards read, noting: 'No other work of Edwards' is so heavily dotted with footnotes containing long extracts from the works of other theologians and divines. In addition to the writings of Solomon Stoddard[44] ... Edwards drew upon the works of sixteen other authors, mostly seventeenth-century English Puritans and dissenting clergy.'[45] Smith then names Flavel in that list of sixteen. Edwards quotes Flavel more than he does William Ames, John Calvin and John Owen combined.

Smith argues that, although Flavel may not be as well known to scholars as others on that list, he is worthy of study. 'All writers cited [by Edwards], with the possible exception of Flavel and Jones, are well known to students of Puritanism.'[46] 'The name of Flavel does not occur in historical studies of seventeenth-century Puritanism as often as it should, and he is less well known than some contemporaries who wrote less and whose works were less influential among the common people. Edwards was nevertheless familiar with many of his books.'[47]

As already noted, Miller contends that Flavel's influence on the Puritan rhetorical technique of 'spiritualizing' is unquestioned. His exploration of Edward's use of that technique naturally includes a discussion of Flavel.

Holbrook, while analyzing the sources of typology in American literature, also notices the connection between Edwards and Flavel. In commenting on the

---

[43] Jonathan Edwards, *The Works of Jonathan Edwards*, Vol. 11, *Jonathan Edwards: Typological Writings*, ed. Wallace Anderson (New Haven and London: Yale University Press, 1993), p. 23.

[44] Solomon Stoddard (1643–1729) was an American Congregational pastor and theologian. He was educated at Harvard, served first as a chaplain in Barbados, and then as pastor in Northampton, Massachusetts. He served in Northampton for sixty years, becoming well known for his preaching, his stand on 'open communion,' and his influence over the entire region's clergy. His successor was his grandson, Jonathan Edwards. Patricia J. Tracy, 'Stoddard, Solomon,' in John A. Garraty and Mark C. Carnes, eds, *American National Biography* (New York: American Council of Learned Societies, 1999).

[45] Jonathan Edwards, *The Works of Jonathan Edwards*, Vol. 2, ed. John E. Smith (New Haven: Yale University Press, 1959), p. 52.

[46] Edwards, *Works*, Vol. 2, p. 52.

[47] Edwards, *Works*, Vol. 2, pp. 60–61.

similarity of theology and approach between Flavel's *Husbandry Spiritualized* and Edwards' writings he writes: 'Flavel's Husbandry Spiritualized is another matter entirely, and has been unjustly represented. He opens this companion work by explaining that it continues an older exegetical method, and delineates a theological position and practice indistinguishable from that of Jonathan Edwards.'[48]

The evidence supports the conclusion that the works of John Flavel were owned by, referred to, quoted by, and exerted an influence upon Jonathan Edwards.

George Whitefield (1714–70), the Calvinistic evangelist noted for his prominent role in the Great Awakening, gives us a glimpse of his evaluation of Flavel. A letter which Whitefield wrote to John Wesley, dated December 24, 1740, and addressing the doctrinal issue of election is included in his published journals. In that letter he chastised Wesley for declaring that no Baptist or Presbyterian writer he had read knew anything of the 'liberties of Christ.' Whitefield, provoked by that comment, responded by naming a few examples of both Baptists and Presbyterians who, in his opinion, were unquestionably prominent and obvious examples of persons who had known the 'liberties of Christ.' He wrote, 'What! neither Bunyan, Henry, Flavel, Halyburton, nor any of the New-England and Scots divines.'[49] This reference reveals the esteem in which Whitefield held Flavel. Only four men were actually named by him to bolster his argument with Wesley. Flavel was one of those four.

Archibald Alexander (1772–1851) was professor at Princeton Theological Seminary and served as that school's first principal from 1812 to 1840. It is argued that he, more than any other individual, set the tone and direction which the seminary followed for the next one hundred years. Christopher Lensch, in a historical examination of early American Presbyterianism, explained the influence Flavel had on Alexander. 'While tutoring away from home, the writings of the Puritan, John Flavel, deeply impressed young Archibald. In fact he counted his own spiritual transformation from a Sunday evening when he was reading a Flavel sermon to friends. Thereupon he drank deeply from many Puritan writers, but confessed his greatest debt to Flavel.'[50] This evaluation is supported by Alexander's own words. He wrote: 'To John Flavel I certainly owe more than to any uninspired author.'[51] Undoubtedly this esteem for Flavel was made known to the hundreds of young men being trained for the ministry at Princeton for those twenty-eight years Alexander was principal.

---

[48] Holbrook, 'Elaborated Labyrinth,' pp. 241–42.
[49] George Whitefield, *George Whitefield's Journals* (London: Banner of Truth, 1960), p. 583.
[50] Christopher K. Lensch, 'Two early American Presbyterian Pastor-Theologians: Samuel Davies and Archibald Alexander,' *WRS Journal* 12/2 (August 2005), pp. 20–26.
[51] Lensch, 'Two Pastor-Theologians,' p. 26 n. 18.

Flavel's writings continued to be republished frequently well into the 1800s. Paul E.G. Cook, in a review of Flavel's *Works* written on the occasion of their 1968 reprinting, stated: 'His collected works were ... republished, on the average, every twenty years until 1823.'[52]

In addition to influencing pastors and theologians, Flavel's *Works* had a widespread influence on laypeople. Research concerning Puritanism in the New World has especially noted Flavel's importance.

C.C. Goen, in comments made on Edwards' use of Flavel in his *Some Thoughts Concerning The Revival*, made a salient comment on the widespread use of Flavel in New England. He wrote that Flavel 'was an English Presbyterian whose writings had long been a staple of New England devotional literature.'[53]

Charles E. Hambrick-Stowe makes the same observation in his *The Practice of Piety: Puritan Devotional Disciplines in Seventeenth-Century New England*. He writes: 'The manuals that had been used in New England since the earliest days of settlement continued to be important, but the new generation of Puritans in both old and New England produced a burst of their own literature. English manuals by Restoration writers such as Flavel, Baxter, and Bunyan ... were imported in large numbers into New England.'[54] Later in his discussion Hambrick-Stowe focuses on the widespread impact that Flavel's written works had in New England. 'The greatest devotional writer for occupational groups was the Englishman John Flavel. His works did not appear in American editions until the early eighteenth century, but they were enthusiastically imported in the closing decades of the seventeenth.'[55]

David D. Hall, in his *Worlds of Wonder, Days of Judgment: Popular Religious Belief in Early New England*, examined the importing, printing and circulation of religious books in late seventeenth-century New England. He noted that the Boston merchants 'ordered and *reordered* the same books repeatedly.'[56] He names Flavel's books as being among those being reprinted due to popular demand.

Lambert, in his investigation of the early eighteenth-century Great Awakening, notes the use of seventeenth-century printed sermons in New England. He represents Mather Byles (1706–88), prominent Bostonian clergyman, grandson of Increase Mather, and publisher of religious literature in eighteenth-century New England, as saying 'that Flavel's sermons reach across the ages and speak "immediately to the Heart" and "set the great Doctrines of

---

[52] Paul E.G. Cook, 'The Works of John Flavel,' *EQ* 41 (1969), pp. 178–80.
[53] Jonathan Edwards, *The Works of Jonathan Edwards*. Vol. 4, *Jonathan Edwards: The Great Awakening*, ed. C.C. Goen (New Haven and London: Yale University Press, 1972), p. 312.
[54] Hambrick-Stowe, *Practice of Piety*, p. 266.
[55] Hambrick-Stowe, *Practice of Piety*, p. 275.
[56] Hall, *Worlds of Wonder*, p. 48.

the Gospel in the most affecting and engaging Lights.'"[57] Lambert also noted that an examination of 'revivalists' libraries' of that time in New England revealed copies of Flavel's writings.[58]

Wills and Names in the New World

Evidence of the popularity of Flavel's works in New England can be seen, not only in libraries and the records of printers and merchants but also in the wills and last testaments of the early inhabitants of the New World. It is not unusual to find Flavel's *Whole Works* mentioned in wills. Although an exhaustive listing of such wills would require research that would take us beyond the focus of this study, even an introductory investigation reveals numerous examples. Two examples are presented here. In 1806 Thomas Snoddy of North Carolina made an 'inventory of the goods and chattles of Samuel Snoddy, deceased.' In addition to items of furniture and kitchen utensils there was 'one large Bible, the works of John Flavel, one confession of faith, some pamphlets.'[59] In 1801, a Benjamin Moody Sr of Massachusetts, who had four children, included a reference to Flavel's *Whole Works* in his will, granting each child 'one fourth part of Rev. John Flavel's works, in two vols, which I possess.'[60] Although we are left to wonder how the two volumes were to be divided between the four children, we do recognize the distinct importance placed upon Flavel's books by Moody. One hundred years after the first edition of the *Whole Works* was printed it was appearing in people's wills. Such references in documents relating to the estates of early Americans are not uncommon.

Another telling hint of the esteem Flavel held in the eyes of the inhabitants of the New World is the rather remarkable occurrence of sons being named after him. Genealogical research finds numerous sons in America being given the names 'John Flavel' or even 'Flavel' to precede their surname, and this occurred in families unrelated to any Flavel ancestors. An exhaustive listing of such occurrences would require research that would take us beyond the focus of this study, but an exploratory investigation results in sufficient examples to suggest that this took place with significant frequency. We offer a few examples here to illustrate this noteworthy occurrence.

As early as the mid-1700s we find inhabitants of New England naming their sons after him. Ellis Bliss (1733–1814) of Connecticut, himself a descendant of those who left England because of persecution on account of their

---

[57] Lambert, *Inventing*, p. 173.
[58] Lambert, *Inventing*, pp. 161–62.
[59] Carol S. Byler, 'Snoddy Family History,' http://bellsouthpwp.net/c/s/csbyler/Genealogy/Snoddy/Snoddy.html, accessed 6 November 2008.
[60] 'Rootsweb: Finding our Roots together,' http://www.rootsweb.com/~maessex/Wills/moodyb.htm, accessed 4 June 2007.

nonconformity, named one son John Flavel Bliss and another Flavel Bliss.[61] Benajah Holcombe (1741–1834) named one of his sons Flavel Holcombe (born in 1781). One of Benajah's grandsons was named John Flavel Holcombe (born in 1803), erasing any suggestion that the name 'Flavel' which had been given to Benajah's son had perhaps come from a source other than the Puritan preacher.[62] James Harvey Neel (born in 1785) of Pennsylvania, himself known as a 'devout Presbyterian,' named one of his sons John Flavel Neel.[63] A member of Harvard's graduating class of 1818 was named John Flavel Jenkins.[64] John Davison (1772–1858) of Vermont recognized as a deacon in his church, named one of his sons Flavel Davison.[65] Ambrose Cowdery Sr (1762–1835) of Connecticut named one of his sons John Flavel Cowdery.[66] The examples are too numerous to list. The frequency of such occurrences, however, is too great to ignore. John Flavel, through his writings, had found an inimitable esteem among the inhabitants of the New World.

The Observations of Scholarly Investigation

We turn our attention to secondary literature which mentions or investigates Flavel's writings and find there additional evidence that he was a significant figure in seventeenth-century English Puritanism.

We have found four Ph.D. dissertations which have looked at Flavel's writings. Thomas Holbrook, in 'The Elaborated Labyrinth: The American Habit of Typology,' examines two of Flavel's treatises and discussed them in light of the development and use of typology in American literature.[67] His concern is not with theology nor with preaching, but with the literary use of typology.

Ralph Gore Jr investigates Flavel's writings in his 'The Pursuit of Plainness: Rethinking the Puritan Regulative Principle of Worship.' As the basis of his insights into Puritan and Presbyterian thought he examines the writings of William Ames (1576–1633),[68] John Owen, and John Flavel. Gore views these

---

[61] John Homer Bliss, *Genealogy of the Bliss Family in America from about the year 1550 to 1880* (Boston: the author, 1881), p. 67.
[62] James and Randal Holcombe, 'Holcombe Family Genealogy,' http://www.holcombegenealogy.com/data/p2.htm#i83, accessed 6 November 2008.
[63] 'Three Rivers Genealogy,' http://www.15122.com/3Rivers/History/CITIES/WMSettlers.htm, accessed 6 November 2008.
[64] 'Surname Site', http://surnamesite.com/harvard/harvard1818.htm, accessed 6 November 2008.
[65] 'Genealogy SF', http://www.genealogysf.com/Stanton-p/p97.htm#i4820, accessed 6 November 2008.
[66] Dale R. Broadhurst, 'The Oliver Cowdery Pages,' http://olivercowdery.com/family/Cdrygen4.htm, accessed 6 November 2008.
[67] Holbrook, 'Elaborated Labyrinth.'
[68] William Ames was educated at Cambridge and while there was converted under the influence of William Perkins. Ames graduated MA in 1601, was elected a fellow of

men as 'theologians representing mature Puritan and Presbyterian thought.'[69] Although his choice to examine Flavel's writings supports our contention that Flavel was indeed an important figure in seventeenth-century Puritanism, his dissertation does not directly intersect with our study.

Sally Ann Stephenson, in 'The Ministerial and Theological Purposes of Jonathan Edwards' Thought: A Study in Source and Context,' maintains that Flavel had an influence upon the thought of Jonathan Edwards. She states Edward's view of the roles played by the human mind and will in conversion and then maintains that Flavel's view was similar.[70] Although she supports this contention with quotations from Flavel, she does not examine Flavel's doctrine in a systematic way. We will interact with her contention at the appropriate place in our argumentation. Beyond that, however, there is nothing in Stephenson's dissertation that overlaps with our study.

Clark Maddux's 'Ramist Rationality, Covenant Theology, and Puritan Poetics' includes eight pages devoted directly to a discussion of the influence of Ramism upon Flavel.[71] This relationship is important to Maddux because he is proposing that Ramist influence on New England Puritanism was more pervasive and long-lasting than has generally been acknowledged. He sees Flavel as a prime example of a 'Ramist Puritan' and a primary influence upon the Puritan poet, Edward Taylor (1642–1729), whose works Maddux examines in detail.

Maddux's discussion most closely intersects with ours on two points: first, when he comments upon the faculty psychology of Flavel; and secondly, when he touches upon the effect Flavel's Ramism has upon the arrangement of his written material. We will discuss Maddux's comments in more detail at the appropriate places in our study, but it should be stated here that the goal of his discussion propels him in a direction different from ours. He does not identify Flavel's view of the effectual call, nor does he address the issue of the theological underpinning of his evangelistic preaching.

Holbrook, Gore, Stephenson and Maddux do not discuss the theology or preaching of Flavel in a way that deals directly with the topic of our study.

---

the university, and ordained. He spent the years until 1610 there as a voice of nonconformity. In 1610, having his degrees and academic duties suspended, he found exile in the Netherlands. There he ministered in an Anglo-Scottish community, took part in the Synod of Dort, became a professor at the University of Franeker, remained involved in English nonconformity, and authored many books and textbooks. He was understood as being 'a leading voice of American and English Puritanism.' Keith L. Sprunger, 'Ames, William (1576–1633),' *ODNB*, http://www.oxforddnb.com/view/article/440, accessed 21 November 2009.

[69] Ralph J. Gore Jr, 'The Pursuit of Plainness: Rethinking the Puritan Regulative Principle of Worship' (Ph.D. diss., Westminster Theological Seminary, 1988), p. 19.

[70] Stephenson, 'Jonathan Edwards' Thought,' p. 152.

[71] Clark Maddux, 'Ramist Rationality, Covenant Theology, and the Poetics of Edward Taylor' (Ph.D. diss., Purdue University, 2001), pp. 170–78.

They do, however, by the attention they give to Flavel, support our contention that he was an important figure in seventeenth-century Puritanism. It should be noted here that we have found no doctoral dissertations which have had as their main focus the writings of Flavel. Certainly none have approached the issue of showing the relationship between Flavel's theology and his preaching.

Two scholarly works other than Ph.D. dissertations give significant attention to John Flavel.

Thomas Lea, in his article *The Hermeneutics of the Puritans*, draws six 'principles of interpretation' that he proposes to be characteristic of the Puritans.[72] In illustrating and supporting his thesis, he leans primarily on the writings of three men, Perkins, Owen, and Flavel. At one point, in which Lea comments upon the practical nature of Puritan preaching, he briefly intersects with a portion of our study. We will comment on that at the appropriate time. He does not discuss the Puritan view of the effectual call, nor the relationship between it and Puritan sermon construction and delivery. It is important to note that he places Flavel alongside of Perkins and Owen, thereby recognizing Flavel's significance.

Norman Fiering interacts with Flavel's writings in his *Moral Philosophy at Seventeenth-Century Harvard: A Discipline in Transition*. Fiering's work relates to ours in those sections where he is discussing the various seventeenth-century views of the relationship between the human will and the human intellect. His discussion applies directly to our evaluation of Flavel's faculty psychology. Fiering includes Flavel in his descriptions, referring to Flavel's ideas as a 'curious blend' of various views.[73] He does not, however, make a connection between the understanding of human psychology which Flavel held and the way Flavel preached. We will interact with Fiering's conclusions when examining Flavel's theological understanding of the human constitution. For now we note that Flavel's theological views warranted being brought into Fiering's discussion of seventeenth-century psychology.

It should also be noted that Fiering recognizes that the various views concerning the intellect and will, their place in saving faith, the effect of sin upon them, and their relationship to each other, indeed have implications for preaching. In a parallel publication Fiering briefly touches on some implications of an 'Augustinian liberty' of the will as opposed to the view

---

[72] Thomas D. Lea, 'The Hermeneutics of the Puritans,' *Journal of the Evangelical Theological Society* 39 (1996), pp. 271–84. The six principles are: Emphasizing the importance of words in the text of Scripture; Recognizing the importance of the context of a statement in Scripture; Being aware of the necessity for critical thinking in understanding and applying Scripture; Using Scripture to interpret Scripture; Striving to understand the literal meaning of a text; and Recognizing the appearance of figures of speech in Scripture.

[73] Norman S. Fiering, *Moral Philosophy at Seventeenth-Century Harvard: A Discipline in Transition* (Chapel Hill: University of North Carolina Press, 1981), p. 126.

contained in what he calls Intellectualism:

> If the will is corrupt, controlled by Satan and unmanageable in its concupiscence or self-love, then only a redeeming love from outside can turn it around toward God. The function of the ministry of the church is to reach the heart or the affections, opening the way with God's assistance for a new will to enter. Intellectualism, on the other hand, may encourage human pride in knowing the way and in the natural man's sufficiency for virtue and even salvation.[74]

Although recognizing that certain views of the human constitution do have implications for the 'ministry of the church' Fiering does not make that the emphasis of his investigation. Therefore his study, although giving significant attention to Flavel, does not pursue the same questions as ours. It does, however, support our conclusion concerning Flavel's importance.

Other scholarly works offer brief examinations of Flavel's writings. Richard Gildrie mentions Flavel as an example of an evangelical who classified moral habits of persons in a particular three-tiered scheme.[75] Peter Toon briefly summarizes Flavel's treatise concerning antinomianism[76] and mentions him as an example of post-1662 nonconformists who possessed the 'Puritan spirit.'[77] E. Brooks Holifield makes passing reference to Flavel's *Sacramental Meditations*.[78] K.M. Campbell, in a paper entitled 'The Antinomian Controversies of the 17th Century,' quotes Flavel as an example of one who argued against antinomian tenets.[79] Hambrick-Stowe's discussion of Flavel focuses on Flavel's use of 'spiritualizing' in his *Husbandry Spiritualized* and *Navigation Spiritualized* and how that compares with other devotional writers.[80]

---

[74] Norman S. Fiering, 'Will and Intellect in the New England Mind,' *William and Mary Quarterly*, 3rd ser., 29 (1972), pp. 515–58, at 551.

[75] R.P. Gildrie, *The Profane, the Civil, & the Godly: The Reformation of Manners in Orthodox New England, 1679–1749* (University Park: Pennsylvania State University Press, 1994). On p. 22 he writes: 'It is within this context of evangelical Christianity that the reformers developed in their popular preaching the three-tiered classification of the moral habits of persons and societies as godly, civil, and profane. This language became particularly prominent in Massachusetts in the 1680s after the synod and also appeared in the works of the popular English evangelical John Flavel at about the same time.'

[76] Toon, *Hyper-Calvinism*, p. 30 n. 34.

[77] Toon, *Puritans and Calvinism*, p. 50.

[78] E. Brooks Holifield, *The Covenant Sealed: The Development of Puritan Sacramental Theology in Old and New England, 1570–1720* (New Haven: Yale University Press, 1974), p. 126. It should be noted that, although Holifield correctly references Flavel's treatise, he gives inaccurate information concerning the place of Flavel's ministry.

[79] K.M. Campbell, 'The Antinomian Controversies of the 17th century,' in Donald Macleod, ed., *Living the Christian Life: Papers from the 1974 Westminster Conference* (London: Westminster Conference, 1974), pp. 61–81, at 72.

[80] Hambrick-Stowe, *Practice of Piety*, pp. 275–76.

William Dyrness discusses Flavel and *Husbandry Spiritualized* in his investigation of the influence of Reformed theology on the visual culture in which it was promoted.[81] Bickel quotes Flavel's sermons as examples of Puritan preaching which emphasized the person and work of Christ.[82] None of these studies have detailed John Flavel's theological understanding of the effectual call, nor do they show the correlation between that understanding and his practice of preaching. We propose to do both in our examination of Flavel.

We draw attention to one reference to Flavel made by Horton Davies in his *Worship and Theology in England.* In his discussion of the 1662 ejection of Puritan ministers from the Church of England, he gives a list of eighteen men 'among the most famous'[83] of those ejected. Flavel is mentioned in the list,[84] along with Owen, Baxter, Charnock,[85] and others. However, after having mentioned him in this legendary group, Davies never quotes or mentions Flavel again throughout his tome.

Such treatment of Flavel is illustrative of what we see in the scholarly literature. Enough is known about Flavel to realize that he was an important figure but little scholarly study of depth has yet been done on him and his theology. We concur with Smith when he noted: 'The name of Flavel does not occur in historical studies of seventeenth-century Puritanism as often as it should, and he is less well known than some contemporaries who wrote less and whose works were less influential among the common people.'[86] It is our intent to address the lack of scholarly inquiry into this important seventeenth-century figure.

Introductory Issues concerning Flavel's Works

Following the Act of Uniformity and his subsequent ejection from the

---

[81] William A. Dyrness, *Reformed Theology and Visual Culture: The Protestant Imagination from Calvin to Edwards* (Cambridge: Cambridge University Press, 2004), pp. 267–69.

[82] Bickel, *Light and Heat*, p. 122.

[83] Davies, *Worship and Theology*, Vol.2, p. 439.

[84] In Davies' list Flavel is spelled 'Favel.' We are not aware of any Favel who was ejected in 1662. This is most likely a typographical error.

[85] Stephen Charnock graduated MA from Cambridge in 1649. He served as a chaplain in a variety of appointments, including regiments in Wales and Ireland, and became a fellow of New College, Oxford. For a time after the Restoration he apparently supported himself by practising medicine. He was implicated in a plot concerning the seizing of Dublin Castle but avoided arrest. After 1675 he co-pastored a church in London with Thomas Watson. Several sermons and treatises of his were published, the best known being his *Several Discourses upon the Existence and Attributes of God*. Richard L. Greaves, 'Charnock, Stephen (1628–1680),' *ODNB*, http://www.oxford dnb.com/view/article/5172, accessed 21 November 2009.

[86] Edwards, *Works*, Vol. 2, pp. 60–61.

Dartmouth church, Flavel began to put into writing some of his thoughts and teachings for publication. The first treatise, *A Saint Indeed*, was written in 1667 when he was thirty-nine years old. Over the next twenty-five years he would produce thirty-three more written works. Most of these were published individually as they were completed. He had nearly completed *An Exposition of the Assembly's Catechism* when he died in 1691. A neighbouring nonconformist minister completed it, and it was published two years later. In 1701, ten years after Flavel's death, his complete works were first collected and published.[87]

Unless otherwise noted, when referring to Flavel's writings we will quote from the six-volume edition of Flavel's complete works published by the Banner of Truth Trust in 1968. This is a reprinting of the 1820 edition of Flavel's *Works* published by W. Baynes and Son.[88] We use this version for two reasons. First, it is the version of Flavel's writings that is readily available to the public, both in libraries and for purchase. Secondly, a comparison of the 1968 reprint with the 1701 first edition of Flavel's *Whole Works* shows that there is very little difference between them. Those differences that have significance to our study will be noted at the proper place in our argumentation.[89]

There are thirty-four individual publications contained in Flavel's *Works*. In addition to those works we have a sermon, a partial sermon, two letters of correspondence with a neighbouring Quaker, and the preface Flavel wrote for a friend's book. There are a few additional letters of Flavel's in the Bodleian Library but the content of those letters is not relevant to our study.[90] A chronological and annotated list of Flavel's works is given in Appendix 5.

One noteworthy introductory issue concerns Flavel's citation of other writers. In his *Works* he quotes or refers to more than 550 different authors,

---

[87] Flavel, *Whole Works* (1701).

[88] John Flavel, *The Works of John Flavel* (6 vols, Edinburgh: Banner of Truth, 1968; first published 1820).

[89] The early publications of Flavel's *Works* contain extensive italicization which, by today's standards, appears unusual and overdone. In places entire sentences, and even paragraphs, are italicized. We have chosen to omit the italicization in our quotations from the 1701 first edition and the 1968 reprint. It is our judgment that this omission will not detract from understanding Flavel's content or emphasis but rather will contribute to an undistracted evaluation of his writings. In cases where retaining the italicization is deemed crucial to understanding Flavel's argument, we have done so. Capitalization and spelling from those versions have been retained.

[90] The Bodleian contains the following correspondence of John Flavel's: rough drafts of two letters which Edmund Elys sent to Flavel (MS J.Walker e.8.39, 40); two letters from Flavel to Elys, dated June 2, 1687 and June 13, 1687 (MS J. Walker c.4.307, 309); and Flavel's letter to J. Thornton, dated August 15, 1684, asking for help in the light of his being hunted down by the authorities which were attempting to confiscate his properties. (Rawl. Lrs. 109.33).

historical figures and contemporaries.[91] The list of those he cited reads like a library catalogue. We note here only a few examples representative of various categories from which he read and quoted. He drew upon Greek philosophers (Plato, Aristotle, Socrates); Greek church fathers (Athanasius, Chrysostom, Clement, Cyril, Irenaeus, Origen); Latin church fathers (Ambrose, Augustine, Cyprian, Jerome, Lactantius, Tertulian; Roman Catholic theologians (Baronius, Bellarmine, Bernard of Clairvaux, Adrian, Suarez); continental Reformers and theologians (Luther, Calvin, Zwingli, Alsted, Bullinger, Buxtorf, Zanchius); Scottish Protestant theologians (Cameron, Durham, Rutherford); Caroline divines (Laud, Taylor, Herbert, Fuller); early Puritans (Ames, Cartwright, Perkins, Rogers); contemporary Puritans (Baxter, Richard Bernard, Burroughs, Caryl, Charnock, Cotton, Goodwin, Owen); and others from divergent perspectives such as Amyraldus, Bucer, Crisp, Davenant, Grotius, Keach, Seneca, and Plutarch. The list is immense in both scope and size.

Evangelistic Intent in Flavel's Publications

An important element of our discussion is the presupposition that it is legitimate to view Flavel's published works as attempts to influence unregenerate readers. We observe that Flavel did not begin publishing his sermons or treatises until his ejection from the church in Dartmouth. It was only in Restoration England that he published. Is this fact an indication that his published sermons were primarily aimed at shoring up the faith of the congregation from which he had been separated? Is it legitimate to treat his published sermons as examples of attempts to communicate to the unregenerate?

Keeble, in his *The Literary Culture of Nonconformity*, suggests that nonconformist authors aimed their publications at readers who could be religiously characterized in one of four ways, 'as unregenerate; as believers who have reached a particular stage of spiritual maturity; as members of particular congregations; and as adherents of a denomination.' He continues: 'The first of these were not commonly intended as the sole readers ... evangelism to the public at large was usually not the main purpose but a subsidiary aim in books primarily directed to the consolation and encouragement of believers, and particularly nonconformists.'[92] We suggest that the evidence within Flavel's works points to an evangelistic concern which he expressed in preaching and which he carried into his published sermon collections and treatises. If Keeble's characterization is correct, Flavel was an

---

[91] Due to the lack of standardized citations in the seventeenth century we are unable to determine with certainty the identity of each person whom Flavel refers to or cites. Those of whom we are confident number 552. There are most likely even more.

[92] N.H. Keeble, *The Literary Culture of Nonconformity in Later Seventeenth-Century England* (Athens: University of Georgia Press, 1987), p. 139.

exception who did indeed intend for many, but not all, of his works to be read by the unregenerate.

Several of his treatises had a distinct and explicit evangelistic purpose. Other treatises written primarily to believers also included material designed for those who were unconverted. All of his sermons, as we will discover later, were preached with the understanding that some in the audience were yet unregenerate. The published versions of those sermons retain those portions which are aimed at conversion.

In the epistle to the readers of *Navigation Spiritualized* Flavel makes his evangelistic aim clear. He is writing to hardened seamen, enjoining them to be concerned for their eternal well-being. 'O Sirs! I beg of you, if you have any regard to those precious, immortal souls of yours, which are also imbarked for eternity, whither all winds blow them, and will quickly be at their port of heaven or hell, that you will seriously mind these things, and learn to steer your course to heaven.'[93] The entire treatise, although containing teaching that is applicable to those already converted, is aimed primarily at unconverted seamen. Flavel emphasizes this purpose: 'I write not for critical and learned persons; my design is not to please your fancies any further, ... if God shall bless these meditations to the conversion of any among you, you will be the gainers, and my heart shall rejoice, even mine.'[94] At the end of the treatise he closes with this prayer: 'O thou, that art the Father of spirits, that formedst and canst easily reform the heart, open thou the blind eye, unstop the deaf ear, let the world [*sic* for 'word'] take hold upon the heart. If thou wilt but say the word, these weak labours shall prosper, to bring home many lost souls unto thee. Amen.'[95] From beginning to end, *Navigation Spiritualized* is written with the conversion of the unregenerate in mind.

In his *Dissuasive*, which was later attached to *Navigation Spiritualized*, Flavel continues with his intent to speak to the unregenerate among seamen and enlists the help of Christian ship captains. 'And O that all pious masters would persuade all those that are under their charge to buy this ensuing treatise, and diligently peruse it.'[96] This same concern is seen in *The Seaman's Companion*. It is addressed 'To all Masters, Mariners, and Seamen; especially such as belong to the Port of Dartmouth, and the Parts adjacent.'[97] The sermons are a mixture of admonition and instruction for the already converted and evangelistic appeal to those not yet converted. A portion of Flavel's design in publishing this little sermon series can be seen in his closing comments to those in charge of the ships. 'But it is my earnest request to you, masters, that have the over-sight, and must give an account for your companies, that you will not

---

[93] Flavel, *Works*, Vol. 5, p. 208.
[94] Flavel, *Works*, Vol. 5, p. 208-209.
[95] Flavel, *Works*, Vol. 5. p. 293.
[96] Flavel, *Works*, Vol. 5, p. 297.
[97] Flavel, *Works*, Vol. 5, p. 342.

only read and consider these things for yourselves, but that you will at fit seasons, especially upon the Lord's day, read and inculcate them upon your servants and company.'[98]

Flavel maintained his evangelistic aim with *Husbandry Spiritualized*. Commenting on his purpose for both *Husbandry Spiritualized* and *Navigation Spiritualized*, he wrote: 'I considered, that if the Pharisees, in a blind zeal to a faction, could compass sea and land, to proselyte men to their party ... how much more was I obliged, by true love of God, and zeal both with seamen and husbandmen, to win them to Christ.'[99] Yet he also readily acknowledged his purpose to write for those who were already converted. Joseph Caryl, who added a preface to *Husbandry Spiritualized*, noted the dual purpose of the treatise:

> This book ... is not calculated only for the common husbandman; persons of any calling, or condition, may find the author working out such searching reflections and strong convictions ... as may prove, if faithfully improved, very useful to them; to some for their awakening, to consider the state of their souls, whether in grace, or in nature; to others for their instruction, consolation, and encouragement in the ways of grace.[100]

This dual purpose, evangelism of the unconverted and edification of the already converted, was not only displayed in Flavel's treatises. It is also seen in his sermons and in his discussion of the task of the preacher. As will be shown later in the study, Flavel understood his audience to contain people at various stages of being effectually called to faith. The fact that a listener was a churchgoer was not seen by Flavel as meaning that that person was converted. Some sermons were weighted with a greater emphasis towards the edification of the regenerate, but the evangelistic aim was never completely absent.

This evangelistic aim is seen clearly when long sermon series are investigated in their entirety. *Fountain of Life* and *Method of Grace*, the two largest treatises of Flavel, which together comprise seventy-seven of his sermons, clearly have a strong evangelistic aim. This aim, not withstanding the corresponding concern to build up his flock, is evident in the doctrines expounded and the application of those doctrines to the reader. In our investigation of the connection between Flavel's understanding of the effectual call and his application of that to evangelistic preaching we will lean heavily on the sermons contained in these two treatises. It is our contention that there was a clear evangelistic intent in both the original preaching and the eventual publication of these sermon series.

This evangelistic intent is seen in the other large collection of sermons, *England's Duty*. As the fourth largest of all of Flavel's individual works, this

---

[98] Flavel, *Works*, Vol. 5, p. 416.
[99] Flavel, *Works*, Vol. 5, p. 5.
[100] Joseph Caryl, in Flavel, *Works*, Vol. 5, p. 10.

treatise consists of the texts of eleven of his sermons preached as a series from Revelation 3:20. This series was preached early in the new climate of liberty that nonconformists experienced after the commencement of the reign of William and Mary.

Apparently there was an extraordinary response to Flavel's preaching of these sermons. In reference to those days he wrote: 'Sowing and reaping times trode so close upon one another, that ... it was the busiest and blessedest time I ever saw since I first preached the gospel.'[101] For only the second time in his writing career, he had another person write a preface for one of his books. Increase Mather's introduction precedes the first sermon and in it he wrote of the response of the people to the preaching of these sermons. 'I am informed by unquestionable hands, that there was a remarkable pouring out of the Spirit when these sermons were *viva voce* delivered, a great number of souls having been brought home to Christ thereby.'[102]

Flavel's aim in the sermons was primarily the conversion of the unregenerate hearers, and secondarily the encouragement of those who had already believed.

> As to the treatise itself, thou wilt find it a persuasive to open thy heart to Christ ... If thou be in thy unregenerate state, then he solemnly demands in this text admission into the soul he made, by the consent of the will; ... If thou hast opened thy heart to him, thou wilt, I hope, meet somewhat in this treatise that will clear thy evidences, and cheer thy heart.[103]

In the preface to *England's Duty*, Flavel made the point that he did not change the sermons significantly for publication. 'The following discourse comes to thy hand in that native plainness wherein it was preached. I was conscientiously unwilling to alter it, because I found by experience, the Lord had blessed and prospered it in that dress.'[104] Increase Mather saw in the treatise an evangelistic purpose. He wrote: 'The Lord grant that the second preaching of them [the sermons] to far greater multitudes by this way of the press, may, by the same Spirit, be made abundantly successful for the conversion and salvation of God's elect.'[105]

This evangelistic intent is also clear when we examine the content of his treatises which were not collections of sermons. We have already noted this intent in *Navigation Spiritualized*, *Husbandry Spiritualized* and *Dissuasive*. It is notable that this intent was also evident to the people of Flavel's day. The following extended quotation of an anecdote shows the evangelistic success of another treatise, *Keeping the Heart*, and the use of that book in Flavel's day for

---

[101] Flavel, *Works*, Vol. 4, p. 3.
[102] Flavel, *Works*, Vol. 4, p. 17.
[103] Flavel, *Works*, Vol. 4, p. 5.
[104] Flavel, *Works*, Vol. 4. p. 3.
[105] Increase Mather, in Flavel, *Works*, Vol. 4, p. 17.

evangelistic purposes.

> Mr. Flavel being in London in 1673, his old bookseller, Mr. Boulter, gave him this following relation, viz. That some time before, there came into his shop a sparkish gentleman to enquire for some play-books; Mr. Boulter told him he had none, but shewed him Mr. Flavel's little treatise of *Keeping the Heart*, intreated him to read it, and assured him it would do him more good than play-books. The gentleman read the title, and glancing upon several pages here and there, broke out into these and such other expressions, What a damnable Fanatic was he who made this book? Mr. Boulter begged of him to buy and read it, and told him he had no cause to censure it so bitterly; at last he bought it, but told him he would not read it. What will you do with it then, said Mr. Boulter? I will tear and burn it, said he, and send it to the Devil. Mr. Boulter told him, that he should not have it. Upon this the gentleman promised to read it; and Mr. Boulter told him, if he disliked it upon reading, he would return him his money. About a month after, the gentleman came to the shop again in a very modest habit, and with a serious countenance, bespoke Mr. Boulter thus; Sir, I most heartily thank you for putting this book into my hands; I bless God that moved you to do it, it hath saved my soul; blessed be God that ever I came into your shop. And then he bought a hundred more of those books of him, and told him he would give them to the poor who could not buy them, and so left him, praising and admiring the goodness of God. Thus it pleased God to bless the sermons, discourses and writings of Mr. Flavel.[106]

Keeping the Heart is just one example of Flavel writing with evangelistic intent woven into the fabric of a treatise mainly aimed at believers. *Hour of Temptation* is another such treatise. Although mainly addressing Christians, Flavel uses the last 'counsel' to direct his words to those who were still unconverted. The eighth counsel is, 'That seeing a day of great trouble is approaching, and all outward comforts ready to take their farewell of you, you should now give all diligence to clear up your title to Christ, and interest in that kingdom which cannot be shaken.'[107] He ends the treatise by urging the reader to make sure that he or she is a genuine believer in Jesus Christ. More examples could be given, but the above will suffice. Flavel's insistence on including an evangelistic intent in his printed sermons and treatises leads us to conclude that he was indeed aiming at the unregenerate in his publications.

This conclusion is in agreement with Flavel's unnamed biographer, who wrote: 'He was a mighty wrestler with God in secret prayer, and particularly begged of him to crown his sermons, printed books and private discourses, with the conversion of poor sinners, a work which his heart was much set upon.'[108]

A mention of Flavel's *The Reasonableness of Personal Reformation, and the*

---

[106] Anon., 'The Life of the Late Rev. Mr. John Flavel, Minister of Dartmouth,' in *Works*, Vol. 1, pp. xiii–xiv.
[107] Flavel, *Works*, Vol. 4, p. 552.
[108] Anon., 'Life of Flavel,' *Works*, Vol. 1, p. xii.

Necessity of Conversion is appropriate here. It was an evangelistic endeavour. Near the end of the work Flavel records his prayer concerning the treatise:

> O my God! ... thou that hast inclined my heart to make this attempt, and encouraged me with hope, that it shall not be in vain to all them that read it, ... I beseech thee, lay the hand of thy Spirit upon the heart and hand of thy servant; strengthen and guide him in drawing the bow of the gospel, and directing the arrows, that they may strike the mark he aims at, even the conviction and conversion of lewd and dissolute sinners. Command these considerations to stay and settle in their hearts, till they bring them fully over to thyself in Christ.[109]

As the title suggests, Flavel appeals to the reason of his readers, but he also purposefully aims at their consciences, attempting to move them toward conversion.

This was the last full treatise that Flavel wrote. It was published in 1691, the year of his death. From the beginning of his publishing career with the printing of *Saint Indeed* in 1667, to 1691 and *Reasonableness and Reformation*, Flavel remained intent on evangelizing the unconverted. He did publish some treatises primarily for the benefit of believers but, as we have previously pointed out, even those discourses often included words directed at readers who were possibly unconverted. It is our conclusion that Flavel's purpose in publishing was both the edification of believers and the evangelization of unbelievers.

This conclusion is not surprising when we realize that the same dual purpose was in Flavel's mind when he was behind a pulpit. Prior to St Bartholomew's Day of 1662 he preached from his pulpit in Dartmouth with both purposes – to edify those already converted, and to see the conversion of the unregenerate take place. When he lost his pulpit he lost his platform for both edification and evangelism. Thus, when he turned to publishing he once again pursued both.

Summary

It is our contention that John Flavel is the ideal subject for the study of the relationship between the Puritan understanding of the effectual call and Puritan evangelistic preaching. We assert that Flavel was an influential member of the Puritan movement. His influence is seen by observing contemporary comments about him by both friend and foe. His impact is also seen in the influence his written works had on contemporaries and on generations which followed. This influence was widespread, including lay people as well as theologians and ministers, some of whom were very influential figures themselves. This influence was manifest in both England and the New World. We have also noted that he was particularly purposeful and earnest in evangelism and was met with a large measure of success in that work. We also note that this evangelistic intent was present in his publications as well as in his preaching. In

---

[109] Flavel, *Works*, Vol. 6, p. 542.

the later sections of this study we will endeavour to show that he was conscious of possessing a well-defined view of the effectual call and deliberately applied that view to preaching. Therefore, we assert that John Flavel is an excellent subject for study concerning the interrelatedness of Puritan theology and the manner and matter of Puritan preaching to the unconverted.

There were undoubtedly other preachers in late seventeenth-century England who possessed a similar theology to Flavel's and who deliberately applied that theology to their work of preaching. However his stature among his contemporaries and the significant influence which his *Works* had on both continents, plus the fact that his *Works* are available today for our examination, set Flavel apart as a particularly appropriate subject of our study.

The unique qualification of Flavel for this study is magnified by the previously demonstrated lack of scholarly examination of Puritan preaching in light of the Puritan view of the effectual call. Our study intends to use the writings of Flavel to explore and describe the interrelatedness of the Puritan understanding of the effectual call with the manner and matter of Puritan evangelistic preaching.

PART TWO

The Theology of John Flavel

Before describing the way in which Flavel's theology affected his preaching it is necessary to examine his writings in order to determine exactly what he believed. Therefore, we now turn to an investigation of the theology of John Flavel. Our investigation is not intended to be an exhaustive analysis of his views of all areas of theology, but rather a focused description of those areas which directly impacted his understanding of the effectual call and which he saw as being directly applicable to the task of evangelistic preaching. Consistent with this purpose we will explore his views of the human constitution, the doctrine of sin, and the effectual call.

It is important to note, however, that Flavel's view of the Christian life was broader than conversion. He did not propose that a person's conversion was the end of God's dealing with that individual, nor did he hold that the Scripture's application to a person's life was confined to the effectual call. God's plan for an individual after conversion involved both sanctification and glorification.

Concerning sanctification, that work of God in a believer's life between the time of conversion and the time of death, Flavel spoke of the believer growing in the love of Christ. In *Sacramental Meditations* Flavel expands upon this thought while exploring the meaning of Ephesians 3:19, 'And to know the love of Christ, which passeth knowledge.' He writes: 'The knowledge of Christ, and his love, is deservedly, in this place, set down among the *desiderata Christianorum*, the most desirable enjoyments of believers in this world ... . Labour to get the clearest and fullest apprehensive knowledge of Christ and his love, that is attainable in this world.'[1] The result of conversion is to bring a person into a relationship with Christ which then introduces the person to an experience of love which earthly existence cannot exhaust. Flavel, through his sermons and writings, addressed this experience of sanctification.

Concerning glorification, that work of God upon the believer after death, Flavel had much to say. In *Soul of Man* Flavel gives considerable attention to the life of the soul after physical death. At one point in the treatise he derives from Hebrews 12:23 the doctrine '[t]hat righteous and holy souls, once separated from their bodies by death, are immediately perfected in themselves; and associated with others alike perfect in the kingdom of God.' Flavel

---

[1] Flavel, *Works*, Vol. 6, p. 456.

continues and explains the purpose of this part of his treatise: 'But the true level and aim of this discourse is at a higher mark, viz. the far more excellent, free, and noble life the souls of the just begin to live immediately after their bodies are dropt off from them by death, at which time they begin to live like themselves, a pleasant, free, and divine life.'[2] The life of the individual with God in heaven was a significant component of Flavel's theology which he explored in his sermons and writings.

Our focus, as has already been stated, will be upon Flavel's view of the human constitution, his doctrine of sin, and the effectual call. Within the category of the effectual call we will look in detail at his views of illumination, conviction, the renewing of the will, and faith. This is undertaken with an acknowledgement of the importance to Flavel of both sanctification and glorification. Our focus, however, is designed to allow exploration of those areas of Flavel's theology which directly impacted his understanding of the effectual call and which he saw as being directly applicable to the task of preaching for conversion.

---

[2] Flavel, *Works*, Vol. 3, p. 22.

Chapter 3

The Human Constitution

We begin the analysis of John Flavel's theology with a focus on his understanding of the human constitution. Although he touched upon this area of doctrine in many of his treatises and sermons, it is in his lengthy *Soul of Man* that we see Flavel's view of man clearly and methodically explained.

In the first major section of *Soul of Man* Flavel presents the human being as a dichotomy consisting of body and soul. He uses many arguments to prove that the soul is a substance (albeit an immaterial substance), then discusses its eternal nature, its various faculties, its origin as immediately created, and its relationship to the body.[1] That aspect of the doctrine of the human constitution which most directly impinges upon our study occurs within Flavel's discussion of the soul's faculties, and it is this aspect upon which we will focus.

The following analysis will use Flavel's *Soul of Man* as the foundation of his view of the soul's faculties, but will incorporate his other writings when necessary. Prior to examining his view of the soul's faculties, however, we draw attention to his understanding of the image of God.

The 'Image of God'

It is notable that Flavel only refers to the image of God once in the entire foundational treatise *Soul of Man*, and that reference is merely a passing comment rather than a vital part of his argument.[2] He discusses the idea of the image of God only six times in all his *Works*.[3] He does not approach the topic

---

[1] Flavel, *Whole Works*, Vol. 1, p. 481. The outline of *Soul of Man*, from which the arrangement of his material can be discerned, is seen in a chart published in the first edition of Flavel's *Whole Works* and entitled 'A Synopsis, or View of the Soul in the State of Composition, in six Particulars, in this first Table of Life.' This table was not included in the 1820 edition of Flavel's *Works* and therefore does not appear in the 1968 Banner of Truth reprint. It is presented in Appendix 4 of this study.

[2] Flavel, *Works*, Vol. 2, p. 539.

[3] The occurrences are as follows: Vol. 1, p. 110 (*Fountain of Life*), in which he comments that Adam was 'created in the image of God,' but does not expound on what that image consists of; Vol. 2, p. 539 (*Soul of Man*) in which he states that sin has 'razed out [of humankind] the Divine image which was its glory;' Vol. 5, pp. 426, 529, Vol. 6, pp. 163–64, 170, which are quoted and discussed above.

of human constitution with the *imago dei* as his starting point, nor, given his definition of it, does it play an important role in his mind as he explains the effectual call and the work of preaching to the unconverted.

In his *Exposition* Flavel helps his readers to explore the Catechism's meaning and implications by posing a series of follow-up questions to each catechism question and answer.

His exploration of the meaning of the *imago dei* occurred when he reached the question, How did God create man? The first answer was that God created man male and female, after his own image, in knowledge, righteousness, and holiness, with dominion over the creatures. Flavel's follow-up questions and answers are given here.

Q. 2. What is meant by the image of God?

A. Not a resemblance of God in any bodily shape or figure, but in holiness; Eph iv. 24. And that ye put on the new man, which after God is created in righteousness and true holiness.

Q. 3. In what graces did man resemble God?

A. In such a knowledge of God himself, and the creatures, which made him happy; Col. iii. 10 ...

Q. 4. In what other graces did this image consist?

A. In righteousness as well as holiness; Eph. iv. 24 ...

Q. 5. What is the first inference from hence?

A. The deplorable misery of the fall; Rom. v. 12 ...

Q. 6. What is the second instruction from hence?

A. The beauty of holiness, which is the image of God, and the excellency of man; Psalm xvi. 3 ...

Q. 7. What is the third instruction from hence?

A. We have infinite cause to bless God for Christ, who repairs this lost image in his people; Eph. iv. 23 ...

Q. 8. What is the fourth instruction from hence?

A. That the despisers of holiness are the despisers of God; for holiness is God's image.

Q. 9. What is the fifth instruction from hence?

A. The excellency of sanctification, which defaces the image of Satan, and draws the image of God upon the soul of man.[4]

---

[4] Flavel, *Works*, Vol. 6, pp. 163–64.

The Human Constitution 65

It is important to note that the idea of knowledge as a part of the image of God is included by Flavel, but he defines it in a certain way. When he mentions knowledge in reference to the image of God he does not mean the capacity or faculty of knowledge. What he is referring to is man's knowledge of God.

He expresses this idea explicitly in his *Touchstone of Sincerity*.

> 'The new man is renewed in knowledge, after the image of him that created him,' Col. iii. 10. The schoolmen, and some of the fathers, place this image or resemblence of God, in the natural faculties of the soul, viz. the understanding, memory, and will: which is an umbrage of a trinity in unity; but it rather consists in the renovation of the faculties by grace; for in this we bear the Divine image upon our souls, and that image or resemblance of God in holiness is the beauty and honour of our souls.[5]

Therefore we see that Flavel understands that the unregenerate person has lost the image of God. He explicitly states this when, later in the *Exposition*, he explores the consequences of Adam's sin: 'Q. 5. What was the evil of punishment? A. *First*, Loss of God's image.'[6]

In Flavel's view the faculties of the soul remain a part of an unregenerate person. However, in the unregenerate the faculties are as yet unrestored and thus unholy and not employed in knowing God or in reflecting God's holiness.

Rather than upholding certain faculties of the soul as being hallmarks of the image of God, Flavel focuses on holiness. In his answer to question 8 (quoted above) he states simply, 'for holiness is God's image.' In his answer to question 6 he refers with equal succinctness to '[t]he beauty of holiness, which is the image of God.' It is not the faculties themselves which Flavel sees as making up the image of God, but the renewing of those faculties in holiness.

In *A Saint Indeed* Flavel refers to the image of God in the context of a discussion of sanctification:

> But by regeneration this disordered soul is set aright again: sanctification being the rectifying and due framing, or as the scripture phrases it, the renovation of the soul after the image of God, Eph. iv. 24 … And thus the soul which sin had universally depraved is again by grace restored and rectified. Thus being presupposed, it will not be difficult to apprehend what it is to keep the heart, which is nothing else but the constant care and diligence of such a renewed man, to preserve his soul in that holy frame to which grace hath reduced it, and daily strives to hold it.[7]

We ask an important question here: By using the word 'renovating' is he meaning that there is some residual presence of the image of God in the sinner which can be improved upon, in contrast to his otherwise stated understanding

---

[5] Flavel, *Works*, Vol. 5, p. 529.
[6] Flavel, *Works*, Vol. 6, p. 170.
[7] Flavel, *Works*, Vol. 5, p. 426.

that the image of God has been 'razed out' by sin? Careful analysis of his argumentation suggests not. We see in the above quotation that in his view the image of God in a person appears after regeneration and consists of a 'rectified' soul and a correct 'framing' of the soul. It is the soul that is 'renovated,' not the image of God. The image was lost by sin. It is put again into the regenerated soul.

The previous quotation from his *Touchstone of Sincerity* shows us that Flavel was aware that his view of the image of God differed from some of the church fathers. It also differed from that of William Ames, a theologian whom he greatly respected[8] and often quoted. In Ames' *The Marrow of Theology* his entire discussion of the human constitution is framed within the concept of the image of God.[9] According to Ames there was an outward and inward image of God. The inward image of God included the perfection of the soul. This perfection consisted, according to Ames, 'not only in those faculties by which it was a free principle of its own actions, in understanding and will, but also being adorned with gifts whereby man was made able, and fit to live well, namely with wisdom, holinesse, and righteousness.'[10] So Flavel parted company with his revered Ames by insisting that the faculties of the soul, in and of themselves, are not part of the *imago dei*. Although Flavel acknowledged his departure from the thinking of the church fathers, he did not draw attention to the fact that he differed also from Ames.

Gavin McGrath does not mention Flavel, but nevertheless his assessment of Richard Baxter's doctrine of the human constitution suggests that Flavel differed from him also. Baxter, in the preface to his *Call to the Unconverted*, wrote: 'there is a twofold image of God in man; the one is natural, and that is, our reason and free-will, and this is not lost. The other is qualitative and ethical, and this is our holiness, and this is lost, and by grace restored.'[11] Flavel never spoke of any such twofold image of God.[12]

---

[8] Flavel referred to William Ames as 'a reverend divine' (Vol. 5, p. 304), 'a learned and judicious person' (Vol. 6, p. 356); and as '[one of] the best expositors' (Vol. 4, p. 523).

[9] William Ames, *The Marrow of Sacred Divinity* (London: Edward Griffin, 1643), pp.37–39; idem, *The Marrow of Theology*, transl. John Eusden (Grand Rapids: Baker, 1968), pp. 105–106.

[10] Ames, *Marrow of Sacred Divinity*, p. 38.

[11] Richard Baxter, *A Call to the Unconverted* (London: R.W., 1658), Preface, p. 55. McGrath discusses this portion of Baxter's argument in 'Puritans and the Human Will,' p. 215.

[12] McGrath argues that the 'image of God' paradigm was a crucial part of the approach of Baxter and Owen to the faculties of the soul, the effect of sin on those faculties, and the renewing of them by grace. Flavel's approach is striking in that it addresses the same issues that McGrath shows Baxter and Owen addressing, yet without reference to the image of God. He simply does not see the *imago dei* as an organizing principle of his theology.

Suzanne McDonald, in 'The Pneumatology of the "Lost" Image in John Owen,' assesses Owen's view of the *imago dei*.[13] Her conclusion is significantly similar to what we see in Flavel.[14] She maintains: 'Across the twenty-four volumes that constitute his collected works, Owen insists with very few exceptions upon the utter loss of the image in all save the elect.'[15] The elect only come to possess the image of God after regeneration. She continues by asserting: 'The loss of the image in all save the elect is a recurring and important theme in Owen, as is the specific association of the image with right relationship with God.'[16] We cannot observe such an importance being placed upon this view by Flavel, but nevertheless Flavel's view echoes that of Owen. McDonald presses the idea that Owen held a unique view: 'Owen is therefore distinctive even within his own tradition for his evident reluctance to speak of any remnant of the image outside the elect.'[17] Our study reveals that there was at least one contemporary within Owen's tradition who held the same position – John Flavel.

As we will see later, Flavel's view of the effectual call significantly shaped his preaching to the unconverted. His view had as a crucial element an understanding of the roles played by the various faculties of the soul in the effectual call. Whether the faculties themselves were considered by Flavel as essential elements of the *imago dei* or not did not affect his view of how the faculties were involved in the effectual call, nor his application of the effectual call to the work of preaching.

As we analyze Flavel's view of the human constitution further, we do so with the understanding that his entire discussion is carried out without any reference to the *imago dei* paradigm. He approaches the subject of the human constitution from a different angle altogether, by exploring what the soul is in its essence, what the soul's faculties are, and what those faculties can, should, and will do in light of the soul's present sinfulness and the grace of God. It is to the topic of the soul's faculties that we now turn.

---

[13] Suzanne McDonald, 'The Pneumatology of the "Lost" Image in John Owen,' *WTJ* 71 (2009), pp. 323–35.

[14] Although McDonald would agree with McGrath that Owen's view of the *imago dei* was important, her assessment of Owen's view of the *imago dei* stands in contrast to that proposed by McGrath. For additional discussion of Owen's view of the *imago dei* that proposes a differently nuanced conclusion than McDonald, see Kelly M. Kapic, *Communion with God: The Divine and the Human in the Theology of John Owen* (Grand Rapids: Baker Academic, 2007), pp. 35–66.

[15] McDonald, 'Pnuematology,' p. 324.

[16] McDonald, 'Pnuematology,' p. 325.

[17] McDonald, 'Pnuematology,' p. 329.

The Faculties of the Soul

Puritan 'Faculty Psychology'

Perry Miller devoted forty pages in his *The New England Mind* to a description of the Puritan understanding of the constitution and psychology of man. He makes the point that the seventeenth-century Puritans held a common view of these issues which was not original to them. 'This doctrine of the psychological process was a part of the intellectual heritage which Puritans accepted without criticism, almost without realizing that it was a doctrine, since to them no other concept was available.'[18] Miller asserts[19] that this 'doctrine' originated with Aristotle; that it was influenced also by the ideas of Plato, the Stoics, and some medieval theologians; and that it then made its way to the Puritans via the German theologians Johann Alsted (1588–1638)[20] and Bartholomaus Keckermann (1571–1609).[21] Miller refers to the Puritan view of human constitution and psychology as an 'inherited psychology,' the 'Aristotelian tradition,' and 'Peripatetic psychology.' He asserts that this inherited faculty psychology was virtually universally accepted by the Puritans. He writes, 'It is difficult to estimate objectively how much Puritanism owed to the traditional and inherited psychological theory, for it is next to impossible to consider Puritanism of the seventeenth century apart from that theory.'[22]

Miller points out its importance to the Puritan task of preaching. 'The faculties could not be quickened until ministers knew what they were, and the manner of teaching depended entirely upon what concept of the faculties the ministers were taught.'[23] John Fulcher, in his 'Puritan Piety in Early New England,' supports Miller's contention by quoting and examining the writings of Thomas Hooker. 'Hooker's emphasis upon the affections, especially in the application of the Word, illustrates Miller's point ... that the final part of the sermon was designed to arouse the affections and, indeed, that the whole sermon was framed according to the faculty psychology.'[24]

---

[18] Miller, *New England Mind*, p. 242.
[19] Miller, *New England Mind*, pp. 243–45.
[20] Johann Heinrich Alsted was a German Protestant clergyman and logician who became a professor at Herborn and then at Weissenburg. He was a member of the Synod of Dort and wrote numerous works, the best known being his *Encyclopedia*, first published in 1630. E.F. Karl Muller, 'Alsted, Johann Heinrich,' *The New Schaff-Herzog Encyclopedia of Religious Knowledge.* Grand Rapids: Baker, 1951.
[21] Bartholomaus Keckermann was a German Calvinistic theologian who became a professor first at Heidelberg. From 1601 until the end of his life he was rector and professor at Danzig. E.F. Karl Muller, 'Keckermann, Bartholomaeus,' *The New Schaff-Herzog Encyclopedia of Religious Knowledge.* Grand Rapids: Baker, 1951.
[22] Miller, *New England Mind*, p. 255.
[23] Miller, *New England Mind*, p. 244.
[24] Fulcher, 'Puritan Piety' p.258 n. 25.

We ask the question: According to the Puritans how many faculties does the soul have and what are they? In each case, those who examine the faculty psychology of Puritan writers mention the intellect (sometimes referred to as the mind, or the understanding), the will and the affections (sometimes referred to as the passions or the emotions).

Fulcher does not explicitly list or categorize the soul's faculties, but in the midst of his examinations of several Puritan preachers he does mention the mind, will and affections. Tipson, as we noted earlier, does not systematically discuss the Puritan view of the faculties of the soul. He does, however, mention the human intellect, will and affections, although not positing that as an exhaustive list of the soul's faculties.[25] Fulcher and Tipson are examples of those who, although not asking our particular question and therefore not giving an explicit answer, nevertheless refer to the seventeenth-century Puritan view of the soul's faculties as including mind, will and affections.

Stephenson examines Jonathan Edwards' view of psychology and describes its similarities and differences with seventeenth-century Puritan thought. She includes Flavel in her discussion.[26] Stephenson's value to our investigation is that in comparing Edwards' view of the soul's faculties to that of his seventeenth-century Puritan predecessors, she discusses those predecessors and their views. It is instructive that when talking of the faculty psychology of seventeenth-century Puritanism she continually speaks of mind, will and affections.[27] Bernard Duffy, in his preface to Yarbrough's *Delightful Conviction: Jonathan Edwards and the Rhetoric of Conversion*, also compares Edwards' thought to that of the previous century and also describes that century's faculty psychology as involving 'the will, the intellect, and the affections.'[28]

Stephen Beck, in 'The Doctrine of *gratia praeparans* in the Soteriology of Richard Sibbes,' understands the early Puritan concept of the faculties of the soul as including those very three faculties. He summarizes the view of the soul's faculties held by Richard Sibbes (1577–1635)[29] as including reason, will

---

[25] Tipson, 'Understanding of Conversion,' pp. 208–15.
[26] The influence that Flavel's writings had on the thought of Edwards would make an intriguing study. Such an inquiry, however, is outside the scope of our study.
[27] For example, when she examines Shepard's view and comments that in his opinion the 'whole soul' consists of 'mind, will and emotions.' Stephenson, 'Jonathan Edwards' Thought,' p. 151.
[28] Stephen Yarbrough and John Adams, *Delightful Conviction: Jonathan Edwards and the Rhetoric of Conversion* (Westport: Greenwood Press, 1993), p. xv. We have been unable to trace the primary documents upon which Yarbrough and Adams base this assertion.
[29] Richard Sibbes was educated at Cambridge, was ordained in 1608, and began ministry as a college preacher. He soon relocated to London and became a well-known preacher and an influential member of those clergy with nonconformist sympathies. In 1626 he was appointed to the mastership of St Catherine's College,

and affections.³⁰ McGrath, in his 'Puritans and the Human Will,' represents the theology of Baxter and Owen – contemporaries of Flavel – as maintaining that the soul's faculties are 'reason, will and affections.'³¹ Anders Lunt, in 'The Reinvention of Preaching,' demonstrates the presence of a faculty psychology within seventeenth-century Puritanism. He also summarizes those faculties as mind, will and affections.³²

Some scholars, although acknowledging the Puritans' awareness of the affections, appear not to treat the affections as a faculty equal to the mind and will. Stephen Yuille, in his brief description of Flavel's faculty psychology, touches upon this discussion: did the Puritan view include the affections as a separate faculty? He writes:

> This tripartite division of the soul [intellect, will and affections as three faculties] is a minor alteration of the more common bipartite division within Reformed theology. Calvin states, 'The soul consists of two faculties, understanding and will' (*Institutes*, I.XV.7). Calvin does not deny the function of the affections, but prefers to include them under the banner of the will. The will, therefore, has two components: inclination (or affections) and choice. Many of the Puritans, however, designate the affections as a faculty in its own right.³³

Miller at times mentions the affections in an equal way with the mind and will, but at other times seems not to treat the affections as a faculty in themselves.³⁴

Cambridge. He was known as 'a reformer, but a cautious reformer, as a puritan, but a moderate puritan.' Mark E. Dever, 'Sibbes, Richard (1577?–1635),' *ODNB*, http://www.oxforddnb.com/ view/article/25498, accessed 21 November 2009.

30 Stephen P. Beck, 'The Doctrine of *gratia praeparans* in the Soteriology of Richard Sibbes' (Ph.D. diss., Westminster Theological Seminary, 1994), pp. 124–31.
31 McGrath, 'Puritans and the Human Will,' p. 212.
32 Lunt, 'Reinvention of Preaching,' pp. 119–35. Lunt speaks as if the faculty psychology of John Locke was present in the previous century but had been overlooked by scholars studying the seventeenth-century works. In actuality Locke's system is a modification of certain aspects of the previous theory. Fiering, although acknowledging the similarities, explains the differences that Locke introduced to faculty psychology (Fiering, *Moral Philosophy*, p. 107). Stephenson explores how Edwards interacted with Locke's thought (Stephenson, 'Jonathan Edwards' Thought,' p. 120.
33 Yuille, *Inner Sanctum*, pp. 35–36 n. 14.
34 Two examples of Miller's lack of clarity on this subject will suffice. On p. 240 of *New England Mind*, he states that 'the distinguishing faculties of the rational creature, [are] reason and will.' Thus he apparently does not include the affections as a faculty, at least not as a faculty in the same sense as the mind and will. Yet on p. 253, when commenting upon the Puritan ideal of human psychology, he states: 'they held to the vision of an ideal state in which all faculties harmonized, in which the passions voluntarily depended upon the will and the will upon right reason.' Thus, he has referred to the affections, or passions, as a faculty.

After plowing through his lengthy chapter on 'The Nature of Man,' one is left unsure of Miller's answer to our question: How many faculties does the soul have and what are they? There are at least two – the mind and the will – but in Miller's presentation we are left unsure concerning the affections.

Norman Fiering carries out his detailed discussion of the seventeenth-century Puritan understanding of the relationship between the will and the intellect with the settled conclusion that those were 'the two faculties of the rational soul.'[35] Although he has a protracted discussion of emotion in seventeenth-century Puritanism and recognizes the affections as an important part of the Puritan view of human psychology, he does not actually call the affections a third faculty of the soul. But Miller, perhaps, and Fiering appear to hold a minority opinion. The majority of scholarship maintains that the faculty psychology of seventeenth-century Puritanism counted the faculties of the soul to be three – the intellect, the will, and the affections.

Miller makes the point that this faculty psychology, although held almost universally among the Puritans, was seldom addressed directly by them. 'They discussed the faculties only in passing references, in incidental exegesis, but with no deliberate concentration, and a casual reader of Puritan sermons might never notice that they contain a version of human psychology unless his attention were expressly called to scattered passages.'[36] He explains further that the Puritans 'explained this or that faculty only when the explanation was called for in a particular text and scarcely ever presented a complete picture of all the faculties in operation together.'[37] Fulcher has examined Thomas Hooker's sermons and supports Miller's assertion. He writes: 'Although Hooker makes no formal attempt to spell out his doctrine in terms of the faculty psychology, his arguments presuppose its categories and relationships, and employ its forms as a theoretical framework.'[38] Fulcher goes on to add: 'Hooker's use of the theory illustrates Miller's contention that the Puritan divines accepted the faculty psychology and incorporated its categories into their theology, at least in its application, without consciously expounding the psychology itself.'[39] Inasmuch as Miller and Fulcher's description is an accurate portrayal of seventeenth-century Puritanism, Flavel must be considered as a notable exception. In various treatises we find him presenting 'a complete picture of all the faculties in operation together' and how they are affected by either sin or grace. Then, most notably, he gives 'deliberate

---

[35] Fiering, *Moral Philosophy*, p. 106.
[36] Miller, *New England Mind*, p. 242.
[37] Miller, *New England Mind*, p. 267.
[38] Fulcher, 'Puritan Piety,' p. 215. These categories of faculty psychology are observable in two treatises of Thomas Hooker: *The Soules Preparation for Christ* (London: Robert Davulman, 1632), and *The Application of Redemption* (London: Peter Cole, 1656).
[39] Fulcher, 'Puritan Piety,' p.215 n. 58.

concentration' to the entire picture of human psychology and attempts a 'formal attempt to spell out the doctrine' in *Soul of Man*.

Early in *Soul of Man* Flavel qualifies his discussion of the soul's faculties. He states, 'It is not my design in this discourse to treat of the several faculties and powers of the soul, or to give you the rise, natures, or numbers of its affections and passions: but I shall confine my discourse to its general nature and original.'[40] This qualification is understood partly as an introduction to the fact that he would devote significant effort in the treatise to addressing the issue of the origin of the soul. This issue is important to Flavel and he explores it as well as the issue of the faculties. Also, it appears that Flavel is aware of some of the more detailed philosophical issues encountered when discussing the faculties of the soul, but chooses not to address all of them. We see this choice of his as a natural reflection of his pastoral and evangelistic zeal. The reader who held a copy of *Soul of Man* was holding a book containing much more than theoretical postulations. It was a book of practical application aimed at the spiritual needs of believers and also at the conversion of unbelievers. As we will see, the self-imposed limits of his discussion of the faculties are especially evident in his discussion of the affections. Nevertheless, his explanation of the 'general nature' of the soul's faculties is comprehensive and methodical and reveals enough about his faculty psychology for us to understand what the various faculties are, in his view, and how they relate to each other.

The Number of Faculties in the Soul

When Flavel comes to enumerate the soul's faculties, he settles on three: the intellect, the will, and the affections. Yuille suggests that 'Flavel seems to fluctuate between a bi-partite and tri-partite division. In the final analysis, the difference is unimportant given the fact that the function of the affections remains the same in both paradigms.'[41] We suggest that a careful examination of the places in which Flavel emphasizes the intellect and will to the exclusion of the affections, in the light of the places in which he is trying to be comprehensive in his definitions, reveals that he indeed holds to a 'tri-partite division.' Yuille's comment that the difference between the two views is unimportant is true in Flavel's case precisely because he actually holds to the 'tri-partite' view. The passage of his writings that suggests a seeming bi-partite view will be discussed when we look at Flavel's view of the steps of the effectual call.

We reiterate that when listing the soul's faculties Flavel names three. He will at times discuss memory, conscience, and reason – but when summarizing succinctly he concludes that these are all part of the understanding. In *Soul of Man* he names the faculties concisely prior to examining each one in more

---

[40] Flavel, *Works*, Vol. 2, p. 495.
[41] Yuille, *Inner Sanctum*, pp. 35–36 n. 14.

detail. 'And being an immortal spirit, fitted and framed to live for ever, I find that God hath, answerably, endued and furnished it [the soul] with an *understanding, will,* and *affections,* whereby it is capable of being wrought upon by the Spirit in the way of grace and sanctification in this world in order to the enjoyment of God, its chief happiness in the world to come.'[42]

We will now turn our attention to Flavel's view of each faculty individually, and then examine how he describes the relationship between them.

The Intellect (including the Conscience)

All that Flavel develops in terms of the place of the mind in the effectual call and in preaching for conversion flows from how he views the capacities of the intellect, and how those capacities are affected by both sin and grace.

The beginning of his discussion of the understanding in *Soul of Man* is worth quoting here. He writes:

> It [the soul] is a vital, spiritual, and immortal substance, endued with an understanding. This is the noble leading faculty of the soul: We are not distinguished from brutes by our senses, but by our understanding. As grace sets one man above another, so understanding sets the meanest man above the best of brutes. Strange and wonderful things are performed by the natural instinct and sagacity of beasts; but yet what is said of one, is true of them all, 'God hath not imparted understanding to them,' Job xxxix. 17. This is a jewel which adorns none but rational creatures, men and angels.[43]

We note that Flavel exalts the human intellect as that which distinguishes man from animals. He does this often. In the *Soul of Man* he states:

> What animal is there in the world, out of whose soul the acts of reason spring and flow, as they do out of human souls? Are they capable of inventing, (or which is much less) of learning the arts and sciences? Can they correct their senses, and demonstrate a star to be far greater than the whole earth, which to the eye seems no bigger than the rowel of a spur? Do they foreknow the positions and combination of the planets, and the eclipses of the sun and moon many years before they suffer them?[44]

He refers to this perspective also in his *Mental Errors*. In warning against the harmful results of intellectual pride, he first acknowledges the value of the intellect. 'Reason, indeed, is the highest natural excellency of man; it exalts him above all earthly creatures, and, in its primitive perfection, almost equalized him with angels, Heb. ii. 7.'[45] In *Reasonableness and Necessity* he writes:

---

[42] Flavel, *Works*, Vol. 2, p. 523.
[43] Flavel, *Works*, Vol. 2, p. 502.
[44] Flavel, *Works*, Vol. 2, p. 518.
[45] Flavel, *Works*, Vol. 3, p. 464.

'Reason exalts man above all earthly beings; it is his dignity and privilege, that God hath furnished him with abilities of mind, to recollect, animadvert, compare, infer, ponder, and judge his own actions.'[46]

His praise for the human mind is sometimes exalted. In the thirty-fifth sermon of *Method of Grace* he is explaining that spiritual blindness is an aspect of God's judgment. He writes of '[f]irst, The subject of this judgment, which is the soul, and the principal power of the soul, which is the mind and understanding faculty; the soul is the most precious and invaluable part of man, and the mind is the superior and most noble power of the soul.'[47]

Flavel sees the human intellect as the highest natural excellency of man, the superior and most noble power of the soul, the leading faculty of the soul, and that which differentiates man from animal. But what exactly is the intellect?

In *Soul of Man* Flavel defines the intellect for us. 'The understanding is a faculty of the reasonable soul by which a man apprehends and judges all intelligible things.'[48] Following this definition he begins a discussion of the various 'uses' or 'powers' of the understanding. He mentions four such powers – the discernment, the direction of the will, the thoughts, and the conscience. In other writings he includes explanations of memory. At times he uses the words 'reason' and 'reflection.' However, when systematizing his view of the mind he limited the powers to four. Therefore, although we acknowledge that he does refer to memory, reason and reflection, it is our conclusion that he includes them under the category of 'thoughts.'

DISCERNMENT: A FUNCTION OF THE INTELLECT

The first ability or function of the intellect which Flavel mentions is that of discernment. He calls it a 'use' of the understanding in man, and writes that it is:

> To distinguish truth from error and falsehood. By this candle of the Lord, lighted up in the soul of men, he may discern betwixt duty and sin, good and evil: It is the eye of the soul, by which it seeth the way in which we should go, and the dangerous precipices that are on either side. It is the soul's taster, and discerns wholesome food from baneful poison, Job xii. 11. 'Doth not the ear (i.e. understanding by the ear) try words, as the mouth tasteth meat?' It brings all things as it were in the lump before it, and then sorts them, and orderly ranks them into their proper classes of lawful and unlawful, necessary and indifferent, expedient and inexpedient, that the soul may not be damnified by mistaking one for another.[49]

---

[46] Flavel, *Works*, Vol. 6, p. 472.
[47] Flavel, *Works*, Vol. 2, p. 464.
[48] Flavel, *Works*, Vol. 2, p. 503.
[49] Flavel, *Works*, Vol. 2, p. 503.

Direction of the Will: Another Function of the Intellect

The second 'use' of the understanding in man touches upon the relationship between the mind and the will. This relationship will be explored in greater detail shortly, but here let us see how Flavel introduces this aspect of the intellect:

> To *direct* and guide us in our practice. This faculty [the understanding] is by philosophers rightly called the ἡγεμόνικον, the leading faculty; because the will follows its practical dictates. It sits at the helm, and guides the course of the soul; not impelling, or rigourously enforcing its dictates upon the will; for the will cannot be so imposed upon; but by giving it a directive light, or pointing, as it were, with its finger, what it ought to chuse, and what to refuse.[50]

It is crucial to this study to note that Flavel viewed the intellect as the leading faculty of the soul. We will explore this view in more detail shortly when we come to describe Flavel's understanding of the relationship between the three faculties.

Also it should be noted that this perspective on the intellect as the 'leading faculty' of the soul has extremely important implications for how the ministry of preaching is to be carried out towards those who are yet unconverted. Those implications will be explored later.

Flavel continues his enumeration of the intellect's functions. 'To this faculty belong two other excellent and wonderful powers of the soul, viz. 1. Thoughts. 2. Conscience.'[51] We will look at them individually.

Thoughts: Another Function of the Intellect

Flavel begins his discussion of thoughts by quoting Zanchius:[52] 'Thoughts are properly the actings and agitations of the mind, or any actual operation of the understanding.'[53] Flavel continues:

> They are the musings of the mind, which are acted in the speculative part of the understanding. It is observable that the Hebrew word שׂוּחַ *suach*, which is used for meditation, or thinking, signifies both to think and to speak in the mind. When the understanding, or mind, resolves, and meditates the things that come into it, that very meditation is an inward speaking, or hidden word in the heart. ... Thoughts are the figments and creatures of the mind: They are formed within it, in

---

[50] Flavel, *Works*, Vol. 2, p. 503.
[51] Flavel, *Works*, Vol. 2, p. 503.
[52] Hieronymus Zanchi (also known as Girolamo Zanchi) was professor at Neustadt an der Haardt, and is considered to be one of the 'architects of Reformed orthodoxy,' along with Theodore Beza, in the generation of theologians following John Calvin's death. 'Protestant Orthodoxy,' *Encyclopædia Britannica Online*. 2009, http://search.eb.com/eb/article-9061606, accessed 10 December 2009.
[53] Flavel, *Works*, Vol. 2, p. 503.

multitudes innumerable. The power of cogitation is in the mind, yea, in the spirit of the mind.[54]

Earlier in *Soul of Man*, when he was delineating differences between the soul and body, Flavel touched upon the issue of memory. He wrote:

> Again, for the being of our souls, if we reflect upon ourselves, we shall find that all our knowledge of them resolves into this, that we are beings conscious to ourselves of several kinds of cogitations; that by our outward senses we apprehend bodily things present; and by our imagination we apprehend things absent; and that we oft recover into our apprehensions things past and gone, and upon our perception of things, we find ourselves variously affected.[55]

In the twenty-first sermon of *Fountain of Life* he is discussing the doctrine '[t]hat the sacramental memorial Christ left with his people, is a special mark of his care and love for them.'[56] He digresses into a discussion of memory:

> Remembrance, properly, is the return of the mind to an object, about which it hath been formerly conversant; and it may so return to a thing, it hath conversed with before, two ways; speculatively and transiently; or affectingly, and permanently. A speculative remembrance, is only to call to mind the history of such a person, and his sufferings: that Christ was once put to death in the flesh. An affectionate remembrance, is when we so call Christ and his death to our minds, as to feel the powerful impressions thereof upon our hearts.[57]

At the end of his discussion of the soul's faculties in *Soul of Man* Flavel summarizes the ability of the intellect to think. 'My thoughts are all formed in my mind or understanding in innumerable multitudes and variety. By it I can think of things present, or absent; visible, or invisible; of God, or myself; of this world, or the world to come.'[58]

CONSCIENCE: ANOTHER FUNCTION OF THE INTELLECT

Another aspect of the intellect, in Flavel's view, is the human conscience. No discussion of his view of the human constitution would be complete without noting his view of the conscience, a very important part of his theology. Its importance will become clearer when we examine Flavel's understanding of the effectual call, see the place that the conscience plays in the effectual call, and then see the implications for preaching which he drew from this understanding.

Great respect is paid to the conscience in Flavel's writings. He sees it as a

---

[54] Flavel, *Works*, Vol. 2, pp. 503–504.
[55] Flavel, *Works*, Vol. 2, p. 500.
[56] Flavel, *Works*, Vol. 1, p. 261.
[57] Flavel, *Works*, Vol. 1, p. 262.
[58] Flavel, *Works*, Vol. 2, p. 523.

powerful aspect of the soul. He uses elevated language when referring to it. 'To my *understanding* also belongs by [*sic*] *conscience*, a noble, divine and awful power.'[59]

> It is a very high and awful power; it is *solo Deo mi nor* [*sic*], and rides (as Joseph did) in the second chariot; the next and immediate officer under God ... . It observes records, and bears witness of all our actions; and acquits and condemns, as in the name of God, for them. Its consolations are most sweet, and its condemnations most terrible: so terrible, that some have chosen death, which is the king of terrors, rather than to endure the scorching heat of their own consciences. The greatest deference and obedience is due to its command, and a man had better endure any rack or torture in the world, than incur the torments of it.[60]

There are times in his writings when he almost seems to elevate the conscience to the same level as the mind, will and emotions – as if it were an equal and separate faculty of the soul. One example is found in his exposition of Mark 16:26 in *Soul of Man*. He is persuading his readers of the truth that one soul is worth more than the entire world and attempts to instill awe in them by causing them to think on the soul's 'noble faculties, and admirable powers.' Here he presents the mind, will, conscience, and affections, in that order, for the readers' contemplation. A careful reading of this section reveals no inconsistency with his already-stated belief that the soul contains only three faculties. Rather, this section of Flavel's writing illustrates the importance with which Flavel views the conscience. It is a particular 'power' of the mind which contributes to the 'intrinsic worth and excellency'[61] of the soul. However, when defining the soul's faculties carefully he always mentions just three: mind, will, and affections, with the conscience seen as one power or function of the intellect.

In this regard Flavel's view is consistent with that of Ames[62] and perhaps differs from that of Perkins.[63] John Eusden, in his introduction to *The Marrow*

---

[59] Flavel, *Works*, Vol. 2, p. 524.
[60] Flavel, *Works*, Vol. 2, p. 504.
[61] Flavel, *Works*, Vol. 3, p. 156.
[62] Beeke and Pederson describe Ames as being considered 'Perkins's most important disciple and heir. Ames's major works were widely circulated and influenced Calvinistic theology in England throughout the seventeenth century.' Joel R. Beeke and Randall J. Pederson, *Meet the Puritans* (Grand Rapids: Reformation Heritage Books, 2006), p. 45.
[63] David Cornick summarizes the significance of Perkins in terms of his influence upon Protestant thought concerning the conscience. He writes that Perkins 'was the first English Protestant theologian to try and supply the need [for a manual for pastoral care that could be used by new clergy]. He wrote treatises on the ministry, and attempted to provide books of guidance for his fellow ministers, based on his own deep pastoral experience, and he was soon imitated, although none attained his

of Theology: William Ames, points out an apparent difference between Perkins and Ames:

> In the opening of *Conscience: Its Law or Cases*, Ames writes that he plans to emulate the approach of his teacher Perkins and will emphasize the practical side of theology. But Ames also wrote as a creative individual and often broke with his colleagues in the Puritan brotherhood. In the *Conscience* reference to Perkins, Ames immediately says that he views conscience as an act of practical judgment not, like Perkins, as a faculty.[64]

Perkins' explanation of the conscience as a separate faculty is not as clear as Eusden would have us conclude. Perkins begins his *Discourse of Conscience* by insisting that conscience, rather than being a faculty in and of itself, is a part of the mind.

> Conscience is a part of the understanding in al [*sic*] reasonable creatures, determining of their particular actions, either with them or against them. I say Conscience is a part of the understanding, and I shew it thus: God in framing of the soule placed in it two principal faculties, *Understanding* and *Will*. ... Now, conscience is not placed in the affections nor will, but in the understanding: because the actions thereof standes [*sic*] in the use of reason.[65]

After making the point that the conscience is a part of the understanding, he then states that 'conscience is not a bare knowledge or judgment of the understanding (as men commonly write) but a naturall power, facultie, or created qualitie, from whence knowledge and judgment proceede as effects.'[66] And so he begins to call conscience a faculty immediately after stressing that it is properly seen as a part of one of the principal faculties of the soul, i.e. the mind. Thus he speaks of a faculty within a faculty.

---

systematic grandeur. ... Conscience was therefore a subject that preoccupied Perkins, and he provided the first extended English Protestant theology of conscience.' David Cornick, 'Pastoral Care in England: Perkins, Baxter and Burnet,' in G.R. Evans, ed., *A History of Pastoral Care* (London and New York: Cassell, 2000), pp. 313–27, at 314–15. Coleman Markham states that 'Perkins' understanding of conscience is the central factor in his writings, the point at which soteriology and ethics, faith and works, are held together.' Coleman Markham, 'William Perkins' Understanding of the Function of Conscience' (Ph.D. diss., Vanderbilt University, 1967), p. 18.

[64] Ames, *Marrow of Theology*, transl. Eusden, pp. 17–18.
[65] William Perkins, *William Perkins 1558–1602 English Puritanist: His Pioneer Works on Casuistry: 'A Discourse of Conscience' and 'The Whole Treatise of Cases of Conscience'*, ed. Thomas Merrill (The Hague: N.V. Drukkerij Trio, 1966), p. 5.
[66] William Perkins, *The Works of William Perkins*, ed. Ian Breward (Appleford, Berkshire: Sutton Courtenay Press, 1970), p. 5. Breward, an authority on Perkins' works, comments: 'He did not entirely escape the danger of treating it [conscience] as a separate faculty, or of giving it an over-rational role.' Perkins, *Works*, p. 64.

But then, Ames does not always maintain his distinctions clearly either. In the *Marrow*, when listing how sin's corruption had reached 'not only to the whole man in general but to each of his parts,'[67] he then speaks of the intellect, the conscience, the will, the affections, and the body. He elevates the conscience to a distinct level of importance even though he makes it clear that he does not consider it a faculty separate from the mind.

This way of speaking about the conscience in Perkins and in Ames reminds us of the language Flavel used when describing the conscience and upon which we have already commented. Perkins, Ames and Flavel all view the conscience as a vitally important part of the human being. All speak of it as being located in the mind. Perkins refers to it as a 'facultie' but in a context in which he has already insisted that it was a part of the understanding. Ames and Flavel do not refer to it as a faculty but only as a power or function of the mind.

Flavel begins his explanation of the conscience by insisting that the seat of it in the human being is the intellect. 'The conscience belongs also to this faculty [the understanding]; for it being the judgment of a man upon himself, with respect or relation to the judgment of God, it must needs belong to the understanding part or faculty.' He then quotes Ames: '"Thoughts are formed in the speculative, but conscience belongs to the practical understanding."'[68]

Fiering, in his *Moral Philosophy at Seventeenth-Century Harvard*, examines in detail the seventeenth-century competing views of human psychology and their implications concerning the relationship between human mind and will. Commenting upon the affect that Ames' writings had on those discussions, Fiering writes: 'According to Ames, as we have already seen, conscience is a complex human endowment. But its most significant characteristic in relation to the matter at hand is that it is not in any sense a separate faculty. It is rather a reflexive power of the intellect.'[69] Flavel's view is consistent with this representation of Ames' thought.

Flavel's view of the conscience as being seated in the mind can also be seen in the arrangement of *Soul of Man*'s material in his 'Synopsis.' As previously stated, the 'Synopsis' is an outline of the entire treatise and was published in the first edition of Flavel's *Whole Works*. In this visual representation of his argumentation Flavel very clearly places his discussion of the conscience under the category of the soul's understanding.[70]

Flavel sees the fact that humans possess a conscience as logically tied to the fact that humans are reasonable beings. In a discussion of the judgment of the last day Flavel states: 'Man is a reasonable being, and every reasonable being, is an accountable being.'[71] He then discusses the guilty consciences of men as

---

[67] Ames, *Marrow of Divinity*, p. 120.
[68] Flavel, *Works*, Vol. 2, p. 504.
[69] Fiering, *Moral Philosophy*, p. 120.
[70] Flavel, *Whole Works*, p. 481. It is presented in Appendix 4 of this study.
[71] Flavel, *Works*, Vol. 1, p. 527.

evidence that they know that they are accountable.

> And what need we seek evidence of this truth, further than our own conscience? Lo, it is a truth engraven legibly upon every man's own breast. Every one hath a kind of little tribunal, or privy sessions in his own conscience, which both accuses and excuses for good or evil, which it could never do, were there not a future judgment, of which it is now conscious to itself.[72]

Reasonable beings are accountable to their creator. Man's conscience, itself seated in that part of the soul which makes him accountable, tells him so.

Flavel rejects the argument that the conscience is a result of education and upbringing. He refers to Scripture and to non-Christian history to prove his point. 'Nor let any imagine, that this may be but the fruit of education and discourse. ... For if so, how comes it to obtain so universally? ... It is evident that the very consciences of the Heathens, have these offices of accusing and excusing, Rom ii. 15.'[73] He then leans on Sir Charles Wolseley's book, *The Unreasonableness of Atheism*,[74] and explains: 'it is hard to imagine, (as an ingenious author speaks) that a general cheat should bow down the backs of all mankind, and induce so many doubts and fears, and troubles, amongst them; and give an interruption to the whole course of their corrupt living, and that there should be no account of it?'[75] The conscience, in Flavel's view, is not a product of human upbringing but an aspect of the human intellect. It is a human capacity shared by all.

Does Flavel give a concise definition of the conscience? A lengthy appendix to Flavel's *England's Duty* is devoted entirely to the issue of the conscience. In it he writes: 'Conscience (as our Divines well express it) is the judgment of man upon himself, as he is subject to the judgment of God. A judgment it is, and a practical judgment too; it belongs to the understanding faculty ... . This self-judgment is the proper office, of the conscience.'[76] In his summary of the soul's faculties, Flavel writes again of the conscience as that which self-judges the soul. The conscience is that '[b]y which I summon and judge myself, as at a solemn tribunal; bind and lo[o]se, condemn and acquit myself and actions, but still with an eye and respect to the judgment of God. Hence are my best comforts, and worst terrors.'[77]

On this point he is in agreement with both Perkins and Ames. Perkins wrote:

---

[72] Flavel, *Works*, Vol. 1, p. 527.
[73] Flavel, *Works*, Vol. 1, p. 528.
[74] Charles Wolseley, *The Unreasonableness of Atheism made manifest, In a Discourse written by the command of a Person of Honour* (London: Nathaniel Ponder, 1669).
[75] Flavel, *Works*, Vol. 1, p. 528.
[76] Flavel, *Works*, Vol. 4, p. 271.
[77] Flavel, *Works*, Vol. 2, p. 524.

> Nay it [conscience] is (as it were) a little God sitting in the middle of men[s] hearts, arraigning them in this life as they shal be arraigned for their offences at the tribunal seat of the everliving God in the day of judgment. Wherefore the temporarie judgment that is given by the conscience is nothing els but a beginning or a fore-runner of the last judgment.[78]

Eusden quotes Ames as writing: 'Conscience ... is a man's judgment of himself according to God's judgment of him.'[79]

According to Flavel, the conscience is not a separate faculty of the soul but a power or function of the intellect. It is that exercise of self-judgment which the soul works upon itself. It is an extremely significant and important function of the intellect. This elevated view of the conscience holds significant implications for the ministry of preaching. We will look at those implications later.

So we see that Flavel expresses the functions of the intellect as falling into four main categories: the discerning of good and evil, the direction of the soul's will, the thinking processes, and the conscience.

The Will

The second faculty of the soul which Flavel names is the will. 'God hath endued the soul of man not only with an understanding to discern, and direct, but also a *will* to govern, moderate, and over-rule the actions of life.'[80] He defines the will in the following way: 'The will is a faculty of the rational soul, whereby a man either chuseth or refuseth the things which the understanding discerns and knows.'[81]

Flavel describes the will as having two 'excellencies,' which are liberty and dominion. He makes the point that the human will cannot be compelled. This is different, he states, from the intellect. 'In this it differs from the understanding, that the understanding is wrought upon necessarily, but the will acts spontaneously.'[82]

The freedom, or liberty, of the will is only absolute in the natural realm. Flavel writes:

> The liberty of the will must be understood to be in things natural, which are within its own proper sphere, not in things supernatural. It can move, or not move the body, as it pleaseth; but it cannot move towards Christ, in the way of faith, as it pleaseth; it can open or shut the hand or eye at its pleasure, but not the heart.[83]

---

[78] Perkins, *Works*, p. 9.
[79] Ames, *Marrow of Divinity*, p. 43.
[80] Flavel, *Works*, Vol. 2, p. 505.
[81] Flavel, *Works*, Vol. 2, p. 506.
[82] Flavel, *Works*, Vol. 2, p. 506.
[83] Flavel, *Works*, Vol. 2, p. 506.

Fiering misunderstands this distinction of Flavel's and, as a part of his assertion that Flavel was 'radical,' explains: 'Thus, it is as though there are two wills in Flavel's analysis, one that usually follows the judgments of the intellect and another that can obey only the judgments of God.'[84] Flavel did not propose two wills, but two spheres – one natural, the other supernatural. The human will has absolute freedom in the natural, which Flavel calls 'its own proper sphere,' but not in the supernatural.

Having intimated that the will's liberty does not extend to things supernatural, such as faith in Christ, Flavel quickly addresses the conundrum of maintaining the will's liberty and also maintaining a belief in efficacious grace. 'True, indeed, it [the will] is not compelled, or forced to turn to God by supernatural grace, but in a way suitable to its nature, it is determined and drawn to Christ, Psal. cx. 3. It is drawn by a mighty power, and yet runs freely; Cant. i. 4. 'Draw me, and I will run after thee.' This is consistent with his earlier contention that the will's liberty is congruent with its nature. Flavel writes: 'it cannot be compelled and forced: Coaction is repugnant to its very nature.'[85]

At this point in his discussion he delves further into the issue of the liberty of the will in the light of efficacious grace. He quotes Thomas Manton (1620–77)[86] at length. It is a passage in which Manton is attempting to refute the views of Pelagius.[87] What is important for our purposes is to discern from Flavel's comments about Manton's quotation the purpose for which Flavel includes it in his description of the human will. Flavel is using the quotation to strike at the idea of an 'indifferent' will.[88] An indifferent will, in Flavel's thinking, implies that it has the power to choose that is not completely attributable to grace. But

---

[84] Fiering, *Moral Philosophy*, p. 127.

[85] Flavel, *Works*, Vol. 2, p. 506.

[86] Thomas Manton was educated at Oxford, following which he was ordained to the diaconate in 1640. He ministered in Devon until the advance of Royalist forces in the Civil War gave him cause to flee to London. There he ministered and participated in the effort to establish Presbyterianism in the London area. During the Commonwealth he became the 'principal presbyterian voice on protectorate committees discussing religious matters.' After the Restoration his nonconformity resulted in a brief time in jail, but he continued ministering and negotiating for tolerance with government authorities. E.C. Vernon, 'Manton, Thomas (*bap.* 1620, *d.* 1677),' *ODNB*, http://www.oxforddnb.com/view/article/18009, accessed 21 November 2009.

[87] This passage is found in Manton's *One Hundred and Ninety Sermons on the Hundred and Nineteenth Psalm* (London: T.P., 1681), p. 252.

[88] Manton writes: 'Now there are others grant the secret influences of God's grace, but make the will of man to be a co-ordinate cause with God; namely, that God doth propound the object, hold forth inducing considerations, give some remote power and assistance; but still there's an indifferency in the will of man to accept and refuse, as liketh him best.' Manton, *Hundred and Nineteenth Psalm*, p. 252.

of one thing Flavel is certain: the human being is in need of efficacious grace. He ends his interaction with Manton by saying, 'but still the pride of nature will not let men see the necessity of divine efficacious influences upon the will, and the consistency thereof with natural liberty.'[89]

After having discussed the liberty of the will, Flavel asserts that the will also possesses dominion. Here he divides the will's dominion into two parts: *imperium despoticum*, and *imperium politicum*.

He explains the first, the *imperium despoticum*, in this way, 'The will, like an absolute sovereign, reigns over the body, i.e. its external members by way of absolute command.' He is quick to mention, however, two limitations to this command. The will cannot restore or repair, merely by its willing, any member of the body which is in some way incapacitated. 'If the soul will the health and life of the body never so intensely and vehemently, it cannot keep off death one moment the longer from it.' Also, the will cannot overrule providence. 'Its sovereignty no way intrenches upon, nor interferes with the dominion of providence.'[90] Flavel is saying that although the human will has great dominion in the natural realm it cannot stave off sickness and death, nor can it interfere with and frustrate the divine will.

Flavel describes the second aspect of the will's dominion, the *imperium politicum*, as follows:

> It [the will] hath a political power over the faculties and passions of the soul, not by way of absolute command, but by way of suasion and insinuation. Thus it can oft times persuade the understanding and thoughts to lay by this or that subject, and apply themselves to the study of another. It can bridle and restrain the affections and passions, but yet it hath no absolute command over the inner, as it hath over the outward man.[91]

Flavel is asserting that the will has control over the other faculties of the soul, but that this control is not absolute. It can persuade the mind.[92] It can restrain the affections. But it can do neither absolutely.

It would be appropriate at this point to take note of some of Fiering's observations concerning Flavel's discussion of the human will. Fiering traces the development of the conflict of ideas concerning human psychology that was present in the seventeenth century. He notes the position of intellectualism which held that the will had no determining power in and of itself but followed

---

[89] Flavel, *Works*, Vol. 2, p. 507.
[90] All three quotations in this paragraph are from Flavel, *Works*, Vol. 2, p. 507.
[91] Flavel, *Works*, Vol. 2, p. 508.
[92] Flavel appears unaware of the problem contained in attributing cognitive powers to the will. For discussions reflecting upon how that problem contributed to the eventual alteration of seventeenth-century faculty psychology, and for the place of Locke and Edwards in that development, see Stephenson, 'Jonathan Edwards' Thought,' pp. 144–49.

absolutely the dictates of the mind. This position, although not expressing it explicitly, suggested some sort of determinism. What was in the mind necessarily determined the will's action. Fiering quotes Thomas Aquinas (1225–74)[93] as representing this view: 'The will necessarily pursues what is firmly held by reason, and that it cannot abstain from that which reason dictates.'[94]

This intellectualism was met with various forms of voluntarism. Fiering explains that Scholastic voluntarism attributed to the human will a self-determining power. This position was a clear reaction against the inferred determinism of the intellectualist position and gave no room for a necessity of action to be placed upon the will. Augustinian voluntarism, on the other hand, while also disavowing the intellectualist position, allowed for divine determinism in relation to the will. It tended to attribute autonomy to the will in reference to the soul's other faculties but not in reference to God.[95]

At the end of Fiering's discussion he examines the view of Ames and comments: 'Reasoning such as Ames's, which contained some combination of Scholastic and Augustinian voluntarism, was common enough in Puritanism in the second half of the seventeenth century.'[96] He then refers to Edward Reynolds (1599–1676)[97] and John Flavel as examples. In his interaction with Flavel's writings he correctly observes Flavel's alteration of a strict scholastic voluntarism. Fiering writes: 'All of this would seem to be in accordance with a Scholastic voluntarism. But Flavel revealed that the will has other limitations and other sources of guidance.'[98]

We return now to our discussion of the limitations on the will which Flavel

---

[93] Thomas Aquinas was an Italian Dominican theologian known for his classical systematization of Latin theology, and is recognized as the Roman Catholic Church's 'foremost Western philosopher and theologian.' 'Aquinas, Thomas, Saint,' *Encyclopædia Britannica Online*, 2009, http://search.eb.com/eb/article-9108661, accessed 10 December 2009.

[94] Fiering, *Moral Philosophy*, p. 114.

[95] Fiering's explanation of scholastic and Augustinian voluntarism is found in his *Moral Philosophy*, pp. 114–27.

[96] Fiering, *Moral Philosophy*, p. 126.

[97] Edward Reynolds was educated at Merton College, Oxford, held a variety of ministerial posts, and then became involved in the reformation of Oxford in the late 1640s. He eventually was made DD, vice-chancellor of Oxford, and dean of Christ Church. He was recognized as one of the leading moderates and following the Restoration he maintained this position, trying to reason with nonconformists, with whom he was theologically sympathetic, as well as with the Church of England authorities. He eventually accepted the bishopric of Norwich. He wrote more than 30 books, one of which – *Treatise of the Passions* – was used as a textbook at Oxford for many years. Ian Atherton, 'Reynolds, Edward (1599–1676),' *ODNB*, http://www.oxforddnb.com/view/article/23408, accessed 21 November 2009.

[98] Fiering, *Moral Philosophy*, p. 127.

recognizes. We will discuss Flavel's 'other sources of guidance' to the will when we explain the relationship between the three faculties.

It is important to note that Flavel sees two cases in which the will cannot exert dominion over the understanding. First of all, the will cannot force the mind to stop thinking on some subjects. This occurs when God is working in the soul to convince it of its own sinfulness. We will note later that a person's realization of, and emotional response to, their own sinfulness is a vital part of Flavel's understanding of the effectual call. The will is also not absolutely able to stop the mind from considering some thoughts when Satan is pressing the soul with temptation.[99] We note that these two exceptions are consistent with Flavel's prior assertion that the 'proper sphere' of the human will's liberty is the natural, not the supernatural. The work of God and Satan on the human will is in the realm of the supernatural and thus not under the will's dominion.

The second case in which the will cannot exercise complete dominion over the mind is when the conscience is stirred up and not at rest. Flavel writes: 'It cannot quiet and compose a raging conscience, and reduce it at its pleasure to rest and peace. This is the peculiar work of God.'[100]

He finishes his discussion of the limitations of the will's dominion by saying: 'These things are exempt from the liberty and dominion of the will of man; but notwithstanding these exemptions, it is a noble faculty, and hath a vastly extended empire in the soul of man.'[101] Later in the treatise, Flavel adds another summary statement: 'It [the will] freely chuseth and refuseth, as my understanding directs and suggests to it. The members of my body, and the passions of my soul, are under its dominion: The former are under its absolute command, the later under its suasions and insinuations, though not absolutely, yet always with effect and success.'[102]

The Affections

The third faculty of the soul, which Flavel names, is the affections. This emotional capacity of the soul is mentioned last, and with it Flavel completes his description of the soul's faculties.

Flavel introduces the subject of the soul's emotions by stating: 'The soul of man is not only endued with an *understanding* and *will*, but also with various *affections* and *passions*, which are of great use and service to it, and speak the excellency of its nature.'[103]

He builds his understanding of the place of emotions around the belief that they fit humankind for happiness, and that this happiness is found in people's

---

[99] Flavel, *Works*, Vol. 2, p. 508.
[100] Flavel, *Works*, Vol. 2, p. 509.
[101] Flavel, *Works*, Vol. 2, p. 509.
[102] Flavel, *Works*, Vol. 2, p. 524.
[103] Flavel, *Works*, Vol. 2, p. 509.

relation to God. He writes:

> The true uses, and most excellent ends for which these affections and passions are bestowed upon the soul of man, are to qualify it, and make it a fit subject to be wrought upon in a moral way of persuasions and allurements, in order to its union with Christ, (for by the affections, as Mr. Fenner rightly observes, the soul becomes marriageable, or capable of being espoused to him) and being so, then to assist it in the prosecution of its full enjoyment in heaven.[104]

Flavel's use of, and concurrence with, William Fenner (1600–40)[105] is significant. Fiering makes the statement that '[p]ossibly the most significant work on the passions that emerged from English Puritanism was William Fenner's little-known *A Treatise of the Affections; or, the Soules Pulse.*' In an extended discussion of Fenner's view of the human affections, Fiering points out that Fenner very definitely rejected the view of the affections as a separate faculty but rather saw them as being located in the will. 'In Fenner the unity of will and higher passion is already accomplished. The passions or affections are only "the motions of the will, by which it goes forth" to the embracing of its object as good or the avoidance of it as evil.'[106] We concur with Fiering's observation. We note that Fenner wrote: 'Saint Paul couples his affections and his will together in one, and his affection that he had to the Thessalonians, he seats in his will.'[107]

This understanding of the place of the affections was one aspect of a view which resulted in a greater emphasis upon the emotions in defining a person's right response to God. Fiering chronicles the thinking and implications of Fenner's view, commenting on 'Fenner's exclusion of reason or rationality as the criterion of religious virtue and piety.'[108] Fenner acknowledged the importance of the intellect but refused to define a proper human response to God in terms of the intellect. The affections, according to Fenner, were key to experiencing God. They were also vital in the process of an unconverted person becoming converted. As Fiering explains:

> Rather than holding up training or habit as the basis of virtue and piety, a concept that makes one's developed character a kind of ineluctable fate dependent upon

---

[104] Flavel, *Works*, Vol. 2, p. 510.
[105] William Fenner was educated at Cambridge, graduating MA in 1619. His ministerial life included a chaplaincy, several vicarships, and some itinerant preaching. He is most known for his ministry at Rochford, Essex, and the publication of his writings, most of which were overseen by Edumund Calamy, his successor at Rochford. A.C. Bickley, 'Fenner, William (*c.*1600–*c.*1640),' rev. Mark Robert Bell, *ODNB*, http://www.oxforddnb.com/view/article/9291, accessed 21 November 2009.
[106] Fiering, *Moral Philosophy*, p. 159.
[107] William Fenner, *Treatise of the Affections; or, the Soules Pulse* (London: R.H., 1642), p. B2.
[108] Fiering, *Moral Philosophy*, p. 160.

environment and circumstances, the theory of spiritual conversion stressed the mutability of the affections, a concept of human nature that allows for the occurrence of radical personality change and salvation for anyone at any time. 'Be a man never so crosse and crooked, never so cruelly and implacably bent to transgresse, yet as long as there are affections in him to be wrought, his heart may be wonne,' Fenner wrote. In other words, without affections, no one would be susceptible to persuasion.[109]

The importance of the affections in the process of a person moving from an unconverted to a converted state is echoed in Flavel. Flavel quoted or referred to Fenner five times in the course of his *Works*. He praised Fenner as 'that great and eminent instrument of God in this work [the work of disquieting people's consciences by preaching].'[110] We observe that Flavel was either unaware of, or chose not to discuss his difference with, Fenner concerning the affections as a separate faculty. What resonated with Flavel regarding Fenner's view of the affections was the practical importance they played in the work of evangelism. Flavel echoed Fenner's vocabulary and emphasis when he spoke of the affections being 'wrought upon' in the process of a person becoming converted.

Flavel sees the affections of the unconverted soul as providing the capacity to desire and as moving a person toward God. 'The soul considered at a distance from God, its true rest and happiness, is furnished and provided with *desire* and *hope* to carry it on, and quicken its motion towards him. These are the arms it is to stretch out towards him, in a state of absence from him.'[111] This, of course, has great implications for preaching to the unconverted. We will explore those implications in due time.

Once the soul is united with God, the affections play an important role in the Christian's experience of God. 'But the soul considered in full union with and fruition of God, its supreme happiness, is accordingly furnished with affections of love, delight, and joy, whereby it rests in him and enjoys its proper blessedness in his presence for ever.'[112]

The very purpose of human emotional capacity is the knowing and enjoying of God:

> These passions and *affections* of my soul are of great use and dignity. I find them as manifold as there are considerations of good and evil. They are strong and sensible motions of my soul, according to my apprehensions of good and evil. By them by [sic] soul is capable of union with the highest good. By love and delight I am capable of enjoying God, and resting in him as the centre of my soul.[113]

---

[109] Fiering, *Moral Philosophy*, p. 162.
[110] Flavel, *Works*, Vol. 4, p. 90.
[111] Flavel, *Works*, Vol. 2, p. 509.
[112] Flavel, *Works*, Vol. 2, p. 510.
[113] Flavel, *Works*, Vol. 2, p. 524.

Although Flavel notes the importance of the affections in the human constitution he does not explore the subject of the soul's emotions in as much detail as he does the soul's intellect and will. After his discussion of the place of the affections, he writes: 'But I must insist no farther on this subject here, it deserves an entire treatise by itself.'[114]

For the purposes of this study it is sufficient to note that Flavel sees the affections as another faculty of the soul in addition to the understanding and the will. Where his discussion of the affections is important to us is in his examination of how they are involved in the effectual call, and what the corresponding implications of that involvement are for the one who preaches to the unconverted.

In summary, Flavel sees the human soul as possessing three faculties: the intellect, the will, and the affections. He divides the intellect's functions into four main categories: the power of discernment, the role of directing the soul's will, the thinking processes, and the conscience. The will is that faculty of the soul which rules and decides. It rules both the body and the other faculties, yet not without some limitations. The affections fit the soul for love for God and happiness in him.

The Relationship between the Intellect, the Will, and the Affections

In our discussion of Flavel's view of the various faculties we have already touched upon the relationship between them. We attempt to expand upon that issue now. Which faculty influenced the other, and what was that influence?

THE WILL'S PLACE AS 'QUEEN OF THE SOUL'

First, we note that according to Flavel the will is the ruling faculty of the soul:

> View its [the soul's] will, and you shall find it like a queen upon the throne of the soul, swaying the sceptre of liberty in her hand ... with all the affections waiting and attending upon her. No tyrant can force it, no torment can wrest the golden sceptre of liberty out its hand; the keys of all the chambers of the soul hang at its girdle, these it delivers to Christ in the day of his power; victorious grace sweetly determines it by gaining its consent, but commits no violence upon it.[115]

We refer to our previous discussion of the will for an explanation of the limitations Flavel sees on the will's dominion. Flavel summarizes those limitations: 'It [the will] freely chuseth and refuseth, as my understanding directs and suggests to it. The members of my body, and the passions of my soul, are under its dominion: The former are under its absolute command, the later under its suasions and insinuations, though not absolutely, yet always with

---

[114] Flavel, *Works*, Vol. 2, p. 510.
[115] Flavel, *Works*, Vol. 3, p. 157.

The Human Constitution

effect and success.'[116] Thus, the will has command, albeit limited in certain respects, over the affections.

THE INFLUENCE OF WILL AND INTELLECT UPON THE AFFECTIONS

In his image of the ruling queen, Flavel includes the affections as the attendants waiting upon the ruler. This presents a picture of the will as having dominion over the emotions. The mind also influences the affections.

In the twenty-fifth sermon of *Fountain of Life* we see Flavel giving counsel to the one who sees his own heart cold and lifeless. Note that he sees the mind as the avenue through which the affections are to be touched:

> If thou wouldst indeed get a heart evangelically melted for sin, and broken with the kindly sense of the grace and love of Christ, thy way is not to force thy affections, nor to vex thyself, and go about complaining of a hard heart, but to set thyself to believe, realize, apply, infer, and compare by faith as you have been directed; and see what this will do: 'They shall look on me whom they have pierced, and mourn.' This is the way and proper method to raise the heart and break it.[117]

We note the interaction of mind and emotions also in Flavel's first definition of the affections. 'These passions and affections of my soul are of great use and dignity. I find them as manifold as there are *considerations* of good and evil. They are strong and sensible motions of my soul, according to my *apprehensions* of good and evil.'[118] The affections result from 'considerations' and 'apprehensions.' Surely Flavel saw the mind as a major influence on the emotions.

THE AFFECTIONS' INFLUENCE UPON THE WILL

The affections then are presented as being under the dominion of the will and susceptible to the influence of the mind. But is there any reciprocal influence of the affections upon the other two faculties? Flavel implies strongly that the affections also influence the will.

We remember Flavel's portrayal of the will and affections in a picture of a royal court. 'View its [the soul's] will, and you shall find it like a queen upon the throne of the soul ... with all the affections waiting and attending upon her.'[119] This presents the will as having dominion over the emotions – the will is the queen. And yet there is an implied susceptibility of the will to the influence of the affections. The attendants are in the same room as the queen and interact with her. We will see the importance of the influence of the affections upon the will in Flavel's thinking when we examine in detail his

---

[116] Flavel, *Works*, Vol. 2, p. 524.
[117] Flavel, *Works*, Vol. 1, p. 319.
[118] Flavel, *Works*, Vol. 2, p. 524; emphasis mine.
[119] Flavel, *Works*, Vol. 3, p. 157.

doctrine of conviction, but here we see the picture emerging that the emotions, although in no way represented as forcing or controlling the will, nevertheless have an influence upon it.

It is at this point in our discussion that some additional interaction with Fiering's reading of Flavel is appropriate. We have already pointed out that Fiering sees in Flavel the view that there are 'sources of guidance'[120] to the will other than the intellect. He notes this as a way of expressing his placing of Flavel in the category of those who advocated some form of confluence between scholastic and Augustinian voluntarism. Later in Fiering's discussion he refers to Flavel's 'confusion' when pointing out the importance Flavel places on the conscience.[121] We contend that the confusion is to be found in Fiering. Later when we discuss Flavel's view of conviction, an integral part of the effectual call, we will see that it includes an emotional response to the conclusions made in the conscience. This movement of the affections has a very definite influence upon the will. Thus Flavel does indeed allow for the affections to influence the will. The affections are one of the 'other sources of guidance' operating upon the will. It is the failure of Fiering to see the link in Flavel's thought between conscience, conviction, and affections that leads Fiering to conclude that Flavel is confused concerning the primacy of the will.

Flavel asserts that the will cannot control the disturbed conscience.

> It [the will] cannot quiet and compose a raging conscience, and reduce it at its pleasure to rest and peace. This is the peculiar work of God. He only that stills the stormy seas, can quiet the distressed and tempestuous soul. The impotence of the will, in this case, is known to all that have been in those deeps of trouble.[122]

Part of the tempest in a soul undergoing conviction is the response of the affections to the conscience's self-judgment. The will cannot ward off that emotional response. Flavel very definitely holds that the affections can indeed influence the will.

This view is not unique to Flavel. In his *Second Epistle of St. Paul to the Corinthians* we find evidence that Sibbes held a similar view. Sibbes writes: 'Carnal wit is a slave to carnal will; and that carnal will is drawn by carnal affections: affections draw the will.'[123] Later, Sibbes writes: 'the affections follow the will.'[124] Beck's summary of Sibbes' view of the relationship between the faculties concludes:

---

[120] Fiering, *Moral Philosophy*, p.127.
[121] Fiering, *Moral Philosophy*, p. 127 n. 49.
[122] Flavel, *Works*, Vol. 2, p. 509.
[123] Richard Sibbes, *A Learned Commentary or Exposition: upon the first Chapter of the Second Epistle of S. Paul to the Corinthians* (London: J.L., 1655), p. 364.
[124] Sibbes, *Second Epistle to the Corinthians*, p. 415.

The Human Constitution

In his exposition of 2 Corinthians we find Sibbes noting on the one hand that 'affections draw the will,' while purporting in the same treatise that the affections follow the will. Though at first sight this appears to be a contradiction, the solution is that Sibbes believed both to be right. He viewed the affections and will interrelated and mutually aiding.[125]

Beck observes in Sibbes the same interrelatedness between will and affections that Flavel describes.

THE RELATIONSHIP BETWEEN THE WILL AND THE MIND

But what of the relationship between the will and the mind? Again, we refer to our previous explanation of Flavel's view of the will. We pointed out that Flavel considers the mind as that which directs the will. He writes: 'This faculty [the understanding] is by philosophers rightly called the ηγεμὸικον, the leading faculty; because the will follows its practical dictates. It sits at the helm, and guides the course of the soul.'[126]

Now we come to a question concerning Flavel's vocabulary and meaning. He refers to the will as the 'queen of the soul,' yet also refers to the intellect as 'the leading faculty of the soul.' Both terms imply primacy, yet when we see them used together we recognize that Flavel allows for some sense of mutual influence between the faculties. In his view the mind is not able to efficiently cause the will to make any decision – such a scenario would be a violation of the will's ruling capacity. However, the mind counsels the will and points it in the direction which the mind has discerned as being right. The will, on the other hand, is able to move the mind off some trains of thought and onto others. As we have already discussed, this dominion of the will over the mind does have some limitations; namely, when God or Satan are working on the mind. And so in Flavel's view the intellect has no dominion over the will, but rather counsels it strongly on what decision is right to make. The will does have dominion over the intellect, but with certain limitations.

McGrath, while attempting to explain the view of Baxter and Owen regarding the relationship between the mind and will, states: 'the intellect discerned between good and evil, but it was the will which then directed the affections and intellect according to its choice.'[127] This is consistent with what we see in Flavel so far as it goes. McGrath does not offer any discussion of any reciprocal influence of the affections on the will, which we do see in Flavel.

In Flavel's view there is a relationship of mutual influence between will and mind. This assertion leads us to the consideration of a particular figurative expression which Flavel repeatedly uses. It is the image of 'the door to the soul.' Which faculty is 'the door to the soul?' Is it the grave counsellor or the

---

[125] Beck, 'Doctrine of *gratia praeparans*,' p. 129.
[126] Flavel, *Works*, Vol. 2, p. 503.
[127] McGrath, 'Puritans and the Human Will,' p. 212.

great prince? Is it the intellect, or is it the will? Here Flavel seems to contradict himself. He calls both the mind and the will the 'door to the soul.' It is our conclusion that this seeming contradiction is a result of Flavel speaking in two different contexts.

When describing the soul itself in terms of its powers and their respective influence upon each other, he resolutely refers to the will as the 'door to the soul.' After discussing the exceptions to the will's dominion (which we have explored already), he writes:

> but notwithstanding these exemptions, it is a noble faculty, and hath a vastly extended empire in the soul of man; it is the door of the soul, at which the Spirit of God knocks for entrance. When this is won, the soul is won to Christ; and if this stand out in rebellion against him, he is barred out of the soul, and can have no saving union with it.[128]

Therefore, when speaking about which faculty of the soul must be won over before the unregenerate becomes a child of God, Flavel unwaveringly propounds that it is the will. When speaking of Christ entering the soul in a saving way, Flavel speaks of the will as being the door through which Christ comes. When the will consents to Christ, the soul is saved.

But when speaking from the perspective of the process through which a person passes when experiencing the effectual call, or when speaking pastorally about how a preacher participates in that effectual call while ministering to a person, he names the intellect as the door of the soul. An example is in his tenth sermon of *Fountain of Life*, on Luke 24:45, 'Then opened he their understandings.' He writes:

> By understanding is not here meant the mind only, in opposition to the heart, will, and affections, but these were opened by and with the mind. The mind is to the heart, as the door to the house: what comes in to the heart, comes in at the understanding, which is introductive to it.[129]

This image of the mind being the door to the soul is the one which Flavel uses most frequently. In the very first of his eleven sermons on Revelation 3:20 he comments, '*at the door*, i.e. the mind and conscience, the faculties and powers which are introductive into the whole soul. The word *door* is here properly put to signify those introductive faculties of the soul, which are of a like use to it, as the door is to the house.'[130]

The failure to distinguish the two contexts in which Flavel uses the term 'door of the soul' can lead to confusion. One might conclude that Flavel is

---

[128] Flavel, *Works*, Vol. 2, p. 509.
[129] Flavel, *Works*, Vol. 1, p. 131.
[130] Flavel, *Works*, Vol. 4, p. 19.

inconsistent, or that he is a strict intellectualist. We assert that he was neither.[131]

This view of the human intellect being the 'door to the soul' expresses itself in significant ways throughout Flavel's theology. We will see when exploring his view of the effectual call that he holds illumination to be the first step of the process and that illumination takes place in the intellect, not the will. Thus, from the practical perspective of the minister, he preaches to the intellect first because it is the 'door to the soul' – the place of the first phase of the effectual call. We will explore Flavel's theology of the effectual call and its implications to the ministry of preaching in due course. The relationship between his view of the intellect, his understanding of the effectual call, and the implications of those two issues for preaching is enormously important to Flavel.

In Flavel's view of the human constitution, the intellect guides the will in an advisory or counselling capacity. We have already noted that he refers to the intellect as the 'leading faculty of the soul.' However, we remind ourselves that no matter how earnestly the mind informs the will, it does not, nor cannot, force any decision. 'The understanding seems to bear the same relation to the will, as a grave counsellor doth to a great prince.'[132]

Yuille, in *The Inner Sanctum of Puritan Piety: John Flavel's Doctrine of*

---

[131] This failure to note differing contexts in which Puritan expressions are found may have been a contributing factor to Miller's somewhat dubious conclusion: 'Therefore, reason, free and independent, is the king and ruler of the faculties, and its consort, the will, is queen and mistress.' Miller, *New England Mind*, p. 247. This conclusion, which leans towards attributing an intellectualist position to the Puritans, is made by Miller in the midst of a discussion of passages in which Puritan writers referred to the will as the ruling faculty. (For the complete discussion, see his chapter, 'The Nature of Man,' in *New England Mind*, pp. 239–79). Fiering, commenting upon Miller's view of the extent of intellectualism in Puritanism, attributes this view partially to Miller's misunderstanding of Ames, and points out that 'Miller also fell into the crucial error of confusing the question of the independence of the will in relation to intellect with the problem of the freedom of the will in relation to divine decrees.' Fiering, *Moral Philosophy*, p. 121 n. 37. Hulse also noted this questionable view of Miller's and concurred with Fiering's evaluation of Miller. 'The instances where he [Miller] did err seem to have been not only quite exceptional but also related to his persistent attempt to present a tension between the Puritans' general intellectual heritage and their pietistical ideas. This tendency may partly explain, for instance, the important misquotation in which he attributed to William Ames the position that the will is subject to the understanding. Norman Fiering, who found Miller's error, is surely right in saying that it could have been inadvertent, and, as Fiering notes, Miller quoted correctly other passages from Ames on the same question.' Hulse, *Adding to the Church*, p. xv. We add to the conversation the idea that Puritan writers, Flavel being an example, used certain phrases (ex. door of the soul, queen of the soul) in different contexts and intended different meanings depending upon the context. A failure to observe the context in which certain phrases were used can contribute to a misinterpretation of the Puritan author's meaning.

[132] Flavel, *Works*, Vol. 2, p. 506.

Mystical Union with Christ, briefly touches upon the faculty psychology of Flavel. He too concludes that Flavel's view is not consistent with a strict intellectualist position: 'Flavel is not suggesting that the will necessarily follows the dictates of the mind. In referring to the mind as the 'leading faculty,' he means that: (1) the will ought to follow the mind; (2) the knowledge of God always begins in the mind; and (3) the will cannot choose that which is unknown to the mind.'[133]

Yarbrough, in his *Jonathan Edwards and the Rhetoric of Conversion*, argues that it was a common view that the intellect had a guiding role in relation to the will. He writes, 'Like most Calvinists prior to Edwards, Stoddard and Cotton adhered to a faculty psychology wherein the intellect led and the heart followed … . Here as elsewhere in earlier Puritan theology, the understanding, properly prepared and set aright by grace, so inclines the will to accept God.'[134]

A discussion of the Puritan view of the soul's faculties can easily result in a presentation of the human soul as containing three distinct and competing entities – a divided soul. Rechtien criticizes the Puritan view of the faculties:

> The traditional understanding of faculties considered them powers of the person acting in a certain way. A faculty was not reified into a thing but as rather a way of existing (*ens quo*, a way by which to exist, rather than *res* or a thing). However, having an overly simplified faculty psychology, Puritans divided the person into faculties as if they were separate things.[135]

But Rechtien's concern, although understandable, is derived without an acknowledgment of the purposes of the Puritan discussion of the faculty psychology. One very significant purpose was practical – they were trying to understand how God would have them preach. Fulcher makes this point when he stresses that for the New England Puritan preacher this faculty psychology was present, but was not dwelt upon in a theoretical fashion. Rather, the preacher was interested in the practical implications of this view upon seeing the unconverted become converted. Fulcher states:

> the interpretation of their [the Puritans'] uses of the categories of faculty psychology, for example, strictly in terms of their intellectual heritage tends to

---

[133] Yuille, *Inner Sanctum*, p. 36 n 16. Yuille's discussion highlights Richard Muller's analysis of Calvin's views concerning the relation between the intellect and the will. He writes, 'Muller makes an insightful observation when he distinguishes between *temporal* and *causal* priority in Calvin's thought. In this paradigm, the will is dependent upon the intellect for its object, because the will is unable to choose the unknown. However, dependence is not the same as determination. The Puritans (including Flavel) adopt this view of the temporal priority of the mind.' Yuille, *Inner Sanctum*, pp. 36–37 n. 16.

[134] Yarbrough, *Delightful Conviction*, p. 96.

[135] Rechtien, 'Logic in Puritan Sermons,' p. 250.

obscure their consuming interest in the salvation of souls. When Shepard tried to stir up the affections of the worshipers in the Cambridge meeting house, he was more concerned with the effect of his preaching upon the congregation than with the theoretical distinctions of faculty psychology.[136]

Stephenson also comments upon the Puritans' use of faculty psychology for shaping their preaching. We view her discussion as being deficient in that she does not see the actual correlation between the faculty psychology and the details of the effectual call. She does not recognize that one purpose of the Puritan preacher holding to his faculty psychology was that it helped inform him of his various responsibilities in the effectual call. Nevertheless, in her comparison of the seventeenth-century Puritan view to that of John Locke (1632–1704)[137] and Jonathan Edwards, she accurately points to the practical nature of the Puritans' view, as well as insisting that the Puritan view did not necessitate a divided soul.[138] Stephenson comments:

> the Puritans had been limited by the scholastic or 'faculty' psychology which tended to picture the mind as a series of entities operating in contradistinction to each other. In his discussion of 'Power' Locke had reduced this idea of faculties as 'distinct Beings that can act' to absurdity … . Edwards later followed this particular argument in his examination of the freedom of the will – though he continued to use the language of faculty psychology. But while this psychology was the only description the Puritans had to work with, they emphasized as far as they could the unity of the faculties especially as they functioned in conversion.[139]

Stephenson continues by looking at some of the works of Solomon Stoddard,[140]

---

[136] Fulcher, 'Puritan Piety,' pp. 309–10.

[137] John Locke was an English philosopher who, although never ordained, held a post at Christ Church, Oxford, for many years. He was also attached as secretary and assistant to prominent politicians. He fled to the Netherlands when the turn of political events necessitated exile. He wrote on a wide range of subjects, and many scholars hold that his works and thought influenced both the European Enlightenment and the Constitution of the United States. His *Essay Concerning Human Understanding* was controversial and gained the attention of Jonathan Edwards. J.R. Milton, 'Locke, John (1632–1704),' *ODNB*, http://www.oxforddnb.com/view/article/16885, accessed 17 December 2009.

[138] Stephenson bases this conclusion concerning Locke and Edwards primarily upon an examination of Locke's *An essay concerning humane understanding in four books* (London: Tho. Basset, 1690), and Edwards' *A treatise concerning religious affections* (Boston: S. Kneeland and T. Green, 1746).

[139] Stephenson, 'Jonathan Edwards' Thought,' pp. 148–49.

[140] Stephenson's conclusions concerning Stoddard are based primarily upon examination of his *A Guide to Christ* (Boston: J. Allen, 1714) and *A treatise concerning conversion* (Boston: J. F., 1719).

Thomas Shepard,[141] and John Flavel. She then states:

> While these men and others like them artificially divided the moment of grace into separate actions for the sake of description, and to serve the purpose of refuting those who sought the 'heat' of affection without the 'light' of a work in the understanding; all of them held that man responded whole-heartedly and instantaneously in conversion. And though conversion in the puritan psychological schema often sounded like an overhaul of a complex machine, freeing the motions of one part after another, the renovation of the soul was for them an internal and immediate act of God.[142]

Beck, in his examination of the theology of Sibbes, also addresses the issue of the faculty psychology presenting the human soul as fragmented and disjointed. He writes:

> Affleck, in mentioning Sibbes' discussion of man's understanding, will, and affections, raises the critical question: "And, this is our problem: can he speak of man this way and still maintain the basic biblical interpretation of man as a unified living being?" We think Sibbes can because, while he speaks of three distinct faculties of man, he clearly speaks of them in strongly interconnected terms.[143]

The conclusion of Beck, Stephenson and others that the faculty psychology was not understood by the Puritans as presenting a divided soul is consistent with our findings concerning Flavel's view. It is true that some of Flavel's discussions of the faculties, taken out of the context of the sermons in which they are found, could be seen as presenting a mechanistic picture which implies a divided human soul, but Flavel would object to that interpretation. He understood there to be three faculties in the human soul, but still one soul. This unity of the soul will be clearly seen when we consider his application of his understanding of the effectual call and its integration with his faculty psychology to the task of preaching.

Summary

So how do we summarize Flavel's view of the relationship between the three faculties? A concise way of stating his view of the relationship is that the will rules, the mind guides, and the affections interact. The will rules the soul, commanding the mind and affections, albeit with a few exceptions which we have already explained. The mind guides the soul, directing the will and

---

[141] Stephenson's conclusions concerning Shepard are based primarily upon examination of his *Parable of the Ten Virgins* (London: J. Haynes, 1660) and *The sound believer a treatise of evangelicall conversion* (London: R. Dawlman, 1649).
[142] Stephenson, 'Jonathan Edwards' Thought,' p. 152.
[143] Beck, 'Doctrine of *Gratia Praeparans*,' pp. 131–32.

affections. The mind's influence on the will is great, but the will retains its liberty and is not forced by the mind, nor necessitated by the mind's conclusion, to any choice. The affections interact with both mind and will. We say 'interact' because, although the greater influence is that of the soul's mind and will on the affections, Flavel acknowledges that the affections can influence the other faculties, especially when the soul is undergoing the divine work of conviction.

We now turn our attention to the next category of John Flavel's theology which needs to be examined – the doctrine of sin.

Chapter 4

The Doctrine of Sin

Flavel's view of the doctrine of sin is most systematically expressed in three treatises. In *Soul of Man* he carefully examines the origin of the soul's sinfulness; in his *Exposition* he discusses the concept of original sin; and in *Method of Grace* he explores the ramifications of sin in the human soul. We will base our presentation of Flavel's view of the doctrine of sin primarily upon his discussions in these three treatises. As is typical of Flavel's preaching and writing, however, he does not save one point of theology for one sermon or treatise only. References to various aspects of the doctrine of sin are distributed throughout his *Works*. We will also refer to important passages in *Husbandry Spiritualized*, *Saint Indeed*, *Touchstone of Sincerity*, *Mental Errors*, and *England's Duty*.

That aspect of the doctrine of sin which most directly touches on our study is Flavel's discussion of the effect of sin on the soul's faculties. Before exploring that feature of his theology it is necessary to sketch briefly the larger picture of his doctrine of sin – especially the origin of sin and the three-fold nature of sin.

Introductory Issues

The Origin of the Soul's Sinfulness

There is no question but that Flavel sees humankind's sin as originating in the sin of Adam. In *Soul of Man* he emphasizes this point with a vivid picture. 'Other sins, like single bullets, kill particular persons: but Adam's sin, like a chain-shot, mowed down all mankind at once.'[1] In his *Exposition* he carefully expresses this doctrine.

> Q. 2. How can we be guilty of Adam's first sin?
>
> A. We are guilty of it, because Adam sinned not only as a single, but also as a public person, and representative of all mankind: ...
>
> Q. 3. How else came we under his guilt?

---

[1] Flavel, *Works*, Vol. 2, p. 539.

The Doctrine of Sin

A. We are guilty of his sin by generation; for we were in his loins.[2]

As previously mentioned, Flavel asserts that every human soul is immediately created. Having made this assertion, but also having contended that our sinfulness is a result of Adam's fall, Flavel feels compelled to address the question of the origin of sin in the soul. He states the problem. 'If the soul be created and infused immediately by God, either it comes out of his hands pure, or impure; if pure, how comes it to be defiled and tainted with sin? If impure, how do we free God from being the author of sin?'[3]

Flavel gives a lengthy and detailed answer to this and other questions concerning the origin of sin in the soul. Fundamental to his explanation is the idea that the soul is created, in a sense, neutral. He quotes Baronius:[4] 'They [souls] are created neither morally pure, nor impure; they receive neither purity nor impurity from him [God], but only their naked essence, and the natural powers and properties flowing therefrom.'[5] The original purity and rectitude of the soul was lost by Adam's sin and is therefore judicially withheld by God. 'As an holy God, he cannot inspire any impurity, and as a just and righteous God, he may, and doth with-hold, or create them void and destitute of that holiness, and righteousness which was once their yea, of happiness and glory.'[6]

How then does the soul come to be defiled with original sin? Flavel asserts that the defilement takes place in the union of the soul to the body. 'It [original sin] comes in neither by the soul alone, nor by the body alone, apart from the soul; but upon the union and conjunction of both in one person. It is the union of these two which constitutes a child of Adam, and as such only we are capable of being infected with his sin.'[7]

Flavel acknowledges that there is a mystery in this and that not everything can be understood. After musing on the mystery, he says: 'Mean time, I think it much more our concernment to study how we may get sin out of our souls, than to puzzle our brains to find out how it came into them.'[8]

---

[2] Flavel, *Works*, Vol. 6, p. 172.
[3] Flavel, *Works*, Vol. 2, p. 519.
[4] Caesar Baronius (1538–1607) was a Roman Catholic cardinal and church historian. Educated in Naples and Rome, he gained a doctorate in 1561. He entered into the Congregation of the Oratory under the leadership of Philip Neri, and remained connected to it the rest of his life. He is best known for his *Annales ecclesiastici*, but also was 'confidant of popes, served on various commissions, undertook the revision and correction of the Roman Martyrology ... and held the post of Vatican librarian.' J. Wahl, 'Baronius, Caesar, Ven.,' in *New Catholic Encyclopedia*, New York: Catholic University of America Press, 2003.
[5] Flavel, *Works*, Vol. 2, pp. 519–20.
[6] Flavel, *Works*, Vol. 2, p. 520.
[7] Flavel, *Works*, Vol. 2, p. 520.
[8] Flavel, *Works*, Vol. 2, p. 520.

The Three Aspects of Sin

In the tenth sermon of his *Method of Grace* Flavel explores the implications of Matthew 9:12 and develops the doctrine '[t]hat the Lord Jesus Christ is the only physician for sick souls.'[9] The 'disease' with which humankind is infected is sin, and Flavel expends considerable effort in explaining the seriousness of this malady. He explains it as having three aspects: guilt, dominion, and inherence.

The guilt of sin is a judicial sentence passed upon all descendants of Adam. 'This is the deepest and deadliest wound the soul of man feels in this world. What is guilt but the obligation of the soul to everlasting punishment and misery? It puts the soul under the sentence of God to eternal wrath.'[10]

As explained earlier, part of this judicial sentence is the creation of the soul in such a way that its union with the body results in immediate sinfulness. Another element of the judicial aspect of sin which Flavel often mentions is the spiritual blindness with which all humankind is born. This blindness will be examined in greater detail when we look at sin's effect on the intellect.

The dominion of sin is the second aspect. This aspect of sin is the effect sin has upon the soul's faculties. This will be investigated in detail in a moment, but here we include Flavel's brief summary. 'Where sin is in dominion, the soul is in a very sad condition; for it darkens the understanding, depraves the conscience, stiffens the will, hardens the heart, misplaces and disorders the affections; and thus every faculty is wounded by the power and dominion of sin over the soul.'[11]

The third aspect is the inherence of sin. By this Flavel means the actual presence of sin in a soul. He calls this 'the very core and root of all our other complaints and ailes. This made the holy apostle bemoan himself and wail so bitterly, Rom. vii. 17. because of "sin that dwelt in him." And the same misery is bewailed by all sanctified persons all the world over.'[12]

How do these three aspects of sin relate to original sin? In his *Exposition* Flavel addresses the topic of original sin. He explains that the term 'original sin' refers both to the judicial guilt of Adam's sin, and to the inner propensity humans have to sin. The catechism's eighteenth question and answer are as follows. 'Quest[ion]. 18. Wherein consists the sinfulness of that estate whereinto man fell? A[nswer]. The sinfulness of that estate whereinto man fell, consists in the guilt of Adam's first sin, the want of original righteousness, and the corruption of his whole nature, which is commonly called original sin, together with all actual transgressions which proceed from it.'[13] A few excerpts from Flavel's exploratory questions and answers show his agreement with the catechism.

---

[9] Flavel, *Works*, Vol. 2, p. 190.
[10] Flavel, *Works*, Vol. 2, p. 191.
[11] Flavel, *Works*, Vol. 2, p. 192.
[12] Flavel, *Works*, Vol. 2, p. 193.
[13] Flavel, *Works*, Vol. 6, p. 172.

The Doctrine of Sin

> Q. 1. How many sorts of sins are all men under?
>
> A. All men are guilty before God of two sorts of sin; of original, and of actual ...
>
> Q. 4. Wherein doth it consist?
>
> A. It consists in two things. First, In our aversion and enmity to that which is good; ... Secondly, In proneness to that which is evil; ...
>
> Q. 5. Is this corruption of nature in all men?
>
> A. Yes; in all mere men, and women, none exempted.[14]

So we see that Flavel interprets the catechism as saying that original sin includes judicial guilt, the absence of original righteousness, and the inner corruption of the soul.

Flavel does not see his three-fold description of sin as conflicting with the doctrine of original sin. When discussing original sin he recognizes the three aspects of sin and partly groups them together under the title 'original sin.' When discussing the three aspects of sin, all that is contained in the idea of original sin is mentioned. These two paradigms are two different ways of explaining the same issue – humanity's sinful condition.

According to Flavel the human condition after Adam's fall and apart from the grace of God includes judicial guilt, an inner propensity to sin, and an actual subjection of the soul's faculties to sin.

Sin's Effect on the Soul's Faculties

Flavel understands that sin rendered the human soul completely unable to respond to God in a saving way. In *Sacramental Meditations* he speaks of the effect of sin on the 'heart' by reflecting on the miraculous nature of saving faith.

> It is the just matter of wonder and astonishment, that ever one spark of faith was kindled in such a heart as thine is; an heart which had no predisposition or inclination in the least to believe: Yea, it was not *Rasa Tabula*, like a clean paper, void of any impression of faith, but filled with contrary impressions to it.[15]

Sin had turned the human heart and inclined it away from God and faith.

In other passages of his writing Flavel describes this effect of sin in relation to the various faculties of the soul. In his view, no faculty of the human soul has been left unaffected by Adam's fall. In a meditation on original sin in his *Exposition*, he writes: 'Q. 6. In what part of our nature doth this sin abide? A. It abides in the whole man, in every part of man, both soul and body.'[16] In

---

[14] Flavel, *Works*, Vol. 6, pp. 172–73.
[15] Flavel, *Works*, Vol. 6, p. 430.
[16] Flavel, *Works*, Vol. 6, p. 173.

Method of Grace, he concurs with a quotation from one he refers to as Zeaem,[17] 'Although the faculties of the soul were not extinguished by the fall, yet their inclination to spiritual objects was wholly lost.'[18] In *Navigation Spiritualized* he describes man in his unregenerate state as having 'all his faculties poisoned [*sic*] and perverted.'[19] In *Saint Indeed*, he summarizes:

> Man, by degeneration, is become a most disordered and rebellious creature, contesting with, and opposing his Maker ... and so is quite disordered, and all his acts irregular: His illuminated understanding is clouded with ignorance, his complying will full of rebellion and stubbornness; his subordinate powers, casting off the dominion and government of the superior faculties.[20]

Indeed, Flavel sees intellect, will, and affections as each being affected by sin.

This view is consistent with the teaching of Perkins and Ames. In Perkins' *The Foundation of Christian Religion Gathered into Six Principles*, he propounds that each of the faculties are corrupted by sin. He mentions the mind, the conscience, the will, the affections, and the body as each receiving its corresponding effect of sin. He wrote that the corruption of sin is '[i]n every part of both body and soul, like a leprosy that runneth from the crown of the head to the sole of the foot.'[21] Ames, in *The Marrow of Theology*, says: 'It is found in Scripture that the same corruption [of sin] is attributed not only to the whole man in general but to each one of his parts.'[22] He goes on to mention the intellect, the conscience, the will, the affections, and the body. Flavel agrees with these two Puritan theologians of previous generations.

We now turn our attention to Flavel's description of sin's effect upon each of the faculties.

Sin's Effect on the Intellect

Flavel explains his view of sin's effect on the intellect by using various motifs. They are spiritual ignorance, natural knowledge juxtaposed against spiritual knowledge, and the relationship between faith and reason. Fundamental to each of these motifs is his understanding of the doctrinal concept of judicial blinding. Also, his emphasis on the Holy Spirit's work of illumination gives insight concerning his understanding of the effects of sin on the intellect. By examining each of these three motifs and two doctrinal concepts, we come to a complete picture of Flavel's view of the intellect of a fallen human.

---

[17] We have not been able to determine with certainty the identity of Zeaem.
[18] Flavel, *Works*, Vol. 2, p. 280 n.
[19] Flavel, *Works*, Vol. 5, p. 269.
[20] Flavel, *Works*, Vol. 5, p. 425.
[21] Perkins, *Works*, p. 151.
[22] Ames, *Marrow of Sacred Divinity*, p. 120.

Judicial Blinding

We begin with the doctrinal concept of judicial blinding. In the thirty-fourth and thirty-fifth sermons of *Method of Grace*, Flavel expounds 2 Corinthians 4:3–4 and develops the doctrine, '[t]hat the understandings of all unbelievers are blinded by Satan's policies, in order to their everlasting perdition.'[23]

In explaining Flavel's view it is important to understand that this blindness and Satan's involvement in it are understood to be a part of God's judgment:

> There are many judgments of God inflicted upon the souls and bodies of men in this world; but none of them are so dreadful as those spiritual judgments are which God inflicts immediately upon the soul; and among spiritual judgments few or none are of a more dreadful nature and consequence than this of spiritual blindness.[24]

The activity of Satan in the blinding of human understanding is not merely an outworking of inherent sin or a consequence of human acts of sin. It is a judicial aspect of the consequences of Adam's fall.

Flavel at times mentions the inherent corruption of the intellect without drawing any correlation between it and Satan's blinding work. When speaking about Christ's role as the Prophet of the church he says: 'It is true, in the state of innocency man had a clear apprehension of the will of God, without a Mediator: but now that light is quenched in the corruption of nature.'[25] When speaking of sin as the disease which Christ heals, he says that 'the dominion of sin darkens the understanding.'[26]

Flavel sees the spiritual blindness of unregenerate people as a judgmental stroke from God. But this condition of the soul can be said to result from a combination of the soul's inherent corruption and the activity of Satan. In *Mental Errors* Flavel combines the two causes. 'Come we next, in the proper order, to consider the principal, impulsive cause of errors; which is SATAN, working upon the pre-disposed matter he finds in the corrupt nature of man.'[27]

This blindness prevents the person from understanding the gospel and therefore from putting his faith in Christ. We will see this consequence most clearly when we consider it in the context of the doctrine of illumination.

Given the importance which Flavel places on the conscience, it is important to note here that this corruption of the intellect by sin involves the conscience as well as the thoughts. Adam's sin 'filled its [the soul's] serene and peaceful conscience with guilt and terror, Tit. i. 15.'[28] When he asserts that all the

---

[23] Flavel, *Works*, Vol. 2, pp. 453, 464.
[24] Flavel, *Works*, Vol. 2, p. 464.
[25] Flavel, *Works*, Vol. 1, p. 121.
[26] Flavel, *Works*, Vol. 2, p. 192.
[27] Flavel, *Works*, Vol. 3, p. 469.
[28] Flavel, *Works*, Vol. 2, p. 539.

faculties are negatively affected by sin he also means that all facets of each faculty are 'poisoned and perverted.'

Spiritual Ignorance

A motif which is closely related to the idea of spiritual blindness is that of spiritual ignorance. In *England's Duty* Flavel explores this concept. 'If knowledge be the key that opens the heart to Christ, as it is plain it is from Luke xi. 52. where Christ denounceth a woe to them that took away the key of knowledge; then ignorance must needs be the shutter that makes fast the door of the heart against Christ.' This ignorance is universal, and is used by Satan to keep the unregenerate in their sinful state. 'Ignorance is Satan's sceptre which he sways over all his kingdom of darkness, and holds his vassals in miserable bondage to him: hence the devils are called, Eph. vi. 12. "The rulers of the darkness of this world."'[29]

Note that it is in the intellect that the battle for the soul begins. For Flavel, a person's deliverance from the rulers of darkness begins when his understanding is healed.

> As soon as ever God opens their eyes; in the same hour they are turned from darkness to light, they are also turned from the power of Satan to God, Acts xxviii. 16 [*sic* for Acts 26:18]. ... O that the great Physician would once apply his excellent eye-salve to your understandings, which are yet darkened with gross ignorance both of your misery and remedy.[30]

Illumination

When analyzing the effect which sin has had on the human intellect it is appropriate to bring the doctrine of illumination into consideration. Flavel's view of this doctrine will be given considerable attention in a later section of this study; however, we should briefly note here its contribution to our understanding of the doctrine of sin.

In the twenty-third sermon of *Method of Grace*, Flavel shows the impossibility of a sinful descendant of Adam believing in Christ apart from divine enabling:

> 'The natural man receives not the things which are of God,' 1 Cor. ii. 14. Three things must be wrought upon man, before he can come to Christ: *His blind understanding must be enlightened*; his hard and rocky heart must be broken and melted; his stiff, fixed, and obstinate will must be conquered and subdued: but all

---

[29] Flavel, *Works*, Vol. 4, p. 44.
[30] Flavel, *Works*, Vol. 4, pp. 44–45.

these are effects of a supernatural power. The illumination of the mind is the peculiar work of God.[31]

Throughout Flavel's *Works* he repeatedly refers to the inability of the unregenerate mind to comprehend the truths of the gospel in a saving way. Without the divine ministry of illumination the sinner cannot come to faith. In an unregenerate soul, saving faith is actually impossible, and this impossibility is partly due to sin's effect on the intellect.

Natural vs Spiritual Knowledge

Sin has introduced into human experience the existence of two kinds of knowledge. In the seventh sermon of *Method of Grace*, Flavel explains:

> There is a *natural knowledge*, even of spiritual objects, a spark of nature blown up by an advantageous education; and though the objects of this knowledge be spiritual things, yet the light in which they are discerned is but a mere natural light. And there is a *spiritual knowledge* of spiritual things, ... the effect and fruit of the Spirit's sanctifying work upon our souls, when the experience of a man's own heart informs and teacheth his understanding, when by feeling the workings of grace in our own souls, we come to understand its nature; this is spiritual knowledge.[32]

His meaning is that the human intellect in its sinful state is capable only of a natural way of knowing. Spiritual knowledge is only possible by the work of the Holy Spirit within the soul.

The two types of knowing are very different in their natures. Flavel makes this point when speaking to the unconverted in the thirty-fifth sermon of *Method of Grace*. 'But O that you would be convinced that your knowledge vastly differs from the knowledge of believers. Though you know the same things that they do, it is a knowledge of another kind and nature.'[33]

In exploring the difference between the natures of the two kinds of knowledge it is helpful to note that the objects of spiritual knowledge are those things pertaining to salvation. Again, in the thirty-fifth sermon of *Method of Grace*, Flavel explains:

> It [spiritual blindness] is a dreadful judgment, if we consider the object about which the understanding is blinded, which is Jesus Christ, and union with him; regeneration, and the nature and necessity thereof. For this blindness is not universal, but respective and particular. A man may have abundance of light and knowledge in things natural and moral; but spiritual things are hidden from his eyes. ... Blindness in part, (saith the apostle) is happened unto Israel? and that

---

[31] Flavel, *Works*, Vol. 2, p. 322; emphasis mine.
[32] Flavel, *Works*, Vol. 2, p. 124.
[33] Flavel, *Works*, Vol. 2, p. 470.

indeed was the principal part of knowledge, viz. the knowledge of Jesus Christ, and him crucified, we see farther than they.[34]

In what way exactly does spiritual knowledge differ from natural knowledge? A hint at Flavel's answer to that question is given in his *England's Duty*. He is trying to encourage the Christian who feels inferior when he compares his own intellectual abilities to those of notable non-Christians:

> You cannot discourse floridly, or dispute subtilely; but can you obey conscientiously, and comply with the manifested will of God tenderly? Then happy art thou. Oh! it is far better to feel a truth, than merely to know it … . Thy little knowledge made effectual by obedience, is more sanctified, more sweet, and more saving than other men's; and therefore of much greater value.[35]

Notice his incorporation of the affections and the will into this discussion of spiritual knowledge. He speaks of 'feeling' a truth, thus implying that the emotions are involved. He also speaks of obedience, thus implying that the will is involved. Mind, will and emotions are all involved in spiritual knowledge.[36]

Spiritual knowledge, in Flavel's view, has an efficacy to it which mere natural knowledge lacks:

> Two things are to be regarded in spiritual knowledge; viz. the quantity, and the efficacy thereof. Your condition doth not so much depend upon the measures of knowledge. … But if that which you do know, be turned into practice and obedience. … If it have influence upon your hearts, and transform your affections into a spiritual frame and temper, … one drop of such knowledge of Christ, and yourselves as this, is more worth than a sea of human, moral, unsanctified, and speculative knowledge.[37]

This efficacy, of course, affects the entire soul – intellect, will, and affections. Flavel often describes it as 'experimental' or 'practical.' More than once he appeals to Hebrews 10:34 to explain this aspect of spiritual knowledge. In *Touchstone of Sincerity*, he writes:

---

[34] Flavel, *Works*, Vol. 2, p. 465.

[35] Flavel, *Works*, Vol. 4, p. 291.

[36] Stephenson, in explaining the historical development of this view of experiential knowledge, traces a line from Calvin, through the Puritans, to Edwards. 'This doctrine of illumination as experiential knowledge – especially as it gained following in sixteenth and seventeenth century England – was to provide Edwards with a considerable background for his own psychology of conversion.' Stephenson, 'Jonathan Edwards' Thought,' p. 135. Beck, in describing the theology of Sibbes, also notes the more-than-intellectual nature of saving knowledge. 'It [saving knowledge] is an apprehending with man's entire being.' Beck, 'Doctrine of *gratia praeparans*,' p. 157.

[37] Flavel, *Works*, Vol. 2, p. 341.

The Doctrine of Sin

> That is a very considerable passage to that purpose in Heb. x. 34. 'Ye took joyfully the spoiling of your goods, (knowing in yourselves) that ye have in heaven a better and more enduring substance.' This knowing in yourselves is by inward and sensible experience, taste and feeling, which is abundantly satisfying to the soul; and stands opposed to all that traditional knowledge we receive from others.[38]

In contrast to spiritual knowledge, natural knowledge is merely intellectual. It does not involve nor transform the entire soul. We see Flavel's comparison of natural to spiritual knowledge in one of his addresses to the unconverted:

> You know spiritual things in another way, merely by the light of reason, ... they know the same things by spiritual illumination, and in an experimental way ... . Their knowledge is practical, yours is idle. ... Their knowledge of God and Christ produces the fruits of faith, ... it hath no such fruits in you; whatever light there be in your understandings, it makes no alteration at all upon your hearts.[39]

Flavel's view of spiritual knowledge is that it is a Holy Spirit-enabled condition whereby a person's intellect perceives the essential saving truths of the gospel and by so doing perceives Christ himself. This spiritual knowledge, although very definitely involving the intellect, also involves the will and emotions. It is a whole-soul response to God.

The Relationship between Faith and Reason

In various parts of his writings Flavel speaks of the relationship between faith and reason. This motif is not in contradistinction with that of spiritual knowledge versus natural knowledge. It is another way of looking at the effect of sin on the human intellect. Not one to rely on only one way of expressing his thoughts, Flavel ranges from one paradigm to another, always with the intent of informing and persuading the hearer.

He expresses his view of the relationship between faith and reason clearly in *Mental Errors*, and so we quote from that work:

> That it is the will of God that reason in all believers should resign to faith, and all ratiocination submit to revelation. Reason is no better than an usurper when it presumes to arbitrate matters belonging to faith and revelation. Reason's proper place is to sit at the feet of faith, and instead of searching the secret grounds and reasons, to adore and admire the great and unsearchable mysteries of the gospel. None of God's works are unreasonable, but many of them are above reason. It was as truly, as ingenuously said by one; Never doth reason shew itself more

---

[38] Flavel, *Works*, Vol. 5, p. 576.
[39] Flavel, *Works*, Vol. 2, p. 470.

reasonable than when it ceaseth to reason about things that are above reason. ... It is not reason, but faith that must save us.[40]

Here he insists that matters of faith are not irrational but supra-rational. That which we can understand is consistent with reason. But there are mysteries in the gospel, and those are meant to be believed in, even if our minds cannot explain them. Reason must sit at the feet of faith.

Flavel seems to reckon this relationship of reason to faith as being a result of sin. It will not be so in heaven because '[t]he soul ... is discharged and freed from all darkness and ignorance of mind, being now able to discern all truths in God, that chrystal ocean of truth.'[41] It was not so with Adam in his pre-fall state. 'In the state of innocency man had a clear apprehension of the will of God.'[42] It is sin which has brought about this necessity of reason to sit at faith's feet.

Sin's Effect on the Will

We turn our attention next to Flavel's description of sin's effect on the 'queen of the soul' – the will. We remember that the will is that faculty which must consent to Christ if the whole soul is to be converted. As we will see when examining Flavel's understanding of the doctrine of faith, he considers the will as the primary seat of faith in the soul. It is with this in view that he occasionally calls the will the 'door of the soul.' If the will holds out against Christ, the entire soul remains unconverted.

Thus it is extremely significant that sin, in Flavel's view, has 'barred the door' of the soul against Christ. 'Every soul comes into the world shut up and fast closed against the Lord Jesus. The very will of man, which is the freest and most arbitrary faculty, comes into the world barred and bolted against Christ. ... This is a dismal effect of the fall.'[43]

He explains in *Method of Grace* that this 'barring of the door' of the will is more than an inability.

> You see where it sticks, not in simple inability to believe, but in an inability complicated with enmity; they neither can come, nor will come to Christ. It is true, all that do come to Christ, come willingly; but thanks be to the grace of God, that hath freed and persuaded the will, else they never had been willing to come.[44]

Thus sin has not merely rendered the will somehow neutrally unable to choose Christ but aggressively set against Christ.

---

[40] Flavel, *Works*, Vol. 3, p. 465.
[41] Flavel, *Works*, Vol. 1, p. 194.
[42] Flavel, *Works*, Vol. 1, p. 121.
[43] Flavel, *Works*, Vol. 4, p. 43.
[44] Flavel, *Works*, Vol. 2, p. 80.

The Doctrine of Sin

Flavel understands that a person's will is changed by sin and thus unable to choose Christ without supernatural intervention. Sin 'made its [the soul's] complying and obedient will stubborn and rebellious.'[45] In *England's Duty* Flavel calls this condition a 'shutting up of the heart against Christ.'[46]

When analyzing the effect which sin has had on the human will, it is appropriate to bring the doctrine of the renewing of the will into consideration. Flavel's view of this doctrine will be given considerable attention in a later section; however, here we should briefly note its contribution to our understanding of the doctrine of sin.

Again, we refer to a portion of the twenty-third sermon of *Method of Grace* which we looked at when considering sin's effect upon the intellect. It also reveals much about sin's effect upon the will. Flavel shows the impossibility of a sinful descendant of Adam believing in Christ apart from divine enabling:

> 'The natural man receives not the things which are of God,' 1 Cor. ii. 14. Three things must be wrought upon man, before he can come to Christ: His blind understanding must be enlightened; his hard and rocky heart must be broken and melted; *his stiff, fixed, and obstinate will must be conquered and subdued*: but all these are effects of a supernatural power.[47]

Throughout Flavel's *Works* he repeatedly refers to the actual inability of the unregenerate will to consent to Christ. Without the divine ministry of the renewal of the will, the sinner cannot come to faith. To unregenerate soul, saving faith is actually impossible, and this is due partly to sin's effect on the will.

Since in Flavel's view the will is the 'queen of the soul,' if the will is changed by sin the entire soul is adversely affected. In *Preparations* Flavel attempts to convince the reader of the enormous significance of having a will submitted to the will of God by contrasting the picture of a restored will with the degree to which sin has affected the natural will. In doing so he reveals the gravity with which he views sin's ruin of the will. With sin having turned the will, it therefore has dominion throughout the entire soul. He writes:

> Look in what faculty the chief residence and strength of sin was, in the same chief residence the power of grace, after conversion, is also: Now it is in the will that the strength and power of sin (before conversion) lay ... . And indeed it was the devil's strong hold, which, in the day of Christ's power, he storms and reduces to his obedience.[48]

This shutting up of the heart against Christ renders faith impossible apart from

---

[45] Flavel, *Works*, Vol. 2, p. 539.
[46] Flavel, *Works*, Vol. 4, p. 43.
[47] Flavel, *Works*, Vol. 2, p. 322; emphasis mine.
[48] Flavel, *Works*, Vol. 6, pp. 23–24.

a direct work of God in the soul. In the twenty-third sermon of *Method of Grace* Flavel explains: 'The impossibility of coming to Christ without the teachings of the Father, will appear from the power of sin, which hath so strong an holdfast upon the hearts and affections of all unregenerate men, that no human arguments or persuasions whatsoever can divorce or separate them.'[49] In Flavel's discussion of the Catechism's question concerning the fall of man into sin he poses and answers a question. 'Q. 4. Did the will of man lose its liberty [original liberty] to good by the Fall? A. Yes, it did, and is so wounded, that it cannot, without thy preventing and regenerating grace, put forth one spiritual and saving act.'[50]

Sin's Effect on the Affections

In addition to the intellect and the will, Flavel mentions the affections as being corrupted by sin. He describes the affections as 'disordered,' 'inverted,' and 'misplaced' by sin. In the tenth sermon of *Method of Grace* he is describing Christ as the only physician for sick souls. In explaining the 'sickness' of the soul, he mentions each faculty and says of the affections: 'Where sin is in dominion, the soul is in a very sad condition; for it ... misplaces and disorders all the affections.'[51]

In *Soul of Man* Flavel asserts that this disordering of the affections which sin has created includes a domination of the affections by the body's sensual appetites, rather than by any desire of God. He writes:

> Our souls are spirits by nature, yet have they naturally no delight in things spiritual: they decline that which is homogeneal and suitable to spirits, and relish nothing but what is carnal and unsuitable to them. How are its affections inverted and misplaced by sin! That noble, spiritual, heaven-born creature the soul, whose element and centre God alone should be, is now fallen into a deep oblivion both of God and itself, and wholly spends its strength in the pursuit of sensual and earthly enjoyments, and becomes a mere drudge and slave to the body. Carnal things now measure out and govern its delights and hopes, its fears and sorrows.[52]

Flavel repeatedly asserts that sin has resulted in the affections now being excited about and desiring that which is wrong rather than that which is right. In the twenty-third sermon of *Method of Grace* he writes of:

> [t]he power of sin, which hath so strong an holdfast upon the hearts and affections of all unregenerate men ... . Sin being connatural, customary, and delightful, doth therefore bewitch their affections and inchant their hearts, to that degree of

---

[49] Flavel, *Works*, Vol. 2, p. 321.
[50] Flavel, *Works*, Vol. 6, p. 168.
[51] Flavel, *Works*, Vol. 2, p. 192.
[52] Flavel, *Works*, Vol. 2, p. 536.

madness and fascination, that they rather chuse damnation by God, than separation from sin.[53]

In the thirty-first sermon of *Method of Grace*, Flavel expands on what the disordering of the affections includes. Not only are the affections now dominated by desires toward what is wrong, but also there is a lack of inclination or strong desire towards God. In this sermon he is exploring the meaning of being 'dead in sin.' He writes:

> They [unconverted people] have no heat or spiritual warmth in their affections to God, and things above; their hearts are as cold as a stone to spiritual objects. They are heated, indeed, by their lusts and affections to the world, and the things of the world: but O how cold and dead are they towards Jesus Christ, and spiritual excellencies.[54]

In addition to the affections being directed in the wrong places, Flavel, in *Preparations*, asserts that sin-tainted affections play an adverse role in temptation. Our corrupt affections are 'the handles of the soul' and thus are worked upon by Satan in his temptations. Flavel explains: 'Our several passions and affections are the handles of his temptations … . The temptation of self-confidence and pride takes hold of a daring and forward disposition, the temptation of apostasy upon a timorous disposition, &c.'[55]

This work of sin has rendered the affections unable to have a proper emotional response to God as it has rendered the mind unable to understand saving truth and the will unable to choose God. Sin has made it impossible for the affections, apart from a work of grace, to respond rightly to God. In the twenty-third sermon of *Method of Grace*, in the same portion we have referred to that relates to sin rendering it impossible for the intellect and will to respond savingly to Christ, Flavel also speaks of the impossibility of a sinful soul responding in an appropriate emotional way to Christ:

> 'The natural man receives not the things which are of God,' 1 Cor. ii. 14. Three things must be wrought upon man, before he can come to Christ: His blind understanding must be enlightened; *his hard and rocky heart must be broken and melted;* his stiff, fixed, and obstinate will must be conquered and subdued: but all these are effects of a supernatural power.[56]

Flavel views the corruption of the soul's emotional faculty as a component of the impossibility of a sinful person coming to faith in Christ apart from a direct work of grace in their life.

---

[53] Flavel, *Works*, Vol. 2, p. 321.
[54] Flavel, *Works*, Vol. 2, p. 427.
[55] Flavel, *Works*, Vol. 6, p. 62.
[56] Flavel, *Works*, Vol. 2, p. 322; emphasis mine.

Summary

Douglas Vickers, in a review of Flavel's *Works*, observes that Flavel integrates his faculty psychology with his understanding of the effect of sin on the human situation. He writes, 'Adopting at many points a faculty classification of understanding, heart, and will, the author [i.e. Flavel] allows no doubt to remain regarding the effects of the fall, the disorder it introduced, the blindness of the intellect, the perversity of the heart, and the enslavement of the will.'[57] We concur with this description.

We offer two quotations from Flavel as we come to providing a summary description of his view of the effect of sin upon the faculties of the soul. In *Method of Grace* he succinctly states: 'Where sin is in dominion, the soul is in a very sad condition; for it darkens the understanding, depraves the conscience, stiffens the will, hardens the heart, misplaces and disorders all the affections; and thus every faculty is wounded by the power and dominion of sin over the soul.'[58] In *Soul of Man* he summarizes the effect of sin on all the soul's faculties: 'It [sin] hath darkened the bright eye of the soul's understanding, ... made its complying and obedient will stubborn and rebellious, ... rendered his tender heart obdurate and senseless.'[59] In Flavel's theology we see that sin has indeed affected all three faculties of the soul. The entire soul is corrupted by sin.

Satan works with the inner corruption which comes from sin to produce blindness in the understanding. The sinful human intellect is not able to perceive the saving truths of the gospel, nor is it able to perceive Christ himself in a saving way. This spiritual ignorance is not merely the result of the soul's inner corruption or of Satan's work, but is a judicial sentence from God on all descendants of Adam. In this sinful state the descendant of Adam is actually unable to come to saving faith without the Holy Spirit's work of illumination in the soul's intellect. Once this illumination takes place, that person can then know with a spiritual knowledge.

The soul's will has been rendered unable to choose Christ. This inability is complicated by actual disinclination concerning God or the gospel. The will is, because of sin, actually set against Christ. Since the will is the primary seat of faith, this effect of sin on the will renders it impossible for the sinner to come to saving faith without the Holy Spirit's work of renewing the will. Once this renewing of the will takes place, the sinner can then believe.

The soul's affections have been disordered by sin. The human heart now desires and loves that which is wrong and experiences negative emotions towards that which is right. Sensual desires now play an inordinate role in the affections. The soul is now easily moved by the temptations of Satan because of the corrupted affections. Indeed, the affections are so corrupted by sin that it

---

[57] Douglas Vickers, 'The Works of John Flavel,' *WTJ* 32 (1969), pp. 92–96, at 95.
[58] Flavel, *Works*, Vol. 2, p. 192.
[59] Flavel, *Works*, Vol. 2, p. 539.

is impossible for them to exercise a proper emotional response to the gospel, to Christ, and to the things of God apart from a work of divine grace in the soul. However, as the Holy Spirit moves an individual sinner through the steps of the effectual call, that person's affections are changed by God and enabled to interact with the intellect and will according to God's original design.

This summary of Flavel's view is consistent with Miller's sweeping commentary on the intersection of the doctrine of sin and faculty psychology in the Puritan mind:

> The description of sin and its effects on the organism might seem one thing to us when given in the terminology of theology and quite another when couched in the vocabulary of psychology, but to the Puritans the two accounts were interchangeable and synonymous. In theology they simply declared that man is corrupt, evil, and impotent; in psychology they gave those adjectives specific meaning by concrete demonstrations of how the mechanism is out of gear, how the ideal reflex created by God is now broken into as many pieces as it has parts, how each part fails to perform its designated function, how the order of the connections is reversed or disfigured, how the higher are unnaturally enslaved to the lower, and how therefore the chaos and depravity become highly explicable.[60]

Flavel's view of sin's effect on the soul's faculties shows no noticeable difference from that of either Perkins or Ames. Perkins explained his view succinctly in *The Foundation of Christian Religion*.

> First, in the mind there is nothing but ignorance and blindness concerning heavenly matters ... . Secondly, the conscience is defiled, being always either benumbed with sin, or else turmoiled with inward accusations and terrors ... . Thirdly, the will of man only willeth and lusteth after evil ... . Fourthly, the affections of the heart, as love, joy, hope, desire, etc., are moved and stirred to that which is evil to embrace it, and they are never stirred unto that which is good unless it be to eschew it.[61]

Ames, in his *Marrow*, echoes Perkins and presages Flavel. He writes:

> It [sin's corruption] is attributed to the intellect, as found in Gen. 6:5, *The imagination and thoughts only evil*; Rom. 8:5–7, *They savor the things of the flesh*. To the conscience in Titus 1:15, *The mind and conscience is defiled*. To the will in Gen. 8:21, *The imagination of the heart of man is evil from his childhood*. To affections of every kind in Rom. 1:24, *To uncleanness in the lusts of their hearts*.[62]

Concerning the doctrine of sin, and particularly sin's effect upon the faculties

---

[60] Miller, *New England Mind*, p. 256.
[61] Perkins, *William Perkins*, p. 151.
[62] Ames, *Marrow*, p. 120.

of the soul, Flavel, in the late seventeenth century, stood in the Puritan tradition which had been exemplified and fostered by Perkins and Ames.

Chapter 5

Effectual Call: Overview and First Step

We now turn our attention to Flavel's view of the effectual call. It is not surprising that the bulk of his thinking concerning this doctrine is found in two of his treatises, *Method of Grace* and *England's Duty*. *Method of Grace* is the second major part of Flavel's pastoral and systematic explanation of the doctrines of salvation. In the first part, which he published as *Fountain of Life*, he looks at the accomplishment of redemption by Christ. In the second part, *Method of Grace*, he examines the application of redemption to the sinner. The effectual call is a major component of this application of redemption.

England's Duty is the fourth largest of Flavel's writings. The entire treatise is based upon Revelation 3:20, 'Behold I stand at the door, and knock; if any man hear my voice, and open the door, I will come in to him, and will sup with him, and he with me.' Flavel goes into great detail concerning the hearing of Christ's voice, which he explains doctrinally as being contained within the effectual call.

In addition to these two treatises, Flavel provides himself with a forum for briefly, yet systematically, explaining the effectual call in his *Exposition*. Therefore *Method of Grace*, *England's Duty*, and *Exposition* will serve as the basis of our evaluation of Flavel's doctrine of the effectual call.

Flavel's Terminology which relates to the Effectual Call[1]

Flavel uses varied nomenclature when referring to the entire process of the effectual call. At times he speaks of vocation, effectual calling, drawing, the application of redemption, and the hearing of Christ's voice. When we consider his usage of each term a consistent and cohesive doctrine emerges, one which includes certain steps in the process of the effectual call. We will look briefly at his terminology, delineate the steps of vocation, determine their order, and note specifically the place of the intellect, will, and affections in the effectual call.

---

[1] Van Beek investigates the words and terms which the Puritan movement either created or which it invested with particular meaning. The phrase 'effectual call' is included in his discussion of terms that 'through their re-definition in Puritan writings ... acquired a new connotation.' Marinus van Beek, *An Enquiry into Puritan Vocabulary* (Groningen: Wolters-Noordhoff, 1969), p. 72. The section on 'effectual call' is found on pp. 74–75.

An examination of the 'Totius Operis' of *Method of Grace* reveals the broader theological context in which Flavel considers the effectual call. He states, 'Redemption hath Two Parts, *viz.* meritorious Impretration, opened Part I. And effectual Application, opened in this 2d Part.'[2] In the beginning of this treatise he explains: 'The application of Christ to us, is not only comprehensive of our justification, but of all those works of the Spirit which are known to us in the scripture by the names of regeneration, *vocation*, sanctification, and conversion.'[3] Flavel understands that vocation, or the effectual call, is one aspect of the application of redemption to the individual human.

When explaining the effectual call to his people by way of his sermons, and to the greater public by way of the printed page, Flavel leans heavily on John 6:44. In this verse Jesus is recorded as saying, 'No man can come to me, except the Father, which hath sent me, draw him.' Flavel's fourth sermon of *Method of Grace* is devoted to explaining the meaning of the verse. He derives from it and from its context the doctrine '[t]hat it is utterly impossible for any man to come to Jesus Christ, unless he be drawn unto him by the special and mighty power of God.'[4] Later in his explanation he lists various steps in this drawing, including illumination and conviction. He seems to equate the effectual call with 'drawing.'

This interpretation of his meaning is confirmed by examining *England's Duty*. In a discourse explaining the 'powerful drawings of the Spirit' he writes: 'When these things are past upon the soul, then it hears Christ's voice, his powerful call.'[5] Flavel uses the terms 'calling' and 'drawing' interchangeably.

As previously mentioned, the entire treatise of *England's Duty* is based on Revelation 3:20 and the example therein of Christ calling to people. 'If any man hears my voice,' Christ says. In the sixth sermon of this treatise Flavel is explaining, with his characteristic detail, the voice of Christ, and he equates it with the effectual call. 'This voice of Christ then, of which the text speaks, is an almighty impression made upon the soul of a sinner from heaven, which is to that soul instead of a voice ... . This inward spiritual impression is Christ's effectual call from heaven.'[6] Hearing Christ's voice is yet another term used synonymously with calling.

Flavel tends to use biblical terminology and intersperse within it nomenclature taken from systematic theologies. In this case, we understand that the terms 'vocation,' 'effectual calling,' 'drawing,' and 'hearing Christ's voice' are used by Flavel synonymously. The term 'application of redemption' covers more aspects of salvation than only the effectual call but does indeed include the effectual call within its sphere.

---

[2] Flavel, *Whole Works*, Vol. 1, p. 248. It is presented in Appendix 3 of this study.
[3] Flavel, *Works*, Vol. 2, p. 19; emphasis mine.
[4] Flavel, *Works*, Vol. 2, p. 69.
[5] Flavel, *Works*, Vol. 4, p. 148.
[6] Flavel, *Works*, Vol. 2, pp. 171–72.

The Steps of the Effectual Call

In Flavel's sermon on John 6:44 he explains the various elements of the effectual call. 'In this order, therefore, the Spirit (ordinarily) draws souls to Christ, he shines into their minds by illumination; applies that light to their consciences by effectual conviction; breaks and wounds their hearts for sin in compunction; and then moves the will to embrace and close with Christ in the way of faith for life and salvation.'[7] It appears from a reading of this section of the fourth sermon of *Method of Grace* that in Flavel's mind there are four steps involved in the effectual call: illumination, conviction, compunction, and the renewing of the will to believe.

However, he does not always speak of four steps. There is a contradiction between *Exposition* and *Method of Grace* concerning the number of steps included in the effectual call. In his exploration of the Catechism Flavel boils the effectual call down to only three steps: illumination, conviction, and the renewing of the sinner's will. Where is compunction – the third step which he had included in *Method of Grace*?

There is a further difference to be found in *England's Duty*. In his fifth sermon in that treatise he discusses Christ's knocking at the soul's door. He writes:

> What are the doors of the soul at which Christ knocks? ... Christ knocks orderly at them all, one after another, for the operations of the Spirit disturb not the order of nature. 1. The first door that opens and lets into the soul is the understanding; nothing passes into the soul, but it must first come through this door of the understanding; nothing can touch the heart or move the affections, but what hath first touched the understanding ... . 2. Within this is the royal gate of the soul, viz. The will of man, that noble and imperial power.[8]

This quotation of Flavel's can be understood only when noting that he is referring to the idea of a 'door to the soul.' He never refers to the affections as being a 'door to the soul,' but, as we have already examined, does describe both the mind and the will with that phrase. In Flavel's view, the affections are effectually wrought upon by God and this is seen especially in the step of conviction. However, the affections are not the entry point, the seat of the first step of the effectual call, nor are they the culmination point, the seat of the last step of the effectual call. Therefore, when speaking of the faculties of the soul which could be considered 'doors of the soul' and applying that to the process of the effectual call Flavel speaks of two steps – one involving the mind and the second involving the will.

Is it possible to systematize these various explanations? Are there two, three, or four steps in the effectual call? Is Flavel propounding outright

---

[7] Flavel, *Works*, Vol. 2, p. 71.
[8] Flavel, *Works*, Vol. 4, p. 89.

contradictions, or is he merely offering variations of the same thoughts? As we examine each step in greater detail we will see that in spite of his sometimes irregular expression of the number of steps, a close examination of all his writings reveals a constant underlying understanding of the effectual call.

Our conclusion is that Flavel sees three distinct steps in the effectual call: illumination, conviction, and the renewing of the will. A detailed examination of his idea of compunction shows that it is included in the broader category of conviction. The seat of illumination and conviction are in the intellect. Conviction begins in the intellect but has great effects upon the emotions. The last step, the renewing of the will, results in faith. This conclusion will be supported shortly as we examine illumination, conviction and the renewing of the will in greater detail.

Before analyzing these steps we must first examine another apparent contradiction in Flavel—that of the order of these steps in the effectual call.

The Order of the Steps of the Effectual Call

In *An Exposition* Flavel mentions the three steps of illumination, conviction and renewing the will, but appears to change their order. Under the title 'Of effectual calling' he begins by quoting the Catechism's question and answer. 'What is effectual calling? A[nswer]. effectual calling is the work of God's Spirit, whereby convincing us of our sin and misery, enlightening our minds in the knowledge of Christ, and renewing our wills, he doth persuade and enable us to embrace Jesus Christ, freely offered to us in the gospel.' Flavel goes on to draw out this teaching with his own questions and answers:

> Q.2. What is the first act of the Spirit in effectual calling?
>
> A. Conviction of sin; ...
>
> Q.4. What is the second act of the Spirit in our effectual calling?
>
> A. The illumination of the mind in the knowledge of Christ; ...
>
> Q. 6. What is the third act?
>
> A. His renewing of the sinner's will, and making it flexible.[9]

Comparison with the fourth sermon of his *Method of Grace* reveals an apparent contradiction. In *Method of Grace* Flavel explains illumination as preceding conviction. In *Exposition* he mentions conviction as the first step in vocation. How do we explain this?

We do so by understanding how Flavel viewed the facts which are illuminated and the relation of conviction to them. In his view, illumination opens the mind to understand the person's dangerous situation as a sinner. At

---

[9] Flavel, *Works*, Vol. 6, p. 193.

that point, conviction occurs. However, illumination is then shed on additional data. The answer to the sinner's danger is Christ, and Christ as the answer is also made known to the sinner in illumination. Therefore, conviction falls within the same time span in which illumination is being accomplished in the mind. Part of illumination precedes conviction, and part of illumination does indeed follow conviction.

With this in mind we look again at Flavel's discussion of the effectual call. 'What is effectual calling? A[nswer]. effectual calling is the work of God's Spirit, whereby convincing us of our sin and misery, enlightening our minds in the knowledge of Christ, and renewing our wills, he doth persuade and enable us to embrace Jesus Christ, freely offered to us in the gospel.'[10] Understanding his view of illumination and conviction (which we will examine in more detail shortly) enables us to see his consistency. Conviction concerning sin and misery was the result of the first part of illumination. Following conviction, further illumination enables the mind to see 'the knowledge of Christ.' This then leads to embracing Christ. Thus, in concurring with the Catechism, Flavel is merely focusing on the second part of illumination and the fact that it is preceded by conviction. We do not believe that there is any fundamental inconsistency with his other writings.

Throughout his writings, in every case in which Flavel discusses the various aspects of the effectual call, except the one passage we referred to in *Exposition*, he explains illumination as preceding conviction. In sermon seven of *Method of Grace*, he mentions the antecedents to faith and lists illumination as the first.[11] In sermon nine he begins a summary of the steps of vocation by saying: 'First, There is an illustrating work of the Spirit upon the minds of sinners, opening their eyes. ...'[12] In the tenth sermon he explains that the 'cure of souls' begins with illumination.[13] In the twenty-second sermon he says that 'illumination is the first act of the Spirit in our conversion.'[14] In *Fountain of Life* he writes: 'As the old, so the new creation begins in light; the opening of the eyes is the first work of the Spirit.'[15] In *England's Duty* he writes that 'the cure of the heart begins at the eye of the mind.'[16] There are more examples but the above will suffice. A reading of his entire *Works* reveals that Flavel understood illumination to precede conviction.

Flavel's order, therefore, of the three steps of the effectual call is: illumination first, then conviction, then renewing of the will. This understanding of the effectual call is not followed by Miller. In his

---

[10] Flavel, *Works*, Vol. 6, p. 193.
[11] Flavel, *Works*, Vol. 2, p. 129.
[12] Flavel, *Works*, Vol. 2, p. 175.
[13] Flavel, *Works*, Vol. 2, p. 198.
[14] Flavel, *Works*, Vol. 2, p. 309.
[15] Flavel, *Works*, Vol. 1, p. 35.
[16] Flavel, *Works*, Vol. 4, p. 54.

interpretation of the Puritan view he writes: 'He [God] regenerates their reasons in order to revivify their wills, and their wills as a preliminary to renewing their affections.'[17] Miller puts the change of the affections last. This is not altogether surprising given his somewhat unclear discussion of the affections with regard to their classification as a faculty of the soul. Miller's summary of the Puritan view agrees with Flavel in asserting that the work of illumination precedes the renewing of the will. Where he differs from Flavel concerns the role of the affections. Flavel very definitely considered the affections as being a faculty of the soul and he believed that this faculty was wrought upon by God in the step of conviction.

Lynn Tipson Jr, in 'The Development of a Puritan Understanding of Conversion,' also arrives at a description of the effectual call that appears different from that which we have observed in Flavel. He writes: 'effectual calling was divided into three links: the effectual preaching of the word, the softening of man's heart by the Spirit, and man's response of faith.'[18] It is important to an understanding of Tipson, however, to note that he describes 'links' involved in the effectual call, not steps. As we noted in Part 1 of this study, Tipson resists giving an explanation of conversion that delineates certain steps. He acknowledges that this description of Puritan theology 'stands counter to a direction frequent in recent studies of Puritanism.'[19] Given that his three 'links' are not meant to be steps of the effectual call which are related to certain faculties of the soul, we do not see Tipson's scheme as necessarily antithetical to that which we have derived from Flavel. Tipson has painted the picture with broader brush strokes and includes the outer call. Flavel paints a finer picture and restricts his painting to the inner call. He acknowledges the outer call but titles it 'revelation' and does not include it in his delineation of the effectual call's steps. He also is careful to integrate faculty psychology with his description of the steps.

Eugene White, in his *Puritan Rhetoric*, after summarizing the 'morphology of conversion' of certain Puritans, expanded his focus to Puritanism as a whole. He writes: 'Although the details of the various treatments of conversion differed somewhat, a remarkable agreement existed concerning the route itself. Knowledge and understanding of Biblical truths always preceded the sequent steps: conviction, "legal fear," humiliation, and, finally, the awareness of the possible presence of faith.'[20] We do see a different 'treatment' of the effectual call in Flavel from that suggested in White's summary, but there is significant agreement between the two. Flavel's view of illumination correlates with White's discussion of knowledge. Flavel's view of conviction correlates with

---

[17] Miller, *New England Mind*, p. 289.
[18] Tipson, 'Understanding of Conversion,' p.242 n. 540.
[19] Tipson, 'Understanding of Conversion,' p. 35.
[20] Eugene E. White, *Puritan Rhetoric: The Issue of Emotion in Religion* (Carbondale and Edwardsville: Southern Illinois University Press, 1972), p. 13.

White's categories of conviction, legal fear, and humiliation. White's last step of faith is encompassed in Flavel's view of the renewing of the will. Certainly White's summary description is consistent with what we see in Flavel in that the process of the effectual call is begun in the mind, continues with an effect upon the emotions, and is finalized in the will.

We note here that White's description of the passivity of individuals in relation to their own faith does not entirely agree with Flavel's emphasis.[21] More discussion of this difference will take place when we look at Flavel's view of the doctrine of faith and when we see how he applied his view of faith to the task of preaching.

Perkins, in his famous *Golden Chain*, describes in words and also in diagrammatic form the 'order of the causes of Salvation and Damnation.'[22] His chart shows three circles which are included in the category of effectual calling: 'effectual preaching and hearing,' '[t]he mollifying of the heart,' and 'faith.' He does not list illumination as a separate category, but includes the idea of illumination in his explanation of the first stage. He writes: 'And inwardly the eyes of the mind are enlightened, the heart and ears open, that he may see, hear and understand the preaching of the word of God.' His description of the 'mollifying of the heart' correlates closely with Flavel's idea of conviction. Perkins writes, 'The second is the mollifying of the heart, the which must be bruised in pieces that it may be fit to receive God's saving grace offered unto it.'[23] He describes four 'hammers' by which the bruising of the heart takes place, and compunction is one of them. Compunction, as we have mentioned, is viewed by Flavel as part of conviction, the second step in his view of the effectual call. Perkins then describes the last step, which is faith. Perkins begins to speak of 'five degrees or motions of the heart' which are involved in the process of a person coming to faith.[24] The first that he mentions is illumination. Thus, when considering faith, he goes back over ground that he had already alluded to in his first step. The result of the five motions, however, is the same as that which Flavel propounds in his view of faith – the person has applied to himself the gospel promises.

We note briefly here one difference in emphasis between the two men

---

[21] White makes a qualifying statement concerning his summary of the Puritan view: 'It [White's own paradigm] is not intended to imply that the Puritan system was rigid or monolithic, or even that the chief architects were consistent within their own writings. The various components of the schema represent general tendencies rather then hermitic units.' White, *Puritan Rhetoric*, pp. 22–23.

[22] Perkins, *Works*, p. 168 (chart).

[23] Perkins, *Works*, p. 228.

[24] For the entire discussion of faith, see Perkins, *Works*, pp. 228–30. The five motions are: (1) knowledge of the gospel by illumination, (2) hope of pardon, (3) hungering and thirsting after the grace which is offered in Christ Jesus, (4) approaching the throne of grace, and (5) a special persuasion whereby the person applies to himself those promises which are made in the gospel.

concerning faith. In Perkins' explanation of faith he does not draw attention to the human will as being the seat of faith. Our observation is that Perkins does acknowledge that saving faith is not merely an intellectual assent, but in the discussion of faith in *A Golden Chain* he is not stressing that point. Flavel, however, does emphasize the correlation between the faculties of the soul and the act of faith.

Thus we see Flavel agreeing with Perkins concerning the movement of the overall process: there is an inner illumination which precedes an involvement of the affections which in turn precedes faith. The descriptions, however, which the two men proffer are quite different. Flavel obviously allows his faculty psychology to influence his arrangement of the steps. Perkins is not as explicit in arranging his presentation according to the faculties of the soul. We contend that in spite of the difference in presentation there is no real difference of substance between Perkins and Flavel concerning the effectual call.

An examination of William Ames' *Marrow of Theology*, however, does present one notable difference with Flavel. In the section entitled 'Calling,' Ames talks of the call as consisting of two parts: the offer of Christ and the receiving of Christ. The offer of Christ consists of an outward and an inner offer. The outward is seen in the preaching of the gospel. The inner offer consists of illumination. The receiving of Christ consists of a passive and an active element. The passive is the renewing of the will. The active element is faith.[25]

We assert that none of this would be argued with by Flavel. We do note, however, that Ames' description does not mention conviction or the emotional element but rather draws attention only to the intellect and will. On the point concerning the place of affections in the effectual call, Flavel sounds closer to Perkins. Ames' silence concerning the place of the affections in the effectual call is not acceptable to Flavel. Indeed, Flavel insists that the effectual call has an emotional element to it. Other than this difference, however, Flavel is in agreement with Ames. Both see the effectual call beginning in the intellect with illumination and culminating in the will with faith.

It is helpful to note that one cause of the differing descriptions of the effectual call is that some Puritans include references to the 'outer call' or the 'outward preaching and hearing' within the category of the effectual call. Perkins and Ames both do so. Flavel approaches his description differently. He acknowledges the outer call but refers to it as 'revelation' and differentiates it from the effectual call. He only refers to that which takes place in the inner workings of the soul as the effectual call. The outer call, of course, is the arena of the preacher's work and thus extremely important to Flavel, but he restricts his discussion of the effectual call to the steps which take place within the

---

[25] Ames, *Marrow of Divinity*, pp. 157–60.

soul.[26]

Another cause of the differing descriptions of the effectual call is that some Puritans, and subsequent scholars, place the seat of illumination as being in the human will as well as the intellect. Flavel divides the faculties of the soul between the steps of the effectual call. Illumination pertains only to the mind. The will is the object of a later step in the effectual call.[27]

We should emphasize, before proceeding to investigate Flavel's view of each of the steps of the effectual call, that his understanding of the various faculties of the soul is an indispensable component of his view of the effectual call. His view of the human constitution gives him a greater ability to construct an understanding of the process of a person being drawn from an unregenerate state into a regenerate state. The faculty psychology of Flavel is inextricably linked with his view of the effectual call. Each step is related to certain faculties. Effectual grace overcomes the effect of sin on the faculties. Miller suggests that such a mindset was common among the Puritans:

> Thus in Puritan philosophy the concept of spiritual regeneration ... was integrated with a concept of the physical powers of the soul ... . The ministers could not keep these two concepts apart, and consequently whenever they descended from the plane of lofty piety to concrete particulars, they had to translate the process and phases of regeneration minutely into the language of the faculty psychology.[28]

This 'translation' is certainly evident in Flavel.

We now turn our attention to a careful analysis of Flavel's view of the first step of the effectual call.

Illumination

As stated earlier, when Flavel speaks specifically of the entire theological category of the effectual call his discussions are concentrated in *Method of Grace*, *England's Duty*, and *Exposition*. However, his explanations of the doctrine of illumination are scattered throughout his *Works*. In *Fountain of Life* Flavel gives a lengthy explanation of illumination as one part of Christ's

---

[26] In stark contrast to Flavel's presentation, McGrath restricts the effectual call to that which happens to a person prior to conviction. 'Following the effectual call came conviction.' McGrath, 'Puritans and the Human Will,' p. 253. Such an understanding of the effectual call is dramatically different from what we find in Flavel.

[27] It is helpful to note that some of the differences in presentations of the doctrine of illumination are due to the fact that some writers use the term 'illumination' in a more all-encompassing way. They speak of illumination as encompassing all that happens afterwards in heart and will as well as that which begins the process in the mind. Flavel dissects the effectual call and only speaks of illumination as a divine work in the mind.

[28] Miller, *New England Mind*, p. 280.

'prophetical office.'[29] In *Soul of Man* and *Seaman's Companion* he delineates the difference between the mind's natural capacity and its capacity after illumination. *Touchstone of Sincerity* and *Sacramental Meditations* also refer to illumination. One does not read Flavel's sermons for very long before being confronted with the doctrine of illumination. Indeed, it is Flavel's repeated emphasis on the doctrine of illumination that shows us the tremendous importance which he gives to this aspect of the effectual call. He draws significant implications from the doctrine of illumination and applies them to the ministry of preaching. Those implications will be seen later in the study.

Here we will examine Flavel's understanding of the doctrine of illumination by first noting the terminology which he used. Then we will examine the information, or biblical data, regarding which illumination occurs, the means of illumination, and its efficacy. We will then consider what Flavel calls 'partial conviction.' Throughout this examination the place of the intellect in Flavel's view of illumination will be noted.

Flavel's Terminology which relates to Illumination

We understand that the terminology already mentioned concerning the effectual call includes the doctrine of illumination. Inasmuch as a term or phrase used by Flavel refers to the effectual call, it includes within it the concept of illumination. But what vocabulary does he use when referring specifically to the first step of the effectual call, that of illumination?

In addition to the term 'illumination,' there is one phrase, 'teachings of the Father,' and there is one motif contrasting ignorance and spiritual knowledge. We will consider each in turn.

It would be helpful at this point to note that Flavel differentiates the terms 'revelation' and 'illumination'. In the ninth and tenth sermons of *Fountain of Life* he discusses Christ's office as the Prophet of the church. We can observe from his discussion and the arrangement of its various parts that Flavel considered illumination and revelation as being related yet different. The ninth sermon is entitled 'The first Branch of Christ's Prophetical Office, consisting in the Revelation of the Will of God.'[30] The tenth is titled 'The Second Branch of Christ's Prophetical Office, consisting in the Illumination of the Understanding.'[31]

He explains the principal difference between revelation and illumination: 'His prophetical office consists of two parts; one external, consisting in a true and full revelation of the will of God to men, ... The other in illuminating the

---

[29] Flavel, *Works*, Vol. 1, p. 131.
[30] Flavel, *Works*, Vol. 1, p. 118.
[31] Flavel, *Works*, Vol. 1, p. 131.

Effectual Call: Overview and First Step

mind, and opening the heart to receive and embrace that doctrine.'[32] Revelation is an external ministry and not necessarily efficacious. Flavel quotes Edward Reynolds to support this point. '"To the spiritual illumination of a soul, it suffices not that the object be revealed, nor yet that man, the subject of that knowledge, have a due use of his own reason; but it is further necessary that the grace and special assistance of the Holy Spirit be superadded, to open and mollify the heart."'[33] In Flavel's thinking illumination is not synonymous with revelation.

As we have already noted, this outer offer of the gospel, which some Puritans presented as a part of the effectual call, is considered by Flavel to lie outside the category of the effectual call. He leans heavily upon the concept of the outer offer when discussing the ministry of preaching, but his discussion of the effectual call is restricted to what God does inwardly in the soul.

In the twenty-second sermon of *Method of Grace* Flavel expounds and applies John 6:45, 'It is written in the prophets, And they shall be all taught of God. Every man therefore that hath heard, and hath learned of the Father, cometh unto me.'[34] Flavel focuses on the phrase 'learned of the Father' and proposes '[t]hat the teachings of God are absolutely necessary to every man that cometh unto Christ, in the way of faith.'[35]

He equates the phrase 'teachings of God' with illumination. 'But to speak positively, the teachings of God are nothing else but that spiritual and heavenly light, by which the Spirit of God shineth into the hearts of men ... . And though this be the proper work of the Spirit, yet it is called the teachings of the Father, because the Spirit who enlightens us is commissioned and sent by the Father.'[36] In his subsequent discussion he delves into various facets of the doctrine of illumination, but it is all considered under the umbrella phrase 'teachings of God.'

We also see a certain motif used by Flavel in discussing illumination, namely 'spiritual knowledge' and its corresponding contrast to 'spiritual ignorance.' In the first sermon of *Fountain of Life* he says: 'The knowledge of Jesus Christ is a fundamental knowledge ... . It is fundamental to all graces; ... Col. iii. 10. "The new man is renewed in knowledge." As the old, so the new creation begins in light; the opening of the eyes is the first work of the Spirit.'[37]

Near the end of *Soul of Man* Flavel discusses spiritual ignorance and knowledge and clearly relates those concepts to illumination. After describing the spiritual ignorance of England's people, he says:

---

[32] Flavel, *Works*, Vol. 1, pp. 118–19.
[33] Flavel, *Works*, Vol. 1, p. 133.
[34] Flavel, *Works*, Vol. 2, p. 306.
[35] Flavel, *Works*, Vol. 2, p. 307.
[36] Flavel, *Works*, Vol. 2, p. 309.
[37] Flavel, *Works*, Vol. 1, pp. 34–35.

And thus they live and die without knowledge; there is no key of knowledge (as it is fitly called, Luke xi. 52.) to open the door of the soul to Christ; he and his ministers, therefore, must stand without; pity they may, but help they cannot, till knowledge open the door: Satan is ruler of the darkness of this world ... that is, of all blind and ignorant souls. Ignorance is the chain with which he binds them fast to himself, and till that chain be knocked off by Divine illumination, they cannot be emancipated, and made free of Christ's kingdom.[38]

We can discern the full content of Flavel's discussion of illumination when we include his use of the terms 'teachings of God,' 'spiritual ignorance' and 'spiritual knowledge.'

The Data regarding which Illumination takes place

An important aspect of Flavel's understanding of illumination is that there is a specific content regarding which the Spirit illumines the human mind. There is a realm of natural knowledge which the human mind does not need the Spirit's enabling to understand. But there is another realm of knowledge that the sinful human cannot understand, at least not in a saving way, unless illumination has taken place in the mind.

In the seventh sermon of *England's Duty* Flavel begins to explain what is contained in that realm of knowledge:

What it is to be truly willing to receive Jesus Christ. ... It implies, and necessarily includes, the right understanding and true apprehension of gospel terms and articles: these must be known, pondered, and duly considered, before the will can savingly open, in an act of consent, to Christ's offer. ... you must exercise your understandings upon the terms and articles of Christianity, or else your consent is rash, blindfold, and unstable.[39]

What are these 'terms and articles' of Christianity? Later in the same sermon Flavel expresses his belief that there must be a realization of the cost involved in believing in Christ, and a subsequent willingness to pay that price. In his explanation of these 'terms,' he also explains that such understanding and willingness is the result of illumination:

Saving faith ... [is] another manner of thing than the world generally understands it to be; and it is impossible for any man's will to open to, and receive Christ, upon terms of such deep self-denial as these, until there be, 1. A conviction of our sin and misery. 2. A discovery of Christ in his glory and necessity. 3. The drawing power of the Spirit upon the soul.[40]

---

[38] Flavel, *Works*, Vol. 3, pp. 187–88.
[39] Flavel, *Works*, Vol. 4, p. 144.
[40] Flavel, *Works*, Vol. 4, pp. 147–48.

In *Saint Indeed* Flavel summarizes the truths which the Spirit illuminates to people by putting those truths into two categories. He mentions these two categories when he speaks in general terms of the want of understanding in the unillumined person, who is '[b]lind; i.e. without spiritual illumination, and so neither knowing their disease, nor their remedy; the evil of sin, nor the necessity of Christ.'[41] This two-fold summary of the data regarding which illumination occurs is consistent with his short statement of this issue in *Method of Grace*: 'You cannot believe till God hath opened your eyes to see your sin, your misery by sin, and your remedy in Jesus Christ alone.'[42] All of the teachings of Scripture that show the human problem in sin and explain Christ as the solution to that problem are unintelligible (as 'spiritual knowledge') to the unillumined person.

Those teachings are numerous. Flavel does not offer any one exhaustive list. Any biblical teaching which contributes to an understanding of humankind's problem of sin or of the solution to that problem in Christ is included.[43]

Insight into those core teachings which Flavel would include can be gleaned from his correspondence with Clement Lake (d.1689), a convert to Quakerism. Flavel stresses the doctrine that he considers to be crucial for a person to possess saving faith and which, in his opinion, is denied by Quaker teaching. He writes:

> If Quakerism subvert the fundamental and essential articles of the Christian religion, then no Quaker that understands and professes the principles of Quakerism can be a Christian. But it does so as will presently appear. For: They deny the existence of the human nature, and satisfaction of the Blood of Christ. 1. They deny the imputed righteousness of Christ, as the matter of our justification. 2. They deny the resurrection of the body and its participation of glory with the soul. 3. They lead men to the covenant of works, and obedience to the light within for salvation.[44]

We note his emphases upon the reality of the humanity of Christ and the substitutionary aspect of Christ's death. In Flavel's view it is crucial to understand who Christ was – that being God, he had also become really human. It is also crucial, in Flavel's mind, to understand that the death of Christ rendered a 'satisfaction' toward God on behalf of the sinner. Thus those putting their faith in Christ are to be relying on that which Christ did in their place or on their behalf, and not on 'obedience' or any other self effort.

This emphasis on relying on what Christ has accomplished rather than upon

---

[41] Flavel, *Works*, Vol. 5, p. 515.
[42] Flavel, *Works*, Vol. 2, p. 129.
[43] In Sermon 22 of *Method of Grace* Flavel lists twelve particular truths which the Spirit illuminates to people as they come to Christ, but does not present the list as exhaustive. Flavel, *Works*, Vol. 2, pp. 310–16.
[44] Flavel, *Flavel, The Quaker and the Crown*, p. 29.

one's own religious striving is reinforced when Flavel asks Lake:

> Are we justified and saved by that very blood of Christ that was shed at Jerusalem, or by some other means than by the blood of the Man Christ Jesus? ...
>
> Is the active and passive obedience, which Christ performed here on earth, in the days of his flesh, the matter of our righteousness before God? Or is it something in ourselves? ...
>
> Must we expect salvation by believing in Christ for righteousness, and applying his righteousness to our souls by faith? Or must we expect it by obedience to the light within us?[45]

All the biblical data which builds the case for one to put such reliance upon Christ and to renounce any reliance upon oneself is data over which the divine work of illumination takes place.

The Means of Illumination

Just as he delineates the data about which illumination takes place, Flavel also explains the means by which illumination takes place. He understands that there are two means by which the sinful human being is illumined. 'And there are two principal ways, by which Christ opens the understandings and hearts of men, *viz.* by his Word and Spirit.'[46] We will look at each in turn.

The first means is the word of God. In *Method of Grace* Flavel states plainly,: 'The law of God hath an enlightening efficacy upon the minds of men ... . When the word comes in power, all things appear with another face: The sins that were hid from our eyes, and the danger which was concealed by the policy of Satan from our souls, now lie clear and open before us.'[47] In *Fountain of Life*, after acknowledging that it is theoretically possible for God to illumine a person's mind by his immediate power, Flavel explains that God has ordained preaching as a means for illumination.

> God will keep up his ordinances among men: and though he hath not tied himself, yet he hath tied us, to them. Cornelius must send for Peter: God can make the earth produce corn, as it did at first, without cultivation and labour; but he that shall now expect it in the neglect of means, may perish for want of bread.[48]

The word of God is one means of illumination.

The second means is the Holy Spirit. In *England's Duty* Flavel labours to explain that the Spirit is the source of efficacy in the bringing of a sinner to

---

[45] Flavel, *Flavel, The Quaker and the Crown*, pp. 29–30.
[46] Flavel, *Works*, Vol. 1, p. 136.
[47] Flavel, *Works*, Vol. 2, p. 297.
[48] Flavel, *Works*, Vol. 1, p. 136.

faith in Christ:

> The principal instrument, by whose efficacy the heart is opened, is the Spirit of God, without whom it is impossible the design should ever prosper: neither ordinances, providences, or ministers can successfully manage it without him … . Ordinances are but as the sails of a ship; ministers as the seamen that manage those sails: the anchor may be weighed, the sails spread, but when all this is done, there is no sailing till a gale come. We preach and pray, and you hear; but there is no motion Christ-ward, until the Spirit of God … blow upon them. Until he illuminates the understanding with divine light … there can be no spiritual motion heaven-ward.[49]

The word of God and the Holy Spirit are understood by Flavel, then, to be the divinely ordained means of illumination.

Illumination as Effectual

Flavel understands this illumination as being much more than merely a presentation of information to the human mind. Rather, it is an actual changing of the human mind. Illumination is effectual – it causes the mind to understand that which previously, because of sin, it could not comprehend.

In the twenty-third sermon of *Method of Grace*, he explains the effectual nature of illumination by using the image of a sundial:

> The understanding faculty, like a dial, is enlightened with the beams of divine truth shining upon it: this no man's teachings can do: Men can only teach objectively, by propounding truth to the understanding; but they cannot enlighten the faculty itself, as God doth, 1 John v. 20. He giveth man understanding as well as instructions, to be understood; he opens the eyes of the understanding, as well as propoundeth the object.[50]

In *England's Duty* he makes the same point.

> There is a new eye created in the mind: 'the Son of God is come, and hath given us an understanding, that we may know him that is true,' 1 John v. 20. … All the angels in heaven, ministers, and Libraries upon earth, cannot create such an eye, give such an illumination; it is only he that 'commanded the light to shine out of darkness, that thus shineth in our hearts, to give the light of the knowledge of the glory of God in the face of Jesus Christ,' 2 Cor. iv. 6.[51]

Flavel's understanding is that the work of illumination is an effectual act of God in the mind of sinful human beings. After briefly touching upon one of

---

[49] Flavel, *Works*, Vol. 4, p. 198.
[50] Flavel, *Works*, Vol. 2, p. 326.
[51] Flavel, *Works*, Vol. 4, p. 50.

Flavel's discussions of illumination, Stephenson rightly states:

> Illumination, a figure used in Puritan discussions of conversion, always referred to God's action upon the understanding. Illumination did not impart new knowledge, but shed light upon the mind hitherto darkened by sin, enabling it to perceive 'savingly' what was known before 'notionally.' It was the giving of new power or ability, but no new faculty or new knowledge was involved.[52]

'Partial Convictions'

Even though he views illumination as being efficacious, Flavel does speak about a condition in which a person experiences illumination to a certain degree and yet true conversion has not happened. In *England's Duty* Flavel calls this condition 'partial convictions.' 'Partial convictions upon the understanding; light and knowledge breaking into the mind, producing orthodoxy of judgment; this seems to be the effectual opening of the understanding to Christ, though alas! to this day they never saw sin in its vileness, much less their own special sin; nor Christ in his suitableness and necessity.'[53]

Flavel's view of partial conviction is clearly integrated with his view of the human constitution and his understanding of the nature of saving faith. In the case of partial conviction, the mind has seemingly understood some gospel truths but the will has not yet submitted to the authority of Christ. In *Method of Grace* he explains what he believes is happening in the heart of a person who is experiencing partial conviction:

> The devil hath deeply intrenched himself, and strongly fortified every faculty of the soul against Christ; the understanding, indeed, is the first entrance into the soul, and out of that faculty he is oftentimes cast by light and conviction, which seems to make a great change upon a man: now he becomes a professor, now he takes up the duties of religion, and passes up and down the world for a convert; but, alas, alas! all the while Satan keeps the fort-royal, the heart and will are in his own possession. ... While the heart stands out, though the understanding be taken in, the soul remains in Satan's possession.[54]

Such a view raises a question concerning this light and conviction which has reached into a person's understanding: how can it be viewed as efficacious illumination if it does not result in faith? Flavel appears to parley with the question by defining and redefining light. The thirty-third sermon of *Method of Grace* is entitled 'Of the Aggravation of the Sin, and Punishment of Unbelief under the light of the Gospel.' It is a sermon based upon John 3:9, 'And this is the condemnation, that light is come into the world, and men loved darkness

---

[52] Stephenson, 'Jonathan Edwards' Thought,' pp.152–53.
[53] Flavel, *Works*, Vol. 4, p. 202.
[54] Flavel, *Works*, Vol. 2, p. 449.

rather than light, because their deeds were evil.' Flavel explains that light can come in two different ways.

> First, In the means by which it is conveyed to us; or Secondly, in the efficacy of it upon our minds, when it actually shines in our souls. Light may come among a people in the means, and yet they actually remain in darkness all the while. As it is in nature; the sun may be up and a very glorious morning far advanced, whilst many thousands are drowning upon their beds with their curtains drawn about them. Light in the means, we may call potential light. Light in the mind, we may call actual light.[55]

Having made a distinction between potential and actual light, he further distinguishes between two kinds of actual light. They are: '1. Common, and intellectual only, to conviction; or, 2. Special and efficacious light, bringing the soul to Christ by real conversion.' This differentiation between common and efficacious light enables Flavel to explain why some people appear to have been illumined when in reality they have not. 'Wherever light comes, in this last sense [efficacious], it is impossible that such men should prefer darkness before it: But it may come in the means, yea, it may actually shine into the consciences of men by those means, and convince them of their sins, and yet men may hate it, and chuse darkness rather than light.'[56] Flavel recognizes that spiritual light can shine into a person's mind and even affect their conscience without it being the efficacious illumination to which he so often refers.

His explanation will remain unsatisfactory to some. It is, in essence, a restating of an observation about various ways which people respond to the gospel, rather than an actual explanation of those responses. It is observable that some people exhibit some degree of understanding concerning the saving gospel truths. Some of them even exhibit some pangs of conscience and emotions which seem the same as that which leads to faith, but these people do not believe. They continue with an unrenewed will. How do we explain this? Is it attributed to a work of the Spirit upon all humankind, giving humankind equal ability to understand? In other words, is it due to some form of prevenient grace? Flavel makes it clear in various places in his writings that he rejects the notion of a prevenient grace which works on all humankind, elect and non-elect, equally. That being the case, what then is this partial conviction? Is it a work of the Spirit upon some of the non-elect, but not all, enabling some to see more than others? If so, how is this uneven distribution of the Spirit's work among those destined to perish explained? Why is this done? Or perhaps partial conviction is a sign that some but not all of the renewing of the mind has taken place? Or perhaps some manifestations of partial conviction are not due at all to the Spirit's work but are merely a natural response of the faculties of the soul? The issue of partial conviction raises many questions.

---

[55] Flavel, *Works*, Vol. 2, p. 440.
[56] Flavel, *Works*, Vol. 2, p. 441.

Here we see Flavel choosing to bypass such questions altogether.[57] Instead he defines 'partial convictions' by the end state of the individual being considered. If the individual eventually truly believes, then that individual underwent effectual illumination. If the individual showed signs of illumination but did not eventually believe, then that individual was merely going through partial conviction. How to explain that partial conviction, its relation to broader purposes of God in salvation, or its implications concerning the renewed (or partially renewed) capacity of the faculties, is not addressed by Flavel.

It is important to emphasize here that, in Flavel's view, that which enables us to distinguish between partial conviction and real illumination is always the eventual effect of illumination upon the person's will. In 'A Sure Tryal', after describing illumination and conviction, Flavel makes a revealing transition into his discussion of the will. He writes: 'To come to the main, for all these [illumination and conviction] are but previous Works, and may signifie something or nothing; the third thing that gives an Interest in Christ, is a deliberate Consent.'[58] We will ahortly examine in detail his understanding of 'deliberate consent,' but for now our attention is focused upon the fact that in Flavel's opinion the outward appearances of illumination and conviction are not sufficient in and of themselves to indicate that true conversion is taking place. They 'may signifie something or nothing.' The real test is what happens in the person's will. When effectual illumination occurs, it will lead to the will of the person submitting to Christ. When partial conviction occurs, the will remains stubborn and in Satan's control.

The recognition of the possibility of partial conviction has direct application to the ministry of preaching. We will investigate this application later in the study. We will also revisit the subject of partial conviction in our discussion of Flavel's view of the doctrine of conviction.

Summary concerning Illumination

In summary, illumination is the first step of the effectual call. The intellect is the seat of illumination. Illumination is the work of God in which he enables the human mind to understand the truths about its own problem of sin and to comprehend the solution to that problem in Christ. Apart from this work of God the sinful human being is not able to understand those truths savingly. God uses two means to perform this work: his word and his Spirit. Using those two means, he brings about an actual change within the human mind which enables it to comprehend what it was previously unable savingly to understand.

---

[57] Flavel is not alone in this. Ames states without any further explanation: 'This [spiritual enlightenment] is sometimes and in a certain way granted to those who are not elected.' Ames, *Marrow of Divinity*, p. 158.

[58] Flavel, 'A Sure Tryal of a Christian's State,' in James Burdwood, *Helps for Faith and Patience in Times of Affliction* (London: Jonathan Robinson, 1693).

There is a condition in some people in which illumination appears to have taken place, but it is shown to be only a partial conviction by the fact that, regardless of whatever light and conviction appeared to be in the mind and emotions, the will of those people is ultimately not bowed to Christ. True illumination always results in a conviction that then leads to the renewing of the will and faith.

Chapter 6

Effectual Call: Last Steps and Summary

Conviction

As stated earlier, Flavel's specific discussions of the whole theological category of the effectual call are concentrated in *Method of Grace*, *England's Duty*, and *Exposition*. However, just as with the doctrine of illumination, his discussions of the doctrine of conviction are scattered widely throughout his *Works*. We do not read Flavel's explanation of illumination without being confronted with the topic of conviction. The two are related to each other in his understanding of the effectual call. This makes sense when we remember that he viewed the conscience not as a separate faculty of the soul but as a power or function of the intellect, and when we realize that the work of conviction involves the conscience.

Here we will examine Flavel's understanding of the doctrine of conviction by first noting how he defines it. Secondly, we will examine the relationship between compunction and conviction. Then we will examine conviction's aim, necessity, means, and efficacy. We will finish by observing Flavel's discussion of partial conviction and his thinking concerning opposition to conviction. Throughout our discussion we will note the place of the affections in conviction.

Definition

We know that when called upon to define precisely the faculties of the soul Flavel saw the conscience not as a separate faculty from the intellect but as one of its powers or functions. A lengthy appendix to *England's Duty* is devoted entirely to the issue of the human conscience. In that appendix he writes: 'Conscience (as our Divines well express it) is the judgment of man upon himself, as he is subject to the judgment of God. A judgment it is, and a practical judgment too; it belongs to the understanding faculty ... . This self-judgment is the proper office, of the conscience.'[1]

This self-judgment of which Flavel speaks is indeed what he means by conviction. We find Flavel's most succinct definition of conviction in the twenty-first sermon of *Method of Grace*: '[c]onviction being nothing else but

---

[1] Flavel, *Works*, Vol. 4, p. 271.

the application of the light that shines in the mind to the conscience of a sinner.'² Thus we understand that conviction is the self-judgment in the conscience of a sinner which is due to the light of illumination. When self-judgment occurs in the conscience, conviction is taking place.

Compunction: The intense Effect of Conviction upon the Affections

Although the seat of conviction is the conscience, and the conscience is a part of the mind, conviction nevertheless involves the affections. In Flavel's view, the illumination of the mind, including the conscience, results in a response from the affections. It is helpful to note a few of his illustrations which show the intense emotional effect of conviction. He speaks of conviction as an arrow, as a cutting of the heart, as a plow, as a magnifying glass, and as a raging sea.

In the sixteenth sermon of *Fountain of Life*, he is discussing the way in which Christ draws people to himself. In this discussion he writes that Jesus 'causes armies of convictions, and spiritual troubles, to begird and straiten them on every side, so that they know not what to do. These convictions, like a shower of arrows, strike, point-blank, into their consciences.'³ In *England's Duty* he writes as if he were unconverted, describing what it is to be convicted. 'I was sitting under the word with a careless wandering heart, as at other times; when lo, above all the thoughts of my heart, an arrow of conviction was suddenly shot into my conscience, which startled, wounded, and disquieted it.'⁴

In *Husbandry Spiritualized* Flavel notes that when engrafting takes place there is a cutting which precedes it: 'The first work about it, is cutting work, Acts ii. 37. their hearts were cut by conviction, and deep compunction; no cyon [scion] is ingraffed without cutting, no soul united with Christ, without a cutting sense of sin and misery.'⁵

In the same treatise he compares conviction to plowing. This is a rather lengthy discussion in which he explains conviction in detail. The emotional intensity of conviction is described like this:

> The plow pierces deep into the bosom of the earth, makes, as it were, a deep gash or wound in the heart of it. So doth the Spirit upon the hearts of sinners, he pierces their very souls by conviction ... . It comes upon the conscience with such piercing dilemmas, and tilts the sword of conviction so deep into their souls, that there is no stanching the blood, no healing the wound, till Christ himself come, and undertake the cure.⁶

In *Navigation Spiritualized* Flavel adds the imagery of a stormy sea to that of

---

² Flavel, *Works*, Vol. 2, p. 297.
³ Flavel, *Works*, Vol. 1, p. 201.
⁴ Flavel, *Works*, Vol. 4, p. 174.
⁵ Flavel, *Works*, Vol. 5, p. 146.
⁶ Flavel, *Works*, Vol. 5, p. 62.

the arrow, and then compounds it with the image of a magnifying glass, all meant to describe a person under conviction:

> Conscience, when awakened by the terrors of the Lord, is like a raging tempestuous sea; so it works, so it roars; and it is not in the power of all creatures to hush or quiet it. Spiritual terrors, as well as spiritual consolations are not known till felt. O when the arrows of the Almighty are shot into the spirit, ... when the venom of those arrows drink up the spirits ... . Conscience is the seat of guilt: it is like a burning glass, so it contracts the beams of the threatenings, twists them together, and reflects them on the soul, until it smoke, scorch, and flame.[7]

These illustrations show that Flavel understands conviction to produce intense emotions in the soul.

As shown earlier when addressing the question of how many steps Flavel sees in the effectual call, he sometimes states compunction as a separate step from conviction, and sometimes does not. How do we explain this?

In Flavel's view, compunction is the emotional effect of conviction. There are times when he is discussing the effectual call from the perspective of the different faculties of the soul and therefore mentions conviction (which is seated in the intellect) and compunction (which is seated in the emotions) as separate parts of the effectual call. An example of this appears in the fourth sermon of *Method of Grace*. 'In this order, therefore, the Spirit (ordinarily) draws souls to Christ, he shines into their minds by illumination; applies that light to their consciences by effectual conviction; breaks and wounds their hearts for sin in compunction; and then moves the will to embrace and close with Christ in the way of faith for life and salvation.'[8]

However, at other times he incorporates the emotional response to the soul's self-judgment into his discussion of conviction. In those cases he refers to both the work of the conscience and its corresponding emotional effect as conviction. An example of this is found in the seventh sermon of *Method of Grace*. 'Believe it, O man! that breast of thine must be pierced and stung with conviction, sense, and sorrow for sin, if ever thou rightly close with Christ by faith... . when men come to see their miserable and sad estate by a true light, it cannot but wound them, and that to the very heart.'[9]

In most of Flavel's discussion, as the illustrations above of arrows, seas, plow, and so on show, the intense emotions arising from conviction are spoken of as part of conviction itself, not as a separate step in the effectual call. Also, as noted earlier, when called upon to state precisely the steps of the effectual call, Flavel names just three: illumination, conviction, and renewing of the will. This three-step scheme includes compunction under the heading of conviction.

The illustrations of compunction raise a question: does Flavel expect that the

---

[7] Flavel, *Works*, Vol. 5, p. 265.
[8] Flavel, *Works*, Vol. 2, p. 71.
[9] Flavel, *Works*, Vol. 2, p. 130.

intensity of emotion would be the same in every convicted sinner? The answer to that question is no. Flavel allows that different people could experience different intensities of emotions and still be considered under conviction. In the seventh sermon of *Method of Grace* he writes: 'It is true, there is much difference found in the strength, depth, and continuance of conviction, and spiritual troubles in converts; but sure it is, the child of faith is not ordinarily born without some pangs.'[10] In Flavel's understanding of conviction it was not the intensity of the emotion that was all-important, but the eventual influence of conviction upon the will.

The Aim of Conviction

Although intense emotion often accompanies conviction Flavel looks beyond the emotion to the desired end. He never considers conviction to be an end in itself. It is always a step beyond illumination and towards faith. He writes: 'Conviction is an antecedent to believing: Where this goes not before, no faith can follow after.'[11] In *Husbandry Spiritualized* he also explains the aim of conviction by using the example of plowing. 'The work of the plow is but ... a preparative work in order to fruit. Should the husbandman plow his ground ever so often, yet if the seed be not cast in, and quickened, in vain is the harvest expected. Thus conviction also is but a preparative to a farther work upon the soul of a sinner.'[12] That 'farther work,' of course, is the renewing of the will to exercise faith.

In *England's Duty* Flavel shows his understanding of the aim of conviction in a discussion in which he warns people against allowing their experience of conviction to dissuade them from believing. 'And on the other side, beware that your convictions and troubles turn not into discouragements to faith; this will cross the proper intention of them: they are Christ's knocks for entrance, and were never intended to be bars or stumbling-blocks in your way to him; not stops, but steps in your way to Christ.'[13] Conviction is meant to lead a person to the next step in the effectual call, which is the renewing of the will.

The Necessity of Conviction

Flavel insists unequivocally that conviction is an absolutely necessary step in the effectual call. In 'A Sure Tryal,' he explains: 'There must of necessity be a full and serious conviction of Sin and Misery without Christ; there's not a Soul that comes to him without such a conviction ... . I take this to be an unquestionable truth, that so much conviction as unbottoms the soul from self-

---

[10] Flavel, *Works*, Vol. 2, p. 130.
[11] Flavel, *Works*, Vol. 2, p. 130.
[12] Flavel, *Works*, Vol. 5, p. 63.
[13] Flavel, *Works*, Vol. 4, p. 106.

righteousness and false hopes, is absolutely necessary.'[14] In *Method of Grace* he writes '[t]hat there is no coming ordinarily to Christ without the application of the law to our consciences, in a way of effectual conviction.'[15] Later in the twenty-fourth sermon he makes the same point, using an illustration from nature.

> Conviction of sin hath the same respect unto sanctification, as the blossoms of trees have to the fruits that follow them: A blossom is but ... an imperfect fruit in itself, and in order to a more perfect and noble fruit. Where there are no blossoms, we can expect no fruit; and where we see no conviction of sin, we can expect no conversion to Christ.[16]

Flavel so believes in the necessity of conviction that he uses the experience of conviction prior to conversion as a sign which a doubting Christian can remember in order to bolster his or her assurance of salvation.

> Hath then the Spirit of God been a Spirit of conviction to thee? ... Not only terrified and affrighted thy conscience with this or that more notorious act of sin, but fully convinced thee of the state of sin that thou art in by reason of thy unbelief ... . This gives, at least, a strong probability that God hath given thee his Spirit.[17]

Likewise, a professing Christian with no signs of conviction in his past might therefore have reason to doubt the reality of his own Christianity. In the twenty-fifth sermon of *Fountain of Life*, Flavel discusses the fact that some people respond emotionally to the gospel but are yet left in an unregenerate condition. He then applies this to the one who has had no emotional response at all to the gospel: 'What cause have they to fear and tremble, whose hearts are as unrelenting as the rocks, yielding to nothing that is proposed, or urged upon them?'[18]

In Flavel's view conviction is an indispensable step in the effectual call. He states simply that 'there can be no conversion without conviction.'[19]

The Means of Conviction

What are the means by which conviction takes place? The means, according to Flavel, are the same two associated with illumination: the word of God and the Spirit of God.

---

[14] Flavel, 'Sure Tryal.'
[15] Flavel, *Works*, Vol. 2, p. 287.
[16] Flavel, *Works*, Vol. 2, p. 336.
[17] Flavel, *Works*, Vol. 2, p. 336.
[18] Flavel, *Works*, Vol. 1, p. 312.
[19] Flavel, *Works*, Vol. 4, p. 105.

Flavel explains that it is the word of God which is used to produce both conviction and compunction in the mind and heart of a sinner. 'The word of God hath a convincing efficacy: it sets sin in order before the soul ... . the convictions of the word are clear and full ... . The law of God hath a soul-wounding, an heart-cutting efficacy ... . No outward trouble, affliction, disgrace, or loss, ever touched the quick as the word of God doth.'[20]

He also explains that the Spirit produces conviction. 'In this order, therefore, the Spirit (ordinarily) draws souls to Christ, he shines into their minds by illumination; applies that light to their consciences by effectual conviction; breaks and wounds their hearts for sin in compunction; and then moves the will to embrace and close with Christ in the way of faith for life and salvation.'[21] Here we note that, as with illumination, conviction and compunction are both attributed by Flavel to the Spirit.

The Efficacy of Conviction

Consistent with Flavel's view of the entire process of the effectual call, conviction is considered efficacious. He deliberately and frequently uses the word 'efficacy' or 'effectual' in his description of conviction. In the twenty-first sermon of *Method of Grace* he writes: 'The word of God hath a convincing efficacy ... . The law of God hath a soul-wounding, an heart-cutting efficacy.'[22] In the twentieth sermon of the same treatise he says that 'there is no coming ordinarily to Christ without the application of the law to our consciences, in a way of effectual conviction.'[23]

In *England's Duty* Flavel describes the interplay of word and Spirit as he explains the efficacy of conviction. 'Now this efficacy is not inherent in the word itself, it works not thus as a natural agent; then all would feel this power, that comes within the sound of it. No, this comes from the Spirit of Christ, speaking in it to the sinner's conscience; when it is the administration of the Spirit, then it becomes thus efficacious.'[24]

Flavel understands conviction as being more than a natural response of the conscience to illumination. Rather, it is an efficacious work of the Spirit upon the conscience that guarantees movement of the soul towards saving faith. We see this clearly in the tenth sermon of *Method of Grace*, when Flavel describes the effect sin had on the conscience and the necessity of a divine work in the soul to reverse it. 'Where sin is in dominion, the soul is in a very sad condition; for it ... depraves the conscience ... . How difficult is the cure of this disease! It passes the skill of angels or men to heal it; but Christ undertakes it, and makes a

---

[20] Flavel, *Works*, Vol. 2, p. 297.
[21] Flavel, *Works*, Vol. 2, p. 71.
[22] Flavel, *Works*, Vol. 2, p. 297.
[23] Flavel, *Works*, Vol. 2, p. 287.
[24] Flavel, *Works*, Vol. 4, p. 175.

perfect cure of it at last, and this he doth by his Spirit.' He continues, '[a]s the dominion of sin depraved and defiled the conscience ... as to disable it to the performance of all its offices and functions; so that it was neither able to apply, convince, or tremble at the word: So, when the Spirit of holiness is shed forth, O what a tender sense fills the renewed conscience!'[25]

This efficacious work also takes place upon the affections as well as the mind. As we have seen, the emotions are stirred in this second step of the effectual call. This stirring is understood by Flavel as more than a natural response of the affections to the illumined mind, as a Spirit-enabled response of the affections. The emotive faculty of the soul is being worked on in this step.

This understanding is evident in what we have shown already of Flavel's statements concerning conviction. When he refers to 'effectual conviction,' we remember that his view of conviction demands that both the mind, which includes the conscience, and the affections are involved. Thus both faculties are the subject of an effectual work of God. When he speaks of a 'heart-cutting efficacy' he is speaking of the affections as well as the intellect, and is likewise attributing the new workings of both faculties to the work of God.

We also see Flavel's belief that the affections are worked upon by God in the second step of the effectual call when Flavel describes Satan's opposition to the effectual call. In the thirty-fourth sermon of *Method of Grace*, Flavel explains how Satan tries to keep the light out of the mind. But then, if Satan has failed and light does enter the mind, 'he labours to obstruct the efficacy and operation of the light; and though it do shine into the understanding, yet it shall be imprisoned there, and send down no converting influences upon the will and affections.'[26] In Flavel's view there is a 'converting influence' of God upon the affections which is part of the effectual call.

In the second step of the effectual call the affections are wrought upon by God as well as the conscience. This view of conviction has implications for the ministry of preaching. We will examine those implications in due time.

'Partial Conviction' vs Preparatory Work of the Spirit

We have considered the issue of partial conviction under our discussion of illumination. There we determined that there is a condition in some people in which illumination appears to have taken place, but it is shown to be only a partial conviction by the fact that the will of those people is not ultimately submitted to Christ.

In addition to this previous discussion it would be appropriate here to emphasize that Flavel never uses the term 'partial conviction' to describe the pre-believing state of a Christian. Rather, he uses the term 'preparatory work of the Spirit' to label the conviction which leads to true faith. It is equally

---

[25] Flavel, *Works*, Vol. 2, p. 192.
[26] Flavel, *Works*, Vol. 2, p. 460.

important to realize that Flavel never uses the phrase 'preparatory work of the Spirit' to refer to those occurrences in the soul of a non-elect person which do not result in conversion:

> The whole world is distinguishable into three classes, or sorts of persons; such as are far from Christ; such as are not far from Christ; and such as are in Christ. They that are in Christ have heartily received him. Such as are far from Christ, will not open to him; ... But those that are come under the preparatory workings of the Spirit, nigh to Christ, ... O what vehement desires! what strong pleas![27]

To understand Flavel correctly, it is important to realize that the 'preparatory workings of the Spirit' are not some work of God or of man in distinction from the effectual call, but rather the initial steps of the effectual call. Thus these preparatory works do not apply to the non-elect or to any apparent illumination or conviction which takes place within them. Flavel reserves the term 'partial conviction' or 'common conviction' for those who show some apparent signs of illumination and conviction but never experience the renewing of their wills:

> And here is the difference betwixt special and common convictions; common convictions come and go, they put the soul in a fright for a day or a month, and then trouble it no more for ever; but special convictions will be continued, one thing backs another; for Christ is in pursuit of the soul, and will give it chase, till at last he overtake, and come up with it.[28]

This understanding of the efficacy of conviction explains why Flavel never uses the term 'partial conviction' as a description of the process through which a true believer comes to faith. When efficacious conviction is occurring in a person's conscience it always leads to faith. Any aborted conviction which does not result in faith receives the label 'partial conviction.' It is impossible, in Flavel's view, for real conviction to miscarry.

It is appropriate at this point in our discussion to address briefly the issue of preparationism. The Puritan view of preparationism has been the subject of much scholarly discussion.[29] Norman Pettit produced an extensive discussion of

---

[27] Flavel, *Works*, Vol. 2, p. 30.
[28] Flavel, *Works*, Vol. 4, p. 103.
[29] The following sources (listed in chronological order) provide a sample of the scholarly discussion of the issue of preparationism in Puritanism: Miller, *New England Mind*; Norman Pettit, *The Heart Prepared: Grace and Conversion in Puritan Spiritual Life* (Middletown: Wesleyan University Press, 1966); Ian Breward, 'Introduction' to Perkins, *Works*; Tipson, 'Puritan Understanding of Conversion'; McGrath, 'Puritans and the Human Will'; John Howard Ball III, 'A Chronicler of the Soul's Windings: Thomas Hooker and his Morphology of Conversion' (Ph.D. diss., Westminster Theological Seminary, 1990); Timothy K. Beougher, 'Conversion: The Teaching and Practice of the Puritan Pastor Richard Baxter with regard to becoming a "True Christian"' (Ph.D. diss., Trinity Evangelical Divinity School, 1990); Beck,

this issue in *The Heart Prepared: Grace and Conversion in Puritan Spiritual Life*, which has been repeatedly referred to by subsequent scholars. He defines preparation as follows: 'By preparation they meant a period of prolonged introspective meditation and self-analysis in the light of God's revealed Word. In this process man first examined the evils of his sins, repented for those sins, and then turned to God for salvation.'[30] He continues: 'In this preparatory process the soul had first to experience contrition and humiliation ... . The preparationists maintained that contrition and humiliation were not in themselves saving graces but preliminary steps, and that while God takes away all resistance, this cannot be done without man's consent.'[31]

He presents the conundrum which he sees as facing the Puritans:

> Under such conditions [being rendered unable by sin to respond to grace], all who looked to the scriptural exhortations to prepare for grace were confronted with a genuine dilemma ... . Those who preached preparation and believed it to be consistent with predestination were concerned with the problem of a possible period of time before conversion that was neither wholly the work of the Law nor entirely beyond man's control.[32]

We observe that the preparationism which Pettit describes is not present in Flavel's writings. This is partly due to the fact that some of what Pettit includes in the concept of 'preparation' is treated by Flavel as steps within the effectual call.[33] For example, the person who is undergoing conviction is not, in Flavel's

---

'Doctrine of *Gratia Praeparans*'; Richard C. Goode, '"The only and principal end": Propagating the Gospel in early Puritan New England' (Ph.D. diss., Vanderbilt University, 1995); Mark E. Dever, *Richard Sibbes: Puritanism and Calvinism in late Elizabethan and early Stuart England* (Macon: Mercer University Press, 2000); Michael P. Winship, *Making Heretics: Militant Protestantism and Free Grace in Massachusetts, 1636–1641* (Princeton: Princeton University Press, 2002); Theodore Dwight Bozeman, *The Precisianist Strain: Disciplinary Religion & Antinomian Backlash in Puritanism to 1638* (Chapel Hill: Omohundro Institute of Early American History and Culture, 2004); David R. Como, *Blown by the Spirit: Puritanism and the Emergence of an Antinomian Underground in Pre-Civil-War England* (Stanford: Stanford University Press, 2004). Pettit opens his bibliography with an annotated list of late nineteenth-century and early twentieth-century sources which inform the discussion of preparationism.

[30] Pettit, *Heart Prepared*, p. 17.
[31] Pettit, *Heart Prepared*, p. 18.
[32] Pettit, *Heart Prepared*, pp. 16–17.
[33] Richard Muller comments: 'Pettit drives too much of a wedge between English Puritan and continental Reformed theology: more attention needs to be drawn to the relation of preparationism to the first use of the law and to the sense of the demands of the Gospel and of the preached Word in Reformed theology.' Richard Muller, 'Covenant and Conscience in English Reformed Theology: Three Variations on a 17th Century Theme,' *WTJ* 42 (1980), pp. 308–34, at 310 n. 7.

view, preparing himself for salvation but is being wrought upon by the Spirit and is in the process of being called to faith. What Pettit has interpreted as preparatory acts outside of the call Flavel describes as a step within the effectual call.[34] Flavel's view of the effectual call does not allow for Pettit's hypothetical 'possible period of time' between being in a state of sin and being wrought upon by the Spirit and drawn to Christ. For Flavel, there is no dilemma.

Theodore Bozeman, in *The Precisanist Strain*, draws attention to the fact that there are different 'strains' of Puritan preparationist theology.[35] He focuses his discussion on the Puritan clergy who held that behavioural change was a prerequisite for salvation. He upholds Thomas Hooker as a particularly suitable exemplar of this position.[36] Bozeman finishes his discussion by asserting: 'With its call for behavioural change as a condition of access to the Atonement, this strain of preparationist doctrine clearly reveals the harder disciplinary accent of the pietist turn.'[37] He then suggests that the presence of this strain of doctrine necessitates revising 'the widely held notion' that Puritan theology was characterized by a belief that change in behaviour followed, rather than preceded, a deep dramatic conversion.

Before this, Bozeman acknowledged that noteworthy Puritans such as Richard Greenham, William Perkins, Richard Sibbes and others did not give evidence of such a view of preparationism in their teaching. We would add Flavel to that list. Flavel very clearly viewed what Bozeman described as certain efforts of human beings to 'prepare' for grace as evidences of the early steps of the effectual call.

Michael Winship, in *Making Heretics: Militant Protestantism and Free Grace in Massachusetts, 1636–1641*, examines the personal, social and theological dynamics which contributed to the Free Grace controversy in Boston during the 1630s, the two main personalities in which were John Cotton and Thomas Shepard.[38] He suggests that differing views of preparationism among Puritan preachers formed one factor in the controversy. 'Quite apart from personality and personal history, however, there is a doctrinal issue [preparationism] that helps explain why Shepard in particular had such trouble bearing a difference with Cotton and, no less important, why Cotton was to get his back up so stiffly as a consequence.'[39] Winship engages in considerable historical sleuthing to uncover the nuances of theological difference between the antagonists. He suggests that Cotton did indeed hold to a form of

---

[34] It seems that clarifying seventeenth-century authors' definitions of the effectual call is an important element in discussing the questions raised by Puritan preparationism.
[35] Bozeman, *Precisanist Strain*, pp. 107–10.
[36] Hooker expounds his view in detail in *The Soules Preparation for Christ*.
[37] Bozeman, *Precisanist Strain*, p. 110.
[38] Winship, *Making Heretics*, pp. 69–82, 267–74.
[39] Winship, *Making Heretics*, p. 69.

preparationism, but that this form was not satisfactory to Shephard. Cotton's approach met with the accusation of being too close to antinomianism. Shepard's approach was met with the accusation of being too close to Arminianism. Winship maintains that these differences were evident in other Puritan clergy.

> While the increasing visibility of radical preachers in London in the 1620s heightened puritan sensitivities to antinomianism/familism, the growing visibility of Arminianism heightened sensitivities to any doctrine that appeared to threaten justification's unconditional nature by emphasizing human works ... . Thomas Goodwin, a friend sharing Cotton's theological emphases though not his absolutism, bitterly attacked Hooker's distended conception of preparation in the 1630s, and even more moderate ministers expressed scepticism.[40]

We agree with Winship's observation that there were differences of opinion among Puritans of that period over preparationism.[41] Our contribution to the discussion is to place Flavel closer to the position of Cotton than to that of Shepard.

We find a striking similarity concerning this issue between Flavel's view and that of Giles Firmin (1614–97).[42] Flavel refers to Firmin's *Real Christian: or a Treatise of effectual Calling*, in three of his own treatises.[43] Firmin entitles chapter one of his treatise: 'Concerning Preparations of the Soul for Christ, in General.'[44] He gives nine fundamental 'posits' that serve as assumptions for his exposition. Three of them are important for our discussion. Firmin explains his second posit: 'Man naturally (especially if he be an adult before God works upon him) is not a subject fit or disposed to receive Christ immediately, when

---

[40] Winship, *Making Heretics*, p. 71.
[41] David Como also acknowledges that 'the doctrine of "preparationism" was not universally or incontestably accepted within mainstream Puritanism.' Como, *Blown by the Spirit*, p. 352.
[42] Giles Firmin began his education at Cambridge but left before completion of his studies for New England, where he practised medicine. After returning to England, and then again to New England, he was ordained a deacon at the First Church, Boston, where John Cotton was minister. He returned a second time to England, was ordained as a Presbyterian, and became vicar of Shalford, Essex. Following the Act of Uniformity he settled in Ridgewell, Essex, and practised medicine. He was an active nonconformist and in 1672 was instrumental in forming a Presbyterian congregation in Ridgewell. He wrote numerous books in which he did not shy away from theological controversy and disagreement with men such as Richard Baxter and John Owen. N.H. Keeble, 'Firmin, Giles (1613/14–1697),' *ODNB*, http://www.oxforddnb.com/view/article/9481, accessed 21 November 2009.
[43] Flavel quotes or refers to Firmin's *Real Christian* a total of seven times in *Fountain of Life*, *Reasonableness and Necessity*, and *Mystery of Providence*.
[44] Giles Firmin, *Real Christian: or a Treatise of Effectual Calling* (London: D. Newman, 1670). The complete discussion is found on pp. 2–29.

offered to him; but before he will receive him, there must be some work of the Spirit upon him, to prepare him, make him willing and glad to receive him.'[45] We note here that the idea of the Spirit preparing the person is not referring to preparation for the effectual call, but for receiving Christ (which is the final step in the call). Flavel agrees, and equates this preparation with the first two steps of the call.

Firmin explains his fifth posit: 'Though God is very various in the manner of his working, when he converts or draws the soul to Christ; yet the work wrought is in all the same; there is no variety in the work wrought.'[46] Flavel would agree with this. The steps of illumination and conviction are always present even if the intensity or personal details differ from person to person. Firmin and Flavel understand that this drawing is a work of God done only on the elect, and that the process is included in the effectual call.

Firmin then proceeds to his sixth posit: 'To say of a man under God's working, that he is but under a preparatory work, and no more, is a difficult thing.'[47] Here we return to our interpretation of Flavel's view and notice the parallel between it and that of Firmin. Flavel and Firmin both see the steps which prepare a person to receive Christ as steps intrinsic to the effectual call. Neither man would describe such steps apart from the effectual call, or as taking place apart from a work wrought in the sinner by the Spirit. Nor would they describe apparent illumination and conviction in those who never put their faith in Christ as being the same thing as that which prepares a person to believe. Both view preparatory work as the first steps of the effectual call, and as something which takes place only in the elect as they are being drawn to Christ.

Opposition to Conviction

Any discussion of Flavel's view of conviction must include an acknowledgment of his understanding that there is opposition to the work of conviction in the soul of man. In *Sacramental Meditations* he writes: 'How many and mighty enemies did oppose the work of faith in thy soul? Among which Satan and thy own carnal reasonings were the principal ... . By them, what strong-holds and fortifications were raised, to secure thee from the strokes of conviction that make way for faith.'[48] In *Method of Grace* he discusses satanic opposition in more detail. He speaks of Satan's labour in obstructing the operation of light in the sinner's soul '[b]y hastening to quench convictions betimes, and nip them in the bud. Satan knows how dangerous a thing it is, and

---

[45] Firmin, *Real Christian*, p. 6.
[46] Firmin, *Real Christian*, p. 17.
[47] Firmin, *Real Christian*, p. 18.
[48] Flavel, *Works*, Vol. 6, p. 430.

destructive to his interest, to suffer convictions to continue long.'[49] The work of conviction is opposed by Satan and by sinful human nature. This opposition does not negate or overcome the efficacy of the call, but it is real and its presence requires certain tasks of the preacher. We will look at those tasks in due time.

Summary concerning Conviction

In summary, Flavel views conviction as the second step of the effectual call. No one arrives at saving faith without having first experienced conviction. The seat of conviction is the conscience, which is one of the powers or functions of the human mind. Conviction is the work of God in which he enables the conscience to respond in self-judgment to the truths which the mind has understood. This conviction produces an effect in the emotions which is called compunction. Compunction is not a mere natural response of the soul's faculty but is a result of the Spirit working on the affections. Both the intellect and the affections are wrought upon by the Spirit of God in the step of conviction. Although the degree of compunction's emotional intensity varies from person to person, it is not unusual for it to be intense and extreme. God uses two means by which he does this work: his word and his Spirit. Using those two means he overcomes natural and satanic opposition to conviction. Conviction and its corresponding compunction are not an end in themselves, but a step between illumination and faith. There is a condition in some people in which illumination and conviction appear to have taken place, but it is shown to be only a partial conviction by the fact that their wills are ultimately not bowed to Christ. True conviction always leads to the renewing of the will and faith.

Flavel draws significant implications from the doctrine of conviction and applies them to the ministry of preaching. Those implications we will see later in the study.

Renewing of the Will

Just as with the doctrines of illumination and conviction, Flavel's discussions of the renewing of the will are scattered widely throughout his *Works*. In examining his view of the renewing of the will, we will lean heavily on the fourth sermon of *Method of Grace* and the fifth sermon of *England's Duty*. In those two sermons he meticulously outlines this third step of the effectual call.

We will examine Flavel's understanding of the renewing of the will by first reinforcing the previous conclusion that it is indeed the third and final step of the effectual call. We will proceed to examine the efficacious nature of this step, and then see how Flavel understands this efficacy as being exercised in a way which maintains the freedom and dignity of the human will. We shall then

---

[49] Flavel, *Works*, Vol. 2, p. 460.

Effectual Call: Last Steps and Summary

comment on the part providence plays in the effectual call. Finally, we will see that faith is the result of this renewing work on the will. After this examination of Flavel's view of the renewing of the will, we will examine his view of saving faith.

Renewing of the Will: Clearly the third and final Step in Vocation

In the fifth sermon of *England's Duty* Flavel explains in detail what he believes is meant by the final step of the effectual call. The sermon is based upon the portion of Revelation 3:20 which reads, 'Behold I stand at the door and knock.' He explains that after making entrance into the soul by the door of the understanding, Christ knocks at the door of the will:

> Within this [the door of the understanding] is the royal gate of the soul, viz. The will of man, that noble and imperial power. Many things may pass into the mind, or understanding of a man, and yet be able to get no further; the door of the will may be shut against them ... . Christ himself stands betwixt these two doors, in the souls of many persons; he is got into their understandings and consciences, they are convinced of the possibility and necessity of obtaining Jesus Christ, but still the door of their will is barred against him.[50]

This illustrates that in Flavel's view the renewing of the will is indeed the final step of a three-step effectual call. It follows illumination and conviction, and the effectual call has not come to completion until it occurs.

Renewing of the Will as Efficacious

Given Flavel's understanding of the deadening effect of sin upon the human will, it comes as no surprise that he speaks of the work of God upon the sinner's will as efficacious. In the fourth sermon of *Method of Grace* he does so clearly: 'Here is much more than a naked proposal made to the will; there is a power as well as a tender; greatness of power; and yet more, the exceeding greatness of his power; and this power hath an actual efficacy ascribed to it, he works upon our hearts and wills.'[51]

Earlier in the same sermon he labours this point while discussing John 6:44, 'No man can come to me, except the Father, which hath sent me, draw him.' He focuses on the words 'draw him' and comments:

> 'That is, powerfully and effectually incline his will to come to Christ: Not by a violent co-action, but by a benevolent bending of the will which was averse;' and as it is not in the way of force and compulsion, so neither is it by a simple moral suasion, by the bare proposal of an object to the will, and so leaving the sinner to

---

[50] Flavel, *Works*, Vol. 4, p. 89.
[51] Flavel, *Works*, Vol. 2, p. 70.

his own election; but it is such a persuasion, as hath a mighty overcoming efficacy accompanying it.[52]

The movement of the will towards faith in response to illumination and conviction is not attributable to the natural power of the human will. Rather, Flavel attributes the movement of the will towards faith to its having been renewed by a supernatural work of the Spirit.

Renewing of the Will as Congruent with the Nature of the Human Soul

This efficacious work of God upon the will does not, however, negate nor overrule the human will's freedom and dignity. Flavel is insistent that the renewing of the will – indeed, the whole three-step process of the effectual call – is done by God in a way that honours and respects the way in which he created the human soul:

> Christ's knocking at the door of the heart implies the method of the Spirit in conversion to be congruous and agreeable to the nature of man's soul ... . There is a great difference between a friendly admission by consent, and a forcible entrance ... . Forcible actions are unsuitable to the nature of the will, whose motions are free and spontaneous; therefore it is said, Psalm cx. 3. 'Thy people shall be willing in the day of thy power.' It is true, the power of God is upon the will of man in the day of his conversion, or else it would never open to Christ; but yet that power of God doth not act against the freedom of man's will, by co-action and force: no, but of unwilling he makes it willing; taking away the obstinacy and reluctancy of the will by the efficacy of his grace, ... and so the door of the will still opens freely.[53]

Later in the same argument he restates this point. 'It must be confessed, that when the day of God's power is come for the bringing home of a poor sinner to Christ, he cannot resist the power of God's Spirit, that draws him effectually ... yet still the soul comes freely by the consent of his will; for this is the method of Christ in drawing souls to him.'[54]

Providence as an Instrument in the Effectual Call

In the fifth sermon of *England's Duty* Flavel asserts that the Spirit uses providence in the process of the effectual call. In his discussion we note that the two means used in illumination and conviction (the Spirit and the word) are acknowledged as also being the means by which God renews the will. However, into the picture Flavel introduces providence:

---

[52] Flavel, *Works*, Vol. 2, p. 68. Flavel is here quoting Salomo Glassius (1593–1656).
[53] Flavel, *Works*, Vol. 4, p. 92.
[54] Flavel, *Works*, Vol. 4, p. 92.

Effectual Call: Last Steps and Summary 149

> By what instruments Christ knocks at the doors, that is, the judgment, conscience, and will of a sinner. And these are two, viz. 1. His word. 2. His providence. Here my work will be to shew you how the Spirit of God makes use both of the word and works of God, to rouse and open the consciences and hearts of sinners. These are the two hammers or instruments of the Spirit, by which he knocks at the door of the heart.[55]

Flavel explains the relationship between God's word and his providences in the effectual call.

> These [providential works of God], in subserviency to the word, are of excellent use to awaken sinners, and make them open their hearts to Christ. God hath magnified his word above all his name; yet there are some of the providential works of God greatly serviceable in this case; the word sanctifies providences, and providences assist the word, and make it work.[56]

The word is the primary instrument of the Spirit, but he also uses providential dealings when drawing sinners to Christ.

The Result of the Renewing of the Will: Faith

Flavel makes it clear that the result of the renewing of the will is faith. In the fourth sermon of *Method of Grace* he uses the terminology of being 'drawn' to Christ, and he equates the end of that process to faith. He mentions illumination and conviction and then finishes: 'and then [the Spirit] moves the will to embrace and close with Christ *in the way of faith* for life and salvation.'[57] In *England's Duty* Flavel expands upon the imagery of opening the soul's door to Christ and equates that with faith. He repeatedly refers to 'opening thy heart to Christ by faith.'[58]

Before looking in more detail at Flavel's understanding of the doctrine of faith, it is helpful to see his understanding of how the renewing of the will relates to saving faith. We see in Flavel's understanding of that relationship an underlying agreement with the view of Ames. Ames discussed this relationship in his *Marrow* when explaining the receiving of Christ for salvation. We quote him here at length, minus the Scripture quotations and Ames' numbering system:

> As for man, receiving [of Christ] is either passive or active ... . The passive receiving of Christ is the process by which a spiritual principle of grace is generated in the will of man ... . The enlightenment of the mind is not sufficient to produce this effect because it does not take away the corruption of the will. Nor

---

[55] Flavel, *Works*, Vol. 4, p. 94.
[56] Flavel, *Works*, Vol. 4, p. 96.
[57] Flavel, *Works*, Vol. 2, p. 71; emphasis mine.
[58] Flavel, *Works*, Vol. 4, p. 112.

does it communicate any new supernatural principle by which it may convert itself ... . Yet the will in this first receiving plays the role neither of a free agent nor a natural bearer, but only an obedient subject ... . Active receiving is an elicited act of faith in which he who is called now wholly leans upon Christ as his savior and through Christ upon God ... . This act of faith depends partly upon an inborn principle or attitude toward grace and partly upon the action of God moving before and stirring up ... . It is indeed called forth and exercised by man freely but also surely, unavoidably, and unchangeably.[59]

Flavel, on this point, can rightfully be characterized as being in agreement with Ames. When the renewing of the will happens to a person, the person is passive. The same person, however, can accurately be termed 'active' in the exercising of saving faith. The active exercise of faith always follows the passive renewal of the will.

This understanding of the passive and active aspects of the third step of the effectual call has significant implications for preaching for conversion, implications which we will explore shortly. Before doing so, we must examine Flavel's theology of faith.

Faith

As we have just noted, Flavel saw faith as that which takes place once the will is renewed. His view of the interconnection between the renewing of the will and the will's exercise of faith can be seen in his arrangement of sermons for *Method of Grace*. In 'Totius Operis' he refers to the fifth sermon as that which addresses the 'Infusion of Life.' He refers to the sixth and seventh sermons as addressing 'Actual Faith.'[60] He moves deliberately from the renewing of the will to the exercise of faith. In the first sentence of the sixth sermon Flavel makes a transition between the two: 'No sooner is the soul quickened by the Spirit of God, but it answers, in some measure, the end of God in that work, by its *active reception of Jesus Christ, in the way of believing.*'[61] Although he does not understand the two, faith and a renewed will, as synonymous, he nevertheless sees them as inextricably entwined in the believer's experience.[62]

---

[59] Ames, *Marrow*, p. 159.
[60] Flavel, *Whole Works*, Vol. 1, p. 248. The 'Totius Operis' is presented in Appendix 3 of this study.
[61] Flavel, *Works*, Vol. 2, p. 102.
[62] In the fifth sermon of *Method of Grace* Flavel responds to the objection that his view of faith following renewing of the will would present the possibility of a renewed person dying prior to exercising faith and thus never realizing salvation. To this objection Flavel states '[t]hat when we speak of the priority of this quickening work of the Spirit to our actual believing, we rather understand it of the priority of nature, than of time.' Flavel, *Works*, Vol. 2, p. 98.

Which Faculty of the Soul is the Seat of Faith?

Seeing the close relationship that Flavel propounds between the human will and faith, it is appropriate to ask if he understands the human will to be the sole seat of faith. Another way of asking the question is: Are the other two faculties of the soul, i.e. the intellect and the affections, involved in faith, or is it only a matter of the will?

Flavel's response to that question is most explicit in the sixth sermon of *Method of Grace*. The Scripture text for that sermon is John 1:12, 'But as many as received him, to them gave he power to become the sons of God; even to them that believe on his name.' The doctrine which he develops from that text is '[t]hat the receiving of the Lord Jesus Christ is that saving and vital act of faith which gives the soul right both to his person and benefits.'[63]

Early in the sermon he stresses that the understanding of man is involved in what he calls 'the receiving act of faith.' 'The receiving of Christ, necessarily implies the assent of the understanding to the truths of Christ revealed in the gospel.'[64] Flavel explains this point further in the seventh sermon of *England's Duty*:

> It [being willing to receive Jesus Christ] implies, and necessarily includes, the right understanding and true apprehension of gospel terms and articles: these must be known, pondered, and duly considered, before the will can savingly open, in an act of consent, to Christ's offer ... ... he that doth not consider, doth not consent; you must exercise your understandings upon the terms and articles of Christianity, or else your consent is rash, blindfold, and unstable.[65]

Flavel explains that this intellectual grasping of gospel information, although crucial, is not in itself faith. In the sixth sermon of *Method of Grace* he distinguishes between intellectual assent and faith: 'assent [to gospel facts], though it be not in itself saving faith, yet is it the foundation and ground work of it.'[66] Later in the sermon he insists on the primacy of the will in saving faith: 'Receiving Christ consists in the *consent and choice of the will*.'[67]

In *Of Antinomianism*, Flavel identifies as one of the errors of antinomianism the view that the nature of saving faith is mere intellectual assent:

> This doctrine is certainly unsound, because it confounds the distinction betwixt dogmatical and saving faith; and makes it all one, to believe an *axiom* or proposition, and to believe savingly in Christ to eternal life. What is it to believe that God laid our iniquities upon Christ, more than the mere assent of the

---

[63] Flavel, *Works*, Vol. 2, p. 104.
[64] Flavel, *Works*, Vol. 2, p. 106.
[65] Flavel, *Works*, Vol. 4, p. 144.
[66] Flavel, *Works*, Vol. 2, p. 106.
[67] Flavel, *Works*, Vol. 2, p. 109.

understanding to a scripture axiom, or proposition, without any consent of the will, to receive Jesus Christ as the gospel offers him?[68]

The answer to his rhetorical question is nothing. Such assent is not saving faith.

So then, which faculty of the soul does Flavel see as the seat of faith – the mind, the will, or both? He answers that question specifically:

> It is disputed by some, whether faith can be seated in two distinct faculties, as we seem to place it, when we say it involves both the approbation of the judgment and the consent of the will. I will not here entangle my discourse with that fruitless dispute. I am of the same judgment with those divines, that think faith cannot be expressed fully by any one single habit, or act of the mind or will distinctly, for that (as one well notes) [here Flavel refers to John Owen's writings on justification] there are such descriptions given of it in scripture, such things are proposed as the object of it, and such is the experience of all that sincerely believe, as no one single act, either of the mind or will, can answer unto: Nor do I see any thing repugnant to scripture or philosophy if we place it in both faculties. Consent (saith Vasquez)[69] seems to denote the concourse of the will with the understanding.[70]

Having argued his case that the seat of faith is both the mind and will, Flavel goes on in the same sentence to stress the importance of the will: 'but to leave that [the question of how two faculties of the soul can be co-seats of faith], it is most certain the saving, justifying act of faith lies principally in the consent of the will.'[71]

We can understand Flavel's view of the primacy of the will in saving faith more fully when we consider his discussion of assent and consent. In the same sixth sermon of *Method of Grace* he reiterates the limits of assent. '*Assent* is too low to contain the essence of saving faith; it is found in the unregenerate as well as the regenerate: yea, in devils as well as men, James ii. 19. it is supposed and included in justifying faith, but it is not the justifying or saving act.'[72] Consent, on the other hand, is viewed differently. In 'A Sure Tryal' Flavel is speaking about gaining assurance of salvation. In his discussion he

---

[68] Flavel, *Works*, Vol. 3, p. 567.

[69] Gabriel Vasquez (c.1549–1604) was a Spanish Jesuit theologian. He entered the Society of Jesus in 1569. He taught at Alcalà, Ocana, Madrid, and Rome, but spent most of his years at Alcalà. He is known for his painstakingly detailed argumentation, his studies of Augustine, his differences with Suarez, and his encyclopedic knowledge of different Schools and authors. Antonio P. Goyena, 'Gabriel Vasquez,' in *Catholic Encyclopedia* (New York: Robert Appleton, 1914), http://oce.catholic.com/index. php?title=Gabriel_Vasquez, accessed 12 December 2009.

[70] Flavel, *Works*, Vol. 2, p. 109.

[71] Flavel, *Works*, Vol. 2, p. 109.

[72] Flavel, *Works*, Vol. 2, p. 114.

acknowledges the place of the intellect in saving faith, but focuses on the part which the will has played:

> You need not make any Doubt or Question after this, Whether Christ be yours, or you be his: Consent is essential to Marriage; there can be no Spiritual Marriage to Christ, but by consent of the Will ... . If you be therefore consenting and willing to be Christ's upon his own terms, there remains no Doubt whether Christ be yours after that Consent.[73]

As was stated earlier, Flavel's view is that the 'justifying act of faith lies principally in the consent of the will.'[74] Flavel states this again in his *Exposition*. 'Q. 4. What is the seat or habitation of faith? *A*. Not only the head or understanding, but principally the heart and will.'[75]

McGrath finds the same understanding concerning the place of the will in saving faith in his investigation of the works of Baxter and Owen. He notes that those two men, both Puritan contemporaries of Flavel, held different views of faith as it relates to the covenant of grace.[76] However, they agreed about the place of the human will in the exercise of saving faith. McGrath introduces a section of his dissertation by saying: 'It will be shown that the nature of this response [the human response to the divine initiative], according to both Baxter and Owen, ultimately involved the prominence, but not dominance, of the human will.'[77] McGrath asserts that although both Baxter and Owen acknowledged that there are intellectual and emotional components to faith, they also agreed that until the will was involved there was no saving faith.[78] In

---

[73] Flavel, 'Sure Tryal.'
[74] Flavel, *Works*, Vol. 2, p. 109.
[75] Flavel, *Works*, Vol. 6, p. 262.
[76] 'Where Baxter and Owen differed on the nature of faith was over the issue of faith as a covenant condition. Baxter ... argued that faith was the condition of the covenant ... . Owen denied this; he argued that while faith was necessary as the human response, Christ's death procured even this faith for the elect.' McGrath, 'Puritans and the Human Will,' p. 225.
[77] McGrath, 'Puritans and the Human Will,' p. 210.
[78] Both Owen and Baxter wrote voluminously and their views on the 'prominence' of the will can be seen in various writings. We note here one example for each that bears out McGrath's contention. On pp. 252–86 of *A Discourse Concerning the Holy Spirit*, Owen offers an extended discussion of regeneration which involves detailed refutations of various opposing views to his own. He entitles one section 'The Will in the first act of Conversion,' in which his view of the prominence of the will is clear. John Owen, *A Discourse Concerning the Holy Spirit* (London: J. Darby, 1674), p. 271. On pp. 254–66 of *The Divine Life*, Baxter explores why 'walking with God' is the only way to express true wisdom. In the discussion he writes: 'And though it be the Understanding which apprehendeth it [goodness], yet it is the Heart or Will that relisheth it ... And therefore I may well say, it is Wisdom indeed when it reaches to

this, Flavel is in complete agreement.

Seeing the human will as being the primary seat of faith, the seat of the justifying act of faith, has clear and significant implications for preaching. We will see those implications in a moment.

Faith and the Affections

We should note, however, that just as the will being considered the primary seat of faith does not exclude a role for the mind, so too the affections are not excluded from the picture of saving faith. In Flavel's view the affections, which were wrought upon by God to respond with compunction towards sin, are now also able to respond with 'approbation' towards Christ. The heart, which once was either indifferent towards Christ or held an aversion towards him, in the effectual call begins to desire him. Thus when saving faith is exercised toward Christ all three faculties of the soul have been changed. Flavel explains it this way: 'To receive all Christ, is to receive his person clothed with all his offices; and to receive him with all your heart, is to receive him into your understanding, will, and affections, Acts viii. 37. As there is nothing in Christ that may be refused, so there is nothing in you from which he must be excluded.'[79]

Flavel does not describe the renewed affections and their now positive emotions towards Christ as a different step in the effectual call. Nevertheless, he does believe that this emotive change happens. Just as the wrought-upon affections experience compunction in relation to sin and its danger, so the affections experience a desire for Christ prior to faith. Flavel explains this desire in the sixth sermon of *Method of Grace*, in the supposed words of a person being drawn to Christ. 'O, saith the soul, how completely happy shall I be, if I can but win Christ! I would not envy the nobles of the earth, were I but in Christ. I am hungry and athirst, and Christ is meat indeed, and drink indeed; this is the best thing in all the world for me.'[80] This desire for Christ is an influence of the affections upon the will, encouraging the will to decide for Christ.

This understanding of what is happening in the sinner's affections during the effectual call correlates exactly with Flavel's summary of the data on which illumination takes place. We have previously noted that he summarized this as pertaining to the 'disease' of sin and its 'remedy' in Christ. Compunction involves the emotional response to the first part of illumination, the comprehension of the biblical data concerning the disease of sin. There is also an emotional response to the second part of illumination – the comprehension

---

the heart.' Richard Baxter, *The Divine Life* (London: Francis Tyton, 1664), pp. 258–59.

[79] Flavel, *Works*, Vol. 2, p. 140.

[80] Flavel, *Works*, Vol. 2, p. 108.

of the biblical data concerning the remedy in Christ. Flavel does not use a title for this response, but he does speak of it and he believes that it precedes faith. The illumined and convicted person now desires Christ, and this movement of the affections contributes to the decision of the will to receive Christ.

Maddux, in his 'Ramist Rationality,' discusses the arrangement of Edward Taylor's poetry and notes Taylor's intent to first influence his readers' minds, then their affections, and then their wills. Maddux contends that this intentional progression from mind to affections to will was partly a result of Flavel's influence. Indeed, he calls it 'the Flavelian method.'

> This strategy was also complementary to the Flavelian method that prevails in the concluding stanzaic portions aimed at engaging the affections. At the close of his meditation, Taylor often endeavors – not always successfully – to achieve a moment of affective resolution, when the sensed-experience of devotion dovetails with the work of understanding and leads to a zealous regeneration of Christian practice.[81]

This Flavelian method, according to Maddux, engages the affections of the reader (or hearer) for the purpose of influencing the will. He has observed precisely the same pattern that we have observed in Flavel's understanding of the effectual call. This role of the emotions has implications for the preacher which Flavel recognized and purposefully applied in his preaching. We will examine his preaching in a moment.

It should be noted that this view of the role of the affections in relation to faith has not always been clearly understood by those contributing to scholarly discussion of Puritanism. Fedderson, for example, when discussing the role of emotions in Puritan preaching, states: 'Implicit in Hyperius' insistence that preachers must concern themselves more with moving affections than proving and confirming doctrine is a recognition that the ground upon which faith is based is emotional rather than intellectual. Faith is a feeling towards and not a knowledge of God.'[82] Our analysis of Flavel's theology reveals a dramatically different picture of faith from that which Fedderson propounds. We suggest that what Fedderson understands to be 'implicit' may well have been a faulty conclusion on his part. Flavel would insist that the affections are enlivened and active during the step of conviction but that faith can in no wise be characterized as 'a feeling.' Faith is very definitely an act of the will. The reason the emotions are the target of preaching is not because they make up the essence of faith, but because they can influence the will towards faith.

---

[81] Maddux, 'Ramist Rationality,' p. 38. We have been unable to examine the primary source used by Maddux in his examination of Taylor.
[82] Fedderson, 'Elizabethan Sermon,' p. 62.

The Object of Faith

What is the object of this saving faith? To whom or to what is the soul consenting? In *Fountain of Life*, Flavel writes of faith appropriating Christ and the benefits of his death.

> Hence also be informed of the necessity of faith, in order to a state and sense of peace with God: for to what purpose is the blood of Christ our sacrifice shed, unless it be actually and personally applied, and appropriated by faith? You know when the sacrifices under the law were brought to be slain, he that brought it was to put his hand upon the head of the sacrifice, and so it was accepted for him, to make an atonement ... . You must also lay the hand of faith upon Christ your sacrifice, not to imprecate, but apply and appropriate him to your own souls, he having been made a curse for you.[83]

The object of faith is Christ. We see again that such an appropriation speaks of more than mere intellectual assent, of a movement of the human will to trust in Christ.

When we consider the object of saving faith, we see Flavel's understanding of the relationship between illumination, the first step of the effectual call, and faith. In the seventh sermon of *Method of Grace* he explains: 'Illumination is a necessary antecedent to faith: You cannot believe till God hath opened your eyes to see your sin, your misery by sin, and your remedy in Jesus Christ alone.'[84] Illumination is an 'antecedent' to faith. The will is enabled to believe in the Christ that the intellect has been enabled to see.

Although the object of a person's faith is Christ, the person's faith is exercised upon Christ with an understanding of what Christ did to remedy the person's problem of sin. In the thirty-fifth sermon of *Fountain of Life*, Flavel develops the doctrine '[t]hat Jesus Christ hath perfected and completely finished the great work of redemption, committed to him by God the Father.'[85] After discussing in great detail the completeness of Christ's sacrifice of himself on behalf of sinners, Flavel begins drawing inferences to apply to the hearers. In the fourth inference he reflects upon the value of faith in God's sight due to the fact that it trusts not in the person exercising the faith but rather in the person of Christ and his accomplishment on the cross. He writes:

> Is Christ's work of redemption a complete and finished work? How excellent and comfortable beyond all compare, is the method and way of faith! Surely the way of believing is the most excellent way in which a poor sinner can approach God; for it brings before him a complete, entire, perfect righteousness; and this must needs be most honourable to God, most comfortable to the soul that draws nigh to God. O what a complete, finished, perfect thing is the righteousness of Christ! ...

---

[83] Flavel, *Works*, Vol. 1, pp. 150–51.
[84] Flavel, *Works*, Vol. 2, p. 129.
[85] Flavel, *Works*, Vol. 1, p. 431.

How pleasing, therefore and acceptable to God must be that faith, which presents so complete and excellent an atonement to him!⁸⁶

Flavel makes the point that faith does not present itself to God, nor any work of the person to God, but rather it presents Christ and his atoning death to God and trusts in it to gain forgiveness and salvation. Thus the atoning work of Christ is understood and trusted in by the person in exercising faith.

Nevertheless, Flavel consistently presents Christ himself as the object of saving faith. Nowhere is Flavel's understanding of the object of saving faith more clear than in the sixth sermon of *Method of Grace*. In that sermon his text is John 1:12, 'But as many as received him, to them gave he power to become the sons of God; even to them that believe on his name.' Early in the sermon he makes the point that 'we are also heedfully to note its [faith's] special object, ἔλαβον αὐτού" The text saith not αὐτα, *his*, but αὐτόν, *him*, i.e. his person.'⁸⁷

Later in the sermon he discusses what the mind must assent to, the heart find desirable, and the will choose; and in each case it is Christ that is the object. Concerning the mind he writes: 'It is evident that no man can receive Jesus Christ in the darkness of natural ignorance: we must understand and discern who and what he is.'⁸⁸ Concerning the affections he writes: 'Our receiving Christ necessarily implies our hearty approbation, liking and estimation; yea, the acquiescence of our very souls in Jesus Christ, as the most excellent, suitable, and complete remedy for all our wants, sins, and dangers.'⁸⁹ Concerning the will he writes: 'Receiving Christ consists in the consent and choice of the will; and this is the opening of the heart and stretching forth of the soul to receive him.'⁹⁰ In each case it is the person of Christ which is the object – first the object that is understood, then the object which is desired, and finally the object which is 'received.' In the *Exposition* he summarizes this point succinctly, 'Q. 7. What is the object of faith? *A.* The primary object of faith is the person of Christ, and the secondary are his benefits.'⁹¹

Faith as an Instrumental Condition of Salvation

As has been briefly noted, there was not complete agreement among Flavel's contemporaries concerning exactly how faith related to the sinner's justification. McGrath shows that Baxter viewed faith differently from Owen. McGrath summarizes:

---

⁸⁶ Flavel, *Works*, Vol. 1, p. 438.
⁸⁷ Flavel, *Works*, Vol. 2, p. 103.
⁸⁸ Flavel, *Works*, Vol. 2, p. 106.
⁸⁹ Flavel, *Works*, Vol. 2, pp. 107–108.
⁹⁰ Flavel, *Works*, Vol. 2, p. 109.
⁹¹ Flavel, *Works*, Vol. 6, p. 263.

Baxter claimed that God established in Christ a *conditional* covenant: available to all who would repent and believe; faith, thus, was the covenant condition. Owen, on the other hand, while equally insistent upon the necessity of faith, denied that God's covenant was conditional; by the death and satisfaction of Christ for the elect the faith of the elect was procured. The human response, according to Owen, was not a faith which fulfilled the covenant condition but a faith which accepted Christ in all *his* covenant righteousness.[92]

Where does Flavel fit in this argument? At one point in the sixth sermon of *Method of Grace* he compares four views of faith in regard to its relationship to justification. In addition to his own view, he looks at the Roman Catholic view, the Arminian view, and then acknowledges the view of Baxter (although without mentioning his name). Flavel writes: 'Some there are also, even among our reformed divines, that contend that faith justifies and saves us, as it is the condition of the new covenant.'[93] Later he contends: 'I acknowledge faith to be a condition of the covenant, but cannot allow that it justifies as a condition.'[94]

He explains his understanding of faith as an 'instrumental condition' of justification. This differs from Baxter's view.

> It [faith] is the instrument of our justification, Rom. v. 1. Till Christ be received (thus received by us) we are in our sins; under guilt and condemnation; but when faith comes, then comes freedom: 'By him all that believe are justified from all things.' Acts xiii. 38. Rom. viii. 1. For it apprehends or receives the pure and perfect righteousness of the Lord Jesus, wherein the soul, how guilty and sinful soever it be in itself, stands faultless and spotless before the presence of God; all obligations to punishment are, upon believing, immediately dissolved; a full and final pardon sealed. O precious faith! Who can sufficiently value it![95]

Flavel's controversy with his Dartmouth neighbour, Philip Cary, over the issue of infant baptism delved into the theology of the covenants and the relationship of faith to the procurement of the benefits of the covenant of grace. This discussion gave Flavel opportunity to clarify his view of faith being a 'condition' to justification.[96] In his *Refutation of Cary's Rejoinder* he notes that Cary was accusing him of holding a view of faith as a 'meritorious condition.' Flavel goes to great lengths to explain how he could consider faith a condition of justification but not a meritorious condition. He writes to Cary: 'You say ... that a condition plainly implies something of merit, by way of condignity or congruity; which is false.'[97] He uses the phrase 'antecedent condition' in

---

[92] McGrath, 'Puritans and the Human Will,' pp. 209–10.
[93] Flavel, *Works*, Vol. 2, p. 118.
[94] Flavel, *Works*, Vol. 2, p. 120.
[95] Flavel, *Works*, Vol. 2, p. 117.
[96] The published interaction between Cary and Flavel is described in Appendix 5 of this study, under *Reply to Cary's Call* and *Refutation of Cary's Rejoinder*.
[97] Flavel, *Works*, Vol. 3, pp. 525–26.

describing faith's relation to the covenant:

> An antecedent condition signifying no more than an act of ours, which, though it be neither perfect in every degree, nor in the least meritorious of the benefit conferred, nor performed in our natural strength: yet, according to the constitution of the covenant, is required of us, in order to the blessings consequent thereupon, by virtue of the promise: And, consequently the benefits and mercies granted in the promise, in this order are, and must be, suspended by the donor or disposer of them, until it be performed. Such a condition we affirm faith to be.[98]

Emphatically denying that faith held any meritorious value, Flavel nevertheless calls it a condition of entering into salvation. It is an instrumental condition, not a condition which justifies based upon its own virtue. It is the instrument by which the sinner takes hold of Christ and applies to himself Christ's righteousness.

Flavel discusses this same relationship between faith and justification in the eleventh sermon of *Fountain of Life*. Here, rather than using the term 'condition,' he calls faith a 'cause' of the remission of sins:

> It is true, the death of Christ is the meritorious cause of remission, but faith is the instrumental applying cause; and as Christ's blood is necessary in its place, so is our faith in its place also. For to the actual remission of sin, and peace of conscience, there must be a co-operation of all the causes of remission and peace. As there is the grace and love of God for an efficient and impulsive cause, and the death of Christ our sacrifice, the meritorious cause; so of necessity there must be faith, the instrumental cause.[99]

It is this relationship with salvation which gives faith its special esteem. Flavel explains: 'Faith, considered as an habit, is no more precious than other gracious habits are, but considered as an instrument to receive Christ and his righteousness, so it excels them all.'[100] In *Fountain of Life* he writes: 'All the graces have done excellently, but faith excels them all: faith is the Phoenix grace, the queen of graces: deservedly it is stiled precious faith, 2 Pet. i. 1.'[101]

It is also this relationship with justification, as an antecedent or instrumental condition or cause, that makes faith absolutely essential for an individual's salvation.

The Necessity of Faith for Salvation

It is beyond question that Flavel deemed faith to be necessary for salvation. In the eleventh sermon of *Fountain of Life*, in which he discusses the necessity of

---

[98] Flavel, *Works*, Vol. 3, p. 527.
[99] Flavel, *Works*, Vol. 1, pp. 151–52.
[100] Flavel, *Works*, Vol. 2, p. 120.
[101] Flavel, *Works*, Vol. 1, p. 452.

the priesthood of Christ, he makes this point. 'Hence also be informed of the necessity of faith, in order to a state and sense of peace with God: for to what purpose is the blood of Christ our sacrifice shed, unless it be actually and personally applied, and appropriated by faith?'[102] In his *Refutation of Cary's Rejoinder*, Flavel emphatically summarizes his defence of his view of faith by saying '[t]hat no adult person, notwithstanding God's eternal election, and Christ's meritorious death and satisfaction, according to the constitution and order of the new covenant, can either be justified in this world, or saved in the world to come, unless he first believe.'[103] In the seventh sermon of *Method of Grace* he states succinctly: 'Faith in its place is as necessary as the blood of Christ in its place.'[104] For Flavel, there is no salvation without faith. This conclusion has strong implications for the work of the preacher. We will examine those implications shortly.

Faith as Spirit-given yet truly a Human Act

It is necessary to add one more explanation of Flavel's to the picture of faith. In his debate with Cary he eventually addresses the paradox that faith is a result of grace renewing the will and yet it can be rightly considered a human act. This view has significant implications for the work of preaching, and so we quote him at length.

> And yet faith, notwithstanding this [that it is a result of grace], is truly and properly our work and duty; and that upon our believing or not believing, we have, or have not, an actual interest in Christ, righteousness, and life. For though the author of faith be the Spirit of God, yet believing, is properly our act, and an act required of us by a plain command; 1 John iii. 23. This is the command of God, That ye believe. And if its being wrought in God's strength makes it cease to be our work, I would fain know what exposition you would give of that place, Phil. ii. 12, 13. Work out your own salvation, &c. for it is God that worketh in you both to will and to do. And as this faith is truly and properly our work, though wrought in God's strength (for it is not God, but we that do believe) so it is wrought in us by him (by our own confession) before the application of pardoning mercy, which is consequent in order of nature thereunto: and therefore hath the true nature of an antecedent condition, which is that I contend for; and did you but understand your own words, you would not contend against it.[105]

The insistence that faith is understood as a human act, even in the light of the effectual nature of grace, is an important emphasis.

We previously made brief mention of a difference between Eugene White's

---

[102] Flavel, *Works*, Vol. 1, p. 150.
[103] Flavel, *Works*, Vol. 3, p. 531.
[104] Flavel, *Works*, Vol. 2, p. 121.
[105] Flavel, *Works*, Vol. 3, p. 534.

presentation of the Puritan understanding of the effectual call and our findings in Flavel. It is appropriate here to delineate this difference. White's presentation characterizes sinners as passive in relation to their own faith. For example, he talks of a sinner coming through steps resembling Flavel's description of illumination and conviction and then finally experiencing 'the awareness of the possible presence of faith. The smallest "spark of faith" which God "kindled in the heart" was a sufficient conversion.'[106] According to White's description, the appearance of faith in the person takes place without any active participation of the individual. Apparently, White believes that people do not exercise faith, they merely become aware that it is present within them. We believe that White has misunderstood the Puritan view of the final stage of the effectual call. He is attempting to explain the final step of the effectual call without recognizing that it contains, to use the language of Ames, both 'passive' and 'active' aspects. The person is passive with regard to the renewing of the will, but is correctly considered to be active in exercising faith. Although Flavel is very aware of the passive aspect of the renewing of the will, we believe that he would take issue with White's presentation precisely because White has omitted the active aspect of exercising faith.

It should be noted that this view of faith as the active aspect of the final step of the effectual call has tremendous implications for the work of preaching for conversion. Those implications were not lost on Flavel. We will investigate those implications below.

Summary concerning the Renewing of the Will and Faith

In summary, the renewing of the will is the third and final step of the effectual call. It follows illumination and conviction. This step is an efficacious act of God upon the will. The result of the renewing of the will is saving faith. Providence, in addition to God's word, is used by God's Spirit to bring about the consent of the will to Christ. Although the will is acted on by God in its renewal, the nature and dignity of the human will is not violated with regard to its exercise of faith. There are cognitive and emotional aspects to faith, and yet the will is the primary faculty of the soul involved in what Flavel calls 'the justifying act of faith.' In that justifying act the person trusts in Christ and Christ's substitution and righteousness. Christ himself is the primary object of saving faith. Faith itself is not meritorious. It is likened to the outstretching of the hand to receive Christ. It is instrumental in the person appropriating Christ to himself and thus being justified on the basis of the merits of Christ. Although attributable to the grace of God, faith is rightly seen as a human act. The person is passive in the renewing of his will but active in exercising faith. There is no such thing as a person whose will has been renewed who then fails to believe. The two are inextricably entwined and occur together. Unless and until a person

---

[106] White, *Puritan Rhetoric*, p. 13.

acts with his will to trust Christ, that person is not justified before God. No matter how much illumination or conviction seems to have taken place within the soul of an individual, unless the person's will is renewed and he exercises faith in Christ, that person has not yet entered into salvation.

Summary of Flavel's View of the Effectual Call

We have attempted to capture the cogent aspects of Flavel's view of the effectual call in Table 1 below. One additional comment is necessary. The work of God upon the affections which follows compunction and results in the sinner desiring Christ could logically be placed in either the second or the third step of the effectual call. Until this point we have discussed it in the second step because of its relation to the affections. Flavel, although speaking directly to this work and its implications for preachers, is not explicit about where he sees it. He treats it almost as a bridge between the second and third steps, as following compunction and preceding faith. We observe that he never considers it an additional step in the effectual call. This Spirit-enabled desire for Christ could be considered a part of the second step in that it involves the work of God on the affections. Also, Flavel titles the third step 'the renewal of the will,' thus pointing to the importance of the will, not the affections, in the final step. If the summary of the effectual call is made without reference to the corresponding responsibilities of the preacher and with the faculties of the soul being the organizing principle, the second step would be a logical place to list it.

However, as we have seen, when Flavel's understanding of the corresponding responsibilities and aims of the preacher are outlined next to the steps of the effectual call we see a logic in listing this newly wrought desire for Christ in the third step. It can be considered a part of it in the sense that it is the last appeal to the hearers' affections prior to the appeal to their will. Also, it leads directly to the exercise of faith. In the preacher's fulfilment of his duties, preaching to this new-found desire for Christ fits organically as the immediate precursor to preaching to the will. We also note that in the great majority of references to conviction Flavel himself focuses upon the emotions related to compunction rather than upon the positive emotion of desiring Christ. Thus we have decided for the table-form summary presentation of the effectual call to present the work upon the affections in which the sinner begins to desire Christ in the third step.

Table 1. Flavel's View of the Effectual Call

STEP IN EFFECTUAL CALL	FACULTY OF THE SOUL RELATED TO STEP	OCCURRENCE WITHIN THE SOUL
1. ILLUMINATION	Intellect	• Intellect enabled by God to understand the 'disease' of sin • Intellect enabled by God to understand the 'remedy' in Christ
2. CONVICTION	Intellect (conscience) and Affections	• Conscience enabled by God to render proper 'self-judgment' upon the soul • Affections enabled by God to respond to self-judgment with compunction
3. RENEWING OF WILL/FAITH	Affections and Will	• Affections enabled by God to begin to desire Christ • Will renewed by God, thus enabled to believe in Christ • Will exercises saving faith

According to Flavel the effectual call consists of illumination, conviction and renewing of the will resulting in faith. The first step of the effectual call is located in the human intellect. Illumination occurs in the mind. Illumination begins by a work of the Spirit which enables the sinner to understand the reality and gravity of his sin problem. The second step of the effectual call is conviction. Conviction occurs in the conscience, which is one of the functions or powers of the mind. Based upon the illumination of the mind concerning sin, the conscience judges the self. The affections are wrought upon by the Spirit and are then stirred up during conviction in such a way as to produce compunction. Upon the agitation of the affections, illumination continues by enabling the convicted sinner to comprehend the solution to sin in Jesus Christ. The wrought-upon affections begin to desire Christ. At this point, both the mind and affections influence the will. It is the will which serves as the location of the last step in the effectual call. In that step the will is renewed. The result of this renewal is that the will decides to exercise saving faith. Although this faith has cognitive and emotive aspects to it, the principal act of saving faith is seated in the will.

Any apparent progress of a person along the path of the effectual call is considered merely a partial conviction unless the person's will is renewed. Likewise, any consent of the will which is not based upon an illumined mind's cogitations and the corresponding conviction is considered spurious and is not saving faith.

This understanding of the effectual call has direct correlations to, and significant implications for, the ministry of preaching for conversion. Flavel was aware of those correlations and implications and purposefully applied them to his work of preaching. We will now turn our attention to this relationship between the effectual call and the work of preaching for conversion, as seen in his writings and sermons.

PART THREE

The Preaching of John Flavel: The Application of his Theology to the Work of Preaching for Conversion

Chapter 7

Factors other than the Effectual Call which influenced Puritan Sermon Construction

We come to the point in our study in which we propose to show the relationship between John Flavel's understanding of the effectual call and the preparation and delivery of his sermons. We contend that within the generally held Puritan homiletic framework Flavel's theology of the effectual call was the most influential factor shaping his preaching for conversion.

We realize that factors within the Puritan homiletic framework also had an influence on Flavel's preaching. Two of those factors deserve special note – Ramism and the 'plain style' preaching advocated by William Perkins.

Ramism

The influence of Peter Ramus (1515–72)[1] on the theology and homiletics of the seventeenth century has attracted a large amount of scholarly attention.[2] The

---

[1] Peter Ramus (Pierre de la Ramée) graduated as Master of Arts in 1536 from the Collège de Navarre, in Paris. He introduced alterations to Aristotelian logic and began teaching these at the Collège du Mans, in Paris, and at the Collège de l'Ave Maria. The novelty of his approach earned him the suppression of his works by Francis I, but this ban was reversed by Henry II. In 1551 Ramus was appointed regius professor of philosophy at the Collège de France. Around 1561 he was converted to Protestantism. His approach to logic and rhetoric significantly influenced academic circles in Europe and England. 'Ramus, Petrus,' *Encyclopædia Britannica Online*, 2009, http://search.eb.com/eb/article-9062635, accessed 12 December 2009.

[2] The following sources (listed in chronological order) provide a sample of the scholarly discussion of the issue of Ramism and its influence upon Puritanism: Miller, *New England Mind*; Walter J. Ong, *Ramus, Method, and the Decay of Dialogue* (Cambridge, MA: Harvard University Press, 1958); Hugh Kearney, *Scholars and Gentlemen: Universities and Society in Pre-Industrial Britain, 1500–1700* (Ithaca: Cornell University Press,1970); Keith L. Sprunger, *The Learned Doctor William Ames: Dutch Backgrounds of English and American Puritanism* (Urbana: University of Illinois Press, 1972); White, *Puritan Rhetoric*; Rechtien, 'Logic in Puritan Sermons'; Donald K. McKim, *Ramism in William Perkins' Theology* (New York: Peter Lang, 1987); Lunt, 'Reinvention of Preaching'; Maddux, 'Ramist Rationality'; James V. Skalnik, *Ramus and Reform: University and Church at the End of the Renaissance* (Kirksville: Truman State University Press, 2002). For

fact that Ramism exerted a significant influence upon Puritanism both in England and New England has been adequately established. For our purposes we draw attention to three aspects of Ramism: Ramus' use of dichotomies, his 'method' in teaching, and his distinctive understanding of rhetoric.

Peter Toon explains that Ramus 'substituted a simple logic for the complicated Aristotelian logic which was taught in the schools of Paris.' Toon continues:

> Two of the key words in his [Ramus'] system are 'dichotomy' and 'method'. He believed that the way to analyse any of the arts, be that art grammar, dialectic, rhetoric or mathematics, was to use dichotomy. That is, embedded in the nature of things he believed there was an inherent dichotomy. Thus in all definitions of the arts there was a dichotomy, as each definition was made up of two parts, each of which subsequently divided into two more parts.[3]

This use of dichotomy was not only verbally expressed but represented visually in bracketed outlines. Walter Ong chronicles Ramus' use of such visual dichotomizing from his earliest writings through his fourth edition of *Training in Dialectic* and then states that 'division by dichotomies, established in 1547, remains from now on in effective control of Ramus' arguments.'[4] This use of bracketing, when applied to any argument, would result in a chart which had the particulars in their many brackets listed on the right side of the page, the one general topic listed on the left side of the page, and a visual connection which would follow a series of dichotomies between the general topic and the many particulars, becoming increasingly particular if it is read from left to right, but increasingly general if it is read from right to left. The visual representation shows the logical relationships between all the propositions on the page.

Ramus' dichotomizing and his 'method' are not synonymous but they are interconnected in his presentation of material. Ong defines 'method' as seen in the works of Ramus. '"Method" (*methodus*), [is] Ramus' term for orderly pedagogical presentation of any subject by reputedly scientific descent from "general principles" to "specials" by means of definition and bipartite division.'[5] Skalnik adds: 'The heart and soul of Ramism was the concept of "method" developed in successive editions of his works, and in particular his works on logic.'[6]

It is necessary to compare Ramist dichotomizing and method with Flavel's approach. Does he exhibit these aspects of Ramism?

---

additional works concerning Ramism, see Ong's extensive annotated bibliography (pp. 377–91), and the copious footnotes throughout Skalnik's book.

[3] Toon, *Hyper-Calvinism*, p. 24.
[4] Ong, *Ramus*, p. 201.
[5] Ong, *Ramus*, p. 30.
[6] Skalnik, *Ramus and Reform*, p. 43.

The most obvious way to answer this question is to examine the charts which Flavel himself gives as overviews of his three largest treatises. These charts reveal much about Flavel's understanding and thinking processes as he planned series of sermons. The charts reveal how each sermon, and its corresponding central doctrine, fits in relation to the other sermons. Each doctrine can be seen in relationship with those already explained and those yet to come. He preached the series 'from the left side of the page to the right,' and from the top of the page to the bottom – thus taking the audience from the general to the particular and covering those doctrines together which were most closely related. Indeed, it is not an overstatement to say that an examination of the charts which Flavel gives as overviews of his *Fountain of Life*,[7] *Method of Grace*,[8] and *Soul of Man*[9] reveals bracketed outlines entirely consistent with what we see in the textbooks of Ramus.

Take, for example, Flavel's *Method of Grace*. First, we note that even the title of the treatise has the word 'method' in it, a marker signifying the influence of Ramist thought. Second, we note the arrangement of material as visually represented in his 'Totius Operis.' (To see this bracketed outline, refer to Appendix 3 of this study.) On the left side of the page he puts the entire treatise in relation to an even broader topic, redemption. His exploration of redemption is dichotomized into 'meritorious impetration', which he designed his treatise *Fountain of Life* to explore, and 'effectual application', which is the subject of *Method of Grace*. For the content of *Method of Grace*, he continues to dichotomize. Moving from left to right on the page, he divides 'effectual application' for consideration 'doctrinally' and 'practically.' The doctrinal consideration is further divided into 'general nature' and 'special nature.' The special nature is in turn divided into 'union with Christ' and 'communion with Christ,' and so the divisions continue from the left side of the page toward the right. Some divisions on the chart result in more than two subdivisions, but this is also consistent with the charts of Ramus himself.

Maddux, in his 'Ramist Rationality,' also points to the 'Epistle to the Reader' which prefaces *Fountain of Life* as evidence of Ramist ideas in Flavel's thought.[10] Maddux focuses his discussion on the implications of Ramism for Flavel's rhetoric, which we will comment on later in this study. We note here that the epistle to which Maddux has drawn attention also has other signs of Ramist influence. In that epistle Flavel discusses the value of 'method' and of presenting truths 'methodically.' He writes: 'A saving, though an

---

[7] Flavel, *Whole Works*, Vol. 1, p. xvi. The chart for *Fountain of Life* is entitled 'Totius Operis', and forms Appendix 2 of this study.
[8] Flavel, *Whole Works*, Vol. 1, p. 248. The chart for *Method of Grace* is also entitled 'Totius Operis', and forms Appendix 3 of this study.
[9] Flavel, *Whole Works*, Vol. 1, p. 481. The chart for *Soul of Man* is entitled 'Synopsis', and forms Appendix 4 of this study.
[10] Maddux, 'Ramist Rationality,' pp. 174–75.

immethodical knowledge of Christ, will bring us to heaven ... but a regular and methodical, as well as a saving knowledge of him, will bring heaven to us.' He spends considerable time extolling the virtue of pursuing a methodical understanding of Christian doctrine. His explanation reflects Ramist influence when he writes: 'It is the frame and design of holy doctrine that must be known, and every part should be discerned as it hath its particular use to that design, and as it is connected with the other parts.'[11] He continues: 'And every single truth also will be much better perceived by him that seeth its place and order, than by any other: for one truth exceedingly illustrates and leads another into the understanding. —Study therefore to grow in the more methodical knowledge of the same truths which you have received.'[12] More comments on the Ramist flavour of this 'Epistle to the Reader' could be made but the above should suffice.

It is true that Flavel exhibits Ramist influence in the arrangement and organization of his sermon series, in his visual presentation of that arrangement, and in his use of 'method.' However, was this Ramist influence a prevailing factor in his mind as he prepared and presented sermons to the unconverted? Or, was he more concerned with the effectual call and its implications for sermonizing? Before attempting to answer these questions we will continue our discussion of Ramism by considering briefly Ramism's implications for rhetoric.

Ong begins his discussion of Ramist rhetoric with the statement, '[i]f the Ramist dialectic is the most central item in the complex of cultural phenomena which make up Ramism, Ramist rhetoric is the most symptomatic item in the same complex.'[13] Ramus divided Aristotle's five-part organization of rhetoric (invention, disposition, memory, eloquence and delivery) into two parts. He insisted that invention and disposition belonged to logic, not rhetoric. The remaining three parts of Aristotelian rhetoric could not practically stand on their own.[14] Ramism, in effect, separated rhetoric from logic. This separation reduced rhetoric to a mere presentation of what was derived in logic. This reduction of rhetoric into a servant of logic, among other consequences, resulted in downplaying oratorical devices and emphasizing propositional statements.

Miller comments on the effect of Ramist rhetoric:

> To understand why contemporaries beheld such marvelous charms in Ramus' method we must compare it with the current Aristotelian instructions, particularly those in the rhetorics, for organizing discourses, with their elaborate rules for the

---

[11] Flavel, *Works*, Vol. 1, p. 21.
[12] Flavel, *Works*, Vol. 1, p. 22.
[13] Ong, *Ramus*, p. 270.
[14] See more detailed discussions of the effect of Ramism on rhetoric in Skalnik, *Ramus and Reform*, pp. 46–62, and Ong, *Ramus*, pp. 270–92.

formal divisions, their intricate devices for digression, and their complex models for exordia and conclusions. Ramus swept all this confusion aside by declaring that a coherent discourse would emerge of itself if axioms were placed one after another in their natural order.[15]

This approach to rhetoric was appropriated heartily by early Puritans, repeatedly taught to Puritan ministerial students, most notably adapted into Puritan preaching theory by William Perkins, and guaranteed a lasting influence upon the Puritan movement through the popularity and use of Perkins' *Art of Prophesying*.[16] Sinclair Ferguson, in his introduction to the 1996 edition of this work, states:

> As is widely recognised today, one of the major educational influences on William Perkins was the new logic associated with the name of the Frenchman, Pierre de la Ramée ... . The modern reader will catch the flavour of this new method by noting the way in which Perkins uses a two-fold division as he explains and analyses the nature of preaching.[17]

Ferguson refers to the Ramist method and draws attention to the dichotomizing inherent in Ramist thinking, and points to those two aspects of Ramism as being discernible in the writings of Perkins.

Ong points to a less explicit, but nevertheless real, connection between Ramist rhetoric and the Puritan plain style of preaching advocated by Perkins. Ong writes, 'the distinctive plain style emerged later, especially toward the opening of the seventeenth century, but it was not prescribed by Ramist rhetoric, although it was made inevitable by the whole mental setting which constitutes Ramism.'[18] The underpinnings of Ramist implications for rhetoric were eagerly practiced by Puritan sermonizers.

Flavel was one of those sermonizers. Maddux, in his discussion of Ramist rhetorical theory as practised by Flavel, labels Flavel a Philippo-Ramist. Philippo-Ramism was a school of thought that blended the views of Philip Melanchthon (1497–1560), which were Aristotelian, and Ramus' views, which stood in contradistinction to Aristotle. It was a partial return from Ramism to Aristotelian thought. Maddux summarizes Philippo-Ramism's effect on rhetoric as enabling speakers to 'celebrate affective speech, while they reject as vain any rhetoric of self-aggrandizement; as they proclaim the importance of originality, they simultaneously presume that truth will present itself in a

---

[15] Miller, *New England Mind*, p. 140.
[16] William Perkins, *The Arte of Prophecying: Or, A Treatise Concerning the sacred and onely true manner and methode of Preaching* (London: Felix Kyngston, 1607).
[17] Sinclair Ferguson, in William Perkins, *The Art of Prophesying with The calling of the Ministry* (Edinburgh: Banner of Truth, 1996), p. xii.
[18] Ong, *Ramus*, p. 285.

predetermined form and enduring fashion.'[19] We agree that Flavel fits this summary description.[20]

Thus we observe that three aspects of Ramism are indeed evident in Flavel's writings and sermons: the use of dichotomies, the particular 'method' used in teaching, and several Ramist implications for rhetoric. And so we return to our questions: Was this Ramist influence a prevailing factor in Flavel's mind as he prepared and presented sermons to the unconverted? Or was he more concerned with the effectual call and its implications for sermonizing?

We will shortly begin our demonstration of Flavel's conscious correlation of his sermon preparation and delivery with his understanding of the effectual call. In addition to that demonstration, we offer here two observations which contribute to the conclusion that the effectual call was a more prevalent and conscious factor in Flavel's sermon preparation than was Ramism.

The first observation is that Flavel does not mention Ramus at all in his *Works*. The significance of this fact is made clear when it is realized that Flavel's writings are replete with citations from the works of others. In his *Works* he quotes or refers to more than 550 different authors, historical figures and contemporaries.[21] The list is enormous both in size and scope. He quotes from the Greek philosophers, church fathers, Roman Catholic theologians of various centuries, Continental Reformers, English and Scottish Protestant theologians, Caroline divines, early and contemporary Puritans, and others. Flavel leaves no doubt that he is aware of writers past and present. Yet, he is completely silent concerning Ramus. He neither mentions nor quotes him.

The second observation relates to the fact that Flavel comments explicitly on the work of preaching. In those comments, as we will show, he draws attention specifically to the steps of the effectual call and the implications of those steps for the work of preaching. No such explicit correlation is made concerning Ramism. Ramism, as well as Ramus, goes unmentioned in all of Flavel's discussion of preaching. Although, as we have shown, his preaching reflects the influence of Ramism, we propose that it was the effectual call which exercised a more conscious and prevalent influence on him as he prepared and delivered sermons to the unconverted.

The Puritan 'plain style'

One additional factor which contributed to the general homiletic framework of Puritan preaching needs a brief comment – the Puritan 'plain style' of preaching advocated by Perkins. The focus of our study does not propel us to

---

[19] Maddux, 'Ramist Rationality,' p. 174.
[20] Further investigation of the accuracy of Maddux's assertion that Flavel was 'Philippo-Ramist' is not germane to our study. Maddux himself did not go to significant lengths to prove it. We know of no one else who uses this label for Flavel.
[21] A fuller discussion of the sources which Flavel cites appears in Chapter 2.

Factors influencing Puritan Sermon Construction 173

undertake a comprehensive investigation of this style of preaching. Adequate scholarly research has been done on this subject.[22] We merely wish to summarize this style for the purpose of comparing it to Flavel's sermons.

Perkins was not the only one to write a preaching manual, but his was arguably the most influential upon the Puritan movement. Paul Schaefer comments that '[a]n entire generation of preachers was indeed shaped by Perkins.'[23] Mitchell, in his investigation of later Puritans, writes:

> Of the older type of English preaching-manual, Perkins' 'Art of Prophesying' is an outstanding example. Its influence and vogue were enormous, owing to the extraordinary contemporary reputation of its author, whose theological works were accorded a place alongside those of Calvin and Hooker. All through the seventeenth, and among dissenters in the following, century, this short work on preaching continued to be recommended and quoted.[24]

Perkins provides his own summary of what preaching involves at the end of *Art of Prophesying*. He elucidates four parts of preaching:

1. Reading the text clearly from the canonical Scriptures.

2. Explaining the meaning of it, once it has been read, in the light of the Scriptures themselves.

3. Gathering a few profitable points of doctrine from the natural sense of the passage.

4. If the preacher is suitably gifted, applying the doctrines thus explained to the life and practice of the congregation in straightforward, plain speech.[25]

Teresa Toulouse points out that in addition to these points there was another part, the 'reasons' for the doctrine, which were usually placed after the doctrine and before the application, and which were called 'uses.' She proposes[26] that scholarship has shown that this inclusion of 'reasons' to the sermon format is

---

[22] For overviews of the historical development, characteristics, and influence of the 'plain style' preaching, see Miller, *New England Mind*; Rechtien, 'Logic in Puritan Sermons'; Horton Davies, 'Ten Characteristics of English Metaphysical Preaching,' in *Studies of the Church in History: Essays Honoring Robert S. Paul on his Sixty-fifth Birthday*, ed. Horton Davies (Allison Park: Pickwick, 1983), pp. 103–48; Jon D. Orten, 'Elizabethan Puritanism and the Plain Style' (Ph.D. diss., University of Minnesota: 1989); Jussely, '*Lectio Continua*'.

[23] Paul Schaefer, 'The *Arte of Prophesying* by William Perkins (1558–1602),' in Kelly M. Kapic and Randall C. Gleason, eds, *The Devoted Life: An Invitation to the Puritan Classics* (Downers Grove: InterVarsity Press, 2004), pp. 38–51.

[24] Mitchell, *English Pulpit Oratory*, p. 99.

[25] Perkins, *Art of Prophesying*, p. 79.

[26] Toulouse, 'John Cotton,' p. 280. We have not been able to examine the primary source on which this assertion is based.

attributable to John Udall (c.1560–92).²⁷ Jussely shows that Perkins was not the sole inventor of the Puritan plain style but that he was its most notable systematiser and propagator.²⁸ Lunt demonstrates that Richard Bernard (1568–1641),²⁹ in *The Faithful Shepherd*, further developed Perkins' preaching theory by emphasizing the application portion of the sermon.³⁰ Lunt ends his discussion of Bernard by saying: 'the sermon structure outlined by Bernard – like that of Perkins – illustrates that a new sermon form, consisting of doctrines, reasons and uses, had clearly emerged and was beginning to spread throughout England.'³¹

Modern scholarship has focused on that formula – 'doctrine,' 'reasons,' and 'uses' – as encapsulating the Puritan sermon form. Although generally accurate, this summary should not be understood as indicating that the Puritan

---

27 John Udall was educated at Cambridge, proceeding MA in 1584. He was ordained deacon, and served as lecturer at Kingston upon Thames. He established a relationship with the printer Robert Waldegrave of London and soon his sermons were in print. His preaching and its subsequent effect upon the parish unsettled the authorities and for the remainder of Udall's life he lived in contention with them. Eventually he was arrested, sentenced to death, and died in prison. His writings continued to be published posthumously. Claire Cross, 'Udall, John (c.1560–1592/3),' *ODNB*, http://www.oxforddnb.com/ view/article/27973, accessed 21 November 2009.

Although we are unable to trace the exact source on which Toulouse's comments are based, we do see in *Amendment of Life*, a publication of some of Udall's sermons, the emphasis upon 'reasons' which she is stressing. John Udall, *Amendment of Life: Three Sermons, Upon Actes 2. verses 37. 38 containing the true effect of the worde of God in the conversion of the goldly* (London: Thomas Man, 1584).

28 Jussely, '*Lectio Continua*,' pp. 25–32.

29 Richard Bernard was educated at Cambridge, proceeding MA in 1598. He was made vicar of Worksop, Nottinghamshire, in 1601. There his nonconformity led to his being deprived of his post. He formed a separatist congregation and continued to minister to them. In 1607 he was convinced by the archbishop of York to conform, and regained his post at Worksop. His outspokenness was then aimed at the separatists, and is reflected in his writings. His later years saw him summoned before the authorities again for nonconformity. He was 'an example of those godly protestants who practised as much nonconformity as they could within the established church.' He left a large number of written works, two of the most popular being *The Faithful Shepherd* and *The Isle of Man*. Richard L. Greaves, 'Bernard, Richard (bap.1568, d.1642),' *ODNB*, http://www.oxforddnb.com/view/article/2249, accessed 21 November 2009.

30 Lunt, 'Reinvention of Preaching,' pp. 49–63. Bernard's emphasis on application is seen in Chapter 10 of *Faithful Shepheard*. He begins it by stating: 'Application is a neerer bringing of the use delivered, after a more generall sort, in the third person, as spoken to persons absent; to the time, place, and persons then present: and uttered in the second person.' Richard Bernard, *The Faithfull Shepheard: Or, The Shepheards Faithfulnesse* (London: Arnold Hatfield, 1607), p. 71.

31 Lunt, 'Reinvention of Preaching,' p. 63.

preacher would not vary from a strict adherence to these three parts. Sometimes the sermon would be arranged under headings such as 'objections,' 'applications,' 'inferences,' and others. Lunt demonstrates that headings such as these were encouraged by Bernard and consistent with Perkins. Many of the different headings were merely variant ways of arranging material that established the doctrine – thus qualifying as 'reasons,' or applying the doctrine to the life of the hearers – thus qualifying as 'uses.'

Involved in the plain style preaching was a deliberate reaction against flowery speech, witticisms, ornate erudition, and what the Puritans considered inordinate self-aggrandizing rhetorical devices. These perceived negative preaching characteristics were what they accused the non-Puritans of employing and which came to be known as hallmarks of 'metaphysical' preaching. Perkins and others insisted that:

> Human wisdom must be concealed, both in the content of the sermon and in the language we use. The preaching of the Word is the testimony of God and the profession of the knowledge of Christ, not of human skill. Furthermore, the hearers ought not to ascribe their faith to the gifts of men, but to the power of God's word (*1 Cor. 2:1, 2, 5*). But this does not mean that pulpits will be marked by a lack of knowledge and education. The minister may, and in fact *must*, privately make free use of the general arts and of philosophy as well as employ a wide variety of reading while he is preparing his sermon. But in public exposition these should be hidden from the congregation, not ostentatiously paraded before them.[32]

A question pertinent to our study is, how do the sermons of John Flavel conform to these basic characteristics of the Puritan plain style preaching? A careful perusal of his sermons reveals a clear resemblance between the two. Flavel always establishes a doctrine, supports it, and then attempts to apply it to the hearer. Although not always titling the headings within his sermon 'reasons' and 'uses,' he certainly follows that general pattern.

He also, in his comments about the work of preaching, speaks directly to the issue of preaching plainly, and does so repeatedly.[33] Flavel argues from the example and teaching of the apostle Paul, the example of Christ, the dictates of prudence, and the experiences of men, to support the precept of preaching plainly. As an example of his thinking on this subject we present an extended quotation from the ninth sermon of his *Fountain of Life*.

> Jesus Christ, our great Prophet, hath manifested to us the will of God plainly and perspicuously … . And so (according to his own example) would he have his ministers preach, 'using great plainness of speech,' 2 Cor. iii. 12. and by

---

[32] Perkins, *Art of Prophesying*, p. 71.
[33] For a sampling of Flavel's comments on preaching plainly, see his *Works*, Vol. 1, pp. 32, 33, 38, 124; Vol. 2, pp. 235, 477; Vol. 4, pp. 9, 342; Vol. 6, p. 572.

manifestation of the truth, 'commending themselves to every man's conscience,' 1 Cor. iv. 2 ... . who ever spake more weightily, more logically, persuasively than that apostle, by whose pen Christ hath admonished us to beware of vain affections and swelling words of vanity? But he would have us stoop to the understandings of the meanest, and not give the people a comment darker than the text; he would have us rather pierce their ears, than tickle their fancies; and break their hearts than please their ears. Christ was a very plain preacher.[34]

Near the end of his life, he summarized succinctly his view of this issue when he wrote to an assembly of preachers: 'I will tell you, a crucified stile best suits the preachers of a crucified Christ.'[35]

Thus we observe that certain aspects of Perkins' plain style are indeed evident in Flavel's writings and sermons, namely the general arrangement of the sermon material along the lines of 'doctrine,' 'reasons,' and 'uses,' and the insistence upon plain speech. However, we ask the question: was this influence a prevailing factor in Flavel's mind as he prepared and presented sermons to the unconverted? And, how does this influence compare in magnitude with his awareness of the effectual call and its implications for sermonizing?

We have already noted the explicit comments by Flavel on the issue of preaching plainly. We note here also that he quotes and refers to both Perkins and Bernard. He is clearly aware of those two early proponents of the plain style of preaching and orders his sermons in a way that reflects the major components of that style.

Toulouse, in her examination of John Cotton's preaching, notes that Cotton worked within the general structure of Perkins' plain style, yet altered it because of overriding theological concerns.[36] Keeble, in his examination of Richard Baxter's sermons, observes that Puritan preachers varied in their details while remaining within a common form.[37] We suggest that Flavel exhibits a similar characteristic. The Puritan plain style of preaching, as advocated by Perkins, is evidently the framework within which Flavel prepares sermons. However, it is only the framework. The details of the sermon are formed and arranged on the basis of other factors.

It is our conclusion that the most important factor shaping Flavel's sermons to the unconverted, other than a general adoption of the plain style method and the aforementioned influence of Ramism, was his understanding of the effectual call. He was fully conscious of the steps of the effectual call – illumination, conviction and the renewing of the will which resulted in faith. He also was cognizant of the order of those steps. In addition, he was fully aware of what each step consisted of – in what faculty of the soul it was seated and what was happening in the soul during that step. He recognized that the

---

[34] Flavel, *Works*, Vol. 1, p. 124.
[35] Flavel, *Works*, Vol. 6, p. 572.
[36] Toulouse, *New England Sermons*, pp. 28–38.
[37] Keeble, 'Baxter's Preaching Ministry,' p. 552.

preacher was to play a part in seeing illumination, conviction and faith take place, and he knew God's part in each of those steps. He firmly believed all of this and he ordered his preaching for conversion accordingly.

Flavel's View of the Role of the Minister

Before showing Flavel's deliberate alignment of the matter and manner of his sermons in a way congruent with his view of the effectual call, it is important to understand his broader understanding of the role of the minister. It is from within that role that he preached, and he did so with a very definite understanding of what he believed to be God's design for the office of minister.

An important aspect of Flavel's thinking is his insistence that the office of minister is not a human invention, but is ordained by God. In *Method of Grace* he writes:

> The Lord Jesus thought it not sufficient to print the law of grace and the blessed terms of our union with him in the scriptures, ... but hath also set up and established a standing office in the church, to expound that law, inculcate the precepts, and urge the promises thereof; to woo and espouse souls to Christ, ... and this not simply from their own affections and compassions to miserable sinners, but also by virtue of their office and commission, whereby they are authorised and appointed to that work.[38]

The Quakers were present in Dartmouth in Flavel's day. Records of public letters between himself and a local Quaker, Clement Lake, show the interaction Flavel had with that sect.[39] One aspect of Quakerism was its dismissal of the idea that the ministerial office was intended for the present day. Flavel was strident in his refutation of that position. In *Fountain of Life* he says, 'for by ministers he now teacheth us, and to that intent hath fixed them in the church, by a firm constitution, there to remain to the end of the world, Matt. xxviii. 20.'[40] He then counters the arguments of those who used Joel 2:28–29 to suggest that the office of minister had become outdated and unnecessary. He finishes his argument by stating:

> ... God hath given ministers to the church for the work of conversion and edification, 'till we all come into the unity of the faith, to a perfect man,' Eph. iv. 11,12. So that when all the elect are converted, and all those converts become perfect men; when there is no error in judgment or practice, and no seducer to cause it, then, and not till then, will a gospel ministry be useless.[41]

---

[38] Flavel, *Works*, Vol. 2, p. 50.
[39] Flavel, *Flavel, the Quaker and the Crown.*
[40] Flavel, *Works*, Vol. 1, p. 125.
[41] Flavel, *Works*, Vol. 1, p. 126.

In four of his written works he refers to Ephesians 4:7–12 when discussing the office or work of the minister.[42] He sees in that Scripture passage a divine validation for the ministerial role. The office of minister, the person filling that office, and the special equipping of that person, are all seen as 'ascension gifts' from Christ to the church.

What then is the purpose of these 'ascension gifts?' Why does God design and provide the ministry? Flavel was certain that he knew what that purpose was, and that purpose became the mandate for anyone, including himself, who filled that role. In *Soul of Man* he states the purpose concisely: 'All Christ's ordinances are instituted, and his officers ordained for no other use or end but the salvation of souls.'[43] In *England's Duty* he places a letter to his fellow preachers as part of the introduction to the sermon series. In this letter he writes: 'Especially and above all, I humbly beseech you, that, having laid aside all designs of smaller importance, you would mind this one thing how you may gain to Christ the souls committed to you, to which all earthly things are to be postponed. This is the labour, this the work incumbent on us.'[44] Later in *England's Duty* he acknowledges that the building up of those who have believed is also within the purpose of the office. He writes: 'The whole frame of gospel-ordinances is declaredly set up for this purpose to bring men to Christ, and build them up in Christ.'[45] Nevertheless, bringing people to faith in Christ was his over-riding concern, and it was so because he saw it as the over-riding purpose of the ministry. We see this understanding of priority in his *Reply to Mr. Philip Cary's Solemn Call*. Flavel is answering the arguments of the Baptist Philip Cary. Flavel notes Cary's comments concerning the importance of baptism and retorts: 'Sir, I thought the most serious practice of a minister had been to preach Christ and salvation to the souls of men, and not to baptize.'[46]

Thus we see that Flavel's understanding of the role of a minister had a great effect upon his preaching. He saw himself as filling an office that had been given by God. The top priority of that office and those who held it was to 'gain to Christ' the souls committed to them.

The minister's paramount task is to lead people to faith in Christ. But, as we have seen in Flavel's discussion of the various steps in the effectual call, so we see again in his discussion of the minister's role, that the power of salvation rests only in God. Flavel makes it clear that the minister filling the role, and even the role itself, does not contain the power to be efficacious. In *Method of Grace* he writes: 'It [the word] derives not this efficacy from the instrument by

---

[42] Discussions of Eph. 4:7–12 in relation to the ministerial office can be found in *Works*, Vol. 1, pp.126, 510; Vol. 4, pp. 119, 124, 201; Vol. 5, p. 532; Vol. 6, p. 182.
[43] Flavel, *Works*, Vol. 2, p. 479.
[44] Flavel, *Works*, Vol. 4, p. 13.
[45] Flavel, *Works*, Vol. 4, p. 201.
[46] Flavel, *Works*, Vol. 6, p. 373.

Factors influencing Puritan Sermon Construction

which it is ministered: let their gifts and abilities be what they will, it is impossible that ever such effects should be produced from the strength of their natural or gracious abilities.'[47] Later he adds: 'It is our great honour, who are the ministers of the gospel, that we are ... workers together with God ... . But if his presence, blessing, and assistance be not with us, we are nothing, we can do nothing.'[48]

Flavel firmly believes that the drawing of people to saving faith is actually accomplished by the Spirit. In *Method of Grace* he explains: 'But all means and instruments employed in this work of bringing men to Christ, entirely depend upon the blessing and concurrence of the Spirit of God, without whom they signify nothing. How long may ministers preach, before one soul comes to Christ, except the Spirit co-operate in that work!'[49] In *England's Duty* he adds:

> From this spiritual presence of Christ, all gospel-ordinances derive all that power and efficacy which is by them exerted upon the souls of men, either in their conversion or edification. This power is not inherent in them, nor do they act as natural, necessary agents, but as instituted means, which are successful, or unsuccessful according as Christ by his Spirit co-operates with them.[50]

Later in the same work he emphasizes this. 'Ministers can but knock at the external door of the senses ... we can reason with sinners, and plead with their souls; but awaken them we cannot, open their hearts we cannot; we can only lodge our messages in their ears, and leave it to the Spirit of God to make it effectual.'[51]

Flavel understands that the minister's performance of his duties, including preaching, is offered to God to be used by him in the process of effectually calling people out of an unconverted state. The exercise of those duties is merely an instrument in the Spirit's hands. He explains:

> Ordinances are but as the sails of a ship; ministers as the seamen that manage those sails: the anchor may be weighed, the sails spread, but when all this is done, there is no sailing till a gale come. We preach and pray, and you hear; but there is no motion Christ-ward, until the Spirit of God ... blow upon them.[52]

This 'blowing upon the sails' by the Spirit cannot be demanded or forced. The Spirit is sovereign, ordaining means by which he will act, but not thereby making himself subservient to those means. Flavel emphasizes: 'Now the Spirit

---

[47] Flavel, *Works*, Vol. 2, p. 57.
[48] Flavel, *Works*, Vol. 2, p. 82.
[49] Flavel, *Works*, Vol. 2, p. 174.
[50] Flavel, *Works*, Vol. 4, p. 32.
[51] Flavel, *Works*, Vol. 4, p. 93.
[52] Flavel, *Works*, Vol. 4, p. 198.

of the Lord is a free agent, not tied to means, time or instruments.'[53] In *Method of Grace* Flavel discusses the sovereignty of the Spirit in bringing people to spiritual life.

> The work you see is the Lord's; when the Spirit of life comes upon their dead souls, they shall believe, and be made willing; till then, we do but plough upon the rocks: yet let not our hand slack in duty, pray for them, and plead with them you know not which prayer, or exhortation, the Spirit of life may breathe upon them.[54]

The exercise of ministerial duties, including preaching, is not efficacious in itself but is an instrument used by the sovereign Spirit.

Flavel often speaks of the role of preaching as that instrument which is highlighted in God's plan for the drawing of sinners to salvation. In *England's Duty* he poses the question: what are the instruments by which the Spirit knocks at the door of the sinner's soul? He answers: 'The word written or preached, but especially preached; to this Christ gives the preference above all other instruments employed about this work.'[55] In formulating the doctrinal point of the third sermon of *Method of Grace* Flavel states this belief succinctly, '[t]hat the preaching of the gospel by Christ's ambassadors, is the mean appointed for the reconciling and bringing home of sinners to Christ.'[56] Later, in the twenty-second sermon of the same collection, he states: 'The teachings of men are made effectual by the teachings of the Spirit; and the Spirit in his teachings will use and honour the ministry of man.'[57]

As previously noted in Part 2 of this study, Flavel's reference to the effectual call includes only the workings of the Spirit on the inner person. Whereas other theologians, Ames being an example, refer to the outer and inner offer of Christ as being under the category of 'calling,' Flavel describes calling differently, leaving the outer offer in a category different from the effectual call. This difference in expression does not, however, mean that Flavel saw little importance on the outer offer of the gospel. On the contrary, in its place it is as necessary as the inner call. The outer offer of the gospel is the means through which the inner effectual call takes place. In the eighth sermon of *England's Duty*, Flavel discusses these two facets using the motif of 'Christ's voice.' He writes:

> We will speak of the divers sorts and kinds of Christ's voices. I am here only concerned with two, viz. 1. His external. 2. His internal voice. 1. There is an external voice of Christ, which we may call his ministerial voice in the preaching

---

[53] Flavel, *Works*, Vol. 4, p. 198.
[54] Flavel, *Works*, Vol. 2, p. 99.
[55] Flavel, *Works*, Vol. 4, p. 94.
[56] Flavel, *Works*, Vol. 2, p. 50.
[57] Flavel, *Works*, Vol. 2, p. 308.

of the gospel ... . The external or ministerial voice of Christ is but the organ or instrument of conveying his internal and efficacious voice to the soul.[58]

Flavel sees the preaching of the gospel as the primary means which the Spirit uses in applying Christ to the sinner's soul. Thus, in Flavel's thinking, the preacher is privileged to participate with the Spirit in something that is as important as election or the atonement:

> Such a happy time [the time in which a person hears the voice of Christ in a saving way] may come, and when it doth, it will be a day for ever to be remembered; because then the first actual application of Christ will be made to your souls; without which all that the Father hath done in election, and the Son in his meritorious redemption, had been of no benefit or advantage to your souls. And, therefore, you shall find that this work of the Spirit stands betwixt both those works, and makes them both effectual to our salvation.[59]

In *Character of a Pastor* he makes this same point as he addresses his fellow preachers: 'The precious and immortal souls of men are committed to us; souls, about which God hath concerned his thoughts from eternity; for the purchase of which Christ hath shed his own blood; for the winning and espousing of which to himself, he hath put you into this office.'[60]

Therefore we see that Flavel's understanding of the role of the minister played a significant part in his preaching. He occupied a role that had been given to humankind by God, a role designed to 'gain people to Christ.' The elect had been chosen of God, and the Son of God had died to redeem them, but all of that would not profit them until the Spirit of God applied Christ to them personally. In this action God had chosen to use the efforts of ministers, especially their preaching. As they preached faithfully and wisely, the outer offer of the gospel went out to all people and the sermons would be used of the Spirit to bring life to the spiritually dead souls of the elect. It was with this understanding that Flavel formulated his sermons. It was within this theological context that he strove to arrange his sermons in a way consistent with what he understood to be God's method of effectually calling people to himself.

---

[58] Flavel, *Works*, Vol. 4, p. 170.
[59] Flavel, *Works*, Vol. 4, p. 185.
[60] Flavel, *Works*, Vol. 6, p. 584.

Chapter 8

Flavel's Alignment of the Matter and Manner of his Sermons with his View of the Effectual Call

The Importance of the Steps of the Effectual Call and their Order

We turn our attention now to Flavel's deliberate alignment of the matter and manner of his sermons with his view of the effectual call. In *Husbandry Spiritualized* Flavel sees the planning of work done by the knowledgeable farmer as an illustration of an effective preacher. 'Should husbandman employ ignoraut [*sic*] persons, that neither understand the rules nor proper seasons of husbandry; how much would such workmen damnify and prejudice him? He will not employ such to weed his fields, as know not wheat from tares; or to prune his trees, that think midsummer as fit for that work as December: much less will God.'[1] The preacher needs to be as aware of the 'rules and proper seasons' of salvation as the farmer is of husbandry.

Flavel does indeed count the understanding of the order of the steps in the effectual call as being important for the preacher to incorporate in his efforts. In *Method of Grace* he writes: 'The very order of the Spirit's work in bringing men to Christ, shews us to whom the invitation and offers of grace in Christ are to be made … . This [i.e. conviction preceding faith] being the due order of the Spirit's operation, the same order must be observed in gospel-offers and invitations.'[2] We will look at this comment in more detail later, but here we note Flavel's concern that the preacher be aware of how the Spirit brings people to Christ and order his preaching accordingly.

Shaping the Sermon in the Light of Illumination

We remember that illumination is the first step in Flavel's view of the effectual call. How did Flavel design his sermons in light of his understanding of illumination and its place in the effectual call? We find the answer to that question both in his direct comments upon preaching and in his sermons themselves.

Flavel speaks explicitly about the role of the minister in the step of illumination. He refers to the minister as the instrument by which God

---

[1] Flavel, *Works*, Vol. 5, p. 26.
[2] Flavel, *Works*, Vol. 2, p. 177.

illumines minds. Speaking of illumination by using the imagery of light, Flavel writes: 'It implies Christ to be the original and fountain of all that light which is ministerially diffused up and down the world by men. Ministers are but stars, which shine with a borrowed light from the sun.'³ Although we recognize his understanding of astronomy to be deficient, we nevertheless understand his point. Illumination comes from Christ, but Christ uses the ministers in this work.

This work involves appealing to people's reason. Sin's devastating effects upon human reason do not mean that the preacher avoids it. 'In a word, these relicts of reason and conscience in men, are fit handles to catch hold on, for the turning them about from Satan unto God.'⁴ Here we see Flavel speaking to other ministers and explaining that the preacher's task involves deliberately appealing to the reason of the unconverted in an attempt to 'turn them unto God.' Indeed, the assumption undergirding the whole of one of his treatises is that the preacher's role in illumination is to appeal to the thinking of the unconverted. He entitles that work '*The Reasonableness of Personal Reformation, and the Necessity of Conversion*.'⁵

We remember that Flavel considers the intellect to be the doorway to the soul. 'The mind is to the heart, as the door to the house: what comes in to the heart, comes in at the understanding, which is introductive to it.'⁶ He uses the imagery of the 'door to the soul' repeatedly and, as seen in Part 2 of this study, most instances pertain to the work of preaching to the hearer's mind. The 'door' through which Christ begins his entry into the life of an unconverted person is the mind. The entry through that door is the work of illumination. The part that the preacher plays in this step is the presentation of the pertinent biblical data to the understanding. It would be difficult to overemphasize the importance of this perspective to Flavel. Preaching for conversion involves helping the hearer to understand truth, and that attempt is the first responsibility of the preacher in cooperating with God in the effectual call.

In the introductory part of *Soul of Man*, Flavel explains what his aim is in the treatise. 'In the prosecution of these two propositions [the two doctrines he is proposing], many things will come to our hands, of great use in religion; which I shall labour to lay as clearly and orderly to the reader's understanding, and press as warmly upon his heart as I can.'⁷ We see here that, even though his ultimate aim includes reaching the reader's heart, he begins with the reader's understanding. This was always Flavel's way of preaching or writing. He preached to people's minds, trusting God the Spirit to use the sermon to produce illumination. 'Jesus Christ instrumentally opens the understandings of

---

³ Flavel, *Works*, Vol. 1, p. 123.
⁴ Flavel, *Works*, Vol. 6, p. 484.
⁵ Flavel, *Works*, Vol. 6, pp. 470–545; emphasis mine.
⁶ Flavel, *Works*, Vol. 1, p. 131.
⁷ Flavel, *Works*, Vol. 2, p. 494.

men by preaching of the gospel.'[8]

The truth that the preacher is to communicate, the gospel, is to be found in the Bible. Other authors and books could be quoted to support an argument or to illustrate a point but the starting point and basis of all sermons is to be the Bible alone. The Bible is the means appointed by God. In his *Exposition of the Assembly's Catechism* he explains this crucial component of the preacher's task:

> Quest. 89. How is the word made effectual to salvation?
>
> A. The Spirit of God maketh the reading, but especially the preaching of the word, an effectual means of convincing and converting sinners ...
>
> Q. 1. What mean you by the word?
>
> A. By the word is meant the word of God, consigned to writing in the books of the Old and New Testament; which though it be ministered by men, yet is no other than the very word of God, and as such to be received.[9]

Although helpless to affect spiritual comprehension in the hearer, the preacher does his part by communicating biblical information to the hearer. Flavel understands that conversion involved the person understanding salvation truths. There can be no proper moving of the person's emotions nor genuine decision of the person's will if there has not first been adequate instruction aimed at the person's mind. To fellow ministers, he says: 'prudence will direct us, to lay a good foundation of knowledge in our people's souls ... . Except you have a knowing people, you are not like to have a gracious people.'[10] In the sixth sermon of *England's Duty* Flavel addresses listeners who have not yet come to Christ. He tells them to think long and hard on what is being presented to them. He then comments, 'for want of this [thinking about the truth] the church is filled with hypocrites, and hell with inconsiderate and rash professors: the more we deliberate the better we shall conclude.'[11] Flavel's preaching for conversion is aimed first at the hearer's intellect.

White, in his *Puritan Rhetoric*, makes a similar observation about Puritan preaching. In an examination of the notes on preaching of Henry Dunster, first president of Harvard, White observes the 'sequential primacy of the intellect' in Puritan preaching. He writes: 'In those parts of the sermon preceding the Application, the speaker's duty was to "reach and inform the Understanding," with emotional evocation being avoided. Even in the Application, appeals to the emotions and to the Will were to be made only after the speaker had applied

---

[8] Flavel, *Works*, Vol. 1, p. 139.
[9] Flavel, *Works*, Vol. 6, p. 270.
[10] Flavel, *Works*, Vol. 6, pp. 570–71.
[11] Flavel, *Works*, Vol. 4, p. 138.

the doctrine to the Understanding.'[12] Flavel is a prime example of one who practised this 'sequential primacy of the intellect' in his preaching, and he did so because of his understanding of the effectual call.

We remember that in Flavel's view there are two crucial areas of biblical data which must be illuminated for the unconverted to move forward in the process of conversion. He refers to these areas as the 'disease' of sin and its 'remedy' in Christ. This summary informs the preacher of the needed content of his sermons. He must preach about the 'disease' and the 'remedy,' about the problem of sin and the solution to this problem which is found in Christ.

Bruce Shelley, in his interaction with Gerald Cragg's discussion of Puritan preaching, makes observations consistent with ours:

> The orbit in which Puritan preaching moved, then, as Gerald Cragg has indicated, was not 'a circle with one centre, but an ellipse with two foci.' There was the preoccupation with sin, involving the threat of damnation, and there was the offer of forgiveness and the assurance of God's grace. Man's plight and God's succor: these were the two great themes of Puritan pulpits.[13]

Cragg further added when commenting upon Bunyan that '[t]he mark of all his mature preaching was the ability to hold the two in equipoise.'[14]

In his *Character of a Pastor*, Flavel again emphasizes the content on which preachers must focus if they wish their listeners to enter into salvation. 'The greatest part of our congregations are poor, ignorant, and unregenerated people that know neither their misery nor their remedy. This will direct us to the great doctrines of conviction, regeneration, and faith.'[15] Flavel's understanding of the effectual call informed his choice of subject matter. He understood that for a person to experience salvation illumination had to take place regarding the the person's 'misery' and 'remedy.' Therefore, Flavel believed that if he wanted to preach in such a way that the hearer would be converted he must begin with those two areas of biblical material.

Flavel not only spoke about the necessity of preaching in this way, but examinations of his sermons and sermon series reveal that he consciously practised this approach to preaching. His sermons are replete with examples of speaking about the 'disease' and the 'remedy.' In some cases the doctrine extrapolated from the Scripture text gives rise to an entire sermon that deals primarily with one or the other. In such cases, however, Flavel often also draws the listener's attention to the other area of truth.

For example, the seventh sermon of *Fountain of Life* deals with John 17:19, 'And for their sakes I sanctify myself.' The doctrine Flavel articulates is '[t]hat

---

[12] White, *Puritan Rhetoric*, p. 21.
[13] Shelley, 'Preaching in early New England,' p. 27.
[14] Gerald Cragg, *Puritanism in the Period of the Great Persecution 1660–1699* (Cambridge: Cambridge University Press, 1957), p. 204.
[15] Flavel, *Works*, Vol. 6, p. 571.

Jesus Christ did dedicate, and wholly set himself apart to the work of a Mediator, for the elect's sake.'[16] The text of Scripture and the doctrine derived from it determine that the sermon will focus primarily upon the 'remedy.' The sermon goes into considerable detail concerning how Christ is the answer for the sinner's plight. Although that plight, the 'disease,' is not the main thrust of the sermon nevertheless it finds its way into the discussion. Flavel's second inference from the doctrine is: 'If Christ hath sanctified or consecrated himself for us; learn hence, what a horrid evil it is, to use Christ or his blood, as a common and unsanctified thing.'[17] He goes on to try to convince the hearers of one particular aspect of their dilemma in sin. By drawing this inference Flavel is making sure that both areas in which illumination for the unconverted is needed, the problem and the solution to the problem, are touched upon.

Flavel's determination to cover both the problem and the solution can be seen not only in individual sermons but also in the way he arranges sermons within a series. We find a clear example of this in *Method of Grace*. The twentieth to twenty-third sermons are presented as a section within the entire sermon series. Significantly, this section begins with sermons which emphasize the 'disease' and ends with sermons that explain the 'remedy.' The twentieth and twenty-first sermons dwell on Romans 7:9, 'For I was alive without the law once, but when the commandment came, sin revived, and I died.' In the twentieth sermon Flavel arrives at the doctrine '[t]hat unregenerate persons are generally full of groundless confidence and cheerfulness, though their condition be sad and miserable.'[18] The entire sermon explores the plight of the unconverted sinner. There is no explanation of the solution to this plight. In the twenty-first sermon Flavel draws a second doctrine from the same Scripture, '[t]hat there is a mighty efficacy in the word or law of God, to kill vain confidence, and quench carnal mirth in the hearts of men, when God sets it home upon their consciences.'[19] His discussion of the efficacy of the word of God reiterates the inability of the sinner to rectify his or her own spiritual situation. Thus the plight of the sinner is further explained. Even his 'Use for Exhortation' section of the sermon is developed in such a way that it further explores the plight of the unconverted. Not until the twenty-second sermon does the remedy for this plight begin to be explained.

In the twenty-second and twenty-third sermons Flavel turns to John 6:45, 'It is written in the prophets, And they shall be all taught of God. Every man therefore that hath heard, and hath learned of the Father, cometh unto me.' In the twenty-second sermon he begins to explore the remedy.[20] Approaching the subject from the foundation laid in the previous two sermons, he explores the

---

[16] Flavel, *Works*, Vol. 1, p. 97.
[17] Flavel, *Works*, Vol. 1, p. 103.
[18] Flavel, *Works*, Vol. 2, p. 288.
[19] Flavel, *Works*, Vol. 2, p. 295.
[20] Flavel, *Works*, Vol. 2, p. 306.

fact that God can overcome the effects of sin. He can illumine sinners and deliver them. There is a way for souls rendered impotent by sin to find relief. He states, 'The soul that is coming to Christ by faith, is taught of God, that though the case it is in be sad, yet it is not desperate and remediless.'[21] The remedy is in Christ and can be appropriated by faith. The twenty-third sermon focuses on 'the teachings of God' and their good effects in the one who has faith. Gone are the threats and presentations of judgment that appeared in the twentieth and twenty-first sermons. He has moved from the 'disease' and is now concentrating on the 'remedy.'

Other examples could be cited, but we will leave these as sufficient. Flavel deliberately preached in such a way as to explain the sinner's problem and solution. This was his duty, as he understood it. This was his participation in his listeners' experience of the effectual call.

The first step of the effectual call involves illumination concerning the human dilemma of sin. Flavel explains this dilemma using the Bible, addressing his sermons to the minds of the listeners, praying that the sovereign Spirit would be pleased to make it effectual, to move the listeners to conviction. For those already convinced of their need, he explains the remedy for sin in Christ. Likewise, he addresses those sermons also to the listeners' minds and waits for the work of the Spirit to move them further in the process of the effectual call, towards faith. In Table 2 (p. 188) we summarize the crucial elements of Flavel's understanding of the preacher's responsibility and aim in the first step of the effectual call. This summary incorporates what we presented earlier in Table 1 concerning the first step.

Table 2. Flavel's View of the Responsibility of the Preacher in the First Step of the Effectual Call

STEP IN EFFECTUAL CALL	FACULTY OF THE SOUL RELATED TO STEP	OCCURRENCE WITHIN THE SOUL	RESPONSIBILITY AND AIM OF THE PREACHER
ILLUMINATION	Intellect	• Intellect enabled by God to understand the 'disease' of sin • Intellect enabled by God to understand the 'remedy' in Christ	• To preach the biblical data relating to the 'disease' of sin • To preach the biblical data relating to the 'remedy' in Christ • To aim for hearers to understand and assent to this biblical data

---

[21] Flavel, *Works*, Vol. 2, p. 312.

Not all scholars have understood this Puritan emphasis upon preaching to the mind. Fedderson, for example, in his 'Elizabethan Sermon,' states that '[b]oth the preacher and the rhetorician attempt to inculcate belief by appealing to the understanding and to the will, but arousing the heart inevitably takes precedence over the informing of the mind.'[22] We suggest that, had he viewed the preaching to the affections through the grid provided by the Puritan view of the effectual call, he would not have posited the eventual preaching to the will in contradistinction to the preaching to the mind. The preaching to the heart does not 'take precedence' over the preaching to the mind, it merely follows in the sequence of the effectual call. We suggest that Flavel would never have discussed the eventual preaching to the will in the way that Fedderson does. Each step in the effectual call demands a certain emphasis and aim of preaching and thus is equally important in its own place. If we were to use Fedderson's terminology, we would say that the intellect 'takes precedence' over the will in the first step of the effectual call. The affections take precedence in the second step. The will 'takes precedence' in the third step.

McGrath touches upon this same sequential relationship between the intellect and will in the work of preaching when he writes: 'It was the preacher's task to be the chief means of God to … address the intellect in order to move the will.'[23] The will may be considered to have 'prominence,' as McGrath expresses it, but only when the foundational work within the intellect has occurred.[24] If we were to use McGrath's terminology after having understood the effectual call and its sequential steps we could just as easily refer to the 'prominence' of the intellect in the first step, or the 'prominence' of the affections in the second step, as we can to the 'prominence' of the will in the last step of the effectual call.

Thomas Lea, in his evaluation of Puritan preaching, which included Flavel's sermons, notes the same progression from intellect to heart. 'They [Puritan pastors] aimed at instructing the mind so that faith and obedience could become possible. They recognized that heat in the pulpit without light from Scripture would not change people. They rejected an appeal for religious feeling without knowledge or instruction.'[25] Lea's observation is entirely consistent with what we see in Flavel.

Shelley expresses the same findings in his examination of New England Puritanism. He states:

---

[22] Fedderson, 'Elizabethan Sermon,' pp. 48–49.
[23] McGrath, 'Puritans and the Human Will,' p. 248.
[24] McGrath speaks of 'the prominence, but not dominance, of the will's response to God's sovereign initiatives in the divine/human encounter.' This reference to the will's 'prominence' over against the mind and the affections is a crucial point of his thesis. 'Puritans and the Human Will,' p. 3.
[25] Lea, 'Hermeneutics,' p. 284.

They [ministers] wanted their people's faith to rest upon sound intellectual conviction. In converting sinners, said Samuel Ward, minister of Old South Church, we must 'imitate God.' We must 'first deal with their understandings; to raise the affections, without informing the mind, is a fruitless, unprofitable labour, and serves but to make zeal without knowledge.'[26]

Ward's words parallel Flavel's thinking.

It is important to emphasize that in Flavel's thinking the second and third steps of the effectual call depend upon the understanding which has taken place in the mind during the first step. No real conviction takes place without illumination having preceded it. Likewise no real bowing of the will takes place without illumination. The importance which Flavel places upon the involvement of the intellect as the precursor to the involvement of the affections and will cannot be overstressed. In the tenth sermon of *Fountain of Life* he states: 'There is little hope of any good to be done upon your souls, till you begin to go alone [get by yourself], and become thinking men and women: Here all conversion begins.'[27] Excitement of the affections which does not spring from the understanding is considered 'zeal without knowledge.' Decisions of the will which are not based upon careful understanding are 'rash' and 'unstable.'[28] No true conviction or true faith will result unless men and women first understand gospel truths.

In Part 2 of this study we discussed Flavel's view that intellectual assent to gospel truths, although not the essence of saving faith, is necessary for it. Flavel writes:

> The receiving of Christ, necessarily implies the assent of the understanding to the truths of Christ revealed in the gospel, ... which assent, though it be not in itself saving faith, yet is it the foundation and ground work of it; it being impossible the soul should receive, and fiducially embrace, what the mind doth not assent unto as true and infallibly certain.[29]

Flavel saw the preacher's role in illumination as one of aiming for the understanding of and assent to gospel truths, and he understood this aim to be foundational for the other steps of the effectual call. Flavel evidenced this understanding both in his explicit discussion of preaching and in the way he preached.

The preacher's task is not complete, however, when his listeners have understood and assented to necessary biblical teaching. For the person to come to Christ he or she must respond to the information with some degree of compunction, which involves both the mind and the emotions, and then bow

---

[26] Shelley, 'Preaching in early New England,' p. 25.
[27] Flavel, *Works*, Vol. 1, p. 141.
[28] Flavel, *Works*, Vol. 4, p. 144.
[29] Flavel, *Works*, Vol. 2, p. 106.

the will to Christ. In other words, conviction and the renewing of the will need to follow illumination. Flavel believes that just as the preacher plays a role in illumination, likewise he has a part in these remaining two steps of the effectual call.

In the Appendix to *England's Duty* Flavel discusses the work of the preacher which follows illumination:

> Ministers had need often to repeat, and inculcate the same truths to their hearers; for the work is not half done, when truth is got into the minds and consciences of men. Our work sticks at the heart, more than at the head; the understanding is many times opened, when the heart and will are locked, and fast barred against it: To open the passages betwixt the head and heart is the greatest difficulty; this is the work of Almighty power. There is knowledge enough in some men's heads to save them, but it hath not its liberty; restrained truth cannot do its office. It is much easier to convince the mind than to change the heart, or bow the will. The hardest part of the ministerial work is to preach truths into the hearts and lives of men. This makes the frequent inculcations of the same truths necessary and safe to the people's souls.[30]

Preaching the truth 'into the hearts and lives of men' is the minister's responsibility in the last two steps of the effectual call: conviction and the renewal of the will that results in faith. We will now turn our attention to how Flavel shaped his preaching in light of his understanding of conviction.

Shaping the Sermon in the Light of Conviction

We have seen that Flavel's understanding of the doctrine of conviction was specific and well defined. Conviction is the self-judgment in the conscience of a sinner which is due to the light of illumination. When self-judgment occurs in the conscience, conviction has taken place. This conviction gives rise to compunction, the emotional response of the soul to the truth. Flavel understood that the preacher should aim at seeing conviction and its corresponding compunction take place in the hearer. He should so shape his sermon that, for those who needed it, their conscience would condemn them and their emotions would be stirred accordingly.

An additional work of God upon the affections results in the person desiring Christ. This work must also be accomplished in order for saving faith to occur. Flavel understood that the preacher also bears a responsibility for this work upon the affections. We have chosen to consider Flavel's view of this responsibility when we turn our attention to the third and final step of the effectual call.

Saving conviction cannot be actually caused by the preacher or his sermon. The sermon is presented to the hearers in dependence upon the sovereign Spirit.

---

[30] Flavel, *Works*, Vol. 4, p. 292.

Nevertheless, Flavel understood that it is the preacher's responsibility to do that which the Spirit of God can and will use to produce conviction in the hearer. We see in both his explicit discussions of preaching and his own example that Flavel deliberately correlated his sermonizing to his understanding of conviction.

Although this second step of the effectual call involves the emotions, it should not be overlooked that it begins in the intellect. Flavel reckoned the conscience as being a function of the mind. He preached accordingly. The beginnings of conviction could occur only if the preacher aimed at helping the hearer 'self-judge' himself as guilty. When this conviction in the conscience was present, the preacher could aim at the hearer's affections, hoping that his efforts would be used by the Spirit to produce compunction in the hearer. Flavel viewed this progression as forming the divine plan for the effectual call and he ordered his preaching accordingly.

As mentioned in Chapter 2, Flavel's sermon series *England's Duty* was attested by witnesses as having resulted in large numbers of conversions. It is a meticulous eleven-sermon series built upon Revelation 3:20, 'Behold, I stand at the door and knock; if any man hear my voice, and open the door, I will come in to him, and sup with him, and he with me.' The emphasis of the individual sermons, as well as the arrangement of them in the series, gives us insight into Flavel's application of the doctrine of conviction to the work of preaching. We will examine the fifth sermon in that series in some detail, for in it he comments on the integration of preaching with the doctrine of conviction.

In this sermon Flavel arrives at the doctrine '[t]hat every conviction of conscience, and motion upon the affections of sinners, is a knock of Christ from heaven for entrance into their souls.'[31] Once again we observe that Flavel mentions conviction and the subsequent God-wrought change in sinner's affections as being related. In Flavel's mind it is the minister's role to aim deliberately for the hearer's conscience and emotions in his preaching. The preacher, in Flavel's view, is to cooperate with Christ 'knocking' at the sinner's soul. This cooperation means aiming to provoke guilt within the hearer's conscience. 'Every knock of Christ disturbs the sinful rest of the soul; it rouseth guilt in the conscience, and puts the inner man into great distress and trouble.'[32]

In the same sermon Flavel explains three ways in which the preached word is used by Christ to affect the conscience and heart of sinners. Here we see Flavel explaining how his understanding of conviction applies to the work of evangelistic preaching. We will follow his three-fold explanation.

First, Flavel states that Christ 'knocks by the particular convictions of the word upon the conscience ... . Ah, when the word shall come home by the Spirit's particular application, like that of Nathan's to David, *Thou art the man*;

---

[31] Flavel, *Works*, Vol. 4, p. 88.
[32] Flavel, *Works*, Vol. 4, p. 101.

then all the powers of the soul are roused and alarmed.'[33] Flavel purposes to be a 'Nathan' to every 'David' in the audience. He aims to confront them with their sin in such a way that conviction and compunction result. This means 'particular convictions' and 'particular applications.' Mere generalities will not suffice. It is his settled conclusion that significant conviction will most likely take place when the preaching is aimed at specific failures in the hearers' lives. He calls this aspect of preaching the 'particular applications.' The closer the application of the word to the situation of the individual, the more powerful the sermon is apt to be. In his treatise, *A Dissuasive*, he boldly talks to sailors about specific temptations they face. In the section dealing with prostitution, he justifies his frankness by comparing it to the errors of other preachers. 'Many men are wise in generals, but very vain ... in their practical inferences. They are good at speculation, but bunglers at application: but it is truth in the particulars, that, like an hot iron, pierces; and, oh! that you may find these to be such in your soul!'[34] Flavel strove not to be a 'bungler' as a preacher. He aimed at the particulars so that his hearers would experience true conviction.[35]

Second, Flavel points to the preacher's use of divine threats of judgment as a way to participate in Christ's knocking at the soul's door:

> Christ knocks in the word by its terrible comminations and awful threatenings, menacing the soul that opens not with eternal ruin; these are dreadful knocks: O sinner, saith Christ, wilt thou not open? Shall all the tenders of my grace made to thee be in vain? Know then that this thy obstinacy shall be thy damnation ... . Will you not come to me that you might have life? Then will I foretell what death you shall die, you shall die in your sins... . These are loud knocks of the word, terrible sounds, yet no more than needs to startle the drousy consciences of sinners.[36]

Flavel's *Works* are replete with examples of his preaching for compunction using 'particular applications' and 'awful threatening.' Sometimes he includes one or both in a single sermon. At other times he builds those elements into a sermon series. He also includes them in his treatises. We offer a few examples. In the application section of the second sermon of *Fountain of Life*, although the weight of the sermon lies elsewhere, Flavel directs 'Inference 5' to describing the woeful consequences of a sinner rejecting Christ.[37] In the

---

[33] Flavel, *Works*, Vol. 4, p. 95.
[34] Flavel, *Works*, Vol. 5, p. 315.
[35] In Sermon 8 of *England's Duty*, Flavel says: 'A general conviction of sin affects a man no more than the sight of a painted lion upon a sign post; but when a particular conviction is set home upon the conscience, by this special inward voice of Christ, sin is then like a living lion, meeting a man in the way, and roaring dreadfully upon him.' *Works*, Vol. 4, p. 181.
[36] Flavel, *Works*, Vol. 4, p. 95.
[37] Flavel, *Works*, Vol. 1, p. 50.

arrangement of *England's Duty* we see what appears to be a calculated aim for conviction built into the overall series. In the early sermons there are only small portions given over to conviction. These build up to the fourth sermon which includes a long section devoted to conviction. Then the entire fifth sermon is designed to produce conviction and includes an attempt by Flavel to belabour 'particular applications.' In his *Soul of Man*, Flavel works tirelessly for conviction in the section in which he explores the state of unbelieving souls after death. He derives the doctrine from 1 Peter 3:19 '[t]hat the souls or spirits of all men who die in a state of unbelief and disobedience, are immediately committed to the prison of hell, there to suffer the wrath of God due to their sins.'[38] He then spends many pages exploring the horror and awfulness of hell, with six propositions and nine inferences.

We could cite many more examples but these are sufficient to illustrate his attempts to participate in this work of the Spirit in conviction. This participation means at least two things. First, for those whose consciences are untroubled he attempts to provoke them to judge themselves as guilty before God and therefore to feel the necessary negative emotions. He understands this to be needed in the early stages of the effectual call. Secondly, however, he understands that others are further along in the process of effectual calling. Some illumination has occurred and they are already experiencing troubled consciences. He attempts to urge them to obey their consciences. Rather than trying to assuage their consciences, he tries in his preaching to build upon the troubles in their consciences and to move them to submit their wills to Christ; and he does all of this by deliberate use of the 'awful threatenings' of the word and 'particular applications.'

Third, Flavel explains in the fifth sermon of *England's Duty* that an additional way of Christ's knocking is through the gracious invitations of forgiveness and life. We will look in detail at this third way in a moment. Suffice it to say here that the gracious invitations are intended for those already experiencing conviction. Flavel deliberately tries to coordinate his sermon with his understanding of what conviction is and how it fits in the effectual call. 'And thus you see how the word preached becomes an instrument in the Spirit's hand, to open the door of a sinner's heart, at which it knocks by its mighty convictions, dreadful threats, and gracious invitations.'[39]

Flavel's comments in *Reasonableness and Necessity* have already been quoted in reference to his deliberate participation in the process of illumination. The passage also shows his conscious intent to cooperate with the Spirit of God in conviction:

> In a word, these relicts of reason and conscience in men, are fit handles to catch hold on, for the turning them about from Satan unto God. When Paul reasoned

---

[38] Flavel, *Works*, Vol. 3, p. 130.
[39] Flavel, *Works*, Vol. 4, p. 96.

with Felix, about temperance, righteousness, and judgment to come, his words laid hold upon these handles, and gave him such a shake, that the text saith, Felix trembled. And, O! that this might take hold of the reason and conscience of every profane reader, and produce some more excellent and lasting effect upon his soul.[40]

We emphasize that Flavel does not shrink from addressing the consciences of his hearers. On the contrary, he sees it as his duty to do so. He is fulfilling his role as a preacher in the process of the effectual call. He tries in his sermons to 'catch hold of the handle' of the hearers' consciences and thereby to turn them to God. In a prayer that he records concerning one of his treatises, and therefore indicative of how he prayed also for his sermons, he writes:

> O my God! thou that hast counted me faithful, and put me into the ministry; thou that hast inclined my heart to make this attempt, and encouraged me with hope, that it shall not be in vain to all them that read it, if it must be so to some; I beseech thee, lay the hand of thy Spirit upon the heart and hand of thy servant; strengthen and guide him in drawing the bow of the gospel, and directing the arrows, that they may strike the mark he aims at, even the conviction and conversion of lewd and dissolute sinners.[41]

Flavel deliberately aimed his sermons at his hearer's consciences, and he did so understanding where conviction lay in the process of a sinner being drawn to Christ.

In *Husbandry Spiritualized* Flavel draws an analogy between preaching for conviction and plowing a field. He finishes his discussion with an original poem that aptly reveals much about his view of conviction:

> There's skill in plowing, that the plowman knows,
> For if too shallow, or too deep he goes,
> The seed is either bury'd, or else may
> To rooks and daws become an easy prey.
> This, as a lively emblem, fitly may
> Describe the blessed Spirit's work and way:
> Whose work on souls, with this doth symbolize;
> Betwixt them both, thus the resemblance lies.
> Souls are the soil, conviction is the plow,
> God's workmen draw, the Spirit shews them how,
> He guides the work, and in good ground doth bless
> His workmen's pains, with sweet and fair success.
> The heart prepar'd, he scatters in the seed,
> Which in its season springs, no fowl nor weed
> Shall pick it up, or choak this springing corn,
> 'Till it be housed in the heavenly barn.

---

[40] Flavel, *Works*, Vol. 6, p. 484.
[41] Flavel, *Works*, Vol. 6 pp. 541–42.

> When thus the Spirit plows up the fallow ground,
> When with such fruits his servant's work is crown'd;
> Let all the friends of Christ, and souls say now,
> As they pass by the fields, God speed the plow.[42]

In Flavel's mind, sermons aimed at conviction are to the conversion of souls as plowing fallow ground is to the reaping of a harvest. The plowing is not the harvesting. It precedes it, yet it is absolutely necessary to it. Preaching aimed at affecting the hearer's conscience is not the act of leading them to Christ, but it is a necessary step in that direction. As the preacher holds onto the plow, guiding it towards the consciences of the hearers, he is participating with God in that step of the effectual call. This is how Flavel viewed and carried out his preaching.

In Table 3 we summarize the crucial elements of the preacher's responsibility and aim in the second step of the effectual call.

Table 3. Flavel's View of the Responsibility of the Preacher in the Second Step of the Effectual Call

STEP IN EFFECTUAL CALL	FACULTY OF THE SOUL RELATED TO STEP	OCCURRENCE WITHIN THE SOUL	RESPONSIBILITY AND AIM OF THE PREACHER
CONVICTION	Intellect (conscience) and Affections	• Conscience enabled by God to render proper 'self-judgment' upon the soul • Affections enabled by God to respond to self-judgment with compunction	• To apply the biblical data relating to sin and its consequences to the hearer in such a way that the hearer 'self-judges' himself/herself as guilty • To provoke and foster the negative emotions of compunction in the hearer • To aim for hearers to personally realize their guilt and feel compunction over sin

Placing the preaching to the affections in the context of the effectual call enables us to understand better the purpose of Puritan appeals to the emotions.

---

[42] Flavel, *Works*, Vol. 5, p. 66.

Much scholarly treatment of Puritan preaching has taken place without a proper understanding of this important context. Maddux, in his 'Ramist Rationality,' speaks to Puritan preaching in general and uses Flavel as one of his examples. The emphasis of Maddux's discussion is on asserting that Flavel put a strong focus on the hearer's emotions. We have noted in Part 2 of this study that at one point Maddux observes in Flavel a progression in verbal argumentation, from mind to affections to will. However, the inclusion of the human will is only a minor part of Maddux's argument. The majority of his discussion presents the affections as the ultimate target of the speaker. He quotes Flavel's 'Epistle to the Reader' in *Fountain of Life* to support his conclusion that Flavel was supremely focused on the affections of the hearer.[43] Apparently Maddux did not investigate the actual sermons of the treatise in as much depth as he did the opening epistle. Had he done so, an understanding of the will as the final goal of preaching would have emerged, as well as a realization that the effectual call was a driving force in Flavel's sermon preparation.

White, in *Puritan Rhetoric*, begins a list of the sermonic characteristics of New England Puritan preachers with '*(1) The ends of the sermon and the duties of the preacher: an incipient conflict.*'[44] He then attempts to explain the conflict between an esteem for the intellect and yet an apparent need for the emotions in preaching. The conflict is more apparent than real. White misses the sequential nature of the effectual call and thus the 'primacy' of the emotions during the step of conviction. We suggest that Flavel would not talk of any 'incipient conflict' between preaching to the intellect and preaching to the emotions. He would begin by preaching to the mind as he participated with God in the work of illumination, and focus more on exciting the emotions as he attempted to participate with God in the work of conviction.

As we saw, Flavel divides his hearers into three categories:

> The whole world is distinguishable into three classes, or sorts of persons; such as are far from Christ; such as are not far from Christ; and such as are in Christ. They that are in Christ have heartily received him. Such as are far from Christ, will not open to him; ... But those that are come under the preparatory workings of the Spirit, nigh to Christ, ... O what vehement desires! what strong pleas![45]

For those whom he perceives to be 'not far from Christ' he recognizes that their consciences are active and that they are experiencing a range of unpleasant human emotions. He seeks to participate in this work of conviction by working with, not against, those emotions.

Once this emotional response takes place in a person's life, Flavel attempts to be the instrument in God's hand to move them closer to faith. The progression of steps in the effectual call serves as the template which Flavel

---

[43] Maddux, 'Ramist Rationality,' pp. 176–78.
[44] White, *Puritan Rhetoric*, p. 15.
[45] Flavel, *Works*, Vol. 2, p. 30.

follows in arranging his preaching. He gives us a window into his thinking concerning arranging his preaching sequentially in correlation with the steps of the effectual call in the introduction to the second part of *Reasonableness and Necessity*. He writes: 'Reason and conscience having been shaming men out of their profaneness, in the former part of this discourse, free grace invites them to the life of holiness, and thereby to the life of blessedness in this second part.'[46] Flavel arranged the first part of his treatise with illumination and conviction in mind and the second part with the renewing of the will and faith in mind. Once again he shows us his clear understanding of the steps involved in the effectual call and the faculties of the soul in which the steps are transpiring, and he orders his writing and preaching accordingly.

As he continues this introduction, we see him cooperating with the work of God in the consciences of his audience:

> My charity commands me to suppose, that some readers stand, by this time convicted in their own consciences, both of the extreme wickedness, and the immediate danger of that profane course they have hitherto pursued, and persisted in … . It is hard to imagine, that so many close debates and reasoning, as you have heard in the former part, should not leave many of you under conviction and trouble of spirit. You see, your own reasons and consciences have condemned you; 'And if our heart condemn us, (saith the apostle) God is greater than our heart, and knoweth all things;' 1 John iii. 20. It is folly to imagine you shall be acquitted at God's immediate bar, who are already cast and condemned at your own privy sessions.[47]

From this point in the treatise Flavel begins aiming to move the convicted person towards desiring Christ and then choosing Christ. After conviction, he aims to usher the hearers into the renewal of their wills, resulting in faith. To that aspect of the preacher's participation in the effectual call we now turn.

Shaping the Sermon in the Light of the Renewing of the Will and Faith

Flavel understood that when a hearer was experiencing conviction the preacher should then be directing his words at that person's will. The effectual call was not yet complete. The hearer undergoing conviction had not yet exercised faith. The preacher's work was not yet finished:

> Christ himself stands betwixt these two doors [the understanding and the will], in the souls of many persons; he is got into their understandings and consciences,

---

[46] Flavel, *Works*, Vol. 6, p. 530.
[47] Flavel, *Works*, Vol. 6, p. 530.

they are convinced of the possibility and necessity of obtaining Jesus Christ, but still the door of their will is barred against him.[48]

In the third and final step of the effectual call the preacher's sermons must knock on the 'door of their will.'

How did Flavel do that? What did he see as being the preacher's role in this 'knocking'? There is no question that he understood his responsibility to include giving the invitation of salvation to the convicted hearer and pressing it upon his or her volition. We will examine this practice in detail in a moment. However, we also note that he was aware of the place of the hearer's emotions in the process of the effectual call and readily appealed to that faculty of the soul as well.

Preaching to the Affections to evoke a Desire for Christ

Flavel understands the affections as a faculty of the soul which can influence the will towards a decision. The will ultimately makes the decision, but the emotions of the soul can influence the will. This influence is especially significant when the emotions are moved by new understanding that has taken place in an illumined mind.

Flavel unashamedly and deliberately preached to the convicted hearer's emotions. At this point in the steps of the effectual call, however, he is focusing upon uplifting the desirability of Christ in the hearer's estimation. His conveying of the threats and judgments had its primary place in conviction. Now that he is aiming for saving faith he tries to preach in such a way that the hearer desires Christ and willingly moves towards Christ:

> In all the foregoing sermons I have been pleading and wooing for Christ. And as Abraham's servant, to win the damsel's consent, told her what treasures his master's son had, so I have laboured to shew you some part of the unsearchable riches of Christ, if by any means I might allure your hearts, and be instrumental to close the happy match betwixt him and you; and (as the apostle speaks) espouse you to one husband, even to Christ.[49]

By preaching in this way Flavel sees himself as being 'instrumental' in the renewing of the will. He sees himself as acting in tandem with the Spirit in the work of the effectual call.

Flavel applies the first sermon of *Fountain of Life* to ministers. 'It is our calling, as the Bridegroom's friends, to woo and win souls to Christ, to set him forth to the people as crucified among them, Gal. iii. 1. to present him in all his attractive excellencies, that all hearts may be ravished with his beauty, and

---

[48] Flavel, *Works*, Vol. 4, p. 89.
[49] Flavel, *Works*, Vol. 4, p. 268.

charmed into his arms by love.'⁵⁰ In the fifth sermon of *England's Duty*, Flavel is meditating upon the fact that the preached word of God is the primary instrument which God uses to 'rouse and open the hearts of sinners.' In his meditation he muses on the importance of the truths that present Christ as desirable as opposed to the truths that produce conviction.

> The Spirit knocks by the gracious invitations of the word, the sweet allurements and gracious insinuations of it; and without this, no heart would ever open to Christ. It is not the frosts and snow, storms and thunder, but the gentle distilling dews and cherishing sun-beams that make the flowers open in the spring ... . Now the gospel abounds with alluring invitations to draw the will, and open the heart of a sinner.⁵¹

More examples could be cited. The above will suffice to demonstrate that Flavel talked clearly about the responsibility of the preacher to evoke in the hearers' affections a desire for Christ.

Flavel not only spoke of this responsibility, but an examination of his sermons reveals that he practised it. Bruce Bickel, although apparently not realizing the relationship between this practice and Flavel's view of the effectual call, nevertheless draws attention to the twelfth sermon of *Method of Grace* as an example of how Puritan preachers laboured to extol Christ as desirable.⁵² In this sermon Flavel derives the doctrine '[t]hat Jesus Christ is the loveliest person souls can set their eyes upon.'⁵³ He then sets out numerous reasons why Christ is worthy of our desire, ending the sermon by asserting: 'If you see no beauty in Christ why you should desire him, it is because the god of this world has blinded your minds.'⁵⁴

In the sixth sermon of *England's Duty* we see Flavel giving most of the sermon to the attempt to create in the hearer a desire for Christ. The doctrine is '[t]hat Jesus Christ is an earnest suitor for union and communion with the souls of sinners.'⁵⁵ He gives nine demonstrations of Christ's desire for communion with the sinner, meditates especially upon the death of Christ for sinners, shows five ways that Christ's seeking of the sinner should evoke 'astonishment' in us, and then begins his various 'uses,' one of which is a four-part list of the advantages which will come to the one who believes in Christ. Almost the entire sermon is an attempt to cooperate with the Spirit of God in evoking in the hearer a desire for Christ.

Flavel purposefully preached to convicted hearers in such a way as to be used of the Spirit to evoke a desire for Christ in their hearts. He did so in a

---

[50] Flavel, *Works*, Vol. 1, p. 40.
[51] Flavel, *Works*, Vol. 4, p. 95.
[52] Bickel, *Light and Heat*, p.123.
[53] Flavel, *Works*, Vol. 2, p. 215.
[54] Flavel, *Works*, Vol. 2, p. 224.
[55] Flavel, *Works*, Vol. 4, p. 113.

deliberate way in conjunction with his understanding of the steps of the effectual call and the faculties of the soul in which those steps took place.

The Preacher's Emotions

It is significant to note that Flavel had much to say, not only about the hearers' emotions, but also about the place of the minister's own emotions in preaching. 'And as the warm rain is most refreshing, so when the word comes warmly, from the melting affections of the preacher, who imparts not only the gospel, but his own soul with it, 1 Thess ii. 8. this doth abundantly more good than that which drops coldly from the lips of the unaffected speaker.'[56] Flavel viewed his own emotions as a preacher to be a crucial part of the process of being used by the Spirit to evoke proper emotions in his hearers.

Not surprisingly his convictions on this subject are stated very clearly in his address to an assembly of ministers. In his *Character of a Pastor* he says: 'Believe it, sirs, all our reading, studying, and preaching, is but trifling hypocrisy, till the things read, studied, and preached, be felt in some degree upon our own hearts.'[57] He insists that the preacher's emotions be engaged with the sermon's message.

Later in the same address he explains in more detail why the preacher's emotions are important to the faithful execution of his role as an instrument of the salvation of his hearers:

> Ministerial prudence will shew us, of what great use our own affections are, for the moving of others; and will therefore advise us, That, as ever we expect the truths we preach should operate upon the hearts of others, we first labour to work them in upon our own hearts. Such a preacher was St. Paul; he preached with tears accompanying his words, Phil. iii. 18. An hot iron, though blunt, will pierce sooner than a cold one, though sharper.
>
> And why, my brethren, do we think, God hath commissionated us, rather than angels, to be his ambassadors? Was it not, among other reasons, for this? Because we having been under the same condemnation and misery ourselves, and felt both the terrors and consolations of the Spirit, (which angels experimentally know not), might thereby be enabled to treat with sinners more feelingly, and affectionately, in a way more accommodate to them, and therefore more apt to move and win them.[58]

Preaching for conversion should involve the preacher's as well as the hearers' emotions. This, in Flavel's view, was important because the emotions of the preacher could be used to spark the necessary emotions in the hearers and thus to see them move towards saving faith.

---

[56] Flavel, *Works*, Vol. 5, p. 77.
[57] Flavel, *Works*, Vol. 6, p. 568.
[58] Flavel, *Works*, Vol. 6, pp. 572–73.

Although the written records of Flavel's sermons cannot fully portray the emotion with which he delivered them, nevertheless we do see evidence that he preached with great emotion. One example will suffice. In the fourth sermon of *England's Duty*, after examining the subject of Christ's patience, Flavel takes aim at those whom he suspects are unconverted.

> The doctrine of Christ's patience puts a great and serious exhortation into my mouth this day, to press one of the greatest duties upon you that ever I pressed in the whole course of my ministry among you: And could I deliver this exhortation to you upon my knees, with tears of blood mingled with my words, might that prevail, I would surely do it.[59]

Over and over again we see examples like this of Flavel practising what he urged upon his fellow ministers. He preached with great emotion, being himself moved by the truth he was explaining and applying to his hearers.

Preaching in the Light of the Issue of Assent vs Consent

When considering Flavel's insistence on preaching to the hearer's will, it is helpful to remember his distinction between assent and consent. He made clear that mere assent was not synonymous with saving faith. Saving faith included intellectual assent, but involved more than that. On the basis of the mind's assent, the will would then consent to Christ. Some hearers lived between the two. They had accepted certain biblical propositions as true but had not bowed their wills to Christ.

The wise preacher was aware of this situation and arranged his sermons accordingly. He would preach certain points within a sermon, or perhaps entire sermons, to the person who stood between assent and consent. Flavel understood this to be one of the duties of a minister who wished to participate in the Spirit's effectual call of his hearers.

In *Method of Grace* we see an example of Flavel performing this duty. In the first paragraph of the ninth sermon, he explains that he has reached a turning point in the series. He is in essence explaining that what he had done in the first eight sermons was to work towards the hearer's assent. Now he is shifting his focus and will work towards their consent. In figurative language he explains his plan:

> The impetration of our redemption by Jesus Christ, being finished in the first part [in *Fountain of Life*], and the way and means by which Christ is applied to sinners in the foregoing part of this treatise; I am now orderly come to the general use of the whole; which in the first place shall be by way of exhortation, to invite and persuade all men to come to Christ; who, in all the former sermons, had been represented in his garments of salvation, red in his apparel, prepared and offered

---

[59] Flavel, *Works*, Vol. 4, p. 79.

to sinners as their all-sufficient and only remedy: And in the following sermons, will be represented in his perfumed garments coming out of his ivory palaces, Psalm xlv. 8. to allure and draw all men unto him.[60]

Flavel deliberately arranged the sermons in this series around the steps of the effectual call. At this point he is giving particular attention to moving hearers' wills to 'come to Christ.'

A submission of the will must take place in order for the person to 'come to Christ.' As we learned in our discussion of Flavel's view of saving faith, he saw faith as seated in both the intellect and the will, but primarily the will. The will is the faculty of the soul that exercises the 'justifying act' of faith. At this point in the effectual call a preacher's appeal to the intellect to understand would be appropriate, especially involving presentations of Christ as the answer to the sinner's predicament. However, these appeals to the intellect are not enough to see saving faith occur. Appeals must now be made to the will of the hearer. The will must bow to Christ.

How did Flavel preach in the Light of the Passive Aspect of the Third Step?

Here we remember that Flavel understood there to be a passive and an active aspect to the third step of the effectual call. The renewal of the will is passive, a divine work of the sovereign Spirit. But saving faith is active, an act of the hearer's will. How did Flavel preach with both aspects in mind?

Our exploration of his application of this awareness to his preaching can be accomplished by examining what he does with the hearer who is caught between conviction and faith and yet is not ready to move forward. He certainly recognizes that such people are in his audience. He has urged them to believe, but they have not yet reached the point at which they have exercised saving faith. They are not rejecting the gospel nor spurning the preaching, but neither are they evidencing saving faith. How does Flavel's theology inform his preaching to that portion of his audience?

Flavel believed that the Spirit was sovereign in his work of making the minister's preaching effectual. He viewed the sinner's will as powerless, without the Spirit's enabling, to exercise saving faith. At times we see him addressing the undecided listener in light of that theological framework – in light of the passive aspect of the third step in the effectual call.

In *Method of Grace* he addresses this kind of listener with the following advice:

> O that I might persuade you to set yourselves in his way, under the ordinances, and cry to him, 'Lord, that my eyes might be opened.' ... If you ask, What can we do to put ourselves into the way of the Spirit, in order to such a cure? ... I say, though you cannot do any thing, that can make the gospel effectual, yet the Spirit

---

[60] Flavel, *Works*, Vol. 2, p. 156.

of God can make those means you are capable of using effectual, if he please to concur with them … . Let me therefore advise, 1. That you diligently attend upon an able, faithful, and searching ministry … . 2. Satisfy not yourselves with hearing, but consider what you hear. Allow time to reflect upon what God hath spoken to you.[61]

We see here that Flavel tells this kind of listener to keep listening to the word of God being preached and to keep thinking about what he has heard. By doing so the listener will keep himself or herself in the place where the efficacious work of the Spirit can occur.

How did Flavel preach in the Light of the Active Aspect of the Third Step?

We turn now to how Flavel applied the active aspect of the third step to his preaching. Saving faith had to be exercised by the hearer for that person to enter into salvation. What was the preacher's role in this? He believed that the preacher was to urge the convicted hearer to believe. In so doing he invited the hearer to respond to Christ in faith. According to Flavel, this was an important aspect of preaching to the will.

It is appropriate here to emphasize that Flavel's proffering of 'gracious invitations' is directly and deliberately coordinated with the steps of the effectual call and with what he perceives to be taking place in the audience's lives. Only those experiencing conviction are ready for the offer. Flavel explains:

> The very order of the Spirit's work in bringing men to Christ, shews us to whom the invitation and offers of grace in Christ are to be made. For none are convinced of righteousness, i.e. of complete and perfect righteousness, which is in Christ for their justification, until first they be convinced of sin; and, consequently, no man will, or can come to Christ by faith, till convictions of sin have awakened and distressed him … . This being the due order of the Spirit's operation, the same order must be observed in gospel-offers and invitations.[62]

We have already referred to the fifth sermon of *England's Duty*, in which Flavel explains three ways in which the preached word is used by Christ to affect the conscience and heart of sinners. We have already discussed the first two – the 'awful threatenings' of the word and 'particular applications.' We now turn our attention to the third way mentioned in that sermon as we consider how his understanding of the final step in the effectual call influenced his preaching. 'And thus you see how the word preached becomes an instrument in the Spirit's hand, to open the door of a sinner's heart, at which it

---

[61] Flavel, *Works*, Vol. 1, pp. 140–41.
[62] Flavel, *Works*, Vol. 2, p. 177.

knocks by its mighty convictions, dreadful threats, *and gracious invitations.*'[63]

Flavel discusses 'gracious invitations' by mentioning several such invitations that are found in the Scripture. He says: 'Now the gospel abounds with alluring invitations to draw the will, and open the heart of the sinner.'[64] He quotes Matthew 11:28, Isaiah 55:1, and John 7:37 as examples. He then concludes: 'This is that oil of the gospel grace which makes the key turn so pleasantly and effectually amongst all the cross wards of man's will.'[65]

But how exactly does Flavel do this? What do his sermons look like when he is proffering the 'gracious invitation?' First of all, it should be noted that he has no one 'formula' or set wording or particular way in which to express the invitation. Often the text of Scripture that he is preaching from determines the vocabulary and imagery that he uses. Although the vocabulary changes the underlying meaning is the same. He is pressing the hearers towards saving faith. He is asking them to bow their will to Jesus Christ in dependence upon him for forgiveness and life. He is aiming for the hearers to exercise their wills in the 'justifying act' of saving faith.

Examples of Flavel proffering God's 'gracious invitations' abound throughout his *Works*. One appears in the seventh sermon of *Method of Grace*. Flavel applies the doctrinal point to unbelievers, 'who from hence must be pressed, as ever they expect to see the face of God in peace, to receive Jesus Christ as he is now offered to them in the gospel. This is the very scope of the gospel; I shall therefore press it by three great considerations.'[66] We note Flavel's repeated use of the word 'press.' The gospel, in Flavel's view, demands that unbelievers be 'pressed' to receive Jesus Christ. He, as a preacher, is informing his audience that he will begin doing so. He follows this statement with two lengthy 'motives' designed to move the hearers towards receiving Christ. He devotes almost a quarter of the sermon to this task.

We also note the language used of 'receiving Christ.' This is taken from the text of Scripture upon which the sermon is based, John 1:12, 'But as many as received him, to them gave he the power to become the sons of God.' Using this text Flavel urges his unbelieving hearers, presses them, to 'receive Christ.' Will they receive Christ, or not?

In the first sermon of *England's Duty*, he uses the picture of a rebel reaching out and receiving his pardon from a prince.[67] Flavel is pressing his hearers to reach out in faith and take what God is offering them. This is figurative language but it is aimed at the hearer's will. Will the hearer receive this offer from God, or not?

In the sixth sermon of the same series he calls for the listener to cast 'thy

---

[63] Flavel, *Works*, Vol. 4, p. 96; emphasis mine.
[64] Flavel, *Works*, Vol. 4, p. 95.
[65] Flavel, *Works*, Vol. 4, p. 96.
[66] Flavel, *Works*, Vol. 2, p. 135.
[67] Flavel, *Works*, Vol. 4, p. 28.

soul at Christ's *feet* with a hearty consent to all his terms.'[68] The image is somewhat different from that used in the first sermon, but the meaning is the same. Also, the intent to press the listener towards a decision involving his or her will is identical. Will the hearer cast himself at Christ's feet, or not?

In the ninth sermon of *Method of Grace*, after a long section in which he obviously works from conviction towards the hearer's will, Flavel issues a final challenge:

> But the last and principal thing is this: ... Hasten to Christ in the way of faith, and you shall find rest; and till then all the world cannot give you rest. The sooner you transact with Christ, in the way of faith, the sooner you shall be at peace and enter into his rest; for those that believe do now enter into rest ... . No sooner do you come to him, and roll your burden on him, receive him as he offers himself, but the soul feels itself eased on a sudden; 'being justified by faith, we have peace with God,' Rom. v. 1.[69]

In this one invitation he uses three different images: 'come to him,' 'roll your burden on him,' and 'receive him.' All are attempts to express the sinner's response of faith to Christ. All are pointed at evoking a response from the hearer. Will the hearer come to Christ? Will she roll her burden on him? Will he receive him?

For another example we find ourselves again examining the fifth sermon of *England's Duty*. After spending the first part of the sermon exploring the meaning and implications of the idea that Christ 'knocks at the door of the heart,' Flavel comes to a section of the sermon which he entitles 'Use, for Exhortation.' Here he begins his invitation, his pointed attempt to engage the hearer's will.

> Christ is now come near us in the gospel, 'Behold he stands at the door and knocks:' and I am here this day to demand your answer, and in his name I do solemnly demand it; what shall I return to him that sent me? What sayest thou, sinner? Wilt thou open to Christ, or wilt thou shut him out ... ?[70]

It is hard to imagine a more pointed and direct presentation. Flavel is practising what he believes to be the preacher's role in the third step of the effectual call. He is inviting and urging the hearer to believe.

But his invitation, his preaching to the will of his hearers in this fifth sermon, is not yet finished. Flavel follows his initial demand for a response with six 'motives' for opening their hearts to Christ. It is instructive for our understanding of his preaching to quote this section of the sermon at length. He continues preaching to the will of his hearers:

---

[68] Flavel, *Works*, Vol. 4, p. 138.
[69] Flavel, *Works*, Vol. 2, p. 171.
[70] Flavel, *Works*, Vol. 4, p. 109.

Once more, let me try the force of a few more arguments upon your hearts, and refute your vain pleas to the contrary; methinks, no heart should be able to resist such motives, and rational persuasions, as these following will be found to be.

Motive 1. You are in extreme need of Christ, you want him more than bread or breath ... . Now there is a plain, present absolute necessity lying upon every one of you to open your hearts to Christ, and that without delay ... .

Motive 2. The Lord Jesus is this day come nigh to every one of your souls ... . He is not only among you with respect to external means, but he is come into your understandings and consciences; yea, some motions of his you may feel upon your affections; there wants but a little more to make you eternally happy. O what would one effectual touch upon your wills be worth now! the head-work is done, but O that the heart-work were done too. You are almost saved, but to be almost saved, is to be wholly and eternally lost, if it go no further. It is a sad thing for a man that hath one foot in heaven to slide from thence into hell; it is sad to be shipwrecked at the harbour's mouth.

Motive 3. Jesus Christ hath unquestionable right to enter into, and possess every one of your souls: ...

Motive 4. Open the door to Christ, for a train of blessings and mercies come in with him; a troop of privileges follow him. In the same day and hour that Christ comes into thine heart, by a full consent and deliberate choice, a pardon comes with him of all the sins that ever thou committedst in thought, word, or action. Will such a pardon be welcome to thy soul? Then let Christ be welcome, ...

Motive 5. Christ this day solemnly demands entrance into thy soul; he begs thee to open to him, 2 Cor. v. 20. he commands thee to open unto him, 1 John iii. 23 ... . This demand is filed and recorded in heaven; at your own peril be it, if you shut the door against him: ...

Motive 6. And so I have done my master's errand, if you now refuse the knock of Christ at your hearts, he may never knock more; and where are you then? There is a knock which will be the last knock, a call which will be his last call; and after that no more knocks or calls, but an eternal silence as to any overture of mercy or grace.[71]

This extended quotation is one more example of how Flavel put into practice his understanding of the minister's role in the third step of the effectual call. The minister was to preach in such a way that he urged his hearers to respond to Christ. This response meant a bowing of the will to Christ in saving faith. Flavel preached with the understanding that his role was to be an instrument in the Spirit's hand to see that come about.

In some of his sermons, like the one just examined, Flavel devoted a significant portion of the sermon to the invitation. This emphasis was by design and was a result of his understanding of the effectual call. In order for the

---

[71] Flavel, *Works*, Vol. 4, pp. 108–11.

preacher to be faithful in his role of seeing people move from unbelief to saving faith he must work hard at helping the listener receive the proffered invitation.

The other sermons in *England's Duty* are worthy of our attention as examples of the extended effort that Flavel gave to the invitation portion of his sermons. We will briefly observe three of them. In the first of the series he urges his hearers to 'embrace the present gracious tender of Christ'[72] and then develops ten additional points aimed at moving the listener to a decision. Those points occupy approximately one third of the entire sermon. In the fourth sermon, after explaining his doctrinal point, he begins addressing the unconverted in his audience urging them to respond to Christ. He develops seven exhortations towards that end.[73] Again, this effort takes up approximately one third of the entire sermon. In the sixth sermon Flavel begins by extrapolating truths about Jesus Christ from the Scripture text. Then he moves to preaching to the hearer's will. 'In the next place, the point naturally leads us to an use of exhortation, to persuade sinners to embrace Christ's motion, subscribe his terms, and debate no more with him, but end the treaty in a cordial present consent; and so close up the match betwixt him and your souls.'[74] He then takes the rest of the sermon, almost forty per cent of it, to work towards that goal. Flavel's understanding of the preacher's role in the final step in the effectual call demanded that he give extended attention in his sermons to moving his hearers from conviction to faith.

At this point in our discussion it is appropriate to comment on the issue of the freedom of the will as it relates to preaching. As we have noticed in our discussion of Flavel's theology in Part 2 of this study, he saw no contradiction between the efficacy of God's Spirit in the effectual call and the human being's free will. This theological issue is particularly pertinent when the minister is preaching to the listener's will. An extended excerpt from the fifth sermon in *England's Duty* shows that Flavel was aware of this issue as he preached:

> Christ's knocking at the door of the heart implies the method of the Spirit in conversion to be congruous and agreeable to the nature of man's soul. Mark Christ's expression in the text; he doth not say, 'Behold I come to the door,' and break it open by violence; no, Christ makes no forcible entries, whether sinners will or not; he will come in by consent of the will, or not at all ... . There is a great difference between a friendly admission by consent, and a forcible entrance: ... in a friendly admission one knocks, and the other opens. Forcible actions are unsuitable to the nature of the will, whose motions are free and spontaneous; therefore it is said, Psalm cx. 3. 'Thy people shall be willing in the day of thy power.' It is true, the power of God is upon the will of man in the day of his conversion, or else it would never open to Christ; but yet that power of God doth not act against the freedom of man's will, by co-action and force; no, but of

---

[72] Flavel, *Works*, Vol. 4, p. 26.
[73] Flavel, *Works*, Vol. 4, pp. 79–86.
[74] Flavel, *Works*, Vol. 4, p. 131.

unwilling he makes it willing; taking away the obstinacy and reluctancy of the will by the efficacy of his grace, ... and so the door of the will still opens freely ... . It must be confessed, that when the day of God's power is come for the bringing home of a poor sinner to Christ, he cannot resist the power of God's Spirit, that draws him effectually: ... yet still the soul comes freely by the consent of his will; for this is the method of Christ in drawing souls to him. There is in the day of a sinner's conversion ... an offer made for the will ...[75]

This extended quotation describes how Flavel saw the preacher's offer fitting into the theological framework of the last step of the effectual call. The preacher would make the offer to the sinner. He would press the sinner to respond. The Spirit would then take that preached offer and use it as an instrument to turn an unwilling sinner into a person willing to bow to Christ. Flavel's sermons show that he laboured to participate in the process whereby the unwilling became willing. This is what it meant to preach with an aim of seeing saving faith occur in the hearers.

The third step of the effectual call involves the hearers' renewed affections beginning to desire Christ. It also involves the Spirit renewing the will of the hearer, and then the hearer exercising saving faith in Christ. Flavel preached to cooperate with the Spirit in helping the convicted hearer feel as much intensity of desire for Christ as was necessary to move them towards bowing their will to Christ. Thus he sought to evoke and encourage their desire for Christ with his preaching. He also urged convicted hearers to remain in the means which God normally used to produce a renewed will – the listening to preaching and the contemplation on what was taught. He then invited the hearers to believe in Christ and earnestly urged them to do so. He did all this realizing that the power to renew the will and draw a person to faith was not in himself or his sermons, but in the sovereign Spirit.

In Table 4 we summarize the crucial elements of Flavel's understanding of the preacher's responsibility and aim in the third step of the effectual call.

---

[75] Flavel, *Works*, Vol. 4, p. 92.

Table 4. Flavel's View of the Responsibility of the Preacher in the Third Step of the Effectual Call

STEP IN EFFECTUAL CALL	FACULTY OF THE SOUL RELATED TO STEP	OCCURRENCE WITHIN THE SOUL	RESPONSIBILITY AND AIM OF THE PREACHER
RENEWING OF WILL/FAITH	Affections and Will	• Affections enabled by God to begin to desire Christ • Will renewed by God, thus enabled to believe in Christ • Will exercises saving faith	• To provoke and foster a desire for Christ in the hearer • To encourage the hearer to remain in the instrumental means of renewal of will • To invite and urge the hearer to put his/her faith in Christ – to consent to Christ

Patrick Pang is an example of those scholars who have noted the Puritan preacher's aim upon the affections of his hearers without realizing the place of the affections in the effectual call. In 'A Study of Jonathan Edwards as a Pastor-Preacher,' he states that 'the Puritans recognized that the road to conversion lay in the appeal to a person's "affections."'[76] However, Pang provides no substantial examination of the Puritan theology of conversion. Therefore he says nothing concerning the points within the process of an unconverted person becoming converted at which it is appropriate for the preacher to aim for the hearer's affections, and those at which the hearer's intellect and will are the proper aim. Having the steps of the effectual call and the faculties of the soul in which they take place clearly in mind gave the Puritan preacher a 'divine roadmap' for preaching. An appeal to the hearers' affections was not random, isolated, or overemphasized. It was planned for both the second and third steps, had separate purposes in those steps, and was only important in that it was based upon a previous emphasis upon the intellect and a final emphasis upon the will. The preacher knew what faculties to aim for and when in the process to take that aim. Flavel possessed this clarity and applied it to his preaching.

Some scholars note the Puritan preaching to the will, but do not adequately address the role of the renewed affections in the process. McGrath is an example. With his focus upon the Puritan view of the interaction of the intellect and the will, he gives much less attention to the affections. Consequently he

---

[76] Patrick Pang, 'A Study of Jonathan Edwards as a Pastor-Preacher' (D.Min. diss., Fuller Theological Seminary, 1991), p. 115.

overlooks the role of the hearers' affections in the work of preaching. He states: 'It was the preacher's task to be the chief means of God to awaken sinners to their danger, to challenge them to a reasonable consideration of the gospel, and furthermore to address the intellect in order to move the will.'[77] Flavel would agree with that statement as far as it goes, but would insist that the preacher's task also includes the responsibility to address the affections – first in the step of conviction, and then in the final step as he seeks to evoke within the hearer a desire for Christ.

The scholarly literature which has looked at Puritan preaching has at times been inaccurate when interpreting the interplay between the Puritan predestinarian theology, which included a strong belief in the inability of the human will due to sin, and Puritan preaching to the will. We have observed in Part 2 of this study the explicit discussions of Flavel concerning the affect of sin on the human will and the reality of the act of faith being an act of the sinner. Likewise, we have shown in this part of the study Flavel's discussion of how he practised the work of preaching in light of that theology. A key to understanding Flavel's view of his responsibility in the third step of the effectual call is the realization that he saw a passive and an active aspect in the third step. Not all scholars have written with this in mind. Bickel, in his *Light and Heat*, exemplifies such scholars. He places great emphasis on the passive aspect of the renewal of the will but does not give equal attention to the active aspect of faith. Likewise he draws a correlation between the passive aspect and its implications for preaching but appears to argue against there being any implication for preaching from the active aspect. He writes: 'They [Puritan expositors] did not invite the hearers to do something with Christ, but they exhorted the audience to plead with God to do something with them.'[78] He continues:

> The Puritans understood God to be the only one who could convince, convict, convert, and comfort the sinner through the Word. The task of His messengers, then, was to communicate that Word by teaching and applying it to the conscience. Preachers were to declare God's mind and heart ... so that the Holy Spirit, who did not work in a vacuum, would use the revealed truth to enable a lost soul to come to Christ.[79]

Note that Bickel does not see the preacher's task as applying truth to the will – only the conscience is mentioned. Later, in an appendix, he contrasts in opposing columns characteristics of 'Puritan Evangelism' and 'Modern Finneyism.' In this contrast he lists as one point in the Puritan column: 'The preacher's role is to preach to the conscience.' Opposite this point in the other

---

[77] McGrath, 'Puritans and the Human Will,' p. 248.
[78] Bickel, *Light and Heat*, p. 138.
[79] Bickel, *Light and Heat*, p. 156.

column he lists: 'The preacher's role is to preach for decisions.'[80] The preaching to the will is absent from his description of Puritan preaching.

Our study of Flavel stands in sharp contrast to presentations of Puritan theology and preaching such as Bickel's. Flavel saw no conflict between preaching to the conscience and preaching to the will. Each had its own place in the process of seeing an unconverted person become converted. Neither was the sum total of evangelistic preaching. Both were needed, as was the preaching to the intellect. Bickel, and others like him, have overlooked this important aspect of Puritan preaching.

In Part 2 of this study we interacted with White's description of the final phase of the effectual call and pointed out that he has apparently omitted any reference to the active aspect of exercising saving faith. Consistent with that omission White's discussion of Puritan preaching is devoid of any acknowledgment of preaching to the will. Although he identifies the will as the faculty of the soul in which the final stage takes place, even referring to the 'ultimately crucial significance of the Will and Affections,'[81] he insists on downplaying any correlation of this significance with the Puritan preacher's responsibility. In light of our examination of Flavel's preaching theory and practice we see that portion of White's presentation as inaccurate.

Toulouse includes observations of Puritan preaching to the will but describes them as representing 'theological ambivalences' within the preacher. She sees a contradiction between the Puritan theology of human inability and the voluntaristic elements of Puritan sermons. She points to Perkins and his sermonic template as showing signs of this supposed contradiction. She writes: 'His [Perkins'] struggle between his sense of his audience's incapacity before God and the need to give them some freer say in matters of their salvation takes shape in the very sermon form he advocates.'[82] She sees the emphasis on the 'Uses' portion of the sermon as containing an inherent inconsistency with the Puritan doctrine of the effect of sin upon the hearers' wills.

Apparently Toulouse did not explore any Puritan writers who discussed the issue of the freedom of the will as Flavel did. Had she done so she would have seen that preaching to the will is not an inconsistency but a fulfilment of the preacher's responsibility. The preaching to the will is presented to the hearer in dependence upon the sovereign Spirit. If God so chooses he can use the sermon, even its urgings upon the audience's will, as an instrument to produce faith. The active aspect of the third step of the effectual call requires a corresponding sense of responsibility from the preacher but this does not represent a contradiction with what the preacher believes about the effect of sin on the hearer's will.

In Flavel's view, all the preacher's efforts at each step of the effectual call

---

[80] Bickel, *Light and Heat*, p. 186.
[81] White, *Puritan Rhetoric*, p. 21.
[82] Toulouse, *New England Sermons*, p. 20.

are merely 'instruments' to be used by a sovereign God. Just as the preacher's efforts to cooperate with God in the first and second steps of the effectual call do not imply that his sermon is effectual in and of itself to produce illumination and conviction, so too his effort to cooperate with God in the last step does not imply that his sermon is in itself effectual in producing the renewing of the will. Just as the preacher's efforts to be an instrument in illumination and conviction do not imply that the sin-damaged intellects and affections of the hearers are anything other than incapable, so too the preacher's effort to be an instrument in the renewal of the will does not imply that sin-damaged wills are anything other than incapable.

Other scholars have noted the practice among Puritan preachers of aiming for the will and have engaged with the question of such an aim's consistency with Puritan theology without seeing it as inconsistent. Fulcher examines Thomas Shepard's preaching and states:

> The exhortations of the minister, urging repentant sinners to heed the call of Christ, are consistent with Shepard's two-fold conception of vocation as both an inward word of the Spirit and an outward word of the minister. If there are those listening whom Christ has chosen to respond to this calling in his Word, the Spirit will minister to them, and they will be able to respond in an act of faith. This [is a] delicate balance between the purposes of Christ and the endeavours of his ministers.[83]

This description of the Puritan preacher's task as a 'delicate balance' is more consistent with Flavel's view and practice than the 'theological ambivalence' proposed by Toulouse. The passive and active aspects of the third step of the effectual call did indeed introduce a balancing act for the preacher, but it was attempted without any sense of theological inconsistency.

We reiterate that in most scholarly studies of Puritan preaching the context of the effectual call has not been understood or clearly explicated. Our exposition of Flavel's view of the effectual call reveals the purposes and aims of his preaching to the human intellect, affections and will. The effectual call becomes the grid through which his preaching for conversion is understood.

Summary

In Table 5 we combine all the cogent elements of each step of the effectual call and show the corresponding aims and responsibilities of the preacher.

---

[83] Fulcher, 'Puritan Piety,' p. 197.

Table 5. Flavel's View of the Responsibilities of the Preacher throughout the Effectual Call

STEP IN EFFECTUAL CALL	FACULTY OF THE SOUL RELATED TO STEP	OCCURRENCE WITHIN THE SOUL	RESPONSIBILITY AND AIM OF THE PREACHER
ILLUMINATION	Intellect	• Intellect is enabled by God to understand the 'disease' of sin • Intellect is enabled by God to understand the 'remedy' in Christ	• To preach the biblical data relating to the 'disease' of sin • To preach the biblical data relating to the 'remedy' in Christ • To aim for the hearer to understand and assent to this biblical data
CONVICTION	Intellect (conscience) and Affections	• Conscience enabled by God to render proper 'self-judgment' upon the soul • Affections enabled by God to respond to self-judgment with compunction	• To apply the biblical data relating to sin and its consequences in such a way that the hearer 'self-judges' himself/herself as guilty • To provoke and foster the negative emotions of compunction in the hearer • To aim for the hearer to personally realize their guilt and feel compunction over sin
RENEWING OF WILL/FAITH	Affections and Will	• Affections enabled by God to desire Christ • Will renewed by God, thus enabled to believe in Christ • Will exercises saving faith	• To provoke and foster a desire for Christ in the hearer • To encourage the hearer to remain in the instrumental means of renewal of the will • To invite and urge the hearer to put his/her faith in Christ – to consent to Christ

PART FOUR

Conclusion

Chapter 9

Summary and Conclusion of this Study

This study has explored the relationship between the theology believed by late seventeenth-century English Puritan preachers and the manner and matter of their evangelistic preaching. The particular aspect of Puritan theology which we focused upon is the effectual call, with two related areas of theology also being investigated, the human constitution and the doctrine of sin. We have shown that within the generally accepted homiletic framework of the Puritan tradition it was the preacher's view of the effectual call that most influenced his preaching for conversion. We used the writings of one particular late seventeenth-century English Puritan, John Flavel, as the object of our investigation.

In a review of numerous studies of Puritan preaching we noted that none have drawn the correlation between the particular view the Puritans held of the effectual call and the manner and matter of their preaching. Some studies investigate Puritan preaching but do not explain that preaching upon theological grounds. Other studies propose reasons for the distinctive organization and delivery of Puritan sermons, but their proposals do not include the theological framework within which the Puritan preacher carried out his work. Other scholars do indeed suggest theological reasons for the construction and delivery of Puritan sermons yet, with two important exceptions, none include the effectual call in their theories. Those two exceptions, Perry Miller and John Fulcher, left certain details of Puritan theology unexplored and arrived at certain conclusions which are inconsistent with our findings. It is noteworthy that very little scholarship since Miller has directly addressed the relationship between the Puritan view of the effectual call and the formation of the Puritan sermon. Our study addressed this neglected area of academic inquiry.

Certain characteristics of Puritan sermons have been observed by numerous scholars. Such characteristics include lengthy explanations about Christ and his death, an emphasis on the love of God, the use of emotion, the use of threats of divine judgment, the weighting of the sermon on the side of application, and intentional movement towards a point of decision. In large part these observations have been made without corresponding suggestions that the Puritan preacher possessed a comprehensive theological framework which gave purpose and coherence to these characteristics. We have shown that it was his theology of how a person moves from an unregenerate to a regenerate state that provided this framework and gave rise to these characteristics.

Scholars of Puritanism have consistently noted the Puritan view that the human soul includes intellect, affections, and will. This view has been called their 'faculty psychology.' The Puritan preacher, it has been observed, was aware of these three 'faculties of the soul' and their interaction with each other. Some scholars have further noted that the Puritan preacher aimed for these various faculties in his preaching. However, no study has shown the correlation between the preacher's concern with those three faculties of the hearer's soul and a theological understanding of how the hearer is moved from an unregenerate to a regenerate state.

We explored the theological foundation of the place of the faculties of the soul in Puritan preaching. We described the theological grid by which the various faculties of the soul were understood and the theological understanding of how the faculties of the soul are involved in the process by which an unbelieving person becomes a believer. We also showed that the Puritan preacher had this theological understanding in mind as he formulated and presented his sermons to hearers he believed to be unregenerate. Our study has shown that, in the case of Flavel, the integration of an understanding of these three faculties with a theology of the effectual call gave direction to the preacher in his sermon construction and delivery.

We assert that this correlation between theology and homiletics is a crucial part of understanding late seventeenth-century Puritan preaching. Our study was designed to investigate this correlation. We also assert that this correlation and its importance can be clearly seen in Flavel's sermons and writings.

We noted Gavin McGrath's observation of 'the rather startling absence of studies on puritan theology which pay attention to the theology of particular individuals. It seems that in the attempt to "discover" the pulse of seventeenth century Puritanism many of the finer details (which help constitute the whole) are forfeited for the sake of the "broad picture."'[1] We deliberately chose to focus on the writings of one Puritan, intending by so doing to contribute to the 'finer details' of the portrait of seventeenth-century Puritanism as well as to a fuller understanding of the relationship between Puritan theology and preaching.

Flavel is the ideal subject for this study. We have shown that he was an influential member of the Puritan movement. We noted and concurred with John Smith's comment when he was observing the use of Flavel by Jonathan Edwards: 'The name of Flavel does not occur in historical studies of seventeenth-century Puritanism as often as it should, and he is less well known than some contemporaries who wrote less and whose works were less influential among the common people.'[2] It has been our intent in this study to

---

[1] McGrath, 'Puritans and the Human Will,' p. 66.
[2] Edwards, *Works*, Vol. 2, pp. 60–61.

address the lack of scholarly inquiry into this important seventeenth-century figure.

We have demonstrated that Flavel's influence can be seen in comments made about him by his contemporaries, both those sympathetic to and opposed to nonconformity. His impact is also noted in the influence which his written works had on contemporaries and on succeeding generations. This influence was widespread, including lay people as well as theologians and ministers, some of whom were very influential figures themselves. This influence was manifest in both England and the New World. We have also noted that he was particularly purposeful and earnest in evangelism and that he met with a large measure of success in that work. We have shown that he consciously possessed a well-defined view of the effectual call and deliberately applied that view to preaching.

There were undoubtedly other preachers in late seventeenth-century England who possessed a similar theology to Flavel's and who deliberately applied that theology to their work of preaching. However, his stature among his contemporaries and the significant influence which his *Works* had on both continents, plus the fact that his *Works* are available today for our examination, sets Flavel apart as a particularly appropriate subject of our study.

In an examination of his writings we observed that several of his treatises were written with an explicitly evangelistic purpose. Other treatises were written primarily to believers and yet included material designed for those who were unconverted. All Flavel's sermons were prepared and delivered with the understanding that some in the audience were yet unregenerate.

We began our investigation of Flavel's theology by examining his view of the human constitution. The aspects of this branch of theology which are salient to our study concern the faculties of the soul and how those faculties interact within the soul – Flavel's 'faculty psychology.' We observed that Flavel saw the human soul as possessing three faculties: the intellect, the will, and the affections. He described the intellect's functions as being four: the power of discernment, the role of directing the soul's will, the thinking processes, and the conscience. The will is that faculty of the soul which rules and decides. It rules both the body and the other faculties, yet not without some limitations. The affections equip the soul for love for God and happiness in him.

We summarized Flavel's view of the relationship between the faculties in this way: the will rules, the mind guides, and the affections interact. The will rules the soul, commanding the mind and affections, albeit with a few specified exceptions. The mind guides the soul, directing the will and affections. The mind's influence on the will is great, but the will retains its liberty and is not forced by the mind, nor necessitated by the mind's conclusions, to any choice. The affections interact with both mind and will. Although the soul's mind and will have the greater influence on the affections, rather than vice versa, Flavel acknowledged that the affections can influence the other faculties, especially when the soul is undergoing the divine work of conviction.

We continued our investigation of Flavel's theology by examining his understanding of the doctrine of sin. We showed that his theology presents sin as having affected all three faculties of the soul. The sinful human intellect is not able to perceive the saving truths of the gospel, nor is it able to perceive Christ himself in a saving way. The soul's affections have been disordered by sin. The human heart now loves that which is wrong and does not desire that which is right. The soul's will has been rendered unable to choose Christ, and is, because of sin, actually set against Christ. Since the will is the primary seat of faith, this effect of sin on the will renders the sinner unable to come to saving faith. However, as the Holy Spirit moves an individual sinner through the steps of the effectual call that person's intellect is enabled to understand, his or her will is renewed and enabled to believe, and the affections are enabled to interact with the intellect and will according to God's original design.

We should emphasize that Flavel's understanding of the various faculties of the soul, and of the effect of sin on those faculties, was a vital component of his view of the effectual call. His view of the human constitution provided him with the ability to construct a coherent understanding of the process through which a person goes when he or she is being drawn from an unregenerate into a regenerate state. The faculty psychology of Flavel was correlated with his view of the effectual call. Each step in the effectual call was related to certain faculties. Also, his view of how sin had debilitated, and how effectual grace would renovate, each faculty contributed to the complete picture of the effectual call.

Our study has also shown that this coherent understanding was then applied to the task of preaching. Scholarly studies of Puritanism have observed that Puritan faculty psychology influenced their preaching. What has not been demonstrated until now is that it is the Puritan view of the effectual call that completes the picture and answers the question of why they preached as they did to the mind, to the affections, and to the will.

Our investigation of Flavel's theology, after examining the human constitution and the doctrine of sin, then focused on the effectual call. We determined that Flavel understood the effectual call to consist of three steps: illumination, conviction, and the renewing of the will resulting in faith.

The first step of the effectual call is illumination. The seat of illumination is the intellect. Illumination is the efficacious work of God in which he enables the individual to understand in his mind the truths about his own problem of sin and to comprehend the solution in Christ to that problem. Apart from this work of God the sinful human being is unable savingly to understand those truths. God's word and his Spirit are the two means God uses to do this work. Using those two means he brings about an actual change within the human mind which enables it to comprehend what it was previously unable to savingly understand. True illumination always results in conviction which then leads to the renewing of the will and faith.

Flavel views conviction as the second step of the effectual call. This is an efficacious act of God upon the mind and the affections. It is not possible for a person to arrive at saving faith without having first experienced conviction. The conscience, which is one of the powers of the mind, is the seat of conviction. Conviction is the work of God in which he enables the conscience to respond in self-judgment to the truths which the mind has understood. Conviction produces an effect in the emotions which is called compunction. Compunction is not merely a natural response but a result of the Spirit working on the affections. Both the intellect and the affections are wrought upon by the Spirit of God in the step of conviction. Using the Scripture and the Spirit as means, God overcomes all natural and satanic opposition to conviction. Conviction is not an end in itself but a step between illumination and faith.

There is a condition in some people in which illumination and conviction appear to have taken place, but it is shown to be only a partial conviction by the fact that their will is ultimately not bowed to Christ. True conviction always leads to the renewing of the will and faith.

The renewing of the will is the final step of the effectual call. This step is an efficacious act of God upon the affections and the will. Following conviction, in which the person's affections have been enlivened to experience compunction, the same enlivened affections now begin to desire Christ. Thus the person's illumined mind and enlivened affections now exert influence upon the will. There is a passive and an active aspect to the third step of the effectual call. The person is passive in the renewing of his will but active in exercising faith. The result of the renewing of the will is always saving faith. Faith is understood to be a human act even though it is attributed to divine grace. The nature and dignity of the human will is not violated in regard to its exercise of faith, even though God acts upon the will in its renewal. There are aspects to faith that involve the intellect and the affections, and yet the will is the primary faculty of the soul involved in 'the justifying act' of faith. In that justifying act the person trusts in Christ and Christ's substitution and righteousness. The primary object of saving faith is Christ himself. Faith itself is not meritorious. It is the instrument by which the person appropriates Christ personally and thus is justified through the merits of Christ. It is an impossibility for a person whose will has been renewed to fail to believe. The exercise of saving faith is absolutely necessary for a person to enter salvation. Until a person acts with his or her will to trust Christ that person is not justified before God. No matter how much illumination or conviction seems to have taken place within the soul of an individual, unless the person's will is renewed and exercises faith in Christ that person has not yet entered into salvation. Providence, in addition to God's word, is used by God's Spirit to bring about this consent of the will to Christ.

Having explored and delineated Flavel's theology, we proceeded to demonstrate his deliberate correlation of his sermon preparation and delivery with his understanding of the effectual call. He was fully aware of the three steps of the effectual call and their order. He entertained no doubts concerning which faculty of the soul each step occurred in and what was happening in the soul during that step. The divine efficacy of each step did not mean an absence of responsibility on the preacher's part. The preacher bore a responsibility to participate with the Spirit in seeing illumination, conviction, and faith take place.

Flavel's understanding of the effectual call determined his choice of subject matter and his starting point. He understood that, for a person to experience salvation, illumination had to take place regarding the subject matter of the 'disease' of sin and its 'remedy.' Therefore, Flavel believed that if he wanted to preach in such a way that the hearer would be converted he must begin with those two areas of biblical data, and he must begin by addressing the mind – pressing for a thorough and new understanding to occur. Although his sermon did not have the inherent power to create the needed illumination, it was the instrument with which the sovereign Spirit could do so.

Flavel understood the first step of the effectual call to involve illumination concerning the human dilemma of sin. He understood the preacher's responsibility to be that of aiming for the hearer's intellect and an assent to essential gospel truths. As the preacher, his role was to explain the hearer's problem of sin by using the Bible, and then to leave the sermons in the minds of the listeners, praying that the sovereign Spirit would be pleased to make them effectual. For those already convinced of their need, he participated in illumination by explaining the remedy for sin that is found in Christ. He left those sermons also in the listeners' minds, in dependence on the work of the Spirit to move them on further in the process of the effectual call.

Flavel understood the second step of the effectual call, conviction, to involve the exercising of self-judgment in which the hearers condemn themselves as guilty in the sight of God. This self-judgment would then lead to compunction, an emotional response to being guilty. Flavel understood his responsibility as a preacher to be that of cooperating with the Spirit in helping the convicted hearer feel as much intensity of negative emotion as was necessary to move them towards faith. Therefore, he aimed for the hearer's conscience and affections and sought to evoke and encourage the emotions of compunction with his preaching.

Flavel's understanding of the effectual call also determined his ending point in evangelistic preaching. He understood that for people to experience salvation their wills must be renewed and they must exercise the 'justifying act' of faith. Therefore Flavel believed that if he wanted to preach in such a way that the hearer would be converted he must ultimately address the hearer's will, pressing the person to exercise saving faith. This pressing for faith, however, would be based upon the assumption that the hearer had already experienced illumination and conviction.

In the third step Flavel would address the convicted hearer by lifting up the desirability of Christ. This deliberate aim at the enlivened affections of the hearer was meant to evoke a desire for Christ which would then influence the hearer's will.

Flavel's appeal to the will of the hearer was undertaken with the realization that there was both a passive and an active aspect to the third step of the effectual call. The renewal of the will itself did not have an active aspect to it. The hearer was a passive recipient of the gracious work of God in renewing his will. However, the exercising of faith was the hearer's act. Flavel understood the preacher's role to be to urge convicted sinners to remain under the sound of preaching and to think about what they had heard. Perhaps, Flavel told them, by remaining in those means they would become the subject of the renewing work of God. However, this was not the end of the preacher's responsibility. The preacher also had a role in seeing the hearer actively exercise faith. In this, the preacher pressed the convicted hearers to bow their wills to Christ and trust him. Flavel evidenced by both his example and his instruction to preachers that faithful preaching for conversion must include a pressing of the hearer's will to believe.

Flavel did not see this appeal to the will as being inconsistent with the rest of his predestinarian theology, nor did he see in the third step of the effectual call any violation of the liberty and dignity of the human will. The preacher would make the gospel offer to the sinner. The Spirit would then take that preached offer and use it as an instrument to turn an unwilling sinner into a person willing to bow to Christ. Flavel saw himself in this way participating in the process whereby the convicted sinner moved towards saving faith.

The effectual call thus provided the Puritan preacher concerned with the conversion of his hearers with a 'divine roadmap' for his sermons. Although the preacher operated within the generally accepted Puritan homiletical framework, which included such factors as Ramism and the Perkins 'plain style' of preaching, it was his understanding of the effectual call which on a conscious level most influenced his sermon preparation and delivery. Illumination, conviction, and faith; the intellect, the affections, and the will. The Puritan preacher integrated the effectual call with his faculty psychology and the result was a template which guided his sermonizing. He began his sermon aiming for the hearers' minds and selected his content on the basis of what gospel truths were needed for conviction and faith. He then aimed for the affections and deliberately attempted to participate in provoking the negative emotions of compunction. Seeing convicted sinners, he then attempted to ignite within them a desire for Christ. And finally he pressed their wills to exercise saving faith. Each step, based upon where in the soul it was taking place and what exactly was occurring, called for a corresponding task on the part of the preacher. Flavel understood this integration of theology and preaching and deliberately pursued the accomplishment of those tasks.

This study is a contribution to the scholarly investigation of both Puritan preaching and Puritan theology. Our findings concerning Flavel's view of the human constitution, sin, and the effectual call have been compared to the views of his Puritan theological predecessors and some contemporaries. We have also interacted with other academic investigations of Puritan theology and noted where our findings have differed. One contribution concerns the issue of preparationism. We have shown how Flavel's view of the effectual call intersects with the issue of preparationism and thus which 'strain' of Puritan preparationist theology he represents. Other contributions of this study to the discussion of Puritan theology, in addition to the delineation of the effectual call, have been noted within the body of our discussion.

Our findings concerning Flavel's integration of his view of the effectual call with his evangelistic preaching constitute our primary contribution to the scholarly discussion of Puritanism. Our study of Flavel suggests that an understanding of the Puritan view of the effectual call, an understanding which has hitherto been inadequately investigated, provides answers to many of the questions which the academic community has concerning Puritan preaching. Inasmuch as Flavel is representative of late seventeenth-century Puritanism, this correlation between theology and preaching offers a fuller explanation for the matter and manner of Puritan evangelistic preaching.

APPENDIX 1

The Compass of *Navigation Spiritualized*

In the first edition of Flavel's *Whole Works* (1701) he includes a graphic in the introduction to *Navigation Spiritualized*. It consists of a compass with thirty-two points, the points corresponding to the chapters of the treatise. Included under each point is a couplet summarizing that chapter. The center of the compass holds a poem encouraging the seaman to read the treatise. This graphic is not included in the 1968 reprint of Flavel's *Works* and therefore we include it here. A photograph of the graphic is followed by a transcription.

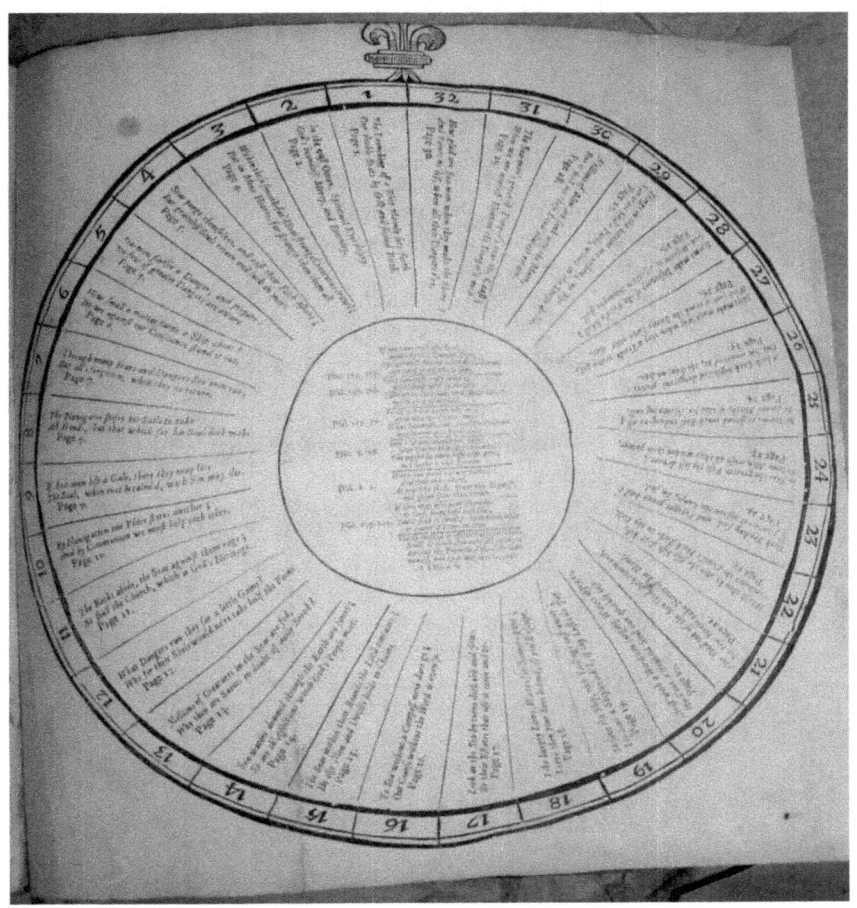

Compass Point	Flavel's Explanation
1	The launching of a ship plainly sets forth our double state by first and second birth.
2	In the vast ocean, spiritual eyes descry God's boundless mercy, and eternity.
3	Within these smooth-fac'd seas strange creatures crawl; but in men's hearts, far stranger than them all.
4	Seas purge themselves, and cast their filth ashore; but graceless souls retain and suck in more.
5	Sea-men foresee a danger, and prepare: yet few of greater dangers are aware.
6	How small a matter turns a ship about? yet we against our conscience stand it out.
7	Through many fears and dangers sea-men run, but all's forgotten, when they do return.
8	The navigator shifts his sails to take all winds, but that which for his soul doth make.
9	If sea-men lose a gale, there they may lie, the soul, when once becalm'd, with sin may die.
10	By navigation one place stores another; and by communion we must help each other.
11	The rocks abide, the seas against them rage; so shall the church, which is God's heritage.
12	What dangers run they for a little gains? Who for their souls would ne're take half the pains.
13	Millions of creatures in the seas are fed, why then are saints in doubt of daily bread?
14	Sea-waters drained through the earth are sweet; so are th' afflictions which God's people meet.
15	The seas within their bounds the Lord contains; he also men and devils holds in chains.
16	To sea without a compass none dare go; our course without the word is even so.
17	Look as the sea by turns doth ebb and flow; so their estates that use it come and go.
18	Like hungry lions, waves for sinners gape; leave then your sins behind, if you'll escape.
19	To save the ship, rich ladings cast away; thy soul is shipwrack'd, if thy lusts do stay.
20	Christ with a word can surging waves appease; his voice a troubled soul can quickly ease.
21	Our food out of the sea God doth command, yet few herein take notice of his hand.

22	Whilst thou by art the silly fish dost kill, perchance the devil's hook sticks in thy gill.
23	Doth trading fail, and voyages prove bad? if you cannot discern the cause, 'tis sad.
24	In seas the greater fish the less devour; so some men crush all those within their power.
25	In storms to spread much sail indangers all; so carnal mirth, if God for mourning call.
26	A little leak neglected dangerous proves: one sin connived at, the soul undoes.
27	Ships make much way when they a trade-wind get, with such a wind the saints have ever met.
28	Storms make discovery of the pilot's skill; God's wisdom in affliction triumphs still.
29	Things in the bottom are unseen; no eye can trace God's paths, which in the deeps do lie.
30	Millions of men are sunk into the main, but it shall not those dead always retain.
31	The sea-man's greatest danger's near the coast; when we are nearest heaven the danger's most.
32	How glad are sea-men when they make the shore? and saints no less, when all their dangers o're.

Poem contained within the Center of the Compass

If you that cross seas,
would by this compass steer;
The greatest storm could do no harm,
nor need you rocks to fear.

This compass truly touch't,
your course will so direct:
That on no rock your souls shall knock;
unless they it neglect.

Could you but learn this art,
then who would you annoy
What inward calms, amidst all storms
might your poor souls enjoy?

Sirs! if you would but take
some pains this art to learn,
you might be then fishers of men,
and make a rich return.

When you have vacant hours,
and time to be alone,

as you'd be blest, grant this request,
and spend some time hereon.

If this may win your thoughts
to God, from self and sin;
you'll find it sweet, to have them meet
as center'd lines in him."

APPENDIX 2

Outline of *Fountain of Life*

In the first edition of Flavel's *Whole Works* there is an outline of *Fountain of Life* given by the author. He entitles this outline 'Totius Operis' and places it before the body of the treatise. It is not included in the 1968 reprint of Flavel's *Works* and therefore we reproduce it here.

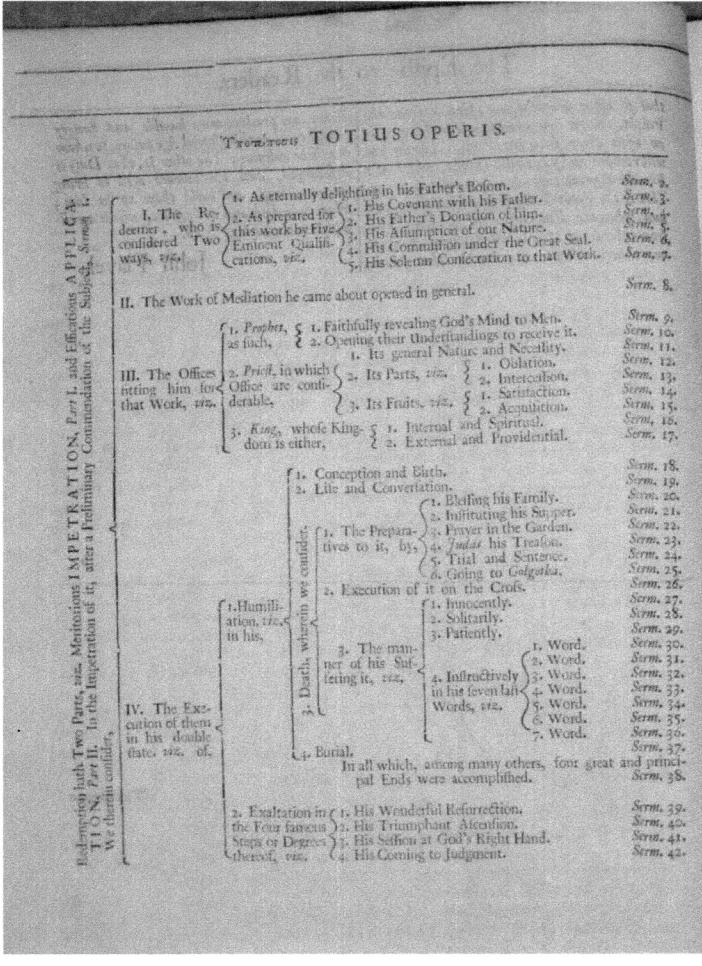

APPENDIX 3

Outline of *Method of Grace*

In the first edition of Flavel's *Whole Works* there is an outline of *Method of Grace* given by the author. He also entitles this outline 'Totius Operis' and places it before the body of the treatise. It is not included in the 1968 reprint of Flavel's *Works* and therefore we reproduce it here. A few handwritten notes from a previous owner can be seen for the tenth through nineteenth sermons.

APPENDIX 4

Outline of *Soul of Man*

In the 1701 edition of Flavel's *Whole Works* there is an outline of *Soul of Man* given to us by the author. He entitles this outline a 'Synopsis' and presents it in two tables. These two tables are placed after the preface and before the body of the treatise. They are not included in the 1968 reprint of Flavel's *Works* and therefore we reproduce them here.

A View of the Soul as separated, considered three ways in this Table of Death.

			Pag.
Firstly, In general Notion, as Soul separated, four ways.	1. The Nature of Separation, and that both	{ 1. Mental and Intellectual, the usefulness of which is shewed.	532
		{ 2. Real and Physical; and that either { 1. *In fieri*, its foregoing pains.	ibid.
		{ 2. *In facto esse*, its dividing stroke.	544
	2. The Notices and Signs of approaching Death, where	{ 1. The Reasons against it are weighed.	571
		{ 2. The Evidences for it are produced.	ibid.
	3. The Changes made by separation, both upon	{ 1. The Body visibly.	554
		{ 2. The Soul more considerably in several respects.	556
	4. The Soul's ability, both to exist and act when separate, proved	{ 1. By its understanding some things now, without Phantasms or help of the Body.	557
		{ 2. The Absurdities of the contrary Hypothesis.	ibid.
Secondly, As a Soul in Christ, in eight Particulars.	1. The proper Season of its separation, which is not,	{ 1. Till the Work of Sanctification be wrought out upon it.	558
		{ 2. Till the whole Work of Obedience be finished by it.	ibid.
		{ 3. And then it goes with all its Graces and Comforts with it.	ibid.
	2. The Ministry of Angels at the time of Separation,	{ 1. Not out of pure Necessity, as though it could not ascend to God without them.	555
		{ 2. But to grace and adorn that day.	ibid.
	3. Their Residence after death opened, both	{ 1. Negatively { 1. They wander not up and down the World.	558
		{ 2. They abide not about our Graves.	559
		{ 3. They are not detained in Purgatory.	ibid.
		{ 4. They fall not into a Swoon, or sleep.	ibid.
		{ 2. Positively, they ascend to God immediately; for { 1. Heaven is ready for them.	ibid.
		{ 2. They are ready for it.	ibid.
		{ 3. Scriptures are for it.	ibid.
		{ 4. Nothing in Reason against it.	ibid.
	4. The Life of holy separate Souls, in respect of their	{ 1. Pleasure, which transcends { 1. All the Sensitive Pleasure here.	561
		{ 2. All the Intellectual Pleasure here.	562
		{ 3. All the Spiritual Pleasure here.	ibid.
		{ 2. Knowledge, which is { 1. More perfect in degree.	562
		{ 2. More easie in its acquisition.	ibid.
		{ 3. Communion with God, which { 1. Excels that here in ten Respects.	563
		{ 2. Admires a double change.	565
	5. The Idea of a Soul in Glory.		568
	6. The Apparitions of departed Souls, where	{ 1. The Arguments for it are produced.	574
		{ 2. Conceptions about it laid down.	575
		{ 3. Reasons against it urged, and Objections answered.	577
	7. The Discourse and Speech of the Spirits of the just.	{ 1. That they do converse in Heaven.	578
		{ 2. Yet without words or sound.	ibid.
		{ 3. By an Act of the *Will*, which is { 1. More clear.	580
		{ 2. More quick.	
	8. Their desires of Re-union, where	{ 1. The Reasons against it are weighed.	581
		{ 2. The Arguments proving it, produced.	582
Thirdly, As a damned Soul, in two things.	1. The Idea or Representation of a damned Soul in respect of	{ 1. The Place where	598
		{ 2. The Misery what	599
		{ 3. The Instrument of its Torments.	600
		{ 4. The Aggravations	602
	2. The various Methods of destroying precious Souls	{ 1. By Satan.	
		{ 2. By Men.	619, &c.
		{ 3. By themselves.	
	The only Season of Salvation noted and pressed upon all.		621, &c.

APPENDIX 5

Annotated Chronological List of Flavel's Works

As stated in Chapter 2, there are thirty-four individual publications contained in Flavel's *Works*. In addition to those works we have a sermon, part of a sermon, two letters of correspondence with a neighbouring Quaker, and the preface he wrote for a friend's book. There are a few additional letters of Flavel's in the Bodleian Library but their content is not relevant to our study.[1]

Determining the year in which each individual treatise was first published is not a straightforward task. In some of the introductions to his treatises Flavel gives the exact date of writing. In most he omits any such reference. In some of those cases we can find clues in Flavel's references to current events or the deaths of notable people that enable us to identify a span of years in which that particular work was written. Entries in biographical dictionaries of the 1800s and other secondary literature that list Flavel's publications are inconsistent. Research in the Bodleian Library and Dr Williams's Library has been helpful in this matter. However, in many cases we have not been able to determine with certainty the original date of publication.

The following is a list of Flavel's writings which are included in his complete *Works*. We list them in the approximate chronological order in which they were written. For those writings for which the original publication dates are not known, a span of years in which we estimate that it was most probably written is given, or an estimated year of publication is suggested followed by a question mark. Following the title and date we have included the volume and page numbers for the 1968 reprint, the approximate length of the work, and a brief annotation. After listing those publications contained in his *Works* we list the additional items written by Flavel, published or unpublished, which are available for our examination.

A Saint Indeed, or The Great Work of a Christian Opened and Pressed – From Proverbs 4:23 (1667), Vol. 5, pp. 417–509 [approximately 41,000

---

[1] The Bodleian contains the following correspondence of John Flavel's: the rough drafts of two letters which Edmund Elys sent to Flavel. (MS J.Walker e.8.39,40.). Two letters from Flavel to Elys, dated June 2, 1687, and June 13, 1687. (MS J. Walker c.4.307, 309). Flavel's letter to J. Thornton, dated August 15, 1684, asking for help in the light of his being hunted down by the authorities which were attempting to confiscate his properties. (Rawl. Lrs. 109.33.).

words]

Not long into his exile from Dartmouth, Flavel addressed this, his first treatise, 'To my dearly beloved and longed for, the Flock of Jesus Christ in Dartmouth, over whom the Holy Ghost hath made me an Overseer.'[2]

This treatise aims at convincing the reader of the importance of 'keeping the heart,' and giving the reader help in doing so. In his introduction Flavel delineates the central doctrine. It is '[t]hat the keeping and right managing of the heart in every condition, is the great business of a Christian's life.'[3] He later summarizes what he understands this 'keeping of the heart' to be: 'to keep the heart is carefully to preserve it from sin, which disorders it; and maintain that spiritual and gracious frame, which fits it for a life of communion with God.'[4] After his introduction the treatise is presented in four major sections: First, what the keeping of the heart supposes and imports. Secondly, why Christians should make this the great business of their lives. The third section is the longest. In it Flavel describes eleven special 'seasons' that call for diligence in keeping the heart. The fourth section focuses on taking the previous three sections and making practical application of them to the readers' lives. This treatise was published repeatedly after Flavel's death under the title *Keeping the Heart*.

Tidings from Rome, or England's Alarm (1668?), Vol. 4, pp. 557–86 [approximately 12,000 words]

One of Flavel's short treatises, *England's Alarm* was written within two years after the Great Fire of London and amidst a growing belief that agents working toward Roman Catholic rise to political power in England were enjoying success.

Flavel begins his treatise with an explanation of his sense of responsibility to the nation. 'Every faithful minister of Christ sustains the relation of a watchman unto the nation wherein he lives, as well as of a pastor to the particular flock over which the Holy Ghost hath set him.'[5] He continues by expressing the urgency of the perceived danger. 'It cannot but much more heighten our fears, if we consider the sad posture we are in at this day of our imminent danger.'[6] He describes the danger and then states his purpose in writing.

> These are some of the principal grounds of England's fear at this day, in reference to the popish party ... . Having thus hinted the grounds of our fears, what remains

---

[2] Flavel, *Works*, Vol. 5, p. 417.
[3] Flavel, *Works*, Vol. 5, p. 425.
[4] Flavel, *Works*, Vol. 5, p. 426.
[5] Flavel, *Works*, Vol. 4, p. 557.
[6] Flavel, *Works*, Vol. 4, p. 564.

but that I next address myself to the principal work designed in these papers; which is to call upon England to awake out of her destructive security, and not to suffer her enemies to surprise her sleeping?[7]

Unlike his other treatises, *England's Alarm* is not based upon a particular Scripture passage or passages, nor is it a development of implications or applications stemming from a derived doctrine. Rather, it is a polemic against 'popery' and a warning against the perceived dangers associated with a possible turning of the state to Roman Catholicism.

Navigation Spiritualized; Or, A New Compass for Seamen, consisting of XXXII points; of Pleasant Observations, Profitable Applications, and Serious Reflections. All concluded with so many Spiritual Poems (1668?), Vol. 5, pp. 206–92 [approximately 39,000 words]

Flavel addressed this treatise 'To all Masters, Mariners, and Seamen; especially such as belong to the Borough of Clifton, Dartmouth, and Hardness, in the county of Devon.'[8] He used activities common to seamen and characteristics of the oceans as illustrations of spiritual truths. The first printing of this treatise included a graphic in the introduction, consisting of a compass with thirty-two points, each point corresponding to a chapter of the treatise. The centre of the compass held a poem encouraging the seaman to read the treatise. This graphic appears in Appendix 1.[9]

Flavel viewed the treatise primarily as an evangelistic tool, an attempt to contribute to the conversion of the people involved in the seafaring industries so prominent in the life of Dartmouth. In his introduction he writes, 'O Sirs! I beg of you, if you have any regard to those precious, immortal souls of yours, which are also imbarked [*sic*] for eternity, whither all winds blow them, and will quickly be at their port of heaven or hell, that you will seriously mind these things, and learn to steer your course to heaven.'[10]

A Pathetical and Serious Dissuasive from the Horrid and detestable Sins of Drunkenness, Swearing, Uncleanness, Forgetfulness of Mercies, Violation of Promises, and atheistical Contempt of Death. Applied by way of Caution to Seamen, and now added as an Appendix to their New Compass. Being an Essay toward their much-desired Reformation, fit to

---

[7] Flavel, *Works*, Vol. 4, p. 569.

[8] Flavel, *Works*, Vol. 5, p. 206.

[9] A careful reading of the 1968 reprint will reveal a reference to the graphic in the introductory epistle prefacing the treatise. The epistle was written by 'T.M.' and he said: 'This collection is prefixed, that at once thou mayest view all the compasses (both speculative, practical, and affectionate) by which thou must steer heavenward.' Vol. 5, p. 212.

[10] Flavel, *Works*, Vol. 5, p. 208.

be seriously recommended to their profane Relations whether Seamen or others, by all such as unfeignedly desire their eternal Welfare (1668?), Vol. 5, pp. 293–342 [approximately 21,000 words]

This treatise was written after *Navigation Spiritualized* and added as an appendix to it. It is unclear when this addition was made, although we know it appears in the first edition of Flavel's *Whole Works*. As the title suggests, the treatise consists of six parts, each part an attempt to dissuade seamen from certain sins. The entire treatise ends by pointing the reader to Christ and forgiveness, thus serving mainly an evangelistic aim.

Husbandry Spiritualized: or, The Heavenly Use of Earthly Things (1669?), Vol. 5, pp. 3–205) [approximately 89,000 words]

Apparently Flavel's *Navigation Spiritualized* met with some success and this encouraged him to turn his attention to the farming community.[11] When commenting on his purpose for both this treatise and *Navigation Spiritualized* Flavel wrote: 'I considered, that if the Pharisees, in a blind zeal to a faction, could compass sea and land, to proselyte men to their party ... how much more was I obliged, by true love of God, and zeal both with seamen and husbandmen, to win them to Christ.'[12] Yet, he also readily acknowledges a purpose in this writing for the one who is already converted. He sees in 'creatures' a spiritual usefulness. He writes that 'they [created things] bear the figures and similitudes of many sublime and heavenly mysteries.'[13] It is Flavel's intent to teach those mysteries to Christians by drawing attention to practices, animals and occurrences common to farmers, hence the subtitle *The Heavenly Use of Earthly Things*.

The treatise consists of four parts. Part 1 comprises twenty chapters; each exploring a 'similitude' Flavel finds in the world of farming. Part 2 consists of four chapters; each dealing with some aspect of caring for fruit trees. Part 3 contains six chapters, each drawing spiritual application from the realm of cattle farming. The fourth and last section of the book is a collection of short 'meditations' on birds, land animals, trees, and a garden.

Each chapter in the first three parts is organized identically. Flavel begins with a two-line rhyme summarizing the chapter. His discussion then proceeds by observation, application, and reflections, and ends the chapter with a poem. The meditations that make up the fourth section of the book are organized differently.

---

[11] In the epistle dedicatory he writes: 'The motives inducing me to this undertaking, were the Lord's owning with some success, my labours of a like nature [*Navigation Spiritualized*].' Vol. 5, p. 5.
[12] Flavel, *Works*, Vol. 5, p. 5.
[13] Flavel, *Works*, Vol. 5, p. 3.

Appendix 5

The Fountain of Life opened up: or, A Display of Christ in His Essential and Mediatorial Glory. Containing Forty-two Sermons on various texts (1671), Vol. 1, pp. 17–561 [approximately 240,000 words]

The largest of Flavel's individual works, this treatise consists of forty-two sermons he preached in Dartmouth. He addressed this collection 'To the Christian Readers, especially those in the Town and Corporation of Dartmouth, and Parts adjacent, who have either befriended, or attended these Lectures.'[14] His original intent was to include more material, but the length of this treatise convinced him to add a second volume later.[15] That second volume would wait nine years and be published as *Method of Grace*.

Flavel envisioned the two treatises, *Fountain of Life* and *Method of Grace*, as forming parts one and two of a discussion of redemption. In the outline at the head of the treatise, entitled 'Totius Operis,' He explains: 'Redemption hath Two Parts, *viz.* Meritorious IMPRETRATION, Part I. and Efficatious APPLICATION, Part II.' In that statement he is referring to the entire *Fountain of Life* as an exploration of the 'meritorious impretration' of redemption.

After one sermon which serves as an introduction to the entire series, Flavel arranges his thoughts in four parts. The first consists of six sermons that examine the Redeemer – Jesus Christ. The second part is made up of only one sermon, which deals in a general way with the topic of mediation. The third part explores in nine sermons the offices which 'befit' Christ for the work of mediation. The fourth part consists of twenty-five sermons which examine how Christ executed this mediation through his humiliation and exaltation.

A Token for Mourners: or the Advice of Christ to a Distressed Mother, Bewailing the death of her dear and only son: Wherein the Boundaries of Sorrow are duly fixed, Excesses restrained, the common Pleas answered, and divers Rules for the support of God's afflicted Ones prescribed (1665–74), Vol. 5, p. 604–66 [approximately 28,000 words]

This work is not a collection of sermons, but rather a short treatise addressing the issue of mourning. Written to his sister, the epistle dedicatory is addressed 'to his dearly beloved brother and sister, Mr. J.C. and Mrs. E.C.'[16] In the

---

[14] Flavel, *Works*, Vol. 1, p. 21.
[15] Flavel writes: 'And it was my purpose at first to have comprised the second part, viz. The application of the redemption that is with Christ unto sinners, in one volume, ... but that making a just volume itself, must await another season to see the light.' Vol. 1, p. 24.
[16] Flavel, *Works*, Vol. 5, p. 604. Flavel's opening sentence shows clearly that the reference to his 'sister' was indeed intended of his biological sister, and was not merely a spiritual term. 'The double tye of nature and grace, beside the many endearing passages that for so many years have linked and glewed our affections so

introduction Flavel describes the loss of his own first wife and son and then recounts a personal visit to his sister's home and the subsequent loss of her child. He seeks to comfort his sister in her grief and, by doing so in writing, comfort others too.

> It is not my design to exasperate your troubles, but to heal them; and for that purpose have I sent you these papers, which I hope may be of use both to you and many others in your condition, since they are the after-fruits of my own troubles; things that I have not commended to you from another hand, but which I have, in some measure, proved and tasted in my own trials.[17]

Flavel lost his first wife prior to 1656. The way in which he refers to this loss in the introduction could be understood to imply that the treatise was written not long after the occurrence.[18] However, in the epistle dedicatory he also mentions the death of his parents, which occurred in 1665. Although the tone of the epistle dedicatory seems to imply a close proximity in time to the family deaths, we have been unable to find any record of this treatise being published until 1674.

Flavel bases his treatise on Luke 7:13 and the biblical account of Jesus encountering the widow of Nain who had just lost her only son to death. After examining the scriptural passage he arrives at the doctrine '[t]hat Christians ought to moderate their sorrows for their dead relations, how many afflicting circumstances, and aggravations soever meet together in their death.'[19] Following this doctrine Flavel arranges his treatise in four parts. In the first part he explains the signs by which acceptable and unacceptable sorrow can be identified. In the second part he seeks to 'dissuade mourners from these sinful excesses of sorrows and keep the golden bridle of moderation upon their passions in times of affliction.'[20] In the third part Flavel examines eleven 'pleas' or justifications for what he calls immoderate grief. And in the fourth and final part he proposes seven 'rules' as 'the means of curing and preventing these sinful excesses of sorrow.'[21]

The Seaman's Companion: Wherein the Mysteries of Providences, Relating to Seamen, are Opened; their Sins and Dangers discovered, their Duties pressed, and their several Troubles and Burdens relieved. In

---

intimately, cannot but beget a tender sympathy in me with you under all your troubles, and make me say of every affliction which befals you, Half's mine.'

[17] Flavel, *Works*, Vol. 5, p. 605.

[18] 'You cannot forget that in *the years lately past*, the Almighty visited my tabernacle with the rod, and in one year cut off from it the root, and the branch, the tender mother, and the only son.' Flavel, *Works*, Vol. 5, p. 604; emphasis mine.

[19] Flavel, *Works*, Vol. 5, p. 612.

[20] Flavel, *Works*, Vol. 5, p. 623.

[21] Flavel, *Works*, Vol. 5, p. 663.

Six practicable and suitable Sermons (1675), Vol. 5, pp. 342–416 [approximately 32,000 words]

As the title indicates, this is a collection of sermons, but unlike the very large *Fountain of Life* there are only six of them. It is addressed 'To all Masters, Mariners, and Seamen; especially such as belong to the Port of Dartmouth, and the Parts adjacent.'[22] The sermons are a mixture of admonition and instruction for the already converted and evangelistic appeal to those not yet converted. A portion of Flavel's design in publishing this little sermon series can be seen in his closing comments to the 'masters,' those in charge of the ships. 'But it is my earnest request to you, masters, that have the over-sight, and must give an account for your companies, that you will not only read and consider these things for yourselves, but that you will at fit seasons, especially upon the Lord's day, read and inculcate them upon your servants and company.'[23]

Divine Conduct, or, The Mystery of Providence, opened in a Treatise upon Psalm 52:2 (1677), Vol. 4, pp. 336–495 [approximately 70,000 words]

Basing this work on Psalm 52:2, Flavel propounds the doctrine '[t]hat it is the duty of the saints, especially in times of straits, to reflect upon the performances of providence for them in all the states, and through all the stages of their lives.'[24]

He develops his treatise in five parts. We will allow him to outline it for us:

First, I shall prove, that the concernments of the saints in this world are certainly conducted by the wisdom and care of special providence. *Secondly*, I will shew you in what particular concernments of theirs this providential care is evidently discovered. *Thirdly*, That it is the duty of saints to advert to, and heedfully observe these performances of providence for them in all their concernments. *Fourthly*, In what manner this duty is to be performed by them. *Fifthly*, What singular benefits result to them from such observations.[25]

This treatise was published repeatedly after Flavel's death under the title *The Mystery of Providence*.

The Touchstone of Sincerity: or, The Signs of Grace, and Symptoms of Hypocrisy. Opened in a practical Treatise upon Revelation 3:17–18 (1678), Vol. 5, pp. 509–604 [approximately 42,000 words]

---

[22] Flavel, *Works*, Vol. 5, p. 342.
[23] Flavel, *Works*, Vol. 5, p. 416.
[24] Flavel, *Works*, Vol. 4, p. 347.
[25] Flavel, *Works*, Vol. 4, p. 349.

In the epistle to the reader that serves as the preface of this treatise, Flavel explains the relation of this work with *A Saint Indeed*.

> Among the difficulties and severities of true religion, the faithful searching, and diligent keeping of our hearts are found in the first and highest rank of difficulties: These two take up the main work of a Christian betwixt them … . I had hopes that these essays for the searching of the heart, might much sooner have followed my former for keeping the heart. But providence hath reserved it for the fittest season.[26]

Thus we see that Flavel envisioned *Touchstone of Sincerity* as logically preceding *Saint Indeed* – both treatises addressing what he considered a primary task of all Christians.

Flavel arranges this treatise in twelve chapters. The first four chapters introduce his subject and support three doctrines which form the foundation of the entire treatise. The doctrines are '[t]hat many professors of religion are under very great and dangerous mistakes in their profession … . That true grace is exceedingly precious, and greatly enriches the soul that possesseth it … . That only is to be accounted true grace which is able to endure all those trials appointed, or permitted for the discovery of it.'[27]

In the remaining chapters Flavel explores the relationship between suffering, the performance of Christian 'duties,' and the possession of certainty of salvation. He leads up to the last two chapters, in which he labours to apply the previous discussion to the conscience and volition of the readers. Chapter eleven is described as '[c]ontaining divers practical instructive inferences from this doctrine; with a serious exhortation to self-trial and thorough examination.'[28] Flavel summarizes the twelfth and final chapter as '[c]ontaining divers helps for the clearing of sincerity and discovery of hypocrisy.'[29]

A Faithful and succinct Narrative of Some Late and Wonderful Sea Deliverances (1679?), Vol. 4, pp. 496–514 [approximately 8,000 words]

This short work, referred to by Flavel as 'this little manual,'[30] is unlike his other writings. It is not a treatise, nor a sermon, but a record of two accounts of dangers at sea in which men experienced 'wonderful sea-deliverances.' In his preface Flavel explains that his purpose in publishing these accounts is to combat what he considers a growing atheistic mindset in his day. 'I am convinced, that if an orderly collection were made of the more remarkable and eminent acts of Divine providence, it would be an excellent compendium or

---

[26] Flavel, *Works*, Vol. 5, p. 509.
[27] Flavel, *Works*, Vol. 5, p. 516.
[28] Flavel, *Works*, Vol. 5, p. 588.
[29] Flavel, *Works*, Vol. 5, p. 595.
[30] Flavel, *Works*, Vol. 4, p. 498.

system of spiritual physic to purge and cure this atheistical generation, wherein the very being of a God and providence are denied by some.'[31]

The first account Flavel gives occurred in 1679, thus we know that this manual was not published before that year. In the *Whole Works* it is placed after *Mystery of Providence*, suggesting that it may have been attached to *Mystery of Providence* in some of its repeated printings.

Sacramental Meditations upon Divers Select Places of Scripture: Wherein Believers are assisted in preparing their Hearts, and exciting their Affections and Graces, when they draw nigh to God in that most awful and solemn Ordinance of the Lord's Supper (1680), Vol. 6, pp. 378–460 [approximately 36,000 words]

This is a collection of twelve sermons intended on preparing the hearer to participate in the 'ordinance of the Lord's Supper.' In the preface Flavel expresses his desire that Christians take part in the Lord's Supper with grace being stimulated within them. 'Even a believer himself doth not eat and drink worthily, unless the grace that is in him be excited and exercised at this ordinance.'[32] He continues to explain that this exciting and exercising of grace would be evidenced in sincere mourning for sin and heartfelt love for Christ. To attain to this mourning and love is not easy. 'To assist thee in this work,' Flavel writes, 'some help is offered in the following meditations.'[33]

Apparently Flavel intended expanding *Sacramental Meditations* in subsequent printings. The author of the biography of Flavel which is prefixed to his *Whole Works* explains this intention. 'He purposed to have enlarged his book of *Sacramental Meditations*, and had most judiciously stated and handled several cases of conscience on that occasion, which he designed to have inserted in the next edition, but lived not to finish them for the press.'[34]

The Method of Grace in the Gospel Redemption. 35 Sermons (1680), Vol. 2, pp. 3–474 [approximately 207,000 words]

This treatise, the second largest of all of Flavel's individual works, consists of the texts of thirty-five of his sermons and was intended as a companion volume to *Fountain of Life*. He refers to the two treatises as 'part 1' and 'part 2' of an exploration of various doctrinal and practical issues pertaining to redemption.[35] His goal had not been completed in the writing of *Fountain of Life*, and his

---

[31] Flavel, *Works*, Vol. 4, pp. 497–98.
[32] Flavel, *Works*, Vol. 6, p. 379.
[33] Flavel, *Works*, Vol. 6, p. 380.
[34] Flavel, *Works*, Vol. 1, p. xiv.
[35] Flavel, *Whole Works*, Vol. 1, p. 248.

determination to finish the task bore fruit nine years later in *Method of Grace*.[36] 'And I consent the more willingly to the publication of this, because the design I first aimed at, could not be entire and complete without it.'[37]

In the first edition of Flavel's *Whole Works* there is an outline of *Method of Grace* entitled 'Totius Operis' which Flavel places before the body of the treatise. In it he explains: 'Redemption hath Two Parts, viz. meritorious Impretration, opened Part I. [i.e. *Fountain of Life*] And effectual Application, opened in this 2d Part ... .' In that statement he is referring to the entire *Method of Grace* as an exploration of the 'effectual application' of redemption.

Flavel divides the treatise into two main parts: an eight-sermon doctrinal consideration of the effectual application of redemption, and then a twenty-seven-sermon practical consideration of it. The second part, being much larger, is divided into four subsections, which he calls exhortation, conviction, examination, and lamentation. The first subsection consists of eleven sermons designed as exhortations to come to Christ; the second of four sermons aimed at conviction; the third of seven sermons intended to enable the hearer to examine his or her 'interest in Christ;' and the final subsection of five sermons representing the present state and eternal future of unconverted people.

Preparations for Sufferings: or the Best Work in the Worst Times. Wherein the Necessity, Excellency, and Means of our readiness for Sufferings are evinced and prescribed; our Call to suffering cleared, and the great unreadiness of many professors bewailed (1681), Vol. 6, pp. 3–83 [approximately 35,000 words]

Flavel states his purpose for this treatise in the epistle to the reader: 'The cup of sufferings is a very bitter cup, and it is but needful that we provide somewhat to sweeten it, that we may be able to receive it with thanksgiving; and what those sweetening ingredients are, and how to prepare them, you will have some direction and help in the following discourse.'[38] Helping people who were going through suffering is his aim.

He arranges the treatise in a total of sixteen chapters. Flavel describes this treatise as that 'which hath once already been presented to the public view.'[39] The chapters do not appear to be texts of individual sermons per se; however, their content had been in some way presented verbally and publicly.

Basing his teaching on Acts 21:13, Flavel uses the first chapter to arrive at the doctrine '[t]hat it is a blessed and excellent thing for the people of God to

---

[36] In the introduction to *Method of Grace*, he writes: 'though it was promised to the world many years past, yet providence hath reserved it for the fittest season, and brought it to thy hand in a time of need.' Flavel, *Works*, Vol. 2, p. 12.
[37] Flavel, *Works*, Vol. 2, p. 12.
[38] Flavel, *Works*, Vol. 6, p. 4.
[39] Flavel, *Works*, Vol. 6, p. 4.

Appendix 5 243

be prepared, and ready for the hardest services, and worst of sufferings, to which the Lord may call them.'[40] The following chapters are investigations of that doctrine's implications for the readers' lives. The various emphases of those investigations are explained in his subtitle.

> *A Practical Treatise of Fear. Wherein the various kinds, uses, cause, effects and remedies thereof are distinctly opened and prescribed, for the relief and encouragement of all those that fear God in these doubtful and distracting times* (1682), Vol. 3, pp. 239–320 [approximately 36,000 words]

In the epistle dedicatory Flavel explains the purpose of this treatise. He refers to the days in which he lived as being 'perilous times.' He then speaks of the value for God's people of having their faith and an assurance of their union with Christ. He explains: 'This so poiseth and steadies the mind, that we may enjoy the comfort and tranquility of a resigned will, when others are at their wit's end. With design to promote this blessed frame, in my own and others hearts in these frightful times, I meditated, and now publish this small tract.'[41]

There are a total of seven chapters in 'this small tract.' He bases it on Isaiah 8:12–14 and uses the first chapter to propose two doctrines: 'Doct. 1. That the best men are too apt to be overcome with slavish fears, in times of imminent distress and danger. Doct. 2. That the fear of God is the most effectual means to extinguish the sinful fear of men, and to secure us from danger.'[42] The following six chapters investigate that doctrine's implications for the readers' lives. The various emphases of his investigations are explained in his subtitle. Chapter six is almost as long as the rest of the treatise. In this chapter he offers twelve 'rules to cure our sinful fears, and prevent these sad and woeful effects of them.'[43]

This treatise and *Refuge* were apparently meant to be companion volumes. In the Table of Contents of the first edition of the *Whole Works* the editor has grouped them together under the title 'Two Treatises, 1. Of Fear. And, 2. Of Evil Days.'[44] And in Flavel's introductory epistle for *Refuge* he refers to both treatises. 'I have endeavoured once more the assistance of poor Christians in these two small treatises, one of fear, the other of preparation for the worst of times.'[45]

---

[40] Flavel, *Works*, Vol. 6, p. 6.
[41] Flavel, *Works*, Vol. 3, p. 240.
[42] Flavel, *Works*, Vol. 3, p. 245.
[43] Flavel, *Works*, Vol. 3, p. 280.
[44] Flavel, *Whole Works*, Vol. 1, title page.
[45] Flavel, *Works*, Vol. 3, p. 322. It should be noted that Flavel's comment is indeed referring to the two treatises, *Fear* and *Refuge*. It is somewhat confusing because in this comment he uses the phrase 'preparation for the worst of times' to refer to

The Righteous Man's Refuge (1682), Vol. 3, pp. 321–413 [approximately 41,000 words]

As mentioned in the discussion of *Fear*, that treatise and this, *The Righteous Man's Refuge*, were apparently published together. Both were intended to give spiritual help to those who were undergoing distressing times. In this treatise's epistle to the reader Flavel writes:

> In consideration of the distress of many unprovided souls for the misery that is coming on them, and not knowing how short my time will be useful to any, (for I know that it cannot be long) I have endeavoured once more the assistance of poor Christians in these two small treatises, one of fear, the other of preparation for the worst of times; which, it may be, is the last help I shall this way be able to afford them.[46]

Flavel begins by using the first chapter to examine Isaiah 26:20 and present it as the foundation for the following chapters. The doctrine he derives from that Scripture verse is '[t]hat the attributes, promises, and providences of God, are the chambers of rest and security, in which his people are to hide themselves, when they forsee the storms of his indignation coming upon the world.'[47] After deriving this doctrine he ends the chapter by listing six propositions, 'which are implied or expressed in the text and doctrine thence deduced.'[48] He then spends the rest of the treatise, eleven further chapters, exploring those six propositions and their application to the readers' lives.

His treatment of the six propositions is unequal. He spends six entire chapters, half the entire treatise, examining the fifth proposition. In discussing it he delineates which attributes of God give security to his people in times of distress. He names divine power, wisdom, faithfulness, the unchangeableness of God, the care of God for his people, and the love of God, and devotes a chapter to each attribute. The twelfth and final chapter of the treatise is devoted to three 'uses' of the previous chapters' discussion.

Antipharmacum Salubernimum: A Serious and Seasonable Caveat to All the Saints in this Hour of Temptation (1682?), Vol. 4, pp. 515–56 [approximately 18,000 words]

Unlike the other treatises which he wrote at approximately the same time, and in the same setting, this treatise is not based upon one Scripture text but rather is a conglomeration of advice to Christians in the face of trials and temptations.

Refuge. This phrase is very similar to the title of a separate treatise *Preparation for Sufferings: or the Best Work in the Worst of Times*.

[46] Flavel, *Works*, Vol. 3, p. 322.
[47] Flavel, *Works*, Vol. 3, p. 327.
[48] Flavel, *Works*, Vol. 3, p. 328.

Each piece of advice, labelled a 'counsel,' is provided with its own Scripture basis. He gives eight 'counsels' and then concludes: 'And now, I have given you my best advice and counsel, to preserve you from the snares and evils that are, and are coming upon the world.'[49]

Although mainly addressing Christians, Flavel uses the last 'counsel' to direct his words to those who are still unconverted. The eighth counsel is '[t]hat seeing a day of great trouble is approaching, and all outward comforts ready to take their farewell of you, you should now give all diligence to clear up your title to Christ, and interest in that kingdom which cannot be shaken.'[50] He ends the treatise urging the reader to make sure that he or she is a genuine believer in Jesus Christ.

Pneumatologia: A Treatise of the Soul of Man (1684–91), Vol. 2, pp. 475–609; Vol. 3, pp. 3–238 [approximately 164,000 words]

The third largest of all of Flavel's individual works, this is not a collection of sermons but a systematic discourse on the subject of the human soul. In his preface Flavel explains the longstanding interest he possessed for this subject. He also reveals how important *Soul of Man* is to him, considering it the second major topic on which he has sought to write. The following quotation from the preface shows how Flavel views this treatise:

> And since the hopes and evidences of salvation began to spring up in my soul, and settle the state thereof, I found these three great words, viz. Christ, soul, and eternity, to have a far different and more awful sound in my ear, than ever they used to have ... . These things have laid some weight upon my thoughts, and I felt, at certain seasons, a strong inclination to sequester myself from all other studies, and spend my last days, and most fixed meditations upon these three great and weighty subjects.[51]

The first of the 'three great and weighty subjects' was covered in the two-part series of *Fountain of Life* and *Method of Grace*. Seeing the positive reception of those treatises Flavel chose to write about the soul. 'I resolved to do what I could; and accordingly some years past I finished and published, in two parts, the Doctrine of Christ; and by the acceptation and success the Lord gave that, he hath encouraged me to go on in this second part of my work, how unequal soever my shoulders are to the burden of it.'[52]

The treatise was written with the purpose of aiding Christians in preparing themselves for death. In his epistle dedicatory he explains:

---

[49] Flavel, *Works*, Vol. 4, p. 557.
[50] Flavel, *Works*, Vol. 4, p. 552.
[51] Flavel, *Works*, Vol. 2, p. 484.
[52] Flavel, *Works*, Vol. 2, p. 484.

And, O that God would grant me my heart's desire on your behalf, in the perusal of it [the treatise]! Even that it may prove a sanctified instrument in his hand both to prepare you for, and bring you in love with the unbodied life, to make you look with pleasure into your graves, and die by consent of will, as well as necessity of nature.[53]

In addition, there is an evangelistic intent in his writing. 'I have also here set before the reader an idea or representation of the state and case of damned souls, that, if it be the will of God, a seasonable discovery of hell may be the means of some men's recovery out of the danger of it.'[54]

The first edition of Flavel's *Whole Works* includes an outline of *Soul of Man* given by the author, entitled a 'Synopsis' and presented in two tables, placed after the preface and before the body of the treatise. The first table is entitled 'A Synopsis, or View of the Soul in the State of Composition, in six Particulars, in this first Table of Life.'[55] It outlines the first half of the treatise. This consideration of the soul's 'state of composition' is divided into six parts, in which Flavel examines the soul's general nature, essential properties, origin, union with the body, love of the body, and the necessity of its separation from the body. The second table, outlining the second half of the treatise, is entitled 'A View of the Soul as Separated, considered three ways in this Table of Death.'[56] In this section Flavel examines the general nature of the human soul after death, the experience of souls in Christ after death, and the experience of damned souls after death.

The Balm of the Covenant Applied to the Bleeding Wounds of Afflicted Saints. to which is added, A Sermon preached for the Funeral of that excellent and religious Gentleman, John Upton, of Lupton, Esq. (1687?), Vol. 6, pp. 83–119 [approximately 16,000 words]

One of the smallest of Flavel's individual treatises, *Balm of the Covenant* was published along with the funeral sermon of John Upton. Flavel is again attempting to give help to Christians who are undergoing suffering and grief. He states his purpose in his epistle dedicatory:

The design of the ensuing discourse, is to evince the truth of what seems a very great paradox to most men, namely, that the afflictions of the saints can do them no hurt, and that the wisdom of men and angels cannot lay one circumstance of

---

[53] Flavel, *Works*, Vol. 2, p. 480.
[54] Flavel, *Works*, Vol. 2, p. 480.
[55] Flavel, *Whole Works*, Vol. 1, p. 481.
[56] Flavel, *Whole Works*, Vol. 1, p. 482.

their condition (how uneasy soever it seems to be) better, or more to their advantage than God hath laid it.[57]

The epistle dedicatory is addressed to Ursala Upton, the widow of John Upton. The Uptons and Flavel had known each other for some years. Flavel had ministered to the Uptons on the occasion of the loss of their child. He reminds Ursala of that time and notes that her husband had encouraged him to put these thoughts in writing, unaware that the occasion upon which they would be eventually published would be his own death.

> It was not without divine direction, that the subject of the ensuing discourse was as pertinently, as seasonably, recommended to me by your dear husband, in the day of your sorrows for your only son. He took, I hope, his portion of comfort out of it before he died, and it is now left as a spring of comfort to you, who then mourned with him, and now mourn for him.[58]

The treatise is based upon 2 Samuel 23:5. After a discussion of that text, Flavel arranges his thoughts around 'three glorious properties of that covenant.' Those three properties are '[t]hat the covenant of grace is able to remove all the causes and grounds of a believer's trouble,'[59] that the covenant 'must be able to do these things at all times, and in all ages,'[60] and 'that it is a sure covenant.'[61] He ends the treatise by applying those 'properties' to the reader's life in a section of 'uses.'

A Sermon Preached for the Funeral of that Excellent and Religious Gentleman, John Upton, of Lupton, Esq. (1687?), Vol. 6, pp. 120–37 [approximately 7,500 words]

A single sermon was preached, as the title explains, at the funeral of John Upton, and was attached to Flavel's short treatise *Balm of the Covenant*. His text is 2 Chronicles 35:24–25. He derives from that passage, and bases the sermon on, the doctrine '[t]hat faithful, active, and public-spirited men in the church of God should not be laid in their graves without great lamentations.'[62]

Vindiciae Legis et Foederis: or, A Reply to Mr. Philip Cary's Solemn Call; Wherein he pretends to answer all the arguments of Mr. Allen, Mr. Baxter, Mr. Sydenham, Mr. Sedgwick, Mr. Roberts, and Dr. Burthogge, For the Right of Believers Infants to Baptism. By proving the law at Sinai,

---

[57] Flavel, *Works*, Vol. 6, p. 83.
[58] Flavel, *Works*, Vol. 6, p. 84.
[59] Flavel, *Works*, Vol. 6, p. 96.
[60] Flavel, *Works*, Vol. 6, p. 108.
[61] Flavel, *Works*, Vol. 6, p. 109.
[62] Flavel, *Works*, Vol. 6, p. 122.

and the Covenant of Circumcision with Abraham, were the very same with Adam's Covenant of Works, and that because the Gospel-covenant is absolute (1688?), Vol. 6, pp. 318–78 [approximately 26,000 words]

Unique among the writings in his *Works,* this and *Refutation of Cary's Rejoinder* record a published dispute between Flavel and Philip Cary over the issue of infant baptism. The biography which prefaces his *Works* comments upon this dispute: 'He [Flavel] never delighted in controversies, but was obliged, contrary to his inclination, to write against Mr. Cary, the principal Anabaptist in Dartmouth, with whom, however, he maintained a friendly and Christian correspondence.'[63] In Flavel's preface to *Reply to Cary's Call* he makes clear that it is the nearness of the opposing author and the potential influence Cary's teaching could have on Flavel's flock that motivates him to respond:

> I cannot now be both silent and innocent; for in this Solemn Call [Cary's book] I find the great doctrines of God's covenants abused by my neighbour; the books dispersed into many families related to me in this place, one of them delivered to me by the Author's own hands, with a pressing desire to give my judgment upon it ... . Thus I am necessarily brought into the field of controversy ... not out of choice, but necessity. And now I am here, I resolve to be only ... an adversary in the controversy, not to the person, especially of my friendly neighbour. Neither would I have appeared thus publicly against him, if differences could have been accommodated, and the evil prevented, in a more private way.[64]

Flavel then proceeds with an examination of Cary's book and a careful polemic against Cary's opinions. Three doctrinal positions of Cary are isolated by Flavel and disputed. They are '[t]hat the Sinai law is the same with Adam's covenant of works, made in paradise,'[65] '[t]hat Abraham's covenant, Gen. xvii. is an Adam's covenant of works also, because circumcision was annexed to it, which obliged men to keep the whole law,' and '[t]hat neither Moses's law, Exod. xx. nor God's covenant with Abraham, Gen. xvii. can be any other than an Adam's covenant of works, because they have each of them conditions in them on man's part; but the gospel-covenant hath none at all, but is altogether free and absolute.'[66]

England's Duty Under the Present Gospel Liberty. From Rev. iii. 20. To which is added, Mount Pisgah; or, a Thanksgiving Sermon for England's Delivery from Popery, Feb. 1688–9 (1689), Vol. 4, pp. 3–306 [approximately 133,000 words]

---

[63] Flavel, *Works*, Vol. 1, p. xiv.
[64] Flavel, *Works*, Vol. 6, p. 322.
[65] Flavel, *Works*, Vol. 6, p. 323.
[66] Flavel, *Works*, Vol. 6, p. 325.

Appendix 5 249

As the fourth largest of Flavel's individual works, this treatise consists of the texts of eleven sermons preached as a series. This series was preached in the early days of liberty that nonconformists experienced after the commencement of the reign of William and Mary. Following the sermons Flavel attached a non-sermon discourse on Romans 1:18 as an appendix. Prefixed to the sermons is a letter written in Latin to 'dearly beloved Ministers of the Gospel.'[67] The editors of the 1820 version of Flavel's *Works* translated this letter into English.

Apparently there was an extraordinary response to Flavel's preaching of these sermons. In reference to those days he wrote: 'Sowing and reaping times trode so close upon one another, that … it was the busiest and blessedest time I ever saw since I first preached the gospel.'[68] For the first time in his writing career he had another person write a preface for one of his books. Increase Mather's introduction precedes the first sermon and in it he writes of the response to the preaching of these sermons: 'I am informed by unquestionable hands, that there was a remarkable pouring out of the Spirit when these sermons were *viva voce* delivered, a great number of souls having been brought home to Christ thereby.'[69]

The Scripture verse upon which this sermon series is based is Revelation 3:20, which reads: 'Behold I stand at the door, and knock; if any man hear my voice, and open the door, I will come in to him, and sup with him, and he with me.' Flavel methodically used the words of that verse as the foundation of his sermons. The first sermon was based upon the word 'Behold;' the second upon the word 'I;' the third upon the word 'stand;' and so on.

His aim in the sermons was primarily the conversion of unregenerate hearers, and secondarily the encouragement of those who had already believed.

> As to the treatise itself, thou wilt find it a persuasive to open thy heart to Christ … . If thou be in thy unregenerate state, then he solemnly demands in this text admission into the soul he made, by the consent of the will; … If thou hast opened thy heart to him, thou wilt, I hope, meet somewhat in this treatise that will clear thy evidences, and cheer thy heart.[70]

Mount Pisgah: A Sermon preached at the Public Thanksgiving, Feb 14th, 1688–9, for England's Deliverance from Popery, upon Deut. iii. 24–25 (1688–9), Vol. 4, pp. 307–35 [approximately 12,000 words]

This single sermon was preached, as the title explains, at a public service of thanksgiving for Protestant success in the Glorious Revolution of 1688. It was attached to Flavel's long treatise *England's Duty*. Beginning with Deuteronomy 3:24–25, he derives and bases the sermon on the doctrine '[t]hat great mercies

---

[67] Flavel, *Works*, Vol. 4, p. 6.
[68] Flavel, *Works*, Vol. 4, p. 3.
[69] Flavel, *Works*, Vol. 4, p. 17.
[70] Flavel, *Works*, Vol. 4, p. 5.

received (though there be yet greater than they to be expected) call for an answerable sense and acknowledgment in the saints.'[71]

He states his purpose at the beginning of the sermon. 'You are called this day to rejoice; I am not only called to rejoice with you in the public mercies of this day, but also to direct you to the best way of improving the mercies you rejoice in, that they may prove introductive to greater mercies than themselves.'[72]

A Coronation-Sermon preached at Dartmouth (1689), Vol. 6, pp. 545–63 [approximately 8,000 words]

This sermon was preached in Dartmouth on the day of the coronation of William and Mary. Flavel used the occasion of the coronation to draw an analogy between it and a soul's conversion. 'Thus I have endeavored to spiritualize and improve the great and solemn actions of this good day.'[73] Basing the sermon upon Song of Solomon 3:1, he moves in his analogy from a coronation to a wedding. 'The coronation-day of a king, is, in a sense, the marriage-day betwixt him and his people.'[74] He then derives, and bases the sermon on, the doctrine '[t]hat the day of a believer's espousals to Christ by faith, is to Christ as the day of a king's coronation is to him, even the day of the gladness of his heart.'[75] Flavel presses the sermon in an evangelistic direction, urging his hearers and readers to 'espouse' Christ as personal king.

ΠΛΑΝΗΛΟΓΙΑ: A Succinct and Seasonable Discourse of the Occasions, Causes, Nature, Rise, Growth, and Remedies of Mental Errors (1690–91), Vol. 3, pp. 413–92 [approximately 34,000 words]

This treatise was published as a compilation of four works. They are titled separately in Flavel's *Works* and, although related theologically to each other, are written in such a way that each stands alone. Two are called appendices to *Mental Errors* and one is an individual sermon. We will consider each separately.

Flavel explains the four works and their relation to each other and to his purposes:

> The book now in thy hands consisteth of four parts, viz. 1. A general discourse of the causes and cures of errors, very necessary at all times (especially at this time) ... . 2. Next, thou hast here the controversies moved by my antagonist [Philip

---

[71] Flavel, *Works*, Vol. 4, p. 312.
[72] Flavel, *Works*, Vol. 4, p. 309.
[73] Flavel, *Works*, Vol. 6, p. 563.
[74] Flavel, *Works*, Vol. 6, p. 546.
[75] Flavel, *Works*, Vol. 6, p. 549.

Appendix 5

Cary] ... . 3. Finding my adversary, in the pursuit of his design, running into many Antinomian delirations, to the reproach and damage of the cause he contends for, I thought it necessary to take the principal errors of Antinomianism into examination, especially at such a time as this, when they seem to spring afresh, to the hazard of God's truth, and the church's peace ... . Lastly, I have added to the former a short, plain, practical sermon, to promote the peace and unity of the churches of Christ.[76]

For only the second time in his writing career he had another person write a preface for one of his books. The actual author of the preface is not known but seven men put their names to it. Increase Mather, the author of the only other preface to a work of Flavel by another, is one of those men.

These seven men had been swept into a controversy which had been sparked by the publication of Tobias Crisp's complete works in the winter of 1689–90.[77] They, along with five other London ministers, had been asked to verify the authenticity of several previously unpublished sermons of Crisp. Their names in Crisp's volume were taken as an endorsement of Crisp's antinomian views and provoked many to consternation, including Richard Baxter. They used the occasion of the publication of Flavel's *Mental Errors*, which included a lengthy appendix arguing against antinomianism, as an opportunity to explain their names' presence in Crisp's works:

The reverend author [Flavel] of the ensuing treatises, having in them explained and defended several gospel-truths, unto which divers things in the writings of the reverend Dr. Crisp, deceased, do seem very opposite; whereas some of us, who subscribed a paper, the design whereof was only to testify, that we believed certain writings of the doctor's never before published, were faithfully transcribed by his son, the publisher of them, which paper is now, by the bookseller, prefixed to the whole volume; containing a large preface which we never saw till after the publication ... and are hereupon by some weak people misunderstood, as if, by that certificate, we intended an approbation of all that is contained in that volume. We declare that we had no such intention: As the paper we subscribed hath no word in it that gives any such intimation.[78]

Not ignorant of the developing controversy over antinomianism, Flavel's publication does more than merely give the misunderstood London ministers an opportunity to explain themselves. He sees the errors of antinomianism as connected to the debate he has been participating in with Philip Cary over infant baptism, and he uses these treatises to attempt to correct the errors.

In *Mental Errors* Flavel first considers 'Twenty general Observations about the Rise and Increase of the Errors of the Times.'[79] These observations are

---

[76] Flavel, *Works*, Vol. 3, pp. 419–21.
[77] A discussion of the controversy can be found in Toon, *Hyper-Calvinism*.
[78] Flavel, *Works*, Vol. 3, p. 414.
[79] Flavel, *Works*, Vol. 3, p. 426.

stated as principles which apply to the church in any situation or time. He then considers sixteen causes of error. The first nine are found in the 'evil dispositions of the seduced.'[80] The next two causes are a consideration of the 'impulsive and instrumental causes, namely, Satan and false teachers.' He then finishes the treatise with five 'special and most successful methods frequently used by them [false teachers], to draw the minds of men from the truth.'[81] Each discussion of a 'cause' of error is followed by a detailed discourse on the corresponding 'remedy.'

> *An Appendix* [to ΠΛΑΝΗΛΟΓΙΑ], *Vindiciarium Vindex: or, A Refutation of the weak and impertinent Rejoinder of Mr. Philip Cary. Wherein he vainly attempts the Defence of his absurd Thesis to the great abuse and injury of the Laws and Covenants of God* (1690–91), Vol. 3, pp. 493–550 [approximately 25,000 words]

This appendix comes as the completion of a printed debate between Flavel and Philip Cary. Cary, a separatist clergyman residing in Dartmouth, began the debate by printing his *Solemn Call*, distributing it in Dartmouth, and asking Flavel for his opinion. Flavel responded with *Reply to Cary's Call*. Cary then printed a rejoinder, giving Flavel a copy while it was still at the printer. Flavel addresses Cary at the beginning of this treatise, *Refutation of Cary's Rejoinder*:

> I have thoroughly considered your reply in the manuscript you sent me, which I hear is now in the press; and in the following sheets have given a full, and (I think) a final answer to whatsoever is material therein: And, it so falling out, that my discourse of *Errors* was just going under the press, whilst your rejoinder was there also, I thought it not convenient to delay my reply any longer.[82]

In the disputation Flavel does not alter his arguments in *Reply to Cary's Call*. Rather, he orients his thoughts into three sections:

> I. I shall clearly evince to the world that Mr. Cary hath not been able to discharge and free his own thesis from the horrid consequents and gross absurdities which I have laid to their charge in my first reply ... . II. That he hath left my arguments standing in their full strength against him. III. And then I shall confirm and strengthen my three positions.[83]

The three are listed in the summary of *Reply to Cary's Call*.

> *The Second Appendix* [to ΠΛΑΝΗΛΟΓΙΑ], *Giving a brief Account of the*

---

[80] Flavel, *Works*, Vol. 3, p. 475.
[81] Flavel, *Works*, Vol. 3, p. 477.
[82] Flavel, *Works*, Vol. 3, p. 493.
[83] Flavel, *Works*, Vol. 3, p. 496.

Appendix 5 253

Rise and Growth of Antinomianism; the Deduction of the principal Errors of the Sect, With modest and seasonable reflections upon them (1690–91), Vol. 3, pp. 551–91 [approximately 17,500 words]

In his introductory paragraphs to this appendix Flavel explains his purpose in addressing the subject of antinomianism.

> The design of the following sheets, cast in as a *Mantissa* to the foregoing discourse of *Errors*, is principally to discharge and free the free grace of God from those dangerous errors, which fight against it under its own colours; partly to prevent the seduction of some that stagger; and, lastly, (though least of all) to vindicate my own doctrine.[84]

Apparently this last purpose in writing was provoked by accusations of antinomian leanings. 'But, notwithstanding my utmost care and caution, some have been apt to censure it [my doctrine], as if in some things it had a tang of antinomianism.'[85] Flavel was apparently eager to clear away any confusion in this matter.

He develops his argument by first discussing four reasons why, in his opinion, the antinomian heresy finds an audience in the hearts of men and women. He then explains the 'chief doctrines commonly called Antinomian.'[86] He lists and briefly summarizes ten errors. The remainder of the treatise is a careful refutation of each error.

Gospel Unity recommended to the Churches of Christ: A Sermon on 1 Corinthians 1:10 (1690–91), Vol. 3, pp. 592–608 [approximately 7,000 words]

A single sermon attached to Flavel's short treatise *Mental Errors* uses 1 Corinthians 1:10 as its text. Flavel derives from that passage, and bases the sermon on, the doctrine that '[u]nity amongst believers, especially in particular church-relation, is as desirable a mercy, as it is a necessary and indispensable duty.'[87] In the epistle to the reader which prefaced *Mental Errors,* he reveals to us his motivation for printing this sermon: 'I have added to the former a short, plain, practical sermon, to promote the peace and unity of the churches of Christ, and to prevent their relapse into past follies.'[88]

The Reasonableness of Personal Reformation, and the Necessity of Conversion: The true Methods of making all men happy in this world, and

---

[84] Flavel, *Works*, Vol. 3, p. 551.
[85] Flavel, *Works*, Vol. 3, p. 551.
[86] Flavel, *Works*, Vol. 3, p. 555.
[87] Flavel, *Works*, Vol. 3, p. 594.
[88] Flavel, *Works*, Vol. 3, p. 421.

in the world to come. Seasonably discoursed, and earnestly pressed upon this licentious age* (1691), Vol. 6, pp. 470–545 [approximately 33,000 words]

A medium-sized treatise, *Reasonableness and Necessity* was not a collection of sermons, but a persuasive for the unconverted. It was an evangelistic endeavour. Near the end of the work Flavel records his prayer for the treatise:

> O my God! ... thou that hast inclined my heart to make this attempt, and encouraged me with hope, that it shall not be in vain to all them that read it, ... I beseech thee, lay the hand of thy Spirit upon the heart and hand of thy servant; strengthen and guide him in drawing the bow of the gospel, and directing the arrows, that they may strike the mark he aims at, even the conviction and conversion of lewd and dissolute sinners. Command these considerations to stay and settle in their hearts, till they bring them fully over to thyself in Christ.[89]

As the title suggests, Flavel appeals to the reason of his readers, but he also aims at the readers' consciences, attempting to move them toward conversion. He begins his introduction: 'Two of the greatest, faithfullest, and most intimate friends in the world, reason and conscience, command me here, in their names, courteously to salute and invite you in.'[90]

The treatise consists of two parts. In the first he addresses the 'reasonableness of personal reformation.' After two chapters of introductory discussion he takes a chapter each to 'censure by reason and conscience' the sins of swearing and blasphemy, drunkenness, uncleanness, and the hatred of the godly. He then begins the second part in which he addresses the 'necessity of conversion' by showing its link with the first part. 'Reason and conscience having been shaming men out of their profaneness, in the former part of this discourse, free grace invites them to the life of holiness, and thereby to the life of blessedness, in this second part.'[91] He divides his arguments into ten parts, always with the conversion of the reader in mind.

The Character of a complete Evangelical Pastor, Drawn by Christ (1691), Vol. 6, pp. 564–85 [approximately 9,000 words]

In 1691 there was an attempt among western nonconformist ministers to formulate a union between their various factions. An assembly was planned for June in the city of Exeter, and Flavel was unanimously chosen to be its moderator. *The Character of a Pastor* is the sermon which he had prepared for this assembly. Although proceedings had begun with Flavel present, and progress towards the union was evident, records indicate that Flavel died on

---

[89] Flavel, *Works*, Vol. 6, p. 542.
[90] Flavel, *Works*, Vol. 6, p. 470.
[91] Flavel, *Works*, Vol. 6, p. 530.

June 26, 1691, without having delivered the sermon. The sermon was printed after his death as a part of *Mr. John Flavell's Remains*,[92] was later included in the *Whole Works*, and is thus found in all later editions of his *Works*.

The sermon is based upon Matthew 24:45–47. From that passage he derives the doctrine '[t]hat our Lord Jesus Christ will amply reward the faithful and prudent stewards of his house, in the day of their account.'[93] His aim in the sermon is the instruction and exhortation of his fellow ministers.

An Exposition of the Assembly's Catechism. With Practical Inferences from each Question: As it was carried out on in the Lord's Days Exercises in Dartmouth, in the first Year of Liberty, 1688 (1692–93), Vol. 6, pp. 138–317 [approximately 79,000 words]

Published posthumously, this last work was being prepared by Flavel when he died. As the title explains, it was not a collection of sermons but an exposition of the Shorter Catechism of the Westminster Assembly. He addressed the one hundred and seven questions of the Catechism by first stating the question and the answer. Then he followed each question and answer with further questions and answers of his own, designed to enable the reader to understand that particular portion of the Catechism and its implications for doctrine and life practices. He had worked through to question 102 at his death.

We are not sure of the identity of the person who authored the preface. In addition to the preface, this person finished the last five questions and readied the manuscript for publication. He states that Flavel had a particular concern that the children of his congregation understood the doctrine explained in the Shorter Catechism. Commenting on the fact that various publications had followed the Shorter Catechism with attempts to expand on it, he stated:

> others have parted the questions and answers into several little ones, under each, to make them more intelligible to younger ones, and more easy to be remembered. Among whom, worthy, orthodox, and excellent Mr. John Flavel may be ranked, who among other of his many most profitable labours, applied himself to the chewing of this bread of life, or crumbling it into smaller pieces, for the convenience of children, and, indeed, of all.[94]

Increase Mather, the only man to write a preface to any work of Flavel's while Flavel was alive, wrote an 'Epistle to the Reader' that was attached to the *Exposition* and which confirms Flavel's intent that this publication be of help to children. 'There are some considerations which may cause the reader to expect … that which is extrordinary [*sic*] in this little manuel [*sic*]; for the author's

---

[92] John Flavel, *Mr. John Flavell's Remains: Being Two Sermons Composed by that Reverend and Learned Divine* (London: Tho. Cockerill, 1691).
[93] Flavel, *Works*, Vol. 6, p. 566.
[94] Flavel, *Works*, Vol. 6, pp. 138–39.

heart was very much engaged in doing this service for Christ, in thus feeding his lambs.'[95]

A Familiar Conference Between a Minister and a Doubting Christian, concerning the Sacrament of the Lord's Supper (1701?), Vol. 6, pp. 460–69 [approximately 4,000 words]

As we mentioned in our discussion of *Sacramental Meditations*, the author of the biography prefixed to the *Whole Works* explains Flavel's intent to address issues of conscience associated with the participation in the Lord's Supper. 'He purposed to have enlarged his book of *Sacramental Meditations,* and had most judiciously stated and handled several cases of conscience on that occasion, which he designed to have inserted in the next edition, but lived not to finish them for the press.'[96] It is probable that *Familiar Conference* is the work to which the biographer was referring. For that reason we suppose that it was first published in 1701.

A very short addition to Flavel's *Works, Familiar Conference* is written as a conversation between a Christian and his pastor. The Christian has never participated in the sacrament of the Lord's Supper and expresses the reasons why. 'I never truly understood the institution, nature, administration, and ends of it, nor the qualifications of those who are to be partakers thereof.'[97] Flavel then uses the dialogue format to address those issues and to urge the Christian to partake.

A Hymn upon Romans 5:6–11 (1701?), Vol. 6, pp. 469–70 [approximately 180 words]

This short poem or hymn, based upon Romans 5:6–11, was probably first published in the first printing of Flavel's *Whole Works*.

A Double Scheme, or Table (1701?), Vol. 6, pp. 586–89 [approximately 1700 words]

The complete subtitle expresses well the aim and content of the table.

> A Double Scheme, or Table; containing, in the first column, The Sins most incident to the Members of particular Churches, plainly forbidden in the Word, and for which God sets Marks of his Displeasure on them. And, in the second,

---

[95] Flavel, *Works*, Vol. 6, pp. 139–40.
[96] Flavel, *Works*, Vol. 1, p. xiv.
[97] Flavel, *Works*, Vol. 6, p. 460.

Appendix 5 257

The Duties enjoined on them in the Scripture, in the conscientious Discharge whereof, they receive signal Fruits of his Favour.[98]

The table is then followed by a short list of six 'Benefits of walking by these Rules.'[99] This short work appears first in the *Whole Works*.

In addition to those writings of Flavel which appear in his *Works* there are four other written pieces available to us which are relevant to our study.

'To the Reader', in *A Cloud of Witnesses* (1670) [approximately 950 words]

Thomas Mall, a contemporary of Flavel, wrote a book in which he collected sayings of martyrs. Part of the title of the book is *A Cloud of Witnessess; or, the Sufferers Mirrour; made up of The Swanlike-songs, and other Choice Passages of several Martyrs and Confessors to the Sixteenth Century.*[100] Flavel provided a preface 'To The Reader' in which he built a case for why Mall's book would be profitable for the reader.

'Correspondence of John Flavel with Clement Lake' (1687) [approximately 1200 words]

Clement Lake was a Quaker who lived in Devon. Upon Lake's death his correspondence with Flavel was published by the Quaker community as an example of Lake's steadfastness when faced with opposition to Quaker doctrine.[101] In addition to two of Lake's letters, the correspondence includes two letters from Flavel to Lake, dated May 2, 1687, and August 7, 1687.

The editor of the recent publication of the correspondence suggests that Lake and Flavel knew each other. The editor's comments summarize Flavel's purpose in writing the letters. 'It is not clear how the two knew each other. It appears that they were close associates prior to Lake's "convincement" or conversion to the Quakers. Flavel appeals to his friend to reconsider his decision, convinced that Lake's optimism is blinding him to the profound

---

[98] Flavel, *Works*, Vol. 6, p. 586.
[99] Flavel, *Works*, Vol. 6, p. 589.
[100] Thomas Mall. *A cloud of witnesses; or, the sufferers mirrour; made up of the swanlike-songs, and other choice passages of several martyrs and confessors to the sixteenth century, in their treatises, speeches; letters, prayers, etc. in their prisons, or exiles; at the bar, or stake, etc. collected out of the ecclesiastical histories of: Eusebius, Fox, Fuller, Petrie, Scotland, and Mr. Samuel Ward's Life of Faith in Death, etc. and alphabetically disposed* (London: Robert Boulters, 1670).
[101] The correspondence can be found in Flavel, *Flavel, the Quaker and the Crown*.

doctrinal differences between Flavel's understanding of true Christianity and that taught by the Quakers.'[102]

'Abraham's Obedience' (date unknown) [approximately 2500 words]

This single handwritten sermon was never published but is preserved in the Bodleian Library. Flavel's text is Genesis 22:2–3. He derives from it, and bases the sermon on, the doctrine '[t]hat God is to be obeyed how cross soever his commands are to our wills; or else, God's will is to take place of our wills; or, this self the nearest self, the highest self is to decrease that Christ may increase.'[103]

The pages containing the sermon are not all present – the last part of the sermon is lost. Our comparison of this handwriting and existing handwritten letters of Flavel lead us to believe that this manuscript is not in his handwriting. The place in which this sermon was preached, the date, and the identity of the one who transcribed it, are unknown.

'A sure tryal of a Christian's state' (1693) [approximately 3500 words]

James Burdwood, a friend of Flavel and fellow minister in Dartmouth, was given the opportunity after Flavel's death to look at some of his papers. Flavel had apparently been working on a discourse on the issue of self-examination. The entire discourse was not in complete form, but the ninth and final section was complete. Burdwood, himself publishing a book entitled *Helps for faith and patience in times of affliction*, decided to include the final section of Flavel's notes as an appendix to his own book. Burdwood wrote:

> Before I had finish'd the foregoing Treatise, there came to my hands, by *God's good Providence*, some Papers of very great concernment to all our Souls for Eternity, being the Conclusion of a Discourse by that Eminent, Learned, and Pious Servant of the Lord Jesus, Mr. *John Flavel*, … Which Papers when I viewed and reviewed, I bless God, I felt so much power in the Contents of them, and so much sweetness, that I thought not fit to eat my Morsels alone, but was strongly imprest to make them publick, which here by the consent of his dear Relations, I presume to do.[104]

Flavel's discourse was based upon 2 Corinthians 13:5 and was aimed at helping those who professed faith in Christ to discern whether or not they had a true 'interest in Christ.' The thrust of this portion of Flavel's writing was, in Burdwood's words, 'concerning Self-examination about a Man's Interest in Christ.' Burdwood printed it, 'hoping it will awaken those that did hear those

---

[102] Flavel, *Flavel, the Quaker and the Crown*, p. 7.
[103] Flavel, 'Abraham's Obedience,' Bodleian Library, MS J. Walker C.7.189.
[104] Burdwood, *Helps for Faith*.

close-trying Truths, to be more exact in their trying Work, and may also excite others to due diligence in that so profitable and too much neglected Duty of Self-examination.'[105]

---

[105] Burdwood, *Helps for Faith.*

Bibliography

Manuscripts

Elys, Edmund. Letters to John Walker containing rough drafts of Elys' letters to John Flavel, March 6, 1703. Bodleian Library, MS. J. Walker e.8.32, 35, 39, 40.
——. 'Reflections: Reflections [by E. Elys] upon several passages in a book [by J. Flavel] entitled, The reasonableness of a personal reformation, and the necessity of conversion, with a letter to Mr. J. Galpine, concerning his printed encomium of J.F.,' 1692. Bodleian Library, G. Pamph. 1061(12).
——. Essay commenting on Flavel's *Fountain of Life*, date unknown. Bodleian Library, MS J. Walker e.8.44.
Flavel, John. 'Abraham's Obedience,' sermon manuscript, date unknown. Bodleian Library, MS J. Walker C.7.189.
——. Letters to Edmund Elys, June 2, 1687; June 13, 1687. Bodleian Library, MS. J. Walker e.8.39, 40.
——. Letter to J. Thornton, August 15, 1684. Bodleian Library, Rawl. Lrs. 109.33.
——. 'Mr. Flavell's legacy to his people annexed to his last will and testament,' date unknown. Bodleian Library, MS C.4. pp. 7–8.
Palke, Thomas. 'Upon the sudden death of the worthy Mr. John Flavell Minister in Dartmouth,' poem, date unknown. Bodleian Library, Walker MS C.4. pp. 7–8.
Quick, John. *Icones sacrae anglicaneae: or The lives & deathss of severall eminent English divines, ministers of the gospell, pastors of churches, & professors of divinity in our own & forreigne universitys*, c.1706. Dr. Williams's Library, MS 38.34, 35.
Smith, Humphries. 'For the Reverend Mr. John Walker, a minister in Exeter' [letter from Smith to Walker], July 26, 1704. Bodleian Library, MS J. Walker c.2.422.

Primary Sources

Ames, William. *Marrow of Sacred Divinity*. London: Edward Griffin, 1643.
——. *The Marrow of Theology*, transl. John Eusden (from 3rd Latin edn, 1629). Grand Rapids: Baker, 1968.
Baxter, Richard. *A Call to the Unconverted*. London: R.W., 1658.
——. *The Divine Life*. London: Francis Tyton, 1664.
——. *Richard Baxter's Catholick Theologie*. London: Nevill Simmons, 1675.
——. *Treatise on Conversion* (abridged from 1657 edn). New York: American Tract Society, 1850.
Bernard, Richard. *The Faithfull Shepheard: Or, The Shepheards Faithfulnesse*. London: Arnold Hatfield, 1607.
Brockett, Allan. ed., 'The Exeter Assembly: The Minutes of the Assemblies of the United Brethren of Devon and Cornwall, 1691–1717, as transcribed by the Reverend Isaac Gilling.' *Devon & Cornwall Record Society* (new series), Vol. 6 (1963).

Burdwood, James. *Helps for faith and patience in times of affliction: To which is added, A Sure Tryal of a Christian's state, by John Flavell late minister (also) in Dartmouth.* London: Jonathan Robinson, 1693.
Calamy, Edmund, and Samuel Palmer. *The Nonconformist's memorial: being an account of the ministers, who were ejected or silenced after the restoration, particularly by the Act of Uniformity, which took place on Bartholomew-Day, Aug. 24, 1662 : containing a concise view of their lives and characters.* London: W. Harris, 1775.
Cary, Philip. *A just reply to Mr. John Flavell's arguments by way of answer to a discourse lately published, entitled A Solemn Call.* London: J. Harris, 1690.
Edwards, Jonathan. *A treatise concerning religious affections.* Boston: S. Kneeland and T. Green, 1746.
——. *The Religious Affections.* London: Banner of Truth, 1961.
——. *Images or Shadows of Divine Things*, ed. Perry Miller, Westport: Greenwood Press, 1977 (first published 1746).
——. *The Works of Jonathan Edwards*, Vol. 2, *Religious Affections*, ed. John E. Smith. New Haven: Yale University Press, 1959.
——. *The Works of Jonathan Edwards.* Vol. 4, *Jonathan Edwards: The Great Awakening*, ed. C.C. Goen, New Haven and London: Yale University Press, 1972.
——. *The Works of Jonathan Edwards*, Vol. 11, *Jonathan Edwards: Typological Writings*, ed. Wallace Anderson. New Haven and London: Yale University Press, 1993.
Fenner, William. *A Treatise of the Affections; or, The Soules Pulse.* London: R.H., 1642.
Firmin, Giles. *Real Christian; or a treatise of effectual calling.* London: D. Newman, 1670.
Flavel, John. *England's duty.* London: [n.p.], 1688.
——. *Flavel, the Quaker and the Crown: John Flavel, Clement Lake, and Religious Liberty in 17th Century England.* Cambridge, MA: Rhwymbooks, 2000 (first published 1687–92).
——. *Keeping the heart* (abridged edn). Wilmington: Sovereign Grace, 1972 [first published 1688].
——. *Mental errors.* London: Thomas Cockerill, 1691.
——. *Mr. John Flavell's remains: Being two sermons composed by that reverend and learned divine.* London: Thomas Cockerill, 1691.
——. 'Observations on Error.' *BT* no. 12 (September 1958), pp. 13–18.
——. *Preparation for suffering.* London: Robert Boulter, 1681.
——. *The reasonableness of personal reformation.* London: Thomas Cockerill, 1691.
——. *The whole works of the Reverend Mr. John Flavel, late minister at Dartmouth in Devon, in two volumes.* 2 vols, London: Thomas Parkhurst, 1701.
——. *The whole works of John Flavel, 2nd edition.* 2 vols, London: [n.p.], 1716.
——. *The Works of John Flavel.* 6 vols, London: Banner of Truth, 1968 (reprint of 1820 edn).
——. 'Unqualified Preachers.' *BT* no. 255 (December 1984), pp. 17–18, 20.
——. *Vindiciae legis.* London: M. Wotton, 1690.
Gibbons, Thomas, and Edmund Calamy. *An English version of the Latin epitaphs in the nonconformist's memorial. To which is added a poem sacred to the memory of the two thousand ministers ejected or silenced by the Act of Uniformity, August 24, 1662.* London: W. Harris, 1775.

Goodwin, Thomas. *Works of Thomas Goodwin*. 12 vols, Eureka: Tanski Publications, 1996 (reprint of 1861–66 edn).
Hooker, Thomas. *The Application of Redemption by the effectual work of the word, and spirit of Christ, for the bringing home of lost sinners to God*. London: Peter Cole, 1656.
——. *The Soules Preparation for Christ, or, A Treatise of Contrition. Wherein is discovered How God breaks the Heart and wounds the Soule, in the conversion of a Sinner to Himself*. London: Robert Davulman, 1632.
Keach, Benjamin. *The banquetting-house, or A feast of fat things*. London: H. Barnard, 1692.
——. *The ax laid to the root: Containing an exposition of that metaphorical text of holy scripture, Mat. 3.10. Part II. Wherein Mr. John Flavel's last grand arguments in his Vindiciarum Vindex, to prove circumcision a gospel-covenant, are answered*. London: John Harris, 1693.
Lake, Clement. *Something by way of testimony concerning Clement Lake of Crediton in Devonshire; with something he wrote in his life time, by way of answer, unto John Flavell, independent preacher of Dartmouth*. London: T. Sowle, 1692.
Locke, John. *An essay concerning humane understanding in four books*. London: Tho. Basset, 1690.
Mall, Thomas. *A cloud of witnesses; or, the sufferers mirrour, made up of the swanlike-songs, and other choice passages of several martyrs and confessors to the sixteenth century, in their treatises, speeches; letters, prayers, etc. in their prisons, or exiles; at the bar, or stake, etc*. London: Robert Boulters, 1670.
Manton, Thomas. *One hundred and Ninety Sermons on the Hundred and Nineteenth Psalm*. London: T.P., 1681.
Owen, John. *A Discourse Concerning the Holy Spirit*. London: J. Darby, 1674.
Perkins, William. *The Arte of Prophecying: Or, A Treatise Concerning the sacred and onely true manner and methode of Preaching*. London: Felix Kyngston, 1607.
——. *The Art of Prophesying with The Calling of the Ministry*, intro. Sinclair B Ferguson. Edinburgh: Banner of Truth, 1996 (first published 1592, 1605).
——. *The Works of William Perkins*, transl. and ed. Ian Breward. 3 vols, Appleford, Berkshire: Sutton Courtenay Press, 1970.
——. *William Perkins 1558–1602 English Puritanist: His Pioneer Works on Casuistry: 'A Discourse of Conscience' and 'The Whole Treatise of Cases of Conscience'*, ed. Thomas F. Merrill. The Hague: N.V. Drukkerij Trio, 1966.
Shepard, Thomas. *Parable of the Ten Virgins*. London: J. Haynes, 1660.
——. *The sound believer a treatise of evangelicall conversion*. London: R. Dawlman, 1649.
Sibbes, Richard. *A Learned Commentary or Exposition: upon the first Chapter of the Second Epistle of S. Paul to the Corinthians*. London: J.L., 1655.
Stoddard, Solomon. *A Guide to Christ*, Boston: J. Allen, 1714.
——. *A treatise concerning conversion*, Boston: J. F., 1719.
Udall, John. *Amendment of Life: Three Sermons, Upon Actes 2. verses 37. 38 containing the true effect of the worde of God in the conversion of the goldly*. London: Thomas Man, 1584.
Whitefield, George. *George Whitefield's Journals*. London: Banner of Truth, 1960 (first published 1738–41).

Wolseley, Charles. *The Unreasonableness of Atheism made manifest, In a Discourse written by the command of a Person of Honour*. London: Nathaniel Ponder, 1669.

Secondary Sources

Books

A'Beckett, W. 'John Flavel.' In *Universal biography*. London: Isaac, Tuckey and Co., 1836.
Aikin, J. 'John Flavel.' In *General biography; or, Lives critical and historical, of the most eminent persons of all ages, countries, conditions, and professions, arranged according to alphabetical order*. London: G.G. and J. Robinson, 1799–1815.
Alexander, H.G. *Religion in England, 1558–1662*. London: University of London Press, 1968.
Allibone, S.A. 'John Flavel.' In *A Critical Dictionary of English Literature, and British and American Authors, living and deceased, from the Earliest Accounts to the Middle of the Nineteenth Century*. Philadelphia: J.B. Lippincott, 1859–71.
Allison, C.F. *The Rise of Moralism: The Proclamation of the Gospel from Hooker to Baxter*. London: SPCK, 1966.
Anon. *Nonconformist Congregations in Great Britain: A List of Histories and other Material in Dr Williams's Library*. London: Dr Williams's Trust, 1973.
Atkinson, Nigel G. *Richard Hooker and the Authority of Scripture, Tradition and Reason: Reformed Theologian of the Church of England?* Carlisle: Paternoster, 1997.
Beeke, Joel R. *The Quest for Full Assurance: The Legacy of Calvin and his Successors*. Edinburgh: Banner of Truth, 1999.
——., and Randall J. Pederson. *Meet the Puritans*. Grand Rapids: Reformation Heritage Books, 2006.
Bickel, R. Bruce. *Light and Heat: The Puritan View of the Pulpit*. Morgan: Soli Deo Gloria, 1999.
Binmore, J.W. *The History of the Baptist Church, Dartmouth*. Dartmouth: Baptist Church, 1950.
Blench, J.W. *Preaching in England in the Late Fifteenth and Sixteenth Centuries: A Study of English Sermons 1450–c.1600*. Oxford: Basil Blackwell, 1964.
Bliss, John Homer. *Genealogy of the Bliss Family in America, from about the year 1550 to 1880*. Boston: the author, 1881.
Bogue, David, and James Bennet. *History of Dissenters from the Revolution in 1688 to the year 1808*. Vol. 2. London: [n.p.], 1809.
Bolam, C.G, and R. Thomas. *The English Presbyterians, from Elizabeth Puritanism to modern Unitarianism*. Boston: Beacon Press, 1968.
Bozeman, Theodore D. *The Precisianist Strain: Disciplinary Religion & Antinomian Backlash in Puritanism to 1638*. Chapel Hill: Omohundro Institute of Early American History and Culture, 2004.
Bremer, Francis J. *Congregational Communion: Clerical Friendship in the Anglo-American Puritan Community, 1610–1692*. Boston: Northeastern University Press, 1994.
——, ed. *Puritanism: Transatlantic Perspectives on a Seventeenth-Century Anglo-American Faith*. Boston: Massachusetts Historical Society, 1993.

———. *The Puritan Experiment: New England Society from Bradford to Edwards.* New York: St. Martin's Press, 1976.
———. *Shaping New Englands: Puritan Clergymen in Seventeenth-Century England and New England.* New York: Twayne, 1994.
Brockett, Allan. *Nonconformity in Exeter, 1650–1875.* Manchester: Manchester University Press, 1962.
———. *The Devon Union List (DUL): A Collection of Written Material relating to the County of Devon.* Exeter: University Library, 1977.
Brook, Benjamin. *The Lives of the Puritans, containing a biographical account of those divines who distinguished themselves in the cause of religious liberty.* 3 vols, London: J. Black, 1813.
Brown, John. *Puritan Preaching in England: A Study of Past and Present.* New York: Charles Scribner's Sons, 1900.
Buswell, James Oliver. *A Systematic Theology of the Christian Religion.* Singapore: Christian Life Publishers, 1994.
Chalmers, A. 'John Flavel.' In *The general biographical dictionary.* London: J. Nichols, 1812–17.
Chambers, J. 'John Flavel.' In *Biographical illustrations of Worcestershire: including lives of persons, natives or residents, eminent either for piety or talent: to which is added, a list of living authors of the county.* London: Longman, Hurst, Rees, Orme, and Brown, 1820.
Cohen, Charles L. *God's Caress: The Psychology of Puritan Religious Experience.* Oxford: Oxford University Press, 1986.
Cole, Benjamin. *Authentic extracts from the lives of John Flavel and Rev. William Tennent.* Brattleborough, Vermont: the author, 1807.
Collier, J. 'John Flavel.' In *A supplement to the great historical, geographical, genealogical and poetical dictionary: being a curious miscellany of sacred and profane history.* London: W. Bowyer for C. Collier, 1727.
Collinson, Patrick. *English Puritanism.* London: Historical Association, 1983.
———. *Godly people: Essays on English Protestantism and Puritanism.* London: Hambledon Press, 1983.
———. *The Elizabethan Puritan Movement.* Oxford, New York: Clarendon Press, Oxford University Press, 1990.
Como, David R. *Blown by the Spirit: Puritanism and the Emergence of an Antinomian Underground in Pre-Civil-War England.* Stanford: Stanford University Press, 2004.
Coolidge, John S. *The Pauline rRnaissance in England: Puritanism and the Bible.* Oxford: Clarendon Press, 1970.
Cragg, Gerald R. *From Puritanism to the Age of Reason: A Study of Changes in Religious Thought within the Church of England, 1660–1700.* Cambridge: Cambridge University Press, 1950.
———. *Puritanism in the Period of the Great Persecution 1660–1688.* Cambridge: Cambridge University Press, 1957.
Cunningham, George G. 'John Flavel, B.A.' In *Lives of eminent and illustrious Englishmen, from Alfred the Great to the latest times, on an original plan.* Glasgow: A. Fullarton, 1836–38.
Cunningham, William. *The Reformers and the Theology of the Reformation.* Edinburgh: T. and T. Clark, 1866.

Curtis, Mark. *Oxford and Cambridge in Transition, 1558–1642*. Oxford: Clarendon Press, 1959.
Dakin, A. *Calvinism*. Philadelphia: Westminster Press, 1946.
Dale, R.W. *History of English Congregationalism*. London: Hodder and Stoughton, 1907.
Davenport, Richard A. 'John Flavel.' In *A dictionary of biography; comprising the most eminent characters of all ages, nations, and professions*. Boston: Gray and Bowen, 1831.
Davies, Horton. *Worship and Theology in England: From Cranmer to Baxter and Fox, 1534–1690*. 2 vols in 1, Grand Rapids: William B. Eerdmans, 1996.
——. *The Worship of the English Puritans*. Morgan: Soli Deo Gloria, 1997.
——, ed. *Studies of the Church in History: Essays honoring Robert S. Paul on his Sixty-Fifth Birthday*. Allison Park: Pickwick Publications, 1983
Dever, Mark E. *Richard Sibbes: Puritanism and Calvinism in late Elizabethan and early Stuart England*. Macon: Mercer University Press, 2000.
Dowey, Edward, Jr. *The Knowledge of God in Calvin's Theology*. Grand Rapids: William B. Eerdmans, 1994.
Durston, Christopher, and Jacqueline Eales. *The Culture of English Puritanism, 1560–1700*. New York: St. Martin's Press, 1996.
Dyrness, William A. *Reformed Theology and Visual Culture: The Protestant Imagination from Calvin to Edwards*. Cambridge: Cambridge University Press, 2004.
Elliott-Binns, L.E. *The Reformation in England*. London: Duckworth, 1937.
Ferrell, Lori A., and Peter McCullough. *The English Sermon Revised: Religion, Literature and History 1600–1750*. Manchester: Manchester University Press, 2000.
Fiering, Norman S. *Moral Philosophy at Seventeenth Century Harvard: A Discipline in Transition*. Chapel Hill: University of North Carolina Press, 1981.
Fincham, Kenneth. *Prelate as Pastor: The Episcopate of James I*. Oxford: Clarendon Press, 1990.
Foakes-Jackson, F.J. *The Church in England*. Cambridge: Cambridge University Press, 1931.
Foster, Joseph. *Alumni Oxonienses. The Members of the University of Oxford, 1500–1714: Their Parentage, Birthplace, and year of Birth, with a Record of their Degrees*, Vol. 2. London: Parker and Co., 1891.
Gee, Henry, and William J. Hardy, eds. *Documents Illustrative of English Church History: Compiled from Original Sources*. London: Macmillan, 1910.
George, Charles, and Katherine George. *The Protestant Mind of the English Reformation*. Princeton: Princeton University Press, 1961.
Gildrie, Richard P. *The Profane, the Civil, & the Godly: The Reformation of Manners in Orthodox New England, 1679–1749*. University Park: Pennsylvania State University Press, 1994.
Gorton, J.A. 'John Flavel.' In *A general biographical dictionary, New edition*. London: Whittaker, 1841.
Goyena, Antonio P. 'Gabriel Vasquez.' In *Catholic Encyclopedia*, New York: Robert Appleton, 1914; online at http://oce.catholic.com/index.php?title=Gabriel_Vasquez.
Greaves, Richard L. *Enemies under his Feet: Radicals and Nonconformists in Britain, 1664–1677*. Stanford: Stanford University Press, 1990.
——. *Saints and Rebels: Seven Nonconformists in Stuart England*. Macon: Mercer University Press, 1985.

Grell, Ole Peter, Jonathan I. Israel, and Nicholas Tyacke, eds. *From Persecution to Toleration: The Glorious Revolution and Religion in England*. Oxford: Clarendon Press, 1991.
Green, Ian. *Print and Protestantism in Early Modern England*. Oxford: Oxford University Press, 2000.
Green, V.H.H. *A History of Oxford University*. London: B.T. Batsford, 1974.
———. *Religion at Oxford and Cambridge*. London: SCM Press, 1964.
Gregory, J. *Puritanism in the Old World and in the New*. New York: Fleming H. Revell, 1896.
Hall, David. *Worlds of Wonder, Days of Judgement*. New York: Alfred A. Knopf, 1989.
Haller, William. *The Rise of Puritanism*. New York: Harper & Row, 1957.
Hambrick-Stowe, Charles E. *The Practice of Piety: Puritan Devotional Disciplines in Seventeenth-Century New England*. Chapel Hill: University of North Carolina Press, 1982.
Heimert, Alan, and Andrew Delbanco. *The Puritans in America: A Narrative Anthology*. Cambridge, MA: Harvard University Press, 1985.
Helm, Paul. *Calvin & the Calvinists*. Edinburgh: Banner of Truth, 1982.
Henson, H. Hensley. *Studies in English Religion in the Seventeenth Century: St. Margaret's Lectures 1903*. London: John Murray, 1903.
Hill, Christopher. *Puritanism and Revolution: Studies in Interpretation of the English Revolution of the 17th Century*. London: Secker & Warburg, 1958.
———. *Society and Puritanism in Pre-Revolutionary England*. New York: Schocken, 1964.
Hindson, Edward, ed. *Introduction to Puritan Theology: A Reader*. Grand Rapids: Baker, 1976.
Holifield, E. Brooks. *The Covenant Sealed: The Development of Puritan Sacramental Theology in Old and New England, 1570–1720*. New Haven: Yale University Press, 1974.
Hook, W.F. *An Ecclesiastical Biography: Containing the Lives of ancient Fathers and Modern Divines, Interspersed with Notices of Heretics and Schismatics, forming a Brief History of the Church in every Age*. London: F. and J. Rivington, 1852.
Hoopes, James. *Sources for* The New England Mind: The Seventeenth Century. Williamsburg: Institute of Early American History and Culture, 1981.
Howell, W.S. *Logic and Rhetoric in England, 1500–1700*. Princeton: Princeton University Press, 1956.
Hulbert, E.B. *The English Reformation and Puritanism, with other Lectures and Addresses by E.B. Hulbert, D.D., LL.D., A Memorial*, ed. A.R.E. Wyant. Chicago: University of Chicago Press, 1908.
Jones, R. Tudur. *Congregationalism in England: 1662–1962*. London: Independent Press, 1962.
Kapic, Kelly M. *Communion with God: The Divine and the Human in the Theology of John Owen*. Grand Rapids: Baker Academic, 2007.
———, and Randall C. Gleason, eds. *The Devoted Life: An Invitation to the Puritan Classics*. Downers Grove: InterVarsity Press, 2004.
Kearney, Hugh. *Scholars and Gentlemen: Universities and Society in Pre-Industrial Britain, 1500–1700*. Ithaca: Cornell University Press, 1970.
Kendall, R.T. *Calvin and English Calvinism to 1649*. Oxford: Oxford University Press, 1979.

Knight, Charles. 'John Flavel.' In *The English Cyclopaedia*. London: Bradbury and Evans, 1856.
Lake, Peter. *Moderate Puritans and the Elizabethan Church*. Cambridge: Cambridge University Press, 1982.
——. *Anglicans and Puritans? Presbyterianism and English Conformist Thought from Whitgift to Hooker*. London: Unwin Hyman, 1988.
Lambert, Frank. *Inventing the 'Great Awakening.'* Princeton: Princeton University Press, 1999.
Lewis, Peter. *The Genius of Puritanism*. Morgan: Soli Deo Gloria, 1996.
Matthew, H.C.G., and Brian Harrison, eds, *Oxford Dictionary of National Biography*, 60 vols, Oxford: Oxford University Press, 2004; online edn at http://www.oxforddnb.com.
Matthews, A.G., and Edmund Calamy. *Calamy Revised: Being a Revision of Edmund Calamy's Account of the Ministers and Others Ejected and Silenced, 1660–2*. Oxford: Clarendon Press, 1988.
Maunder, Samuel. 'John Flavel.' In *The biographical treasury*. London: Longman, Orme, Brown, Green, & Longmans, 1841.
McKim, Donald K. *Ramism in William Perkins' Theology*. New York: Peter Lang, 1987.
Mclachlan, H.J. *Socinianism in Seventeenth Century England*. London: Oxford University Press, 1951.
McNeill, John T. *The History and Character of Calvinism*. New York: Oxford University Press, 1954.
Middleton, Erasmus. 'John Flavel.' In *Evangelical biography*. New ed., London, 1816.
Miller, Perry. *The New England Mind: The Seventeenth Century*. Cambridge, MA: Belknap Press, 1982.
——. *The New England Mind: From Colony to Province*. Cambridge, MA: Harvard University Press, 1953.
Mitchell, W. Fraser. *English Pulpit Oratory from Andrewes to Tillotson: A Study of its Literary Aspects*. New York: Russell & Russell, 1962.
Moorman, John R.H. *A History of the Church in England*. New York: Morehouse-Barlow, 1963.
Morgan, John. *Godly Learning: Puritan Attitudes towards Reason, Learning, and Education, 1560–1640*. Cambridge: Cambridge University Press, 1986.
Müller, E.F. Karl. 'Alsted, Johann Heinrich,' 'Keckermann, Bartholomaeus.' *The New Schaff-Herzog Encyclopedia of Religious Knowledge*. Grand Rapids: Baker, 1951.
Murray, Iain H. *Sermons of the Great Ejection*. London: Banner of Truth, 1962.
New, John F. *Anglican and Puritan: The Basis of their Opposition, 1558–1640*. London: Adam & Charles Black, 1964.
Nuttall, Geoffrey F. *The Holy Spirit in Puritan Faith and Experience*. Oxford: Basil Blackwell, 1946.
——. *The Puritan Spirit: Essays and Addresses*. London: Epworth, 1967.
Ong, Walter J. *Ramus, Method, and the Decay of Dialogue*. Cambridge, MA: Harvard University Press, 1958.
Patrides, C.A., ed. *The Cambridge Platonists*. Cambridge: Cambridge University Press, 1969.
Pettit, Norman. *The Heart Prepared: Grace and Conversion in Puritan Spiritual Life*. New Haven: Yale University Press, 1966.

Pullan, Leighton. *Religion since the Reformation: Eight Lectures preached before the University of Oxford in the year 1922, on the Foundation of the Rev. John Bampton, M.A., Canon of Salisbury.* Oxford: Clarendon Press, 1924.
Reid, W. Stanford, ed., *John Calvin: His Influence in the Western World.* Grand Rapids: Zondervan, 1982.
Richardson, Caroline F. *English Preachers and Preaching, 1640–1670: A Secular Study.* New York: Macmillan, 1928.
Rivers, Isabel. *Reason, Grace, and Sentiment: A Study of the Language of Religion and Ethics in England, 1660–1780.* Cambridge: Cambridge University Press, 1991.
Rooy, Sidney H. *The Theology of Missions in the Puritan Tradition.* Grand Rapids: William B. Eerdmans, 1965.
Rose, H J. 'John Flavel.' In *A New General Biographical Dictionary.* London: B. Fellowes, 1853.
Russell, Percy. *A Short Account of the Congregational Church in Dartmouth founded under the Leadership of John Flavell, 1662.* Dartmouth: Chronicle Printers, 1956.
——. *Flavel Memorial United Reformed Church (formerly Congregational) Dartmouth: Founded by John Flavel in 1662: A Short History of the Congregational Church in Dartmouth.* Dartmouth: Flavel Memorial United Reformed Church, 1974 (revision of 1956 work).
Ryken, Leland. *Worldly Saints: The Puritans as they really were.* Grand Rapids: Academie Books/Zondervan, 1986.
Sachse, William L. *Restoration England 1660–1689.* Cambridge: Cambridge University Press, 1971.
Schneider, Herbert W. *The Puritan Mind.* Ann Arbor: University of Michigan Press, 1958.
Shaw, William A. *A History of the English Church during the Civil Wars and under the Commonwealth, 1640–1660.* 2 vols, New York: Burt Franklin Reprints, 1974 (1900 edn).
Skalnik, James V. *Ramus and Reform: University and Church at the end of the Renaissance.* Kirksville: Truman State University Press, 2002.
Sprunger, Keith L. *The Learned Doctor William Ames: Dutch Backgrounds of English and American Puritanism.* Urbana: University of Illinois Press, 1972.
Steck, James S. *The Intellectual Pleasures of the Puritans.* Shippensburg State College faculty monograph series, Vol. 2, no. 1, ed. Dilys M Jones. Shippensburg: Shippensburg Collegiate Press, 1967.
Thomas, Keith V. *Religion and the Decline of Magic: Studies in Popular Belief in Sixteenth and Seventeenth Century England.* New York: Oxford University Press, 1971.
Toon, Peter. *The Emergence of Hyper-Calvinism in English Nonconformity, 1689–1765.* London: Olive Tree, 1967.
——. *Puritans and Calvinism.* Swengel: Reiner, 1973.
Toulouse, Teresa. *The Art of Prophesying: New England Sermons and the Shaping of Belief.* Athens: University of Georgia Press, 1987.
Tracy, Patricia J. 'Stoddard, Solomon.' In John A. Garraty and Mark C. Carnes, eds, *American National Biography,* New York: American Council of Learned Societies, 1999.
Trueman, Carl R, and R Scott Clark, eds. *Protestant Scholasticism: Essays in Reassessment.* Carlisle: Paternoster, 1999.

Turner, G. Lyon, ed. *Original Records of early Nonconformity under Persecution and Indulgence*, Vol. 1. London: T. Fisher Unwin, 1911.
Tyacke, Nicholas. *Anti-Calvinists: The Rise of English Arminianism, c.1590–1640*. Oxford: Clarendon Press, 1987.
van Beek, Marinus. *An Enquiry into Puritan Vocabulary*. Groningen: Wolters-Noordhoff, 1969.
Vaughan, Alden T, ed. *The Puritan Tradition in America 1620–1730*. Columbia: University of South Carolina Press, 1972.
Wahl, J. 'Baronius, Caesar, Ven.', In *New Catholic Encyclopedia*, New York: Catholic University of America Press, 2003.
Waller, J.F. 'John Flavel.' In *The Imperial Dictionary of Universal Biography*. London: W. Mackenzie, 1863.
Wand, J.W.C. *Anglicanism in History and Today*. New York: Thomas Nelson, 1962.
Watkins, J. 'John Flavel.' In *The universal biographical dictionary.* New ed., London: [n.p.], 1821.
Watt, R. 'John Flavel.' In *Bibliotheca britannica*. Edinburgh: A. Constable, 1824.
Watts, Michael R. *The Dissenters: From the Reformation to the French Revolution*. Oxford: Clarendon Press, 1978.
——. *The Dissenters: The Expansion of Evangelical Nonconformity*. Oxford: Clarendon Press, 1995.
White, B.R. *The English Puritan Tradition*. Nashville: Broadman Press, 1980.
White, Eugene E. *Puritan Rhetoric: The Issue of Emotion in Religion*. Carbondale and Edwardsville: Southern Illinois University Press, 1972.
Willey, Basil. *The Seventeenth Century Background: Studies in the Thought of the Age in Relation to Poetry and Religion*. London: Chatto & Windus, 1950.
Winship, Michael P. *Making Heretics: Militant Protestantism and Free Grace in Massachusetts, 1636–1641*. Princeton: Princeton University Press, 2002.
Wood, Anthony à. 'John Flavel.' In *Athenae oxoniensis*. New ed., London: Lackington, Hughes, etc., 1813–20.
Yarbrough, Stephen R. *Delightful Conviction: Jonathan Edwards and the Rhetoric of Conversion*. Westport: Greenwood Press, 1993.
Yuille, J. Stephen. *The Inner Sanctum of Puritan Piety: John Flavel's Doctrine of Mystical Union with Christ*. Grand Rapids: Reformation Heritage Books, 2007.

Articles
Alain, J.C. 'William Perkins: Plain Preaching.' *Preaching* 11 (1996), pp. 42–45.
Barry, Jonathan. 'The Seventeenth and Eighteenth Centuries.' In Nicholas Orme, ed., *Unity and Variety: A History of the Church in Devon and Cornwall*, pp. 81–108. Exeter: University of Exeter Press, 1991.
Bennett, Christopher. 'The Puritans and the Direct Operations of the Holy Spirit.' In *Building on a Sure Foundation: 1994 Westminster Conference*, pp. 108–22, London: Westminster Conference, 1994.
Brauer, Jerald C. 'Reflections on the Nature of English Puritanism.' *ChH* 23 (1954), pp. 99–108.
——. 'Conversion: From Puritanism to Revivalism.' *Journal of Religion* 58/3 (1978), pp. 227–43.
Budgen, Victor. 'How Flavel held his Hearers.' *Reformation Today* no. 63 (September–October 1981), p. 24.

Campbell, K.M. 'The Antinomian Controversies of the 17th Century.' In Donald Macleod, ed., *Living the Christian Life: Papers from the 1974 Westminster Conference*, pp. 61–81. London: Westminster Conference, 1974.
Christianson, Paul. 'Reformers and the Church of England under Elizabeth and the early Stuarts.' *JEH* 31 (1980), pp. 463–82.
Cohen, Ronald D. 'Puritan Education in Seventeenth Century England and New England.' *History of Education Quarterly* 13 (1973), pp. 301–307.
Collinson, Patrick. 'A Comment: Concerning the Name Puritan.' *JEH* 31 (1980), pp. 483–88.
——. 'England and International Calvinism, 1558–1640.' In M Prestwich, ed., *International Calvinism, 1541–1715*, pp. 197–223. Oxford: Clarendon Press, 1985.
Cook, Paul E.G. 'The Works of John Flavel.' *EQ* 41 (1969), pp. 178–80.
Cornick, David. 'Pastoral Care in England: Perkins, Baxter and Burnet.' In G.R. Evans, ed., *A History of Pastoral Care*, pp. 313–27. London and New York: Cassell, 2000.
Donagan, Barbara. 'Godly Choice: Puritan Decision-Making in 17th Century England.' *Harvard Theological Review* 76 (1983), pp. 307–34.
Edwards, Otis C., Jr. 'Preaching in New England.' *Anglican Theological Review* 71 (1989), pp. 191–200.
Fiering, Norman S. 'Will and Intellect in the New England Mind.' *William and Mary Quarterly*, 3rd ser., 29 (1972), pp. 515–58.
Fincham, Kenneth, and Peter Lake. 'Popularity, Prelacy and Puritanism in the 1630s: Joseph Hall explains himself.' *English Historical Review* 111 (1996), pp. 856–81.
Fletcher, Anthony. 'The Enforcement of the Conventicle Acts, 1664–1679.' In W.J. Sheils, ed., *Persecution and Toleration*, Studies in Church History, Vol. 21, pp. 235–46. Oxford: Blackwell, 1984.
Greaves, Richard L. 'Amid the Holy War: Bunyan and the Ethic of Suffering.' In Anne Laurence, W.R. Owens and Stuart Sim, eds, *John Bunyan and his England, 1628–88*, pp. 63–75. London and Ronceverte: Hambledon Press, 1990.
Green, I.M. 'Bunyan in Context: The Changing Face of Protestantism in Seventeenth-Century England.' In *Bunyan in England and Abroad: Papers delivered at the John Bunyan Tercentenary Symposium, Vrije Universiteit Amsterdam, 1988*, ed. M. van Os and G.J. Schutte, pp. 1–27. Amsterdam: VU Press, 1990.
Hoopes, James. 'Jonathan Edwards's Religious Psychology.' *Journal of American History* 69 (1983), pp. 849–65.
Hulse, Erroll. 'Adding to the Church: The Puritan Approach to Persuading Souls.' In David Bugden, ed., *Adding to the Church: Being Papers read at the 1973 Westminster Conference*, pp. i-xv, 7–19. London: Westminster Conference, 1973.
Keeble, Neil H. 'Richard Baxter's Preaching Ministry: Its History and Texts.' *JEH* 35 (1984), pp. 539–59.
Knox, R. Buick. 'The History of Doctrine in the Seventeenth Century.' In H Cunliffe-Jones, ed., *A History of Christian Doctrine*, pp. 427–51. Philadelphia: Fortress Press, 1978.
Lake, Peter. 'Conformist Clericalism: Richard Bancroft's Analysis of the Socio-Economic Roots of Presbyterianism.' In W.J. Sheils and Diana Wood, eds, *The Church and Wealth*, Studies in Church History, Vol. 24, pp. 219–29. Oxford: Blackwell, 1987.

——. 'The Problem of Puritanism.' In Francis Bremer, ed., *The Worlds of John Winthrop, England and New England, 1588–1649*. Millersville: Millersville State University, 1999.

Lea, Thomas D. 'The Hermeneutics of the Puritans.' *Journal of the Evangelical Theological Society* 39 (1996), pp. 271–84.

Lensch, Christopher K. 'Two early American Presbyterian Pastor-Theologians: Samuel Davies and Archibald Alexander.' *WRS Journal* 12/2 (August 2005), pp. 20–26.

McDonald, Suzanne. 'The Pneumatology of the "Lost" Image in John Owen.' *WTJ* 71 (2009), pp. 323–35.

McGee, J. Sears. 'William Laud and the Outward Face of Religion.' In R. DeMolen, ed., *Leaders of the Reformation*, pp. 318–44. Selinsgrove: Susquehanna University Press, 1984.

McKim, Donald K. 'Some aspects of Death and Dying in Puritanism.' In Robert V Schnucker, ed., *Calviniana: Ideas and Influence of Jean Calvin*, pp. 165–83. Kirksville: Sixteenth Century Journal Publishers, 1988.

Muller, Richard A. 'Covenant and Conscience in English Reformed Theology: Three Variations on a 17th Century Theme.' *WTJ* 42 (1980), pp. 308–34.

Murray, Iain H. 'John Flavel.' *BT* no. 60 (September 1968), pp. 1–10.

——. 'Faithful unto Death.' *BT* no. 27 (April 1962), pp. 1–14.

Murray, John J. 'John Flavel and the Problem of Providence.' In *Triumph through Tribulation: Papers from the 1998 Westminster Conference*, pp. 99–118. London: Westminster Conference, 1998.

O'Malley, James W., 'Content and Rhetorical Forms in Sixteenth-Century Treatises on Preaching', in James Murphy, ed., *Renaissance Rhetoric*. Berkeley: University of California Press, 1983.

Poe, Harry L. 'Bunyan's Departure from Preaching.' *EQ* 58 (1986), pp. 145–55.

Rechtien, John G. 'Logic in Puritan Sermons in the Late Sixteenth Century and Plain Style.' *Style* 13 (1979), pp. 237–58.

Rogal, Samuel J. 'Samuel Pepys at Church: One View of Restoration Pulpit Oratory.' *Historical Magazine of the Protestant Episcopal Church* 44 (1975), pp. 211–40.

Rupp, Gordon. 'Devotion of rapture in English Puritanism.' In R. Knox, ed., *Reformation Conformity and Dissent*, pp. 115–31. Oxford: Clarendon Press, 1977.

Shelley, Bruce L. 'Preaching in early New England.' In *Evangelical Roots: A Tribute to Wilbur Smith*, ed. Kenneth S. Kantzer, pp. 17–33. Nashville: Thomas Nelson, 1978.

Spurr, John. 'The Restoration Church of England, 1646–1689.' In Christopher Durston and Jacqueline Eales, eds, *The Culture of English Puritanism, 1560–1700*, pp. 234–65. New York: St. Martin's Press, 1996.

Tipson, Baird. 'The Elusiveness of "Puritanism."' *Religious Studies Review* 11 (1985), pp. 245–56.

Toulouse, Teresa. '"The arte of prophesying": John Cotton and the Rhetoric of Election.' *Early American Literature* 19 (1984-85), pp. 279–99.

Tyacke, Nicholas. 'Puritanism, Arminianism and Counter-Revolution.' In Conrad Russell, ed., *The Origins of the English Civil War*, pp. 119–44. London: Macmillan, 1973.

VanderMolen, Ronald J. 'Providence as Mystery, Providence as Revelation: Puritan and Anglican Modifications of John Calvin's Doctrine of Providence.' *ChH* 47(1978), pp. 27–47.

Vickers, Douglas. 'The Works of John Flavel.' *WTJ* 32 (1969), pp. 92–96.

Wakefield, Gordon S. 'The Puritans.' In C Jones et al., eds, *The Study of Spirituality*, pp. 437–45. Oxford: Oxford University Press, 1986.

Wallace, Dewey D., Jr. 'The Image of Saintliness in Puritan Hagiography, 1650–1700.' In *The Divine Drama in History and Literature: Essays presented to Horton Davies on his Retirement from Princeton University*, ed. J.E. Booty, pp. 23–43. Allison Park: Pickwick Publications, 1984.

Windeatt, Edward. 'Devonshire and the Indulgence of 1672.' *Congregational Historical Society Transactions* 2 (1902), pp. 159–70.

——. 'John Flavell: A notable Dartmouth Puritan and his Bibliography.' *Transactions of the Devonshire Association* 43 (1911), pp. 172–89.

Dissertations

Ball, John H., III. 'A Chronicler of the Soul's Windings: Thomas Hooker and his Morphology of Conversion.' Ph.D., Westminster Theological Seminary, 1990.

Barber, Robert L., Jr. 'The Puritan Connection between Prayer and Preaching.' D.Min., Fuller Theological Seminary, 2000.

Beck, Stephen P. 'The Doctrine of *gratia praeparans* in the Soteriology of Richard Sibbes.' Ph.D., Westminster Theological Seminary, 1994.

Beougher, Timothy K. 'Conversion: The Teaching and Practice of the Puritan Pastor Richard Baxter with regard to becoming a "True Christian".' Ph.D., Trinity Evangelical Divinity School, 1990.

Chalker, William H. 'Calvin and some Seventeenth Century English Calvinists: A Comparison of their Thought through an Examination of their Doctrines of the Knowledge of God, Faith, and Assurance.' Ph.D., Duke University, 1961.

Elliott, Bruce S. 'The Wrights of Salvation: Craft and Conversion among 17th Century English Puritans.' Ph.D., University of California, Berkeley, 2001.

Farrell, Earl T. 'The Doctrine of Man and Grace as held by the Reverend John Flavel.' B.D., Duke University, 1949.

Fedderson, Kim M. 'The Rhetoric of the Elizabethan Sermon.' Ph.D., York University (Canada), 1985.

Fulcher, John R. 'Puritan Piety in early New England: A Study in Spiritual Regeneration from the Antinomian Controversy to the Cambridge Synod of 1648 in the Massachusetts Bay Colony.' Ph.D., Princeton University, 1963.

Gillespie, J.T. 'Presbyterianism in Devon and Cornwall in the 17th Century.' M.A., University of Durham, date unknown.

Goode, Richard C. '"The only and principal end": Propagating the Gospel in early Puritan New England.' Ph.D., Vanderbilt University, 1995.

Gore, Ralph Jackson, Jr. 'The Pursuit of Plainness: Rethinking the Puritan Regulative Principle of Worship.' Ph.D., Westminster Theological Seminary, 1988.

Holbrook, Thomas Arthur. 'The elaborated Labyrinth: The American Habit of Typology.' Ph.D., University of Maryland, 1984.

Jussely, David H. 'The Puritan Use of the *Lectio Continua* in Sermon Invention (1640–1700).' Ph.D., University of Southern Mississippi, 1997.

Klein, Phyllis G. 'Impertinent Itinerants: Literary Representations of radical Protestant Evangelism in England, 1660–1775.' Ph.D., University of Denver, 1994.

Lunt, Anders Robert. 'The Reinvention of Preaching: A Study of Sixteenth and Seventeenth Century English Preaching Theories.' Ph.D., University of Maryland, 1998.
Maddux, Clark. 'Ramist Rationality, Covenant Theology, and the Poetics of Edward Taylor.' Ph.D., Purdue University, 2001.
Markham, Coleman. 'William Perkins' Understanding of the Function of Conscience.' Ph.D., Vanderbilt University, 1967.
McGrath, Gavin J. 'Puritans and the Human Will: Voluntarism within Mid-Seventeenth Century English Puritanism as seen in the Works of Richard Baxter and John Owen.' Ph.D., University of Durham, 1989.
Meyers, Patricia R. 'Rhetoric of Seventeenth-Century New England Puritan Occasional Sermons.' Ph.D., Arizona State University, 1992.
Orten, Jon D. 'Elizabethan Puritanism and the Plain Style.' Ph.D., University of Minnesota, 1989.
Pang, Patrick. 'A Study of Jonathan Edwards as a Pastor-Preacher.' D.Min., Fuller Theological Seminary, 1991.
Pipa, Joseph A., Jr. 'William Perkins and the Development of Puritan Preaching.' Ph.D., 1985.
Poe, Harry L. 'Evangelistic Fervency among the Puritans in Stuart England, 1603–1688.' Ph.D., Southern Baptist Seminary, 1982.
Stephenson, Sally Ann. 'The Ministerial and Theological Purposes of Jonathan Edwards' Thought: A Study in Source and Context.' Ph.D., University of Pennsylvania, 1983.
Tipson, Lynn Baird, Jr. 'The Development of a Puritan Understanding of Conversion.' Ph.D., Yale University, 1972.

Websites

'Genealogy SF', http://www.genealogysf.com/Stanton-p/p97.htm#i4820, accessed 6 November 2008.
'Rootsweb: Finding our Roots together,' http://www.rootsweb.com/~maessex/Wills/moodyb.htm, accessed 4 June 2007.
'Surname Site', http://surnamesite.com/harvard/harvard1818.htm, accessed 6 November 2008.
'Three Rivers Genealogy,' http://www.15122.com/3Rivers/History/CITIES/WMSettlers.htm, accessed 6 November 2008.
Broadhurst, Dale R. 'The Oliver Cowdery Pages,' http://olivercowdery.com/family/Cdrygen4.htm, accessed 6 November 2008.
Byler, Carol S. 'Snoddy Family History,' http://bellsouthpwp.net/c/s/csbyler/Genealogy/Snoddy/Snoddy.html, accessed 6 November 2008.
James and Randal Holcombe, 'Holcombe Family Genealogy,' http://www.holcombegenealogy.com/data/p2.htm#i83, accessed 6 November 2008.

Index of Authors and Subjects

Act of Uniformity 33–34, 36, 51, 144
Alexander, Archibald 44
Alsted, Johann 53, 68
Ames, William 43, 47–48, 53, 66, 77–81, 84, 93, 102, 113–14, 122, 132, 149–50, 161, 180
Anabaptists 248
Anderson, Wallace 43
Antinomianism 14, 15, 20, 27, 50, 142, 144, 151, 251–53
Aquinas, Thomas 84
Aristotle 9, 12, 53, 68, 170–71
Arminianism 5, 21, 144, 158
Assent 33, 122, 151–52, 156–57, 187, 189, 201, 213, 222
Augustine 53, 152

Baptists 44, 178, 248
Baronius, Caesar 53, 99
Baxter, Richard 6–7, 30–31, 37–38, 41, 42, 45, 51, 53, 66, 70, 91, 141, 144, 153, 157–58, 176, 247, 251
Beck, Stephen 69, 90–91, 96, 106, 141
Beeke, Joel 4, 77
Bernard, Richard 53, 174–76
Bickel, Bruce 18–19, 27, 51, 199, 210–11
Bozeman, Theodore 143
Bradford, John 28
Brauer, Jerald 5
Brockett, Allan 38–39
Burdwood, James 258
Byles, Mather 45

Calvin, John 43, 53, 70, 75, 94, 106, 173
Calvinism 20–21, 30, 36, 41, 44, 68, 75, 77, 94
Campbell, K.M. 50
Cary, Philip 158, 160, 178, 247–48, 250–52
Caryl, Joseph 53, 55
Charnock, Stephen 42, 51, 53
Church of England 6, 33, 34, 36–37, 51, 84
Collinson, Patrick 3, 4, 28
Como, David 142, 144
Compunction 16, 117–18, 121, 134–37, 139, 146, 154, 162–63, 189–92, 195, 213, 221–23
Congregationalists 38, 43
Conscience 7, 58, 72–81, 85, 87–88, 90, 92, 100, 102–03, 112–13, 117, 131, 134–36, 138–41, 146–47, 149, 159, 163, 176, 183, 186, 190–97, 203, 206, 210–11, 213, 219, 221–22, 226, 240–41, 254, 256
Consent 56, 88, 92, 108–109, 126, 132, 142, 148, 151–53, 156–57, 161, 164, 198, 201–202, 206–209, 213, 221, 246, 249, 258
Cook, Paul E.G. 45
Cornick, David 77–78
Cotton, John 15, 25–27, 53, 94, 143–44, 176
Covenant theology 5, 9, 14, 48, 127, 142, 153, 158–59, 246–48, 252
Cragg, Gerald 185
Crisp, Tobias 20, 53, 251

Davies, Horton 7–8, 10, 51, 173
Declaration of Indulgence 34
Declaration of Liberty of Conscience 34–35, 40, 56, 248–49, 255
Dent, Arthur 28
Determinism 84
Dowden, Edward 23
Downe, Anne 34
Duffy, Bernard 69
Dunster, Henry 184
Dyrness, William 51

Edwards, Jonathan 42–45, 48, 51, 69, 70, 83, 94–95, 106, 209, 218
Edwards, Otis C., Jr 25
Efficacy 16, 106, 124, 128–29, 131, 139–

41, 146–48, 178–79, 186, 207–208, 222
Election 17, 18, 26, 27, 44, 56, 67, 131, 132, 141, 145, 148, 153, 158, 160, 177, 181, 186
Elys, Edmund 36–38, 41, 42, 52, 233
Eusden, John 77–78, 81
Evangelism 18–21, 37, 39–41, 53–58, 61, 72, 87, 190–95, 210–11, 219–24

Faculty psychology 9–10, 16, 31, 48, 49, 68–97, 112–13, 120, 122–23, 218–20, 223
Fedderson, Kim 21–24, 27, 155, 188
Fenner, William 86–87
Ferguson, Sinclair 171
Fiering, Norman 49–50, 70, 71, 79, 82–84, 86, 90, 93
Finney, Charles 18–19, 210
Firmin, Giles 144–45
Flavel, Richard 33
Free Grace Controversy 143
Fulcher, John 14–17, 68–69, 71, 94, 212, 217

Galpine, John 39
Geere, Allen 33
Gildrie, Richard 50
Glorification 17, 18, 27, 61–62
Glorious Revolution 35, 249
Goen, C.C. 45
Goodwin, Thomas 53, 144
Gore, Ralph, Jr 47–48
Greaves, Richard 30, 35, 51, 174
Green, I.M. 4, 32
Green, Ian 41
Greenham, Richard 28, 143

Hall, David 41
Haller, William 17–18, 27
Hambrick-Stowe, Charles 4, 45, 50
Heads of Agreement 38
Hemmingsen, Niels 22
Hill, Christopher 5
Holbrook, Thomas 42–43, 47, 48
Holifield, E. Brooks 3, 50
Holy Spirit 7, 16, 17, 39, 56, 58, 73, 92, 102, 105, 107, 112, 113, 116–20, 125–29, 131–32, 136, 138–50, 153, 160–63, 179–84, 187, 190–96, 198–203, 206–208, 210–12, 220–23, 249, 254
Hooker, Thomas 14–15, 68, 71, 141, 143–44, 173
Hoopes, James 11
Hulse, Erroll 40, 93
Hyper-Calvinism 20
Hyperius, Andreas 22, 24, 155

imago Dei (Image of God) 63–67
Intellectualism 50, 83–84, 93
Interregnum 36–37

Jeffries, Dorothy 35
Jenkins, William 35
Jussely, David 19–20, 27, 173–74
Justification 14–15, 17–18, 20, 27, 116, 127, 144, 152, 157–59, 203, 238

Keckermann, Bartholomaus 68
Keeble, Neil 6–8, 53, 144, 176

Lake, Clement 40, 127–28, 177, 257
Lake, Peter 4–5
Lambert, Frank 39, 45–46
Law 29–30, 128, 138–39, 142, 156, 177, 186, 247–48, 252
Lea, Thomas 49, 188
lectio continua 19
Lensch, Christopher 44
Liberty of Conscience 34
Locke, John 70, 83, 95
Logic 11, 13, 24, 26, 68, 79, 167–68, 170–71, 176
Love of God 6–7, 55, 159, 217, 236, 244
Lunt, Anders 9–11, 70, 167, 174–75

Maddux, Clark 48, 155, 169
Mall, Thomas 257
Manton, Thomas 82–83
Mather, Cotton 41–42
Mather, Increase 38, 41, 45, 56, 249, 251, 255
McDonald, Suzanne 67
McGrath, Gavin 30–32, 66–67, 70, 91, 123, 141, 153, 157, 188, 209, 218
Means 7, 12–14, 16, 30, 128–29, 131–32, 138–39, 146, 148, 179–81, 184, 188,

Index 277

203, 206, 208–10, 213, 220–21, 223, 238, 244, 246
Meyers, Patricia 9, 11
Miller, Perry 11–17, 32, 42–43, 68, 70–71, 93, 113, 119–20, 123, 141, 167, 170, 173, 217
Mitchell, W. Fraser 21, 27, 173
Morrice, Elizabeth 33
Muller, Richard 94, 142

Nonconformists(-ity) 6, 15, 20, 30, 33–39, 42, 47–48, 50, 52–56, 69, 82, 84, 144, 174, 219, 240, 254

O'Malley, James 22
Ong, Walter 168, 170, 172
Owen, John 30–32, 37, 41, 43, 47, 49, 51, 53, 66–67, 70, 91, 144, 152–53, 157–58
Oxford Act (File-Mile Act) 34

Pang, Patrick 209
Pelagius 82
Perkins, William 5, 6, 13, 22, 25–27, 29, 47, 49, 53, 77–80, 102, 113–14, 121–22, 143, 167, 171–76, 211, 223
Pettit, Norman 141–43
Philippo-Ramism 171–72
Plain style preaching 8, 11, 13, 19, 21, 167, 171, 172–77, 223
Plato 53, 68
Poe, Harr. 20–21, 27, 40
Predestination 18, 142, 210, 223
Preparationism 15–16, 130–132, 140–145, 224
Presbyterians (-ism). 35, 37–38, 44–45, 47–48, 82, 144
Providence 83, 129, 147–49, 161, 221, 238–41, 244, 258

Quakers (Quakerism) 52, 127, 177, 233, 257–58
Quick, John 39

Ramism (Ramist logic) 11, 13, 24, 167–72, 176, 223
Ramus, Peter 167
Randal, Jane 33
Reason 58, 66, 69–81, 84, 86, 93, 102, 107–108, 120, 125, 183, 193, 197, 254
Rechtien, John 11, 94, 167, 173
Restoration 36, 39, 40, 42, 45, 51, 53, 82, 84
Reynolds, Edward 84, 125
Rhetoric 9–10, 13, 17, 19, 21, 23–24, 43, 121, 167–72, 175, 184, 188, 196
Rogers, Richard 28–29, 53
Roman Catholics(-ism) 5, 23, 34, 53, 84, 99, 152, 158, 172, 234, 235

Sacraments 12, 34, 76, 241, 256
Sanctification 14–15, 17–18, 20, 27, 61, 62, 64–65, 73, 116, 138
Satan 50, 64, 85, 91, 103–04, 111–12, 126, 128, 130, 132, 140, 145–46, 183, 193, 221, 252
Shelley, Bruce 8, 185, 188
Shepard, Thomas 14–16, 95–96, 143–44, 212
Sibbes, Richard 69, 90–91, 96, 143
Skalnik, James 168, 170
Smith, Humfries 37
Smith, John E 43
Stephenson, Sally Ann 42–43, 48, 69, 70, 83, 95–96, 106, 130
Stoddard, Solomon 42, 43, 94, 96
Stoics 68

Taylor, Edward 48, 155
Test Act 34
Tipson, Lynn Baird, Jr 27–31, 69, 120, 141
Toon, Peter 3, 5, 20, 27, 50, 168, 251
Topsham Assembly 38
Toulouse, Teresa 24–27, 173–74, 176, 211–12

Udall, John 174
Union with Christ 86, 169, 243

Vasquez, Gabriel 152
Vickers, Douglas 112
Voluntarism 30, 32, 84, 90

Walker, John 36–38
Wesley, John 44
White, Eugene 120–21, 160–61, 184, 196,

211
Whitefield, George 44
Wilcox, Thomas 28
Winship, Michael 143–44
Wolseley, Sir Charles 80
Wood, Anthony 37

Yarbrough, Stephen 69, 94
Yuille, Stephen 70, 72, 94

Zanchi, Hieronymus (Zanchius) 53, 75
Zeaem 102

www.ingramcontent.com/pod-product-compliance
Lightning Source LLC
Chambersburg PA
CBHW061434300426
44114CB00014B/1677